# COMPARING SPECIAL EDUCATION

# COMPARING SPECIAL EDUCATION

*Origins to Contemporary Paradoxes*

John G. Richardson
and Justin J. W. Powell

Stanford University Press
Stanford, California

Stanford University Press
Stanford, California

Library of Congress Cataloging-in-Publication Data

Richardson, John G.
    Comparing special education : origins to contemporary paradoxes /
John G. Richardson and Justin J. W. Powell.
        p.   cm.
    Includes bibliographical references and index.
    ISBN 978-0-8047-6073-7 (cloth : alk. paper)
  1. Special education—Cross-cultural studies.   I. Powell, Justin J. W.
II. Title.
    LC3965.R43   2011
    371.9—dc22                                        2010039809

# CONTENTS

# ACKNOWLEDGMENTS

The collaboration that led to this book began, as has become commonplace, with an email exchange across many time zones and bilateral comments on current research. We owe many thanks to David Baker for encouraging that initial communication six years ago, for inviting us to present our research in a special session at the centennial American Sociological Association (ASA) meeting in Philadelphia in 2005, and for generally supporting our work on the (comparative) institutional analysis of special education. We presented further iterations at the ASA meetings in 2007 in New York and in 2009 in San Francisco, and we would like to offer our thanks to the participants for their helpful comments. And we owe a special thanks to Doug Judge, whose research collaboration into the case law for juvenile corrections was always strengthened by his theoretical contributions.

For the funding of research stays for the first author in Berlin and London and for workshops held in Berlin and San Francisco, we gratefully acknowledge the financial support of the German-American Academic Relations Foundation (*Stiftung Deutsch-Amerikanische Wissenschaftsbeziehungen im Stifterverband für die Deutsche Wissenschaft*). We also thank the German Academic Exchange Service (DAAD) and the Volkswagen Foundation for fellowships granted to the second author that provided time in scholarly environments conducive to research and writing: the American Institute for Contemporary German Studies of the Johns Hopkins University in Washington, DC, and the Department of Social Policy at the London School of Economics and Political Science. We wish to thank colleagues and staff members in those organizations and at Western Washington University and the Social Science Research Center Berlin (*Wissenschaftszentrum Berlin für Sozialforschung*) for providing collegial environments in which to work.

Our grant also funded a workshop on disability history in Berlin in 2009 that provided an opportunity to present parts of the book. For their interest and commentary, we thank Catherine Kudlick, Michael Bochow, Michael Rasell, and Lisa Pfahl, who also read and commented on draft chapters, as did Leon Kinsley. Angelika Schmiegelow Powell proofread the bibliography, which we much appreciated.

Alongside the anonymous reviewers for Stanford University Press, a number of colleagues read full drafts of the manuscript, from which it benefited greatly. For their comments, we are especially grateful to Bernadette Baker, James Carrier, and Sally Tomlinson, each of whom inspired us with their own studies of special education. We thank our editor, Kate Wahl, for her continuous encouragement during these difficult times for scholarly book publishers.

Finally, we are grateful to our families, especially to Geraldine Walker and to Bernhard Ebbinghaus, for their support for and patience with our unending fascination with the development of special and inclusive education throughout the world.

*JR & JP*
*Bellingham & London, May 2010*

# PREFATORY NOTE ON LANGUAGES OF DIS/ABILITY AND "SPECIAL EDUCATIONAL NEEDS"

The issue of categorical boundaries and the process of labeling determine many contours of the phenomenon of disablement. Its significance derives from consequences of group belonging for every individual's sense of self and identity. However, this "belonging" is often involuntary, and such categorical memberships are frequently stigmatized. Individual life courses are shaped by disciplinary discourses and professional actions, in many instances according to bureaucratic classificatory practices. Language also plays a central role in contemporary identity politics. Furthermore, the tremendous shifts over the past decades in categorical labels and their meanings require reflection on continuity and change, because the use of euphemistic and politically correct terms may deflect or subvert more substantive demands for equality and improvements in service delivery. Frequently, new categories are championed by a diverse set of interest groups. Battles ensue, as resources must be redistributed to meet newly defined, but authorized demands, such as "special educational needs." Yet "far from being 'scientific facts' based on objective, universally understood definitions of difference, the categories and labels assigned in different societies are contingent, temporary, and subjective" (Barton and Armstrong 2001: 696; see also Chapters 6 and 8).

How people are talked about, how dis/ability is understood, and why certain terms are used in a particular cultural context cannot be relegated to the sidelines. Instead, historical and comparative analyses of categories and the classification systems they comprise tell much about the ideologies, values, and norms underpinning certain institutional arrangements, organizational forms, and policies. For example, in the United States over the past several decades, the categories of special education have been based on individual impairment and disability definitions, despite the growth of sociopolitical models of disability and rights-based legislation (see Chapter 5). In Germany in 1994, categories that fell under the "need to attend a special school" (*Sonderschulbedürftigkeit*) were replaced by pedagogical support categories, suggesting that school-based criteria should replace clinical priorities. Whereas the U.S. categories have always focused on individuals (wherever on the "normal curve" of measured intelligence they were found), the German categories have been transformed from organizational-administrative categories to those based on individual pedagogical supports (see Powell 2010). However, such changes in terminology may not affect either the categorical boundaries drawn in schools or the consequences of being classified if the (segregated or separate) school structures are not simultaneously transformed. In fact, countries routinely modify the labels within a classification as a response to scientific developments, as a gesture of goodwill, as an attempt to defuse the stigmatization and discrimination that often result from classification, or as a means to comply with the precepts of national and international bodies, such as the World Health Organization with its *International Classification of Functioning, Disability and Health (ICF)* (WHO 2001; see also Bowker and Star 1999).

The *ICF* has replaced the simplistic, linear model of impairment causing disability leading to handicap with a "bio-psycho-social" model that describes body functions and structures as well as activities and participation shaped by environmental characteristics. By including all of these factors, the model aims to ensure that the relationships between individuals and environments and functioning and disability can be recognized in the contexts in which they originate. In its recognition of the importance of contextual factors in the process of being disabled by barriers, the *ICF* signifies the increasing global influence of sociopolitical conceptualizations of disability, even within the clinical professions, international governmental and nongovernmental organizations, and national bureaucracies. The transformation of the disability research agenda reflects parallel attempts in scientific thought and in the international disability movement to shift away from purely biomedical discourse and toward addressing ethical, social, and legal implications. The debate surrounding implementation of the *ICF* emphasizes the fundamental dilemma of providing a universal linguistic and conceptual framework for disability across languages and cultures. And although it recognizes that the experience of disability is unique to each individual whose personal differences and varying physical, social, and cultural contexts influence those experiences (Üstün et al. 2001), the *ICF*'s model has only just begun to be applied in educational contexts (see, for example, Florian and McLaughlin 2008).

In special education, the overarching cross-national categories proposed by the Organisation for Economic Cooperation and Development (OECD 2004, 2007) follow a resource-based definition of "special educational needs" that orients itself to "additional resources to access the curriculum" and reclassifies national categorical data into just three categories: (a) children with disabilities; (b) children with learning difficulties; and (c) children with disadvantages. This typology emphasizes the main groups served by special education programs and policies. Such efforts at international standardization increase the risk of losing nuances of meaning that reflect particular cultural developments, which offer insights into the social construction of disability. This is especially so as the analyses reach beyond the developed democracies to the majority world. Yet such comparative data also demonstrate forcefully that the subject of special education and dis/ability is indeed global and universal. At the same time, considerable disparities emphasize the importance of social, political, and economic contexts, above individual characteristics, in analyzing student disablement, achievement, and attainment.

In many countries, the social status of people with disabilities has witnessed a remarkable shift over the past few decades. Yet myriad challenges remain, despite the human rights revolution in concert with the global disability movement and stronger within-nation minority groups, striving for emancipation, whose continued awareness-raising and political action is still crucial. Such national and local politicized groups of disability activists and academics may well choose terms different from those which political correctness would dictate—and such differences help to illuminate aspects of the disablement phenomenon. Within the Anglophone world, international debates continue to question the use of such terms as "the handicapped" and "the disabled." Yet there is no consensus regarding even the terms "disabled person" and "people with disabilities" (see Zola 1993). Throughout this book, we have largely unified the disability terminology used to reflect the current North American standard ("people first") language, except when a historical term provides enhanced understanding of a cultural context or is crucial for an argument. For non-English words, where possible, we include the original term after the translation.

In the end, like the categories themselves that await social situations to acquire their ultimate meanings, groups and individuals with and without disabilities must define for themselves which specific connotations they give to these categories, stretching or even rejecting the original impetus or official claim (see Corbett 1995; Hacking 1999). The global disability movement emphasizes the participatory principle "nothing about us, without us" (Charlton 1998). Yet we also emphasize that the "resource-labeling dilemma" remains in force in most education and social policies, as the receipt of additional and specialized resources continues to require bureaucratic classification in most countries analyzed herein. The ambivalence accorded the reification of disability categories in social science research is also a hallmark of special education. It must be tolerated if the research is to speak to contemporary dilemmas of equality and difference in education that begin with how we speak of ourselves and each other.

# COMPARING SPECIAL EDUCATION

# FROM ORIGINS TO CONTEMPORARY PARADOXES IN SPECIAL EDUCATION

OVER THE PAST SEVERAL DECADES, special education has been the subject of a renascent interest, promoted by a global commitment to the rights of children generally and to their right to schooling specifically. Countries around the world have expanded their commitment of provisions to students with special needs. For some, this expansion has been a surge; for others, it has been a gradual increase—a continuation of policies, programs, and practices long in place. The salience of, even the controversy surrounding, special education has led its ideals and practices to turn the tables on regular education. At the very least, special education has moved out from under the shadows of regular education. In many respects, special education has seized the limelight, illustrating the diverse future of schooling itself, even as it offers its expertise in meeting the learning needs of diverse student bodies.

Some of the heightened focus on special education has been unwanted, coming from statistical evidence showing an overrepresentation of racial and ethnic minorities and migrant populations in many categories of special educational needs. The often well-meaning or benign intentions of policies have been thwarted by practices that victimize many with inaccurate diagnoses and stigmatizing labels. Inclusive education and individualized supports attempt to reduce the unintended or unanticipated negative consequences of classification and separation or segregation, emphasizing that all learners have needs to be met and contributions to make.

Special education research sheds light on key issues in schooling, such as the importance of expectations for education and different measures of achievement and attainment, the professionalization and politics of teaching, the economics of education finance, the nexus of education and social policies, and broader cultural conceptions of disability and meritocracy.[1] As we argue herein, thinking about disability and early forms of special schooling preceded compulsory schooling and massification, and thus such analysis shows that disability and disadvantage are not marginal to schooling, they are central.

As a means to absorb problems of instruction in regular education and school failure, special education provisions, whether segregated schools or separated classes or supports provided in inclusive settings, can enhance learning experiences as they alleviate the strains teachers face on a daily basis. In this respect, special education has held a latent organizational power, even if the main supply of students has come from regular education classes. Yet this indirect power has been the source of its vulnerability, for it is often treated as a second-class citizen in terms of resources and recognition—and in terms of spatial position in countries that maintain segregated or separate settings. Nonetheless, this mixture of latent power and vulnerability, resulting in ambivalence, also gives special education and student disability a multidimensionality that often surpasses traditional instruction in regular education— and that demands research from multiple perspectives if we are to fully understand it (see Peters 1993; Skrtic 1995). It is no wonder, then, that much of the literature on special education concerns the politics that surround special and inclusive education, defining policy and pervading practice (see, e.g., Brantlinger 1997). Over the past few decades alone, this literature has grown in volume and diversity. Such productivity has, it seems, aggravated differences in viewpoint, theoretical framework, and methodological strategy. Like the students it serves, special education research is diverse, frequently focused only on one category of student. However, research on special education spans disciplines that range from education and psychology to sociology, history, and political science. Yet because special education remains a secondary area in these disciplines, research results are often not recognized in the mainstream of each discipline—and even less across the boundaries of scientific communities. This presents a challenge to the accumulation of knowledge about special education at different levels of analysis.

In fact, as we show, the range in conceptions of disability, in participation rates, and in the settings experienced by students with special educational needs is vast, even among the developed democracies. Such international and intercultural differences call for comparative and historical analysis if we want to explain how these persistent differences in special education systems came to be and have evolved. This book addresses this continuing diversity as a source of both enrichment and challenge. Theoretically and methodologically, one of the least prevalent perspectives is that of macrosociological and intercultural comparison. Yet we propose that any hope of understanding the diversity found among groups of disadvantaged students and those with special educational needs as well as the tremendous range of institutional and organizational responses to that diversity requires explicit comparative strategies. And such comparisons must go beyond collecting descriptions of national situations, as valuable as these may be (see Mazurek and Winzer 1994; Artiles and Hallahan 1997; Armstrong, Armstrong, and Barton 2000; Barton and Armstrong 2001). Thus far, too few studies of special education have explicitly compared the development and consequences of special education across countries (but see Carrier 1984; Fulcher 1991; Peters 1993; McLaughlin and Rouse 2000; Powell 2011). Utilizing a historical and cross-national comparative approach, this book explores the complexity and richness of special education as a key aspect of schooling by *comparing* across time and place, instead of viewing it at the micro level of individual interaction.

Neither comparative education nor educational sociology has given much sustained attention to special and inclusive education. Yet ongoing debates about inclusive education and rapid shifts in understanding the phenomenon of disablement emphasize the importance and richness of this field of inquiry.

Beyond the significant discrepancies across time and place, the comparative sociology of special education may track variations in institutional and organizational responses. What learning opportunities do national education systems provide that also prepare youth to transition from school to further education, vocational training, work, and active citizenship? Whether special education has a negative or a positive effect on the life chances of those who participate in its programs, the considerable national and historical differences raise questions antecedent to those of education outputs. How did these systems develop and why? Whose interests are served by special education expansion and persistence?

As governments and international organizations alike rely more than ever on benchmarks of student competencies, performance, and achievement as well as on curricular standards to guide policy change and legitimate resource distribution, the growing proportion of students considered to have special educational needs has been widely debated; however, the myriad factors leading to this pattern need further explanation, as there is no consensus as to why this is so—or whether it is a positive or a negative development. Research thus needs to examine diverse historical and cultural understandings of "student disability" and "special educational needs" as well as the school structures providing learning opportunities. Especially as international benchmarks of school performance become ever more influential, the difficulties of constructing and utilizing cross-national datasets on education provisions and placements must be addressed (see Baker and LeTendre 2005). Part 2 presents comparative and historical research strategies for the in-depth analysis needed to make sense of the tremendous variance in special and inclusive education cultures and structures, even among developed countries.

## THEORY AND SPECIAL EDUCATION

Attempts to theorize special education as a system, to not take these complex institutional arrangements for granted, are relatively rare (but see Tomlinson 1982). In *Theorising Special Education*, Catherine Clark, Alan Dyson, and Alan Millward (1998) tackle this challenge, declaring it inescapable. From the premise that any and all purposeful actions in special education are implicit theories, the authors highlight the many difficulties encountered when one attempts to extend the range, precision, and coherence of theory beyond local and particular practices. The goal of developing "theory proper," a reference to a single, general theory, is always constrained in some way by the diversity of local practices and viewpoints. Yet this goal is not simply an ideal, for "if action is ultimately to be rational in the sense that its purposes and its means of achieving those purposes are to be opened to principled and methodologically rigorous scrutiny, then the construction of 'theory proper' is essential" (Clark et al. 1998: 3). The importance of extending theory beyond the diversity of local practices is that doing so renders action rational and accountable to the canons of scientific investigation.

The prospects for developing a theory proper, or general theory, were not entirely bleak for these authors. The way around the dilemma, the only viable path to a general theory, was to go up a level from the knowledge that was foundational to special education, namely, the facts of psychology and medicine focused on the individual. This upward movement, as it were, would challenge the rules and sorts of evidence of psychology and medicine by emphasizing the social processes that constructed psychological and medical knowledge as educationally relevant facts. As a consequence of this shift, the "the process of theorizing [as] socially and historically located" is accentuated (Clark et al. 1998: 4). Such a shift achieves two things: the diversity of types of theory is no longer a problem, but is indeed celebrated, and the search for a single theory of special education that can explain the complexity and contingency of disability and of special education systems implicated in the theory's construction recedes as a precondition for research and explanation.

Although optional, the goal of developing a general theory was nonetheless strongly endorsed. Against warnings about the difficulties of developing such a theory, the authors closed their work with a suggestive proposal that endorsed a general theory of special education. With penetrating insight and rich terms, they suggested that "dialectical analysis" might be especially useful as a theoretical perspective. They proposed a compelling idea: that "apparently stable phenomena—such as special needs education in a given national or local context—are actually the product of multiple forces and processes which temporarily find a point of resolution, but which create endemic stresses in that resolution which ultimately cause it to break apart" (Clark et al. 1998: 170). Such an idea, they believed, had much explanatory power, specifically, the ability to relate the complexity of special needs education to the complexity of the processes that produced it, to include historical dimensions in analyses, and finally, to include the role of power, translated as the forces that reflect the groups that control how special needs education is produced and sustained over time.

By raising the level of causality and emphasizing social and historical contexts, the authors of *Theorising* certainly advanced the discussion of theory in special education. Yet by accentuating the social processes that produce psychological and medical facts, they may have overreached. The socially constructed nature of psychological and medical evidence does not by itself dispose of such evidence. The processes that produce psychological and medical facts do throw light on just how fluid and variable foundational knowledge can be. Yet social construction is neither more valid nor more general; it is another level that interacts with psychological processes and medical dynamics. The two levels are mutually contingent, and thus which level is more foundational varies by time and place—as does the interest of scholars of different disciplines.

## DISCIPLINARY CONVERGENCE?
## INTERCONNECTEDNESS AND THE CONCEPT OF "FIELD"

Although the strategy of privileging a higher level can complicate more than it simplifies, the premise that the process of theorizing is socially and historically located has support from disciplines seemingly far removed from special education. In her exploration of the similar theoretical changes that have occurred in physics and literature, Katherine Hayles notes their common shift away from classical approaches to causality, in which objects and events are seen as discrete and "occurring independently of one another and the observer," and toward a picture of reality that sees "objects, events, and observer as belonging inextricably to the same field" (Hayles 1984: 9). This concept of field, which refers to a point of convergence that arises independently, yet simultaneously within disciplines, called for a very different image of what should be studied and how. It was first evident in physics and mathematics, in the philosophy of science and linguistics, and in the structure of literary texts. Soon following these disciplines were the social sciences, in which the concept of field challenged standard, variable-based analyses. Following in the footsteps of

Max Weber (1958), Howe states that "elective affinities," or the "logic of the interrelationships of networks of meanings of possible actions" (1978: 382), between social, cultural, and historical features become the objects of interest.

The most notable change in what is studied and how it is studied is captured by the concept of interconnectedness. Elaborated most in physics, objects are not seen as discrete, but as being profoundly influenced by the disposition of the other. Their location within the field of objects binds them inextricably to each other; their interconnection constitutes an emergent whole that is more than the sum of the parts.[2] Just as objects are inextricably connected to each other, so also are observers connected to the objects that comprise their discipline, and theory can be entrapped by this connection. Inextricably connected objects require a specific language of causality that uses such untidy terms as "nonlinear," "chaos," and "unpredictable."

Such a concept of interconnectedness, we argue, fits special education and disability well. The rise of attention given to special education from multiple disciplines derives in large part from its strategic interconnection to regular education, its close ties to families and their cultural contexts, and the needed collaboration across the genetic, biological, behavioral, and social disciplines, as evidenced in support teams in schools or in the multistage classification process based on educational, medical, and social recommendations. As we emphasize herein, the case of special education offers insights for institutional and organizational analysis. The multitude of professions, from pedagogy to psychology, that is engaged in the field results in opportunities to continuously renegotiate boundaries. Yet as special education has become more visible within and between nations, its practices have become subjected to a degree of scrutiny that is often motivated by the goal of uncovering what is really going on below the surface—extensive bureaucracy, battles for professional control, and challenges to secure financing and moral support. Empirical regularities, such as gender and ethnic disproportionality, are viewed as dilemmas, fueling cycles of reform—or at least debate.

Special education programs are deeply interconnected to myriad organizations in the fields of education and training, especially in those countries whose schools provide a range of therapeutic and other services. Special education also is inextricably bound to other parts of education systems as well as other key institutions, such as the health-care system, labor markets, and juvenile justice. In terms of individual life courses, special education is preceded by family life and ascriptive group memberships; it is followed by work, further education, or social assistance. This intermediate position means that special education is persistently subject to a variety of influences, some compatible with its principles, goals, and practices, others definitely not.

The concept of interconnectedness suggests that to fully grasp special education, we ought to study it not only directly, but also indirectly, from the angle of relevant institutions and organizational fields that address the ever-changing population of children and youth served by special education. Thus, to more fully understand special education, we should also study such processes as juvenile delinquency, school dropout, vocational training, and educational and social stratification. Such a kaleidoscopic perspective resonates with relevant literature across the social sciences. In the study of crime, Rusche and Kirchheimer (2003) linked imprisonment and the dynamics of the labor market, and Melosi and Pavarini (1981) joined analyses of the prison and the factory. In the study of national differences in bureaucratic organization, Crozier (1964) derived differences from national culture; Dobbin (1994) linked national railroad policies to political cultures; and Guillén (1994) connected models of management with national culture. And in the study of "mental retardation," Farber (1968) showed how the epidemiological rate of mental retardation is linked to shifts in the labor market, which results in those so labeled being defined as a surplus population. All of these examples go beyond mere juxtapositions. They demonstrate how institutions are symbiotic and that they evolve through particular combinations and complementarities with other institutions (see, for example, the literature on varieties of capitalism, Hall and Soskice 2001).

Ignoring special education systems' interconnectedness with other fields promotes discrepancies between levels, particularly between the micro level of the classroom and the macro level where collective outcomes result. For example, a conspicuous and enduring feature of special education is the discrepancy between the best intentions of teachers, psychologists, counselors, parents, and administrators and outcomes that were neither wanted nor entirely anticipated. Analyses of individuals in school are often insufficient to explain the outcomes of special education and the effects of additional resources on the one hand and stigmatization on the other (as in the resource-labeling dilemma). The enduring patterns of ethnic and gender disproportionality in special education are among the most conspicuous examples of such discrepancies between goals and outcomes. These outcomes do not necessarily result from prejudicial intentions; on the contrary, they often result from well-meaning or benign intentions or even from the absence of intentions. Yet they are stubborn regularities found across time and place, across nations that differ substantially in political and economic structures. This feature of special education has much in common with, and thus much to learn from, the dynamic of collective action, which is a mutual dynamic for how individual decisions result in unintended outcomes and how collective outcomes reflect and reinforce individual interactions and decisions.[3] For special education, such empirical regularities as the disproportionate representation of groups along the lines of socioeconomic status, ethnicity, gender, and ability may affirm individual perceptions, which can, in turn, perpetuate such outcomes as self-fulfilling or self-sustaining prophecies. The considerable disparities in "classification thresholds"—understood as the culturally determined propensity to be classified as having special educational needs in a given geographic area—underscore the need to assess the positive and negative results of being classified as having special educational needs (Powell 2003b, 2010). Such perpetuations are not just social dynamics; they can be reinforced by historical legacies that continue to shape the perceptions and vocabularies that compose the practices of special education in the present. Explicit analyses of institutionalization processes are required to determine how and why these systems developed, thereby shedding light on the ways in which children are taught and supported. Despite the tremendous rise of outcome assessment, evaluation, and control at all levels of education, information on the consequences of special education participation on subsequent educational careers and life chances is just beginning to be collected systematically. Which data are collected and which indicators are constructed depends on theoretical principles.

## BARRIERS TO THEORY-BUILDING ABOUT
## SPECIAL EDUCATION DEVELOPMENT

Theories of special education development are certainly acquainted with interconnectedness. Yet such familiarity is largely indirect, employing different terms and concepts. For example, the importance of contextualizing special education generally and inclusive education particularly is increasingly acknowledged. This is owing to persistent disparities across and within nations. Context here means institutions and their network structures, macro environments that vary in shape and effect. In many other accounts, context and contextualization often refer to within-school settings or to the overlap of individual status characteristics, such as the considerable influence of "gender, poverty, language, ethnicity, and geographic isolation" (Mitchell 2005: 2). Without doubt, these characteristics are significant. Yet these students' location in particular institutional contexts, education systems, economies, political structures, and communities of religious, class, and ethnic divisions is the source of these characteristics' influence—and meanings. Race and ethnic affiliations do not inherently affect schooling, and explanations of ethnic and racial disparities in special education founded on presumptions of inherent difference are both ahistorical and misleading. Much like the classicism of physics and literature, the classicism of special education has consisted of themes, mainly at the individual level, that have plagued attempts to fully grasp the institutional interconnectedness of special education.

There is a notable tendency to portray the origins of special education in positive terms, and to link its contemporary, explosive growth to this confident, optimistic vision. The history of special education is often projected as a story of liberation, a movement away from exclusion toward a normalization of rights that entitle full membership and participation (Wang and Reynolds 1996). This depiction of historical change is explained in teleological terms, for the fundamental purpose of special education is akin to a mission to free individuals and groups from unjust restrictions. Especially in long-term perspective, there is much that supports such accounts. Poorhouses and asylums, dungeons of bondage, despair, and death, were prominent forms of controlling indigent blind, deaf, "mad," and "crippled" children and adults. The closure of large institutional confinements and the rise of individualized rehabilitative treatments provided by professionals were doubtless considerable advancements. Yet despite the nadir of modern history experienced under Hitler's disablist and racist regime, eugenic thoughts, policies, and practices are still with us (see Snyder and Mitchell 2006; Poore 2007; Powell 2011).

Such developments reveal an uneven history, discontinuous on one level, continuous on another. Indeed, as is clearly the case in several of the countries analyzed herein, increased segregation and inclusion rates can occur simultaneously as the population of students defined as having special educational needs continues to grow. As we show, this expansion occurs because of changing education ideologies, societal values, and dis/ability paradigms; the diffusion of compulsory schooling, worldwide human rights charters and equal rights legislation, and considerable resources devoted to schooling; the priorities of nation-states and governance structures; and the broadened awareness of disabilities and special educational needs and professional activities, not only within schools but also throughout contemporary societies.

The story of progress and the rhetoric of transformation have prevailed, over evidence of considerable continuity, in such aspects as structures (segregated schools, separate classrooms) and cultures (students in special education are classified as "abnormal" learners and thus stigmatized). At a general level, such a narrative of progress appears linear: more is better. Yet the challenge is one of incorporation, membership, and meaningful participation, which make up the model of inclusive education and social inclusion. But as one descends from the general, the narrative becomes complicated; empirically, the variance increases. Such complications are not limited to failures and digressions. The more revealing challenge is to explain the evidence of continuity, of institutional persistence in the face of tremendous advocacy and social movement mobilization for change. Shifts in disability labels, resting on professional knowledge or fashions and medial awareness raising, can mask the persistence of structural forms and social categories across different times and places. Unmasked, the narrative of progress reveals itself to be euphemistic change over substantive development, paradigm shifts without the transformation of practices.[4]

A recent example of this phenomenon can be found in 2006. A quarter century after the 1981 International Year of Disabled People, the UN General Assembly adopted the International Convention on the Rights of Persons with Disabilities (ICRPD) treaty. Its goal is to promote and protect the human rights, dignity, and freedom of disabled people around the world (UN 2006; see also Quinn and Degener 2002; Chapter 6). Crafted by a diverse coalition of nongovernmental, international, and local organizations and by dedicated individuals in the global disability movement (e.g., Charlton 1998), the ICRPD was the first human rights treaty adopted in the twenty-first century.

As of March 2010, 144 countries had signed the ICRPD, and 82 countries had ratified it.[5] And yet it indicates once again that the rhetoric of progress is disconnected from the global reality of ongoing oppression and discrimination. As did its predecessors, the ICRPD aims to raise awareness about disability while it insists on the reduction of discriminatory practices and stigmatization that have limited the participation and contributions of people with disabilities throughout history.

The narrative of progress not only shapes the everyday assessment of special education but also the character of debates and the strategy of research, which, when it goes beyond a cross-sectional snapshot, more often than not focuses on incremental change within the system instead of structural transformation, a more radical type of institutional change. Beyond the debate within the discipline, the disputes and contentions about special education are frequently characterized as politics, where the implied analogy is the realm of electoral contests with winners and losers. Without diminishing the political and normative character of such debates, their characterization as political inserts an *essentialism* into analyses and explanations by accentuating motives, beliefs, and attitudes of particular actors as major forces behind the dynamics of special education. The constant flux of labeling, the number of and changes in categories, the rise or decline of participation rates, and the persistence of institutional patterns are seen as outcomes resulting from wins, losses, and stalemates in a political and cultural struggle over special and inclusive education. They are said to be the results of human agency, a causal force that is often invoked when structural determinants and historical context are less visible or are difficult to measure (Fuchs 2001).

Alternatively, this volume shifts the attention onto institutional and structural patterns that are antecedent to the motives and intentions of individuals and groups. The politics of special needs education occurs within specific institutional conditions and decision-making processes, which must, in turn, be anchored to specific historical times and places. The choices that are most often made do not pierce foundational assumptions, remaining in line with the institutional logic of the education system. From this angle, the politicization of inclusive education is largely a projection of debates in western countries, which have exported this framework as applicable to countries that are widely different in economic level, cultural tradition, and political system.

When, however, systematic comparisons are made between and across nations, regions, or localities, the intentions and motives of key actors can appear as fluid and momentary and recede as decisive causal forces. The political struggles over special education in western European countries reflect, among other things, the structural ramifications that resulted from prior and ongoing reforms of schooling more generally, such as reforms that imply substantial secondary enrollments and expansion in higher education. Too often, structural differences have been masked as battles of ideology and culture without subjecting such clashes to the in depth analyses required to explain these decision-making contexts at the micro, meso, and macro levels.

The language of essentialism is especially evident in the pervasive use of dichotomies and categorical binaries. Significant and durable inequalities in advantages relate to unequal binary categories (such as female/male, black/white) more so than to individual behavioral differences (Tilly 1998). Such distinctions as abled/disabled, gifted/learning disabled, and inclusive/segregative parallel—or reinforce—such distinctions as high track/low track, majority/minority, and graduate/dropout. The prevalence of dichotomies may not in itself be pernicious. The dichotomy between impairment and disability is an example of a distinction that, having spurred ongoing debates, has clarified the importance of process and context: one may have an impairment, but that may not by itself result in disablement in a particular environment. Disablement results from the interaction of an individual within a specific context that inhibits functioning, which may or may not be relevant in schooling; hence, the prevalence of disabilities among children and youth is not the same as the proportion of a student body with special educational needs. Rather, the tyranny of dichotomies, their falseness, arises when they inhibit concept clarification and, worse, repel empirical verification, especially when they artificially reduce the continuum or obscure the relationality of dis/ability.

If the distinctions of a dichotomy are taken to be qualitatively real, they take on the qualities of essences. Consequently, dichotomies become tyrannical to the extent that those falling on one side of the dichotomy are presumed to be homogenous and stable. Critiques of dichotomies often revolve around the vexing evidence that distinctions contain more variation within than between them. Yet bemoaning and critiquing the meaning and precision of dichotomies sustains their tyranny. If critiques are to be fruitful, such distinctions as "ab/normal" learners or "dis/abled" students cannot be thought of as static states or entities; rather, they must be thought of as variables, for they vary in prevalence and intensity and across time and space.[6]

## CENTRAL DIMENSIONS AND SOCIAL LOGICS

Building on the perspective outlined above, this volume undertakes two related objectives. The first is the primary empirical objective of identifying the variable patterns and conditions that constitute special education within institutions and organizations and as it is widely understood and practiced throughout the world. Similarities and differences within and across nations in special education participation rates, in categories and types of schools, and in stated goals of education and their reflection in national policies vary across time and space—even as the necessity of having special education programs and professionals has been increasingly taken for granted. The relationship between special and general education is not a generalized background context, but is a variable that differs significantly between as well as within nations. The relations between parental authority and professional expertise and between public schooling and state authority are variables. To comprehend special education without reifying individual differences, such variable patterns are best revealed and explained through historical and comparative analyses.

The second objective follows upon the first. This is the more theoretical challenge of interpreting patterns found across countries. To meet this challenge, we are guided by a concentration on three features: two denoted as *central dimensions*, and the third, as *social logics*. Mindful of the barriers to a general theory of special education development, we focus on two central dimensions as forces that have shaped and continue to shape special education, affecting how special education varies across time and space, yet with patterned regularity. Two major dimensions are analyzed: (1) the continuum of institutionalized organizational forms, from segregated settings to inclusive classrooms; and (2) the continuum of education governance, from centralization to decentralization. The former pertains to the major institutions, historical and contemporary, that have comprised "special education," broadly construed as those institutions founded to serve as well as control people with disadvantages and disabilities: the workhouse and the asylum, the houses of refuge and reformatory, the hospitals for deaf and blind people, daycare centers, and special classes and schools. As we emphasize, the history of special education is not solely a movement from exclusion to inclusion, but rather a continuous struggle between authorized segregative settings and (increasingly widely) advocated inclusive environments. A major premise guiding our analysis is that segregative institutions have not been wholly supplanted anywhere, although in some countries they have declined over recent decades, replaced by community living arrangements and inclusive classrooms. Indeed, it is their continuity, as legacy or entrenched institutional persistence, that offers far more explanatory power for contemporary patterns than does the belief, however hopeful and warranted, in a progressive movement toward inclusion. We argue that a full understanding of the remaining barriers to inclusion is required if such barriers are to be removed in democracies striving to maximize the "capabilities" (see Nussbaum 2006) and participation of every citizen.

The second dimension pertains to the locus of state authority and power. The workings and meaning of special education are significantly impacted by the national political structure, by the degree of centralization or decentralization of education governance. Prominent examples of decentralized educational structures that reflect decentralized political systems are those in the United States and England. Contemporary Germany, responding to the abuse of centralized power from 1933 to 1945, moved in the direction of decentralization of education governance, especially in compulsory schooling. In France, by contrast, a historically highly centralized state has exerted more uniform authority over local and regional communities and their schools; yet France has also shifted away from centralization in education. Such designations are neither essential nor stable properties. Centralized systems cannot be neatly distinguished from decentralized systems because a variety of dimensions that impact schooling may be more or less affected by particular governance structures (Meyer 2009). Furthermore, although countries may remain highly centralized or decentralized for long periods of time, they can and have changed.

We explore the impact of governance on (special) education systems. The twin dimensions of segregation / inclusion and centralization/decentralization frame the analyses presented. These dimensions are not, however, sufficient by themselves. Although they identify the central patterns that have structured special education, they require interpretation. The two dimensions are clearly related; indeed, as we show, they interact. Knowing how they have interacted and trying to determine how they will continue to interact can tell us what to observe and measure and how to interpret the patterns that are revealed. Most of all, their interaction requires that we probe into the *social logics* that influence their continuity, their resistance to reforms, and the persistence of outcomes that happen in spite of the best of intentions.

An assumption that guides all chapters is that comparing similarities and differences in special education systems exhibits identifiable and meaningful logics. Institutions are social patterns that have achieved a certain state or property (Jepperson 1991). The concept of "institutional logic" reaches beyond the symbolic to specific organizational structures that are politically defended, constrained technically and materially, and therefore historically specific (see Friedland and Alford 1991). Thus, there is not just one institution or "institutionalization" of special education, there are many, as the resulting nation- and region-specific continua of organizational forms and the diversity of corporate and individual actors involved attests. For example, in the United States the logic that undergirds schooling is separation or allocation among tracks within comprehensive schools. By contrast, Germany, despite its eventful and severe twentieth century, exhibits an extraordinary continuity in the social logic of schooling: stratified and spatially segregated school types reserved for particular classes of students. For both of these countries, as for most others, inclusive education calls the institutional logic of the education system into question, as it would fundamentally change the methods or even the possibility of selecting students based on cultural preferences regarding dis/ability, socioeconomic status, gender, race and ethnicity, or other characteristic. Thus far, however, in both countries, inclusive schooling is not only possible, it has been proven successful. Nevertheless, it remains a local or regional innovation that, depending on local school contexts, awaits effective scaling-up to be realized everywhere. Is inclusive education only compatible with the logic of Western mass schooling or is it not more in line with the logic of education in developing countries? By comprehending the logics in comparing similarities and differences, we are better equipped to resist the seductions of historical linearity and the dangers of essentialism and of false dichotomies. Observing and interpreting special education systems comparatively enhances comprehension and sharpens efforts to improve the opportunities for students as it catalogs a range of barriers but also delineates the potentials for change.

This book is about one of the most significant intellectual reversals in the contemporary era—the belief, reinforced by legislative mandates, that individuals considered to have special educational needs *can* and indeed *should* be educated with the intent similar to that which is accorded their peers. The legitimation and (ongoing) expansion of special education is among the most significant worldwide processes in education of the past hundred years, and especially of the past several decades. In contemporary conflicts about education standards and accountability for the school performance of *all* students, special education plays a key role as it redraws the boundaries between exclusion and inclusion and distinguishes between those who will become educated and those who will remain less educated. In societies increasingly transformed by scientific advance, by information technologies, and by knowledge exchange, we recognize those who are disadvantaged in learning processes as deserving of significant supports and services, yet there is no global consensus on how and where these should be provided. Analyzing the cross-national differences and similarities can help us learn from others to better understand reform risks—and potentials.

## ORGANIZATION OF THE BOOK

Part 1 of the book, The Origins of Special Education, reaches back to the key questions and ideas of the French and English Enlightenments to explore how these helped structure the institutions and organizational forms in education, poverty amelioration, and juvenile delinquency we largely take for granted today. In this era, leading thinkers held foundational debates about the human senses, knowledge, and educability; about charity and philanthropy; and about citizenship and the nation-state. Although these were not mainly directed to issues of schooling, they did have important implications for the first attempts to provide treatment and care as well as education and training. It was in this time that thinkers, nascent professions, and the state first formulated organized and authorized responses to officially defined needs. In England, the problem of pauperism and the responses of charity were not solely state-dominated—although the Poor Laws were national in scope—but rather a complex array of working-class schools and reformatories operated locally, emphasizing work. This ultimately led to a path of *punitive* benevolence. By contrast, in France, the path was one of *paternalistic* benevolence, built upon networks of the Catholic Church and its organized charity. But it was national legislation and the establishment of charitable and later educational institutions (by such eminent individuals as Abbé Charles-Michel de l'Épée, Valentin Haüy, and Edouard Seguin) researching a range of maladies that did most to focus attention on differences of body and mind not as economic problems, but rather as national responsibilities to provide education and treatment, which developed as a national ideal alongside equality.

Indeed, compulsory schooling became simultaneously a key to citizenship and the widely favored alternative to pauperism, child labor, and delinquency. Then, following T. H. Marshall [1950] (1964), we delineate three stages in the development of individual rights—from civil to political to social. These have complements in the organizational forms that developed to serve myriad goals, such as asylums, prisons, workhouses, industrial schools, and state hospitals. Here, the dynamics of change are both top-down, from royal authority to local communities to secure civil and political rights, and bottom-up, especially for social rights. As we see in the case of people with disabilities, the fight for these rights and their guarantee has been seriously compressed into the post–World War II period, even if the general development more nearly followed a sequence of civil rights in the eighteenth century, political rights in the nineteenth century, and social rights in the twentieth century.

Part 2 of the book, Comparing Special Education, joins large-N variable-based and small-N case-based comparative studies. Utilizing international surveys of special education participation rates, undertaken by the United Nations, we attempt to determine the reason for differences in placement rates in special education in 1957 and 1970. Beyond the obvious effects of economic development (Putnam 1979), we find the influence of membership in nongovernmental organizations, as an indicator of connection to world culture, to be a key factor in varying levels of special education. Distinguishing patterns across nations, the Western (largely European) model joins democratic principles with bureaucratic organization, whereas the non-Western (African, Asian, Latin American) model connects the traditional influence of patrimonial authority with elements of democratic participation. Bringing the analysis forward, we compare the institutionalization of expanding special education systems and their divergence over the twentieth century. This contrasts two of the main models in special education: the separate class (found in the United States) and the segregated school (found in Germany). Thus, even within the Western model of providing significant special education services, major differences remain in the differentiation of classification systems as well as in the learning opportunities that a wide range of structures provide. Consequently, the outputs of schooling, whether measured as achievement or attainment, or simply as years of schooling, vary considerably. Contrary to popular hypotheses, these countries do not suggest convergence in schooling. Although participation rates and inclusive education have risen in many European countries, segregation and separation persist, as do the outcomes of low-level certification and labor market marginalization. The results of such stigmatization and social exclusion are dependence on social assistance or, worse, deviance and criminality. Special education and disability policy must be viewed together if we are to grasp the tremendous costs of the systemic production of less-educated persons, a key theme of Part 3, Contemporary Paradoxes.

In Part 3, we focus on a number of contemporary paradoxes evident in comparing special education systems across time and space. Cross-national analyses of special education participation show continued and increasingly rapid expansion over time. More recently, however, calls for education for all have broadened. Article 24 of the ICRPD (UN 2006) calls for inclusive education programs to replace the existing settings that continue to segregate and separate students. As mentioned, we find a paradoxical rise in both segregation and inclusive education rates, which emphasizes the legitimacy of special education despite international efforts to further inclusive schooling. Yet another paradox is that paternalistic benevolence seems charitable, but this pathway led to the institutionalization of highly segregative special education systems, such as those in France and Germany. Although they seem to protect instead of punish children and youth, because they are segregative and highly stigmatizing, they reduce opportunities to participate, result in poor school outcomes, and lead to labor market exclusion. By contrast, it is the punitive benevolent special education systems, such as those found in England and the United States, that have emphasized school integration and, more recently, the importance of inclusive education. These systems emphasize individual investment in education and work and consequently have fewer provisions for social assistance. By legalizing individual education rights, these punitive systems also encourage individuals with disadvantages and disabilities to participate in schooling, even if labor market marginalization remains ubiquitous. A third paradox is that the expansion of education has resulted in rising standards for achievement and norms for attaining school-leaving credentials that have led to less-educated persons becoming more stigmatized; school failure is no longer commonplace and thus requires explanation. Finally, in the United States, rights to education in the juvenile justice system are being guaranteed at the same time as participatory rights are being restricted within special education for certain groups of students. The "education revolution"—including education for all and inclusive education—returns schooling and control to the same organizational forms that were established and debated during the Enlightenment. The risks and benefits of punitive versus paternalistic benevolence can be measured only by comparative research on special education systems.

The paradox of simultaneously rising rates of segregated schooling and inclusive education is resolved by the global diffusion of special education and categorical awareness of student disability that leads to continued increases in overall population size. In comparing countries, a significant finding is that centralized education governance is associated with more inclusive education, challenging countries with decentralized power that wish to meet international ideals in education.

Emphasizing the complementarities between education and disability policies, we uncover a further paradox in the United States between rights, liberties, and education in "least" and "most" restrictive settings, that is, inclusive education and correctional facilities. In the legalization of American education, case law reflects the logic of expanded inclusion in mass public schooling. If the reform school provided the model for organizational management, then the classification of delinquents confined in reformatories had its counterpart in ability grouping and tracking in public education. As public education was massified and increasingly oriented itself to higher education, behavior rose to a dominant frame of reference for underachievement, misconduct, and failure. Delinquency enters schooling and schooling is now inserted into the criminal justice system as an inviolable right. As special education participation rates expand, delinquency and public education are brought closer still, and the organizational mediator of this growing isomorphism falls increasingly to special education. The legal languages of special education and juvenile delinquency seem to rely more than ever on each other; both have traditionally served the most disadvantaged youth.

In many Western societies, the paradigm shift from medical to social-political or minority-group models of disability has gained strength over the past several decades. Yet the institutions and organizational forms of special education have changed radically in only a few societies. Indeed, the structures of most special schools and classrooms around the world have changed far less than the names we use to identify them. Analyses must reach far back to grasp continuities and uncover euphemistic relabeling  for example, the shift from educability to mainstreaming and integration to inclusion—especially if international and comparative work is to successfully measure and monitor institutional change and in so doing offer suggestions for innovation. Special education and student disability offer a valuable test of the persistence of structures even as new ideas and models that diffuse rapidly are touted as hallmarks of our enlightened era. If special education is challenged by global intentions to further develop inclusive education, national resistance to inclusive education is the struggle faced in and by a world that often idealizes, but seems hesitant or unwilling to press for the transformation of schooling needed to realize it.

## PART ONE

# THE ORIGINS OF
# SPECIAL EDUCATION

THE FOUNDATIONS OF THE CONTEMPO-
rary paradoxes in special education—such as the inter-
locking of the institutions and organizations built around the right to schooling and those established to control social deviants and the simultaneous rise
of segregation and inclusion in recent decades—were laid far back in time.
The origins of special education are with us today in the ideas, interests, and
institutions that, despite their variability across nations, harken back to
shared Enlightenment concepts. These concepts guided key personalities
and influenced not only their writing of seminal works, but also the types
of organizations—charitable, educational, medical, and penal—that they
founded. We argue that Enlightenment debates and concepts are the true
ideational origins of special education, which antedated compulsory schooling,
and that these concepts, conflicts, and even organizational solutions can be
found in contemporary societies. Moreover, in tracing the institutionalization

paths, we see durable affinities indicating cultural continuities that we analyze in later chapters.

We begin by addressing the origins of special education. Use of the term
"origins" reminds of Marc Bloch's care in distinguishing its two meanings:
as "beginnings" and as "causes" (Bloch 1964: 29–35). The dangers to historical
interpretation come when the two meanings are contaminated. The time, or
point, when something originates can be as difficult to define as it is elusive.
Each origin point has its own antecedent, luring us ever further back in time.
And invoking causes can be intended as an ideological means to render judgments on the present, not to understand it or to explain it. Bloch concluded
that "a historical phenomenon can never be understood apart from its moment in time" (Bloch 1964: 35). Despite being a good example of Bloch's
concerns, the question of the origins of special education is a credible one,
because it is too seldom posed even though the institutions and many organizations founded then still exist today and thus offer insights into the principles and norms that emanate from them.

With Bloch's admonition in mind, it is helpful to begin with a historical
lesson: the reference to *special education* is a comparatively recent convention,
only becoming established by the end of the nineteenth century. Yet theories
and practices in contemporary special education were evident by the middle
of the eighteenth century and can be extended back further as one relaxes
definitional criteria, looking for functional equivalents that carried the names
of earlier eras. When "special education" became a commonly understood referent is one moment in time among others. In fact, moments prior to the
coupling of "special" with "education" are equally, if not more, significant.
Dis/ability and ab/normality were defined and understood as crucial concepts
long before the expansion and differentiation of education and criminal justice systems. Their significance lies in their long-term imprints. Defined in an
earlier moment in time, they cast an intellectual legacy, especially as the basis
for professional knowledge, that resulted, among other things, in the construction of "special education" as a commonly understood referent.

Thus, we focus here on the philosophical development of the eighteenth-
century Enlightenment as a collection of important moments in time that
preceded and influenced the construction of special education as we know it
today. The significance of Enlightenment thought, principally in its English

and French genres, cannot be detached from late nineteenth-century "special education." If the two are not linked, the origins of special education can be misplaced, attributed to later celebrated intellectual and institutional entrepreneurs whose visions seem "ahead of their times."[1]

The same error can tarnish the interpretation of Enlightenment thought. The works on blind and deaf people and the subsequent construction of large organizations for their treatment and education can be seen as the result of initiatives, struggles, and achievements of early thinkers who influenced subsequent generations. Such contributions should be embedded in the broader economic, social, and cultural contexts that stimulated the rise of such entrepreneurial thought and favored its objectification into institutional form. A focus on such contextual circumstances does not diminish the role of individuals; rather, it illuminates how ideas arose and how they survived to have long-term influence as they guided subsequent institutionalization processes.

If the moment when "special education" became a commonly understood referent cannot be taken as the origins of special education, and if we resist the temptation to reach further and further back in time, we are left with a complicated analytical and interpretative problem. Analytically, the question of what constitutes special education is key, for if there are several moments in time in which "special education" was formed, then there are several origins of special education. We must not, then, seek the solitary *origin* of special education, but rather the *origins*. Like public education, the labor movement, established religions, and indeed the nation itself, special education reoriginates repeatedly as fundamental challenges and solutions are debated and devised, as we discuss in the later chapters.

The origins of special education are the moments in time that (re-)activate or (re-)direct organizational designs, pedagogical foci, and instructional practices that impact those students considered to have special educational needs, students who are seen as deviating from explicit or implicit norms in ever-more standardized, age-graded educational curricula and pathways. Such moments in time do not arise solely with entirely novel ideas and strategies, especially given the continuity represented in significant nationally and internationally renowned organizations whose histories stretch back hundreds of years. We argue that the principles that shape special education today are informed by existing institutional arrangements that owe crucial characteristics to

Enlightenment thought. We begin to chart this history of the origins of special education in the mid–eighteenth century and concentrate on significant circumstances in tracing this developmental process. What principles thread through diverse moments in time? When viewed through continuity and change in the intellectual foundations of special education institutions, how similar or different are the mid–eighteenth century and the mid–twentieth century sociologically?

This is the challenge addressed in Part i. The chapters are composed on two key assumptions: there are multiple origins of special education, and their sociological affinities reveal an interpretable continuity. This continuity is not, however, to be taken as a "narrative of progress" that presumes some necessary historical linearity. We emphasize that the history of special education cannot be reduced solely to a unidirectional progressive movement, from the outside to the inside, from exclusion to inclusion. Indeed, we attend to the paradox of simultaneously rising participation rates in segregated special and inclusive education; furthermore, periods of severe oppression, or backlash, against reform movements as well as demographic shifts in some countries have altered the course of special education expansion. Similarly, the origins of special education cannot be glibly equated with the harsh sins of exclusion. Indeed, the widespread institutionalization of special education throughout the developed world (and beyond) has made "education for all" possible, with special educators often leading the way to pedagogical innovation, especially in regard to individualized instruction and supports. Replacing the simple hope for progress and linearity with historical contingency, we reveal the conditions that thread together otherwise diverse moments in time.

Chapter i, "Special Education Ideas and Institutions: The Enlightenments, Human Nature, and Disability," plumbs the intellectual depth of French and English thought, particularly how debates, published writings, and the exchange of letters raised fundamental questions about the workings of the human senses and how they limit or actually yield knowledge itself. The implication raised by such inquiries, directly and indirectly, was the question of the "educability" of those with senses different in some ways, such as blind and deaf people. A broader question arose: could such individuals and groups be taught and thus participate in society in ways others do? The question of the educability of children, youth, and adults with perceived impairments was largely posed as a philosophical inquiry, one that was supplementary to questions presumed to be deeper in meaning and broader in scope, such as the perfectibility of the human mind and the progress of humankind. Nonetheless, the implications of such philosophical inquires soon raised other questions—those of method and practice. As Chapter 1 explores, Enlightenment thought contributed, unintentionally, to the attraction of large, formal organizations—even "total institutions" (Goffman 1961)—as sites for the care, treatment, and education of persons with disabilities recognized as deserving specific services or treatment. By the close of the eighteenth century, the construction of such institutions for people with hearing or visual impairments, and later for those with mental illnesses or disabilities, had commenced. From this perspective, one origin of special education was the implementation of Enlightenment ideas in the form of asylums and institutions maintained by the state, the church, and charities.

The contribution of Enlightenment thought to the education of people with impairments began at the philosophical level and ended at the institutional and organizational levels. Such an outcome may appear ironic if the construction of such structures is interpreted through a lens of confinement and social control. Although such motivations were present, there were broader forces at play that presented different perspectives, including the perspective that the residential institutionalization of persons with visual, hearing, and cognitive impairments was necessary for their treatment, indeed their education. Thus, the eighteenth century joined novel ideas to nascent institutional and organizational forms, setting into motion a dynamic that would reach across the nineteenth to the twentieth century.

Chapter 2, "Economic Change, State Making, and Citizenship," takes up this development in ideas and institutions, tying both to the formation of the nation-state in general and to the extension of citizenship rights in particular. We examine the extension of citizenship as a general process that is relatively independent of the many social and cultural differences that otherwise distinguish nations. Beyond differences in the relative weight of certain ideas, nations often exhibit similarities in their institutional histories. However, the tremendous variance found in contemporary special education reflects complex institutionalization processes and sustained national (and regional) differences that demand further comparative analysis. We explore the relevance of T. H. Marshall's sequence of civil to political to social rights ([1950] 1964) as a theoretical framework to guide and interpret national similarities and differences in special education systems, affected as they are by broader shifts in disability paradigms, increases in human rights and antidiscrimination legislation, and the massive expansion of all levels of education worldwide (Powell 2011). As citizens with disabilities work to establish their rights in the areas of education, political participation, and labor markets, we see social movements press for these rights by emphasizing the power of citizenship (Janoski 1998: 232).

Furthermore, as a companion to Marshall's sequence of citizenship rights, we draw on Karl Polanyi's (1957) concept of a *double movement*, as it also provides a theoretical tool to help explain the origins of and contemporary developments in special education. Like Marshall's sequence of the extension of rights, Polanyi's concept highlights the inherent antagonism between laissez-faire market economies and the collective response of protection against their social effects. Polanyi's double movement also refers to a general process, external to the clash of political ideologies and motivations; thus, it constrains nations in similar ways that cannot be explained by differences in ideology or motivation. The combined strength of Marshall's sequence and Polanyi's double movement sharpens an understanding of the conditions leading ultimately to the global diffusion of special education provisions. The status of people with disabilities, their education-based but limited citizenship, and the social welfare state developed to care for but also to control them was reared and reformed in recent decades on the basis of models born centuries ago. To reveal the influence of these origins of special education facilitates our understanding of contemporary patterns of segregation and inclusion, of guaranteed human rights and limits placed on liberty.

## CHAPTER I

# IDEAS AND INSTITUTIONS

*The Enlightenments, Human Nature,
and Disability*

> If one steps back from the present into the past, what patterns,
> what structures does one discover in the successive waves of this
> movement, if one looks not from us to them, but from them to us?
> Norbert Elias, *The Civilizing Process*

THE EDUCATION OF CHILDREN WITH
disabilities long preceded the formal expansion of public
education. The established organizational forms for the education of the
blind, deaf, and "dumb"; the "feebleminded" and "insane"; disorderly, criminal, pauper, dependent, and neglected youth were diverse—from charitable
asylums and orphanages to hospitals and various reformatories. Setting aside
superficial differences in name, size, and administration, the universality of
these organizational forms is compelling. In societies with widely different
religious, cultural, political, and economic systems across Europe, such organizations for disabled children and youth were established. The differences
lay in their relative importance and the timing of their founding.

Asylums, orphanages, hospitals, workhouses, and reformatories have their
own and conjoint histories that are more than subordinate chapters in the
chronology of national education systems. If we retrieve these histories, we

find continuities that offer a broader context for understanding the different structures of contemporary special education. Today, disabled children and youth are classified into special education categories, and their subsequent placement in a particular organizational structure may be thought of as a form of confinement. Such placement has affinities to "binding out" a child as an apprentice, a process that confers certain education benefits while placing limits on liberty. Special education programs that segregate children and youth may be thought of as places of well-meaning confinement. Today's special schools for children with disabilities may be considered as modern-day replacements for asylums; special schools for youth with challenging emotional or social behaviors, as variants of houses of correction or reformatories. At minimum, such a thought experiment underscores the way in which more recent terms, such as "handicapping conditions" or "special (educational) needs," have historically been intertwined with poverty and laboring classes and thus with exclusion and stigma. Yet such an experiment accentuates what has been an education transformation of enormous scope: forms and places of punishment and degradation have moved from historically isolated locations to become legally guaranteed provisions and thoroughly legitimate and ubiquitous sites within systems of mass education.

This chapter explores the eighteenth-century Enlightenment as the ideological origin of what would be called "special education" by the end of the nineteenth century. As indicated by its title, this chapter focuses on the interplay of ideas and institutions. An ironic feature of this intellectually rich century was how the flurry of international exchange of ideas that covered the decades from 1700 to the 1780s ended with the rise of institutions that brought forth segregated organizations in which deaf and blind people, the mad, paupers, and criminals lived. The contradiction between the ideas that enlightened thinking celebrates, such as freedom from errors and fallacies, and the construction of large-scale institutions and state-sponsored organizations to care for and control those considered "abnormal" or deviant has not gone unnoticed; neither has it been fully explained.

The exploration of this inaugural era of special education is organized around, first, the trinary structure of Enlightenment thought, referred to as the *official, counter,* and *periphery* Enlightenments and, second, the sequential order of institutionalization and the founding of organizations to carry out the ideas advanced among the leading thinkers and supported by state initiatives.

Enlightenment thought is commonly divided into central bodies of ideas. The official Enlightenment accentuates reason as the source of truth and understanding. The counter Enlightenment, that of Romanticism, accentuates the moral and the spiritual as sources truer than the rational. By including deliberations about people who suffered social disadvantages and people with disabilities, in particular blind and deaf people, we enlarge the number of contributors to Enlightenment thought and thus modify the standard framework. As part of the philosophical treatises on human nature that preoccupied official thought, social and physical deviance became convenient subjects for debate as a methodological means to expand the philosophical questions about the origins of human senses and knowledge. This is the periphery Enlightenment. Although it was not of the stature of either the official or the counter Enlightenment, it came increasingly into public view. The periphery Enlightenment, we argue, represented a core problem to both the official and the counter Enlightenments. The capacity of blind and deaf people to participate in society was a vexing question that led to the larger question of their capacity to be educated. The late eighteenth-century flurry of institution building and establishment of organizations of what would become known as special education would most likely not have happened as it did without the ideas of the periphery Enlightenment.

From this trinary structure of Enlightenment thought, we propose that the manner in which these three schools of thought are interrelated influenced broader cultural conceptions of appropriate and deviant behavior generally and how individuals with disadvantages and disabilities were viewed and treated concretely. Most important is the degree of independence of the periphery Enlightenment, for this determined the seriousness that was extended to reforming the conditions of poverty and treating the afflictions of poor people and those with disabilities. And although the periphery Enlightenment was evident in all national Enlightenments, its autonomy relative to other thought varied, and thus did its long-term impact on the education of these groups. Which groups became the focus of national attention was contingent on the content, structure, and autonomy of the periphery Enlightenment.

Next we consider the sequential order of institutionalization and the founding of organizations to carry out the ideas advanced among the leading thinkers and supported by state initiatives. Although England and France erected
large-scale institutions at strikingly similar times, within this general sequence
there are critical distinctions: Were they constructed as local or national institutions? Was temporal priority given to the social deviancies of pauperism, vagrancy, and delinquency or to the differences perceived among people with
sensory or physical impairments or mental illnesses and disabilities? We propose that the priority given by specific countries to particular organizational
forms and the general institutionalization processes informs our understanding
of the structures of contemporary special education and criminal justice.

Comparing the two developmental paths in England and France, specifically, we find that the former exhibits a combination of decentralized authority with the prior construction of reformatory institutions to deal with social
deviance. This temporal sequence facilitated a long-term path of *punitive benevolence*. In contrast, in France the combination of centralized authority
with the prior construction of eminent national institutions for a select group
of blind and deaf people facilitated a long-term path of *paternalistic benevolence*. The contrast of England and France illustrates the specific structures of
Enlightenment thought and specific trajectories in the formation of "benevolent" institutions and organizations to address disadvantage, disability, and
deviance—one leading to a punitive model, the other to a paternalistic model.
Benevolence was never, of course, purely benevolent, as punitive intentions
were ingrained in these institutions.[1]

## THE TRINARY STRUCTURE OF ENLIGHTENMENT THOUGHT

### *The Official Enlightenment:*
### *John Locke and the Theory of Human Nature*

At the dawn of the eighteenth century, John Locke affirmed the end of ab-
solutism by announcing a new theory of human knowledge. Locke rejected
the existence of innate ideas. In the place of Cartesian belief that (much)
knowledge originates from ideas of the intellect itself, such as infinity and
the existence of God, Locke proposed to view the human mind as a blank
slate. In doing so, he made the origin of human knowledge an empirically

understandable question, able to be grasped through observation and experimentation. Locke argued that knowledge derives from the sensory perceptions that come from experiences. This was not substantially different from what Thomas Hobbes proposed thirty years earlier in his *Leviathan* ([1651] 1991). However, Locke's timing was more auspicious. In Alfred Cobban's terms, "For a hundred years, Europe contrived to live on his ideas, modifying and developing them in all directions, but making no fundamental change" (Cobban 1962: 16).

Locke's theory proposed that ideas derive from perceptions that are mediated by one or more of the senses. The centerpiece of his theory of knowledge is the distinction between primary and secondary qualities and the corresponding distinction between simple and complex ideas. Simple ideas come from one sense only, such as "light and colours come in only by the eyes, [whereas] all kinds of noises, sounds, and tones, only by the ears" (Locke [1689] 1998: book ii, chapter 3). Simple ideas, such as solidity, derive from the real, indivisible qualities of objects themselves; that is, they are inseparable from matter itself. Other ideas, such as space, rest, and motion, derive from more than one sense. These ideas are removed from the material content of objects and result from the active reflection of the mind.

A key element of Locke's *Essay Concerning Human Understanding* is his doctrine of abstract ideas. At the core of all ideas, whether simple or complex, is the material reality of matter itself. The process of forming complex ideas is the active mental operation of combining simple ideas. Abstract ideas derive from reflecting upon the material impressions made on the senses. The generality of abstract ideas is based on that which is common to these particular impressions. The process of abstraction, for Locke, is essentially the mental operation of combining and distinguishing, out of which process emerge words that have a general reference. At all times, however, the priority of matter remains the central causal force.

Locke's distinction between simple and complex ideas invited critiques from numerous quarters and on several grounds. As Leslie Stephen noted, "He, like Descartes, is trying to get outside of himself. His distinction assumes that universal perceptions must be independent not only of the constitution of this or that man, but of the constitution of man generally" (Stephen 1902a: 37). Locke's materialism, however attractive to those impatient with philosophical abstractions or with theological or absolutist obscurities, was advanced with the aid of logical inconsistencies. Locke maintained his theological beliefs, namely, the existence of God, while proclaiming that all knowledge derives from the senses. This coexistence of a material empiricism with abiding theological beliefs underscores how Locke's theory of knowledge did not rest on logical consistency. To be sure, its positive reception was promoted by its apparent superiority over the Cartesian doctrine of innate ideas. Yet the true superiority of Locke's theory rested more on a promise that was ironically akin to Cartesian assumptions. Much like Descartes' pure ideas, Locke's materialism was founded on a singular criterion for truth. As Stephen put it: "[G]et rid of the ideas which do not correspond to actual facts, and of the truths which cannot be tested by experience, and philosophy will be restrained once and for ever from these fruitless and endless attempts to raise its flight above the atmosphere" (Stephen 1902a: 35). Aside from critiques that profited from his logical inconsistencies, Locke's distinction between simple and complex held out the promise of universal perceptions founded on dynamics that transcended individual differences. Like Descartes, Locke was "trying to get outside of himself"; and it could be said that like John Locke, European cultures and nations at the beginning of the eighteenth century were trying to get outside themselves.

The elevation of Locke to theoretical preeminence was forged by concepts and arguments beyond a philosophy of knowledge and understanding. Locke's *Essay*, published in 1689, parallels in many respects his *Two Treatises of Government*, published a year later. A major link between the two works, a link between his theory of knowledge and his theory of civil government, was his concept of *property*. Much as his sensationalist theory of knowledge answered the search for universal perceptions, his conception of property answered the growing swell to replace traditional justifications of absolutist power with the authority of civil government.

Like the logical inconsistency in his theory of knowledge, Locke rejected innate ideas with an attribute that was equally antecedent and inviolable. For Locke, an individual's property was much more than the product of industry and labor. The property of each man was distinctive, for it was "in his Person." The true meaning of property extended beyond the necessities of life, for God gave it "to the use of the Industrious and Rational" and not "the Fancy or Covetousness of the Quarrelsom and Contentious" (Locke [1689] 1998: sec. 34). Property was "outside" the constitution of any one individual, for it was freedom from necessity; thus the lack of freedom on the part of servants and children was owing not to a deficiency in material resources, but to their bondage to the necessities of surviving. And as a consequence, they could not exercise reason. Thus, in Locke's terms, "we are born free as we are born rational" (Locke [1689] 1998: sec. 61), and "[T]he freedom then of man and liberty of acting according to his own will, is grounded on his having reason, which is able to instruct him in that law he is to govern himself by, and make him know how far he is left to the freedom of his own will" (sec. 63).

Locke's conception of property rested on distinguishing man as *animal laborans* (laboring animal) from man as *animal rationale* (rational animal). The former is common, encompassing what God had put on the earth for human survival and defining what needs to be appropriated for continued existence (Arendt 1989). Yet the products of labor, of the body, disappear upon being consumed and must therefore be remade time and again. Labor is the least private of activities. As such, labor is akin to the primary qualities of material objects, to impressions that are given to us by way of one sense only. The products of labor encompass only primary ideas. In contrast, the products of the hands are the result of reason and knowledge and have thereby a longevity that extends across generations and immediate geographic place. The products of reason and reflection encompass secondary qualities and are thus founded on complex ideas inaccessible through labor. Possession of property presupposes access to reason, which, conversely, entails a distance from the necessities of existence.

### *The Counter and Periphery Enlightenments*

The counter Enlightenment coexisted as an intellectual movement parallel to the official Enlightenment. It opposed the dominant ideas of universal reason and individual rights and their implied consequences for traditional authority and the institutions of the *ancien régime*. Much like the official Enlightenment, the counter Enlightenment took variable forms, both within and across nations (Berlin 1968). In England, the official Enlightenment and the ideas of Locke and George Berkeley were not without their antagonists; likewise for the philosophes in France and the *Aufklärung* in the German-speaking lands.

An accepted term for those philosophical and literary rejections of official Enlightenment thought is Romanticism, or the counter Enlightenment.[2] Romanticism viewed traditional authority as a prerequisite to social order, sentiment as superior to reason, and social inequalities as more deeply embedded than notions of individual rights and liberties could overturn.

Those who supported Romanticism needed Locke in order to amplify the depth of their repudiation (Berlin 1999: 49). However, paralleling the scholarly exchanges between the official and the counter Enlightenments was a much less visible—and thus an apparently less prominent—reply to Locke. This discourse, the periphery Enlightenment, took up the Lockean thesis at its most empirical and practical level: not as a "philosophical contrary" to reason and individual rights, but as a "practical contrary" to the very capacity to reason and to exercise rights. It was not confined by scholastic boundaries; its laboratory was the margins of society. The periphery Enlightenment addressed Lockean ideas with observations on real, empirical cases: the poor, the blind and deaf, and the insane.

In England, the home of Locke and Berkeley, the counter Enlightenment and the periphery Enlightenment were intricately connected, overlapping in timing and substance. For both, the central problem of the laboring poor was its perpetuation; the inheritance of pauperism seemed impenetrable by reasonable and "traditional" reforms. In France, the focus was on the sensory qualities of blind and deaf people and of people with mental illness or disability— conditions demanding explanation independent from personal failure or as manifest threats to social order. For the major figures of the French Enlightenment, the example of blind people was taken up first, for it offered direct access to the theory of the senses. Their writings signaled a direction that seemed to be within reach, namely, the construction of organizations for the care and education of the blind, the deaf, and the insane.

The exploration of the relationship between the counter and periphery Enlightenments in England and in France will enable us to better understand why each nation embarked on the socially changing and financially costly path of erecting large-scale institutions. The paths from Enlightenment ideas and their subsequent institutions were paved by interrelation and timing: the degree of autonomy of the periphery Enlightenment and its place in the chronology of Enlightenment thought.

*England.*    With the advent of the eighteenth century, the acknowledged eminence of Newton and Locke encountered a number of changes that had begun to menace "English thought" as a dominating discourse of "the upper-half English" (Viner 1968: 29). For England, these changes were concretely economic, specifically the problems of labor and pauperism. The problems of labor and poverty had long been prominent, but they now took a different turn by altering not only man's relation to nature, but also—and even more so—man's social relations.[3] The national context was both collectively and interpersonally defined by the changing relations between the gentry and the laboring class, aptly summarized by E. P. Thompson as a "patrician society" and a "plebian culture" (Thompson 1974; also Thompson 1978).

If we confine our attention to those whose writings posed a direct challenge to scholastic philosophy in general and to Locke in particular, we encounter a genre of literature that was as much a critical commentary on philosophy as it was a sociological commentary on the changing economic relations that were pervading English society. As a critical commentary, this genre was a counterbalance to the philosophy of Locke most principally by its elevation of the ideal and the sublime over the rational; as a sociological commentary, it drew upon the economic, the salient condition of English society, as a way to reveal the limitations and folly of rational-sounding reforms designed to alleviate poverty. This genre reflected the crisis of the patrician class—the erosion of deference across social relations—prompting a romantic nostalgia for politeness and civility, modes of conduct that were superior to reason and were the "true basis" upon which social relations should be constructed.

Among the best representatives of this counter Enlightenment, right under the nose of Locke, was Anthony, Earl of Shaftesbury (1671–1713). Shaftesbury directly countered Locke's treatises on human nature and knowledge. Less direct, if even concerned with Locke and official philosophy at all, were Bernard Mandeville (1670–1733) and Daniel Defoe (1659? –1731?). The temporal coincidence of these three demonstrates the substantive overlap of the English counter and periphery Enlightenments. Both Mandeville and Defoe used the problems of poverty and begging on the periphery of English society as their way to rebuke official philosophy, and to discredit the presumptively counter Enlightenment thought of Shaftesbury. This temporal and substantive overlap had considerable implications not only for the construction of segregated institutions, but also for the construction of popular education in particular. But first the counter thought of Shaftesbury.

Although certainly not rejecting human reason and the knowledge gained from it, Shaftesbury nonetheless reversed the official argument: he began with the affections, which would then stimulate and direct reason. For Shaftesbury, the "natural affections" came first, not merely in daily conduct, but as the only true means to an ethical and virtuous life. The virtuous man was sociable, for to be nice to others makes us feel good, a sentiment that precedes and is superior to any utilitarian calculation of rewards (Broadbent 1964: 81). Such sentiments, which enable sociable interactions, constitute an individual's "natural moral sense" (Shaftesbury [1711] 1964: 262), something conceived by Shaftesbury as an endowed, internal capacity that could be as much abused through false pursuits as enhanced through social affections. Yet this moral sense was neither a simple reflection of the senses nor an auxiliary extension of reason (Hazard 1963: 337).

Shaftesbury's emphasis was on societies as a *whole*, envisioned much like we comprehend nature as the totality of beings. The order, harmony, and proportion of nature are the same in society. The associating inclination that binds family members is replicated in the ties that join individuals and groups into a nation. The sum of relations and their affections is a series of social networks that constitute, as a whole, a multidimensional, but hierarchical society. The *social* chain of being was a hierarchy of associations, from the laboring multitude to the gentlemanly class, from the manual trades to the professions.

For Shaftesbury, the associating inclination that was especially binding was *politeness*. This style of interaction was the truest, for it was the furthest from calculating self-interest. Of course, from the vantage point of the society as a whole, Shaftesbury's "culture of politeness" was not strictly a new conception of moral goodness or altruism, nor was it a new form of sociability. It was an existent style and discourse best exemplified by a gentry class that "acted as a master metaphor" to remake the world "in a gentlemanly image" (Klein 1994: 7, 9). However, Shaftesbury's conception of politeness was broader than the gentry, for it had *pedagogical* implications that would reach to the construction of special education at the beginning of the twentieth century. As Ernest Tuveson (1953: 275) summarized: ". . . with Shaftesbury we begin to see conduct in terms of what we should now call 'normal' instead of in terms of obedience to divine or natural law; and with Shaftesbury we begin to think of departures from desirable behavior as the 'abnormal' and 'maladjustment' rather than 'sin.' The villains become environment and training, rather than the hereditary 'degenerate nature of man.'"

Shaftesbury's romantic and poetic counter Enlightenment was widely admired within and beyond the shores of England. Yet it was also the object of derision by the figure that was most conspicuously noted for his cynical scrutiny of the avowedly good and virtuous intentions of social reforms. Bernard Mandeville's *The Fable of the Bees*, published in 1714, shares Shaftesbury's wish to explain the workings of society, or, in Shaftesbury's terms, its order, harmony, and proportion. Yet in contrast to Shaftesbury, Mandeville began with a decidedly different conception of man's nature. Mandeville's position was Hobbesian, conceiving individuals as naturally selfish and "full of vice." However, the outcome of multiple individuals pursuing their private vices was not disorder and corruption; on the contrary, the result was "public benefits" that are unforeseen and unintended.

Although a harsh critic of Shaftesbury, viewing him as a typical patrician removed from the reality of the actual lives of men, Mandeville did share Shaftesbury's presumption that society was a residual outcome of multiple individual behaviors. Yet for Shaftesbury, society was a natural outcome; for Mandeville, public benefits were artificial and contrived outcomes. This was a critical difference, for it led Mandeville to "test" his thesis by subjecting the goodness of reform intentions to close scrutiny. In his scrutiny of charity and charity schools, Mandeville levied unrelenting critiques, taking aim at the real motives behind such schools, at the real forces that sustained them, and at the real consequences for poor youth subject to such coercive schooling. With Mandeville and Defoe, the critique of social reforms became a literary genre that greatly extended the distance from the official Enlightenment to the periphery Enlightenment.

What the senses were to Locke and the affections were to Shaftesbury, the passions were to Mandeville. The roles played by pity, charity, pride, vanity, frailty, and enthusiasm were as determining of knowledge and behavior as were the senses. But Mandeville's strategy for demonstrating the impact of the passions—his methodology, as it were—was quite different from that of

both Locke and Shaftesbury. Similar to both men, Mandeville addressed issues of difference and deficiency in human knowledge, yet he did so from a
very different angle. Like the senses, the passions deceived, but not from the
absence of one or another, for "the Seeds of every Passion are innate to us and
no body comes into the World without them" (Shaftesbury [1711] 1964: 281).
The root of the deception, then, was social: charity was, in reality, pity, and as
a consequence, the motivation for one's conduct became disparate from what
one truly felt or offered as an explanation. One felt pity, but acted beneficently
as charity. Because charity yields more approval than does pity, the root of
charitable behavior must remain obscure. People would thus participate in the
deception and thereby sustain hypocrisy as a rule of social exchange.

Mandeville's thesis of private vices and public benefits followed the rule
of unintended consequences. In his attack on charity, he noted that "where
it is too extensive, [it] seldom fails of promoting Sloth and Idleness, and is
good for little in the Commonwealth but to breed Drones and destroy
Industry" (Mandeville [1714] 1988: 267). Even when almshouses were erected
by good intentions, the motives of those who kept them going were quite different. To offset this variable in the motives of those who erected institutions,
charity must be governed by a constant: "All must be set to work that are nay
ways able, and Scrutinies should be made *even among the Infirm*" (Mandeville [1714] 1988: 267–268, emphasis added). The deceit of charity schools was
the same as the falsehood of almshouses. As Mandeville "would have none
neglected that are helpless," charity extended to those who can labor undermined its purpose and deceived the public, indeed the nation. The deceptions
that could arise from charity were pronounced when extended to schools for
the poor, and the motives for the erection of charity schools were considered
especially pernicious. The poor children of charity schools would learn manners and civility. A broad benefit was espoused by clergy who preached the
spiritual returns that came from fulfilling such a Christian obligation. The
deception of charity schools was thus twofold: their promotion on religious
grounds sustained their construction for reasons other than genuine benevolence; and the more the poor were forced to learn manner and civility, "the
more unfit they'll be when grown up for downright Labor." Because knowledge "both enlarges and multiplies our Desires," the working poor "should
be confin'd within the Verge of the Occupations" (Mandeville [1714] 1988:

288). For children of the poor, reading and writing were as harmful as they were irrelevant; thus, going to school was idleness.

The principle that charity weakened the nation was advanced with equal force by Mandeville's contemporary, Daniel Defoe. For Defoe, the real problem of the laboring poor was not so much their lack of manners and civility or absence of skills, but their "Temper": "mutinous when they want employment and idle and saucy when they have it" (Defoe 1724). With the decline of "The Great Law of Subordination," the curse that befell England was an insolence that spread through the laboring poor. Where the insolence of the poor was stimulated by a rise in wages, it was further aggravated by a complicity of the gentry, a comparable display of slothful behavior. The mutuality stemmed from "unseasonable Lenity, Kindness, and Tenderness" on the part of masters toward servants. With the weakening of the boundary distinguishing masters and servants, neither knew how to behave. The "law of subordination" rested on maintaining the social hierarchy, definitively and intentionally.

In England, although there was investment in discussions of human knowledge, the eminently practical issues of labor and poverty were more central: all must work that are able (or can be forced) to do so. Fear reined that charity and education, too freely given to those who should work, would threaten the balance of a class-based society that was on the verge of industrialization. As we shall see, the discourse in France took a different, more academic or abstract direction, and its focus was not on the macro questions of classes, but rather on micro-level issues of individual sensing or understanding and its relevance for the theory of knowledge.

*France.* In contrast to the English preoccupation with the practical applications of scientific knowledge, the French were not so restrained from the various modes of intellectual critique, be it wit and humor or scholastic commentary. To the French philosophes, Enlightenment writings were informed more by political questions than by economic problems. Less constrained by industry and an expanding factory system, French philosophes attended indirectly to problems of labor and poverty.

The French thinkers were, however, direct heirs to the writings of Locke and Berkeley. The sources of human knowledge, of the *understanding*, were taken up with equal intensity, as if the philosophes were obligated to continue that which the English had begun. The "political" dimension of the French Enlightenment constrained philosophes to remain closer to the core questions posed by Locke about the origins and mechanics of human nature. As a consequence, the philosophes confronted the topic of the human senses each in their own way. Condillac's *An Essay on the Origin of Human Knowledge,* published in 1746 (1974), and *Treatise on the Sensations,* published in 1754 (2002), bear the imprint of Locke's *Essay* throughout; Helvétius's *De l'Esprit,* published in 1758 (2005), elaborates on Locke's notion of tabula rasa; and Holbach's *System of Nature,* published in 1770 (2007), is a radical extension of Lockean materialist principles. In contrast to the more macro topics of labor, property, and class relations that preoccupied the English Enlightenment, the French Enlightenment was occupied by the more micro topics of the senses, particularly of vision and hearing.

The focus of the French philosophes on the senses of blind and deaf people returns us to Locke. In his *Essay,* Locke briefly discussed what would widely become known as "Molyneux's Problem" (Thomson 1974). A friend of Locke, William Molyneux had proposed a question to him in a personal letter, which prompted Locke to insert a brief reference to it in his chapter "On Perception." Molyneux posed to Locke the "problem" of a man born blind, but later enabled to see. The problem, as Molyneux framed it, was whether the man would recognize a sphere and a cube by sight alone, having learned to do so from touch. Molyneux's answer was that the man would not be able to distinguish the two objects, for he lacked the experience that would permit his new sight to tell the difference. Locke agreed, affirming "that the blind man, at first sight, would not be able with certainty to say which was the globe, which the cube, whilst he only saw them; though he could unerringly name them by his touch, and certainly distinguish them by the difference of their figures felt" (Locke [1689] 1998: II, 9).

Although Locke inserted a brief, but approving discussion of Molyneux's problem, it was Berkeley who addressed its broader meaning and implications in his first major work, *A New Theory of Vision,* published in 1709 (1919). This compact essay is remarkable for its technical strength and its theoretical organization. Berkeley demonstrated a keen grasp of optics and proceeded through a number of questions by examining the evidence for and against them. As he proceeded, he summarized the evidence with interpretations that are often given in propositional form. Although Molyneux's problem is one such question addressed, the defining background is Locke's theory of knowledge in general and its implications for abstract ideas in particular.

Among Berkeley's summary propositions, likely the most significant is his assertion that objects perceived by sight and sensed by touch are not the same; that is, there is no necessary connection between the sense of touch and the sense of sight (Berkeley [1709] 1919). As he argued, the "extension" of objects perceived by sight is distinct from the "ideas" of touch (CXXVII). Berkeley's explanation, or his *theory,* for this distinction between sight and touch is the significance of experience. The empirical measure of experience is its role in the perception of the location of objects in external space, or the distance of objects from one's vision of them. Berkeley claims that the judgments made of the distance of objects, as well as their form and motion, "is entirely the *result of experience*" (XX, emphasis in original). Interpreting this, he notes the relation between distance from the eyes and "confusion"; and in propositional form, he summarizes: "And this being found constantly to be so, there arises in the mind an *habitual* connection between the several degrees of confusion and distance. The greater confusion still implying the lesser distance and the lesser confusion the greater distance of the *object*" (Berkeley [1709] 1919: XXI, emphases in original). In effect, as Berkeley concludes at the outset of his essay, "distance of itself, and immediately, cannot be seen" (XX). Knowledge is thus not the immediate result of sense perception. Rather, we perceive distance, and thereby know objects in external space, by relying on other ideas. We "estimate" more than sense the distance of objects, and such estimations are "acts of judgments" that are "grounded on experience" more than direct sense impressions.

Berkeley's emphasis on experience by no means replaces sense impressions entirely. Rather, he distinguishes between seeing and vision, a difference between direct, or immediate, perception and indirect, or intermediary, perception (Pitcher 1977: 9). Direct perception, or seeing, is a sense impression that does not entail intellectual reflection. Yet for Berkeley, there really are no perceptions that are immediate, deriving solely from the material content of objects. If perception of distance derives from "the angle of the optic axes," then "it would follow that a man blind from birth made to see, should stand in need of no new experience, in order to perceive distance by sight" (Berkeley [1709] 1919: XLII). This, of course, was sufficiently disproved. The evidence surrounding Molyneux's problem seemed irrefutable.

In Molyneux's problem, there was something for both Locke and Berkeley. In spite of Berkeley's divergences from Locke's sensationalist theory of knowledge, both converged on the importance of experience. Sight and touch are indeed distinct senses, yet if they agree, they can do so only through experience. Thus, Locke may have mentioned Molyneux's problem more as a prompt to consider what would be in the absence of "the most comprehensive of all our senses" (Locke [1689] 1998: II, 9). The example of blindness offered a real means to engage in a thought experiment that was informed by prevailing Enlightenment thought, but was also laden with considerable practical implications. Such implications were made concrete by stories of surgeries that allowed individuals to regain their vision after years of blindness. The theoretical attraction of blindness gained adherents as the ideas of Locke and Berkeley diffused beyond the boundaries of England. This was especially the case for the Enlightenment in France.

The bridge that joined the theoretical ideas of Locke and Berkeley to the French Enlightenment were reports of a successful experiment on a young man blind from birth, but enabled to see during his early teens. William Cheselden published his account of this extraordinary event in *Philosophical Transactions* (1727–28). Berkeley referred to Cheselden's report as vindication of his original theory of vision, which had been articulated through reason only. But Cheselden's observations would be taken up by Voltaire, Diderot, and Condillac, among others. Each in their respective way highlighted blindness as an especially revealing example of Enlightenment thought.

In his *Elements of Sir Isaac Newton's Philosophy,* Voltaire referred to Cheselden's observations, proclaiming that "[this] Experiment confirmed all that *Locke* and *Berkeley* had therein rightly foreseen" (Voltaire 1967: 64). The very fact that Voltaire included Cheselden's experiment in his handbook on Newtonian physics defined the event as a milestone and made it available to a broader audience. It was Denis Diderot, however, who expanded upon the apparently successful experiments on blind individuals. His "Letter on the Blind for the Use of Those Who See" is exemplary. Published in Diderot's

*Thoughts on the Interpretation of Nature* ([1749] 1999), "Letter on the Blind" (64) consists of three parts, each relatively even in length. It begins with a discussion, an imaginary exchange, with a blind man of Puisaux, a technique that Diderot employs to examine the very structure and validity of such experiments as the one reported by Cheselden. It closes with a discussion of Molyneux's problem. In the center, Diderot focuses on Nicholas Saunderson, the "extremely successful professor of mathematics at the University of Cambridge." The ordering of Diderot's "Letter on the Blind" presumes to give Saunderson the most significance, if only because of its centrality in the composition. As a preliminary, however, the discussion with the blind man of Puisaux anticipates and accentuates Diderot's discussion of Saunderson; in fact, all three segments are interdependent, for as Paulson notes, "the real interest of the *Lettre* lies in its articulation of the rhetorical and speculative modes of writing on blindness" (1987: 64).

Diderot's discussion of the blind man of Puisaux identifies the number of ways in which blindness was *not* the affliction as it had so popularly been viewed. Diderot enumerates a number of positives: the difficulty blind people have in finding things "makes them orderly"; the blind man "is a good judge of symmetry," for he "studies by his touch that disposition required between the parts of a whole"; although deprived of seeing the beauty of nature, the blind man's ideas of beauty, "though less extensive, are more definite than those of many keen-sighted philosophers who have written prolix treatises on the subject"; the blind man "has a surprising memory for sounds, and can distinguish as many differences in voices as we can in faces"; the blind man "is so sensitive to the least atmospheric change, that he can distinguish between a street and a closed alley"; the blind man "can turn small articles on the lathe, and do needlework; he levels with a square; he puts together and takes to pieces simple machines"; he "judges the duration of time much more accurately than we by the succession of actions and of thoughts" (Diderot [1749] 1999: 150).

The thrust of Diderot's enumerations is intended, in large part, to erase the popular view that the state of blindness is one of diminished capability and of self-imposed inferiority. It is precisely the opposite, Diderot tells the reader. The blind man feels no less capable, for "we have such a strong desire to exaggerate our qualities, and make little of our defects." In the matter of ethics, the blind man has an "extreme abhorrence of theft," due to the ease with which people could steal from him and because he could so easily be seen if he himself stole. Just as the blind "judge beauty by touch," the absence of sight enables the blind man to *feel* the ethical and to adhere to its require- ments with a more sincere, if not required commitment. With subtlety, Diderot asks: "Do not we ourselves cease to be compassionate when distance or the smallness of the objects produces on us the same effect as deprivation of sight upon the blind?" (Diderot [1749] 1999: 156). With a reference to dis- tance, Diderot implies that a more natural compassion is the compensation for the absence of sight. Similarly, the absence of sight gives the blind man a freedom from the many social conventions that are without functional rea- son and that are, as philosophers expound, a principle source of man's in- authenticity. The absence of sight, alternatively viewed, is a gift insofar as it gives to the blind an ability to penetrate and know the nuances of the social world as well as the natural world. Blind people touch both worlds at a level that may be accessible to seeing people; but as Diderot implies, this is rarely achieved.

From his enumeration of the blind man's qualities and strengths, Diderot turns to the remarkable achievements of Nicholas Saunderson. Like the blind man of Puisaux, Diderot emphasizes how Saunderson "saw by means of his skin." Being sensitive to subtle changes in air movements, Saunderson could detect movements in distant objects that would escape others. Such ability, Diderot suggests, is much like the skill of a draughtsman, who with very few lines captures the wholeness of an image. From a very few sensations, blind people may detect distant changes and extrapolate to whole images. But the subtle meaning of Diderot's praise of the powers of blind people is best con- veyed in his portrayal of an exchange between Saunderson and a clergyman summoned to Saunderson's bedside at the time of his death. In response to the clergyman's argument that the wonders of nature were certainly proof of the existence of God, Saunderson replied that although he could not see the wonders of nature, he nonetheless believed in their "admirable design and order" and in the existence of a divine maker. His "evidence" for the admira- ble design and order of nature was certainly of another kind. Strikingly, Saun- derson's reply to the clergyman turned to a scolding rebuke of the "blindness" of inferring features of nature from one's own circumstance and thus of presuming such admirable design and order have always existed:

A moment ago I reproached you for estimating the perfection of things by your own capacity; I might accuse you here of measuring duration by your own existence. You judge the phases of the world's existence to be like the ephemeral insect of yours. The world seems to you eternal, just as you seem eternal to creatures which last only a day; and the insect is more reasonable than you. What a prodigious series of ephemeral generations witness to *your* eternity, what an immense tradition! Yet we shall all pass away without a possibility of denoting the real extent which we took up, or the precise time of our duration. Time, matter, and space are perhaps but a point (Diderot 1999: 175, emphasis in original).

Clearly, Diderot intends here to underscore the intellectual depth of Saunderson. Although most have sight, this does not ensure vision.

### The Sequential Order of Institutions

*The Demographic Factor.*   Remarkably, the production and flow of Enlightenment thought occurred while a very different phenomenon was unfolding. In the renowned phrase of Michel Foucault, the "Great Confinement" of "troubling" people had commenced in the latter decades of the seventeenth century, evident in the construction of "hospitals, prisons and jails," which soon constituted "an entire network" that spread across Europe. Foucault dates the start of this sweeping change with the founding in Paris of the Hôpital Général in 1656 (Foucault 1988: 39), which had no medical function, but whose purpose, rather, was to maintain social order. Yet as Erik Midelfort (1999) makes clear, in Germany some hospitals operated on the medieval tradition of caregiving, whereas others took up a therapeutic model of treatment; however, the daily lives of those confined to these hospitals differed little. To Foucault, the movement toward confinement was a common response across Europe, triggered by economic dislocations that threatened the "social sensibility" of monarchical and bourgeois power. In its general form, this threat was the rising level of poverty; in its specific form, it was the appearance of the "vagabond." To the monarchical and bourgeois sensibilities alike, the vagabond represented a threat to traditional arrangements, beliefs about work, and community order.

The central motivation behind the founding of the Hôpital Général, which diffused to towns across Europe, was to prevent "mendicancy and idleness as the source of all disorders" (Foucault 1988: 47). Poverty was generally widespread, but especially conspicuous was the mobility of poor people. With the expanding number of wandering poor, necessitating an "economy of makeshifts" (Hufton 1974; Farr 2000: 15–43), a perception grew that distinguished the "true poor" from the "healthy beggars." The former were deserving of pity and voluntary charity, whereas the latter were despised, "perceived as a class apart" (Payne 1975: 186) and subject to harsh discipline. Thus began a new "vocabulary of itinerant poverty" (Hufton 1972: 99).

The increased tendency to distinguish the undeserving beggar from the truly deserving poor reflected the decline in traditional modes of absorbing poverty. As long as begging was domiciled, forms of charity were well established and widely practiced. With the expansion of vagabondage, giving to the poor was increasingly resented, for "in Christian doctrine the spontaneous generosity of the donor was what mattered: to give under compulsion was no virtue" (Hufton 1974: 202). The understood exchange between the pauper and the community was broken. Under traditional charity, voluntary almsgiving was meaningful; its reward was its virtuousness. The gifts remained in the community and rewards could be gleaned from charity in exhibiting one's status and piety. But with the expansion of the vagrant poor, discipline replaced virtue as a dominant motivation, and extracting work became the compensation for charity. And with the decline in voluntary, spontaneous giving, the religious basis for charity and benevolence was slowly eroded. This was a change of considerable scope.

With the advance of a merchant economy, the house of correction was constructed as a means to stem the social problem of vagabondage. Begun first in Amsterdam, the workhouse spread to other cities as a model of benevolent treatment of the "able bodied" poor (Sellin 1944: 1). The house of correction was common to all; it symbolized the end of the "dishonoring penalties of the past" and the advent of an enlightened correction. As Foucault noted as well, the house of correction was especially adaptive, at once supplying cheap labor during times of high employment and absorbing poverty during economic downturns (Foucault 1988: 50–52). At a minimum, the house of correction inaugurated the movement to confine troubling people.

From the house of correction, subsequent institutions would be established, expanding the vocabulary of itinerant poverty in ways that reflected the types of organizations and the sequence of foundings.

*The Cultural Factor.* An important aspect of the eighteenth century was the parallel between Enlightenment thought and the institutionalization processes and the resultant establishment of organizations. The turn to large-scale, rationalized organizational forms was led by the reform of prisons in England beginning in the 1760s. This motivation to reform was stimulated, to be sure, by the revelations and writings of John Howard. Howard's reception was enhanced by his ability to join spiritual concerns and rational objectives, effecting a movement away from the cruel confinement of the old prisons (Ignatieff 1978). Furthermore, a movement to reform prisons fit well with the economic interests of urban merchants and factory owners, members of the "middling" occupations that needed a disciplined labor force. Yet economic motives were only one part of a larger context that not only favored reform, but also favored enacting it through the construction of large organizations, such as the penitentiary. As John Bender shows, the movement away from the old prisons (in England) filled a widening cultural gap brought on by the erosion of the *ancien régime,* particularly the deference given by plebs as reciprocity for the paternalism of the gentry (Bender 1987). This older, "cultural hegemony" was now undermined by the new factory system that was, at least nominally, based on the freedom of labor. The new penitentiary, as a cultural imaginary, required more than a one-person reformer and particular economic interests; it required imaginings in a parallel cultural system that could give it legitimacy, in architectural design as well as in philosophical terms. Part of this parallel system was the literature of novels, from Daniel Defoe to Henry Fielding, among others.

In England, a reimagining of the relation between human nature and physical space occurred. Imagining the new prison coincided with the central, "official" ideas of Locke and his descendants. From the philosophical theses advanced by Locke to the architectural designs planned by noted legal and social reformer Jeremy Bentham ([1787] 1995) in what he called the "Panopticon,"[4] the common contribution was to "locate reality in the instantaneous present of impressions and [to stress] the constructed, 'fictional' aspect of concepts such as self, character, justice, law, nature, final causation, and stable or self-evident notion of which they refused to accept" (Locke [1689] 1998: 35). It was the novel that provided the story of Locke's ideas, particularly in relation to the prison and confinement. With the erection of new penitentiaries in the late eighteenth century, the English Enlightenment, at least the official Enlightenment as articulated by Locke, found its concrete, practical application.

We argue that the counterpart to the new penitentiaries in England was the French establishment in the 1780s of national institutions for deaf and blind people. Just as English prison reform reflected the main intellectual focus of the English Enlightenment, so did the institutions for the deaf and the blind reflect the French Enlightenment. Yet aside from the obvious difference between the kinds of institutions, the contrast is important in a more crucial respect. The motivation and goal of prison reform in England was closely tied to the belief that criminals could be reformed and thereby made available to join the laboring class. Yet the deaf and the blind could not be so reformed. The "Molyneux problem" discussed from Locke to Diderot was almost wholly unanswerable. Given the extreme rarity of cases whereby an individual blind at birth could be surgically or therapeutically given eyesight at a later age, the case for the *education* of the blind (and deaf) was problematic at best. It had to be founded on grounds other than rehabilitation. Why, then, did such national institutions arise in France?

In fact, the justification for the education of the deaf and blind as a national project was not far removed from that advanced for prison reform in England: the common motivation for both was to enhance their integration into a new economic order. Such a motivation was voiced by Valentin Haüy (1745–1822),[5] the founder of the national institute for the young blind in Paris:

No, we never pretend that those of the blind who even discover the most shining parts shall enter into competition, either in the liberal sciences or mechanical arts, with scholars or artisans who are blessed with the use of sight, even when their talents arise not above mediocrity; but when any or all of these provinces are not properly supplied with persons who to the advantage of sight add professional abilities, the blind may then exert their powers, whether natural or acquired, as well in promoting private as public utility; and in this view it requires no mighty effort of courage to recommend them to the public benevolence and attention; and though their talents should not be sufficient to pre-engage the general taste in their favour, or the necessity of employing them, so considerable as to open a resource for their exigencies, yet the force of humanity alone may be adequate to produce an effect so desirable (Haüy 1894: 23).

Yet like the case for prison reform in England, such a strict economic motivation, although necessary, was not sufficient. The claim that the education of the blind was reasonable and thus legitimate was also made on noneconomic grounds, such as the utility of moral benefaction and restoration. As stated well by William Paulson: "The existence of special institutions for the teaching of the blind is justified not by virtue of their educability or resemblance to the seeing, but by virtue of the difficulty of teaching them, *the irreducible character of their difference*" (Paulson 1987: 96, emphasis added). The founding of national institutions for blind people, as for deaf people, was the extension of charity given to "appropriate objects of pity and compassion." Yet like the deserving poor, the blind had to be *worthy* of education.[6]

Working in the tradition of the French *Annales* school of historical writing that gives priority to *longue durée* (long-term historical structures), Zina Weygand (2009) has charted the pivotal periods in the establishment of new representations of blindness and institutional structures in France. She emphasizes that the intellectual and institutional contributions of Diderot, l'Épée, and Haüy in Paris were crucial in establishing the "ideology of the moral, intellectual, and professional education of the indigent blind" (Weygand 2009: 8) alongside the age-old alms-seeking, but that elsewhere in France completely insufficient services and support for education and independence existed, which perpetuated the charity model. Not until the innovation of tactile reading by Louis Braille and the resulting widespread access to written culture would blind people secure a fundamentally different representation and emphasis, one of access to education, through an innovative medium that facilitated learning.

*Alternative Institutional Paths: Punitive vs. Paternalistic Benevolence*

Above, we delineated philosophical similarities and differences with reference to the institutions and organizations founded by leading thinkers as they sought to put their ideas into practice. From this long-term historical perspective, the following principles and activities were found to varying degrees: charity and begging, confinement and punishment, productivity and working, education and schooling. The conception of alternative institutional paths of benevolence as *paternalistic* or *punitive* is guided by how the movement from apprenticeship to compulsory education was interrupted by either state intervention to care for persons with disabilities and illnesses or the control of delinquency and the regulation of child labor. The former is indicated by an earlier founding of state institutions for blind and deaf people and people with mental illnesses or disabilities, whereas the latter is indicated by an earlier founding of prisons and reformatories for delinquent youth. The judgment that such earlier institutional activities influenced benevolence to be paternalistic or punitive is a thematic characterization, a judgment about the dominant cultural view of benevolence toward populations considered to be deviant or disabled. Such a judgment borrows especially his "law of sequence," from the classic analysis of the morphology of folktales by Vladimir Propp ([1928] 1968). Similar to the *place* of an event in the flow of the folktale, it is the place of specific institutions in the broader, temporal *narration* of institution building that is the determining criterion for distinguishing the two alternative institutional paths (see also Marin 1978). Charting the establishment of national institutions and policies provides the sequence of these alternative institutional paths.

In Table 1.1, we compare the dates of institutional foundings and legislation for England and France. This selection of founding or enactment dates is bound by national legislation pertaining to apprenticeships and the dates on which free and compulsory schooling was enacted. The legislation pertaining to apprenticeship is identified as a beginning event because it is a critical indicator of the decline of traditional mechanisms as a means to both absorb poverty *and* instruct the young. Legislation pertaining to apprenticeship signified the improving material conditions brought by a market economy, yet indicated as well what such improvement brought with it—in Polanyi's rich terms, "an avalanche of social dislocation" (Polanyi 1957: 40). As noted earlier, the establishment of houses of correction that followed apprenticeship legislation reflects the attempt to counter social dislocations and as such, represented the mix of traditional arrangements with innovative views. Between the house of correction and the enactment of compulsory schooling lie the

TABLE 1.1. Comparing dates of institutional events: England and France

| England | Year | France |
|---|---|---|
| Workhouses | 1605 | |
| | 1611 | Workhouses |
| | 1656 | Hôpital Général |
| | 1750 | National Institute for Deaf-Mutes |
| Deaf school (first) | 1760 | |
| Prison reform | 1774 | |
| | 1785 | National Institute for Blind Youth |
| Juvenile reformatory | 1788 | |
| | 1834 | "Lunacy": asylums, psychiatry |
| | 1853 | Juvenile Reformatory (Metray) |
| "Lunacy": Metropolitan Poor Commission | 1867 | |
| Compulsory education: Elementary Education Act | 1870 | |
| | 1882 | Compulsory education |

*Sources*: Cooke-Taylor (1894); Pritchard (1963); Goldstein (1987); Foucault (1988); Heywood (1988); Davis (1995); Sewell (1996); Farr (2000). See also Richardson (2006) for more detailed list of events.

founding dates for juvenile reformatories and industrial schools, legislation on child labor, and state institutions to serve (and control) deaf and blind people and people with mental illnesses or disabilities.

This binary comparison reveals two patterns. The first is a common sequence: houses of correction are followed by institutions for the deaf and blind, which are followed by institutions for the "insane," ending with the enactment of compulsory education. For houses of correction, the difference between countries in years is negligible; for institutions for those with sensory impairments, the difference is only ten years; and for enacting compulsory education, the difference is only twelve years. This common sequence suggests a temporal similarity, despite national differences. For both countries, the institutional path to compulsory education began with a response to the decline of apprenticeship. The answer to this challenge to community life came in the form of legislation enabling local communities to erect workhouses wherein poor people could be confined and required to work.

From this legislative effort flowed subsequent institutional events: the establishment of benevolent institutions for people with disabilities and of reformatories to deal with crime and delinquency.

The second pattern, however, reveals critical junctures that reflect important cultural differences. The contrast between England and France is in large measure a contrast between decentralized and centralized national governance, which, in turn, defines the locus of authority over education. For England, decentralization reflected the prevailing influence of economic constraints; the major legislative preoccupation from 1802 to 1844 was the series of *Factory Acts* that sought, among other things, to enforce inspection of the treatment and education of child labor (Kydd [1857] 1966). Thus, popular education was inextricably connected to the economics of rising industrial employment.

Both countries had established workhouses in the early 1600s. Yet for England, the critical institutional event was prison reform, leading to establishment of the first juvenile reformatory, which occurred during the late decades of the eighteenth century. The comparable events for France do not occur until the middle of the nineteenth century. For France, the institutional events that paralleled prison and delinquency reform in England were the founding of the Hôpital Général (and its subsequent diffusion to many localities) and national institutions for the deaf and blind. In both England and France, schools for the deaf were formed within a decade of each other, but such schools in England were local organizations, whereas France established a national institution. Thus, the later decades of the eighteenth century were a turning point, decisive in shaping not only the subsequent course of institutional foundings, but also the educational intent of these institutions. The education of the "special classes" bears the imprint of these divergent paths. For England, the imprint was punitive benevolence, defined by the tight coupling of poverty and youth delinquency and accentuated by a decentralization of power. For France, the imprint was paternalistic benevolence, defined by the national stature of institutions for the deaf and blind, a stature that reinforced national ideals as superior to punitive institutions and practices (Richardson 2009).

*The Path of Punitive Benevolence.*    The social dislocations that came in the wake of large-scale economic development began much earlier in England than in France. For England, the problems of pauperism would become a persistent matter of statutory law as the Poor Laws replaced the Statute of Artificers. But although the Poor Laws were national in scope, their administration was entirely local. English decentralization was solidified early by the disconnection between the legal coherence of the Poor Laws and their fragmentation at the local level (Webb and Webb 1963: 223).

The succession of acts and statutes related present laws to their antecedents, and their cumulative reiteration around problems of vagrants, beggars, sturdy rogues, criminals and lunatic paupers tells a meta-narrative of English benevolence. A key element of English benevolence was the role of *inter vivos* charity, or "associated philanthropy," in which funding for the relief of the poor came from a large number of benefactors. This mode of charity established the key distinction between voluntary and endowed benefaction. Although similar in function, they were legally quite distinct. An orphan home maintained by voluntary subscriptions was relatively ignored by the law, whereas institutions maintained by charitable trust in perpetuity were the objects of periodic scrutiny. Both arrangements would have their nineteenth-century educational legacies. The endowed track would lead to a network of charity, workhouse, district, and separate schools tied to the state by way of the Charity Commission and subject to periodic royal investigations (Chance 1897). The voluntary track, in contrast, led to three marginal types of school, namely, ragged schools, industrial schools, and reformatory schools. These were born of the humanitarian sentiment that argued for separate residential institutions for the children of the "perishing" and "dangerous" classes (Guthrie [1860] 1973; Rubinstein 1969: 8; Carpenter 1970: chapter 2; Babler 1978). Also, a nearly invisible network of working-class schools existed largely beyond and outside the scope of state regulation.

The scale of these working-class "private schools," as Phil Gardner terms them, cannot be determined, for "there are no key dates, no 1833 or 1846; no great names . . . there is *no traceable institutional foundation*" (Gardner 1984: 11, emphasis added). They had no official place; rather, they were part of the daily routines of factories. Although invisible to official agencies, their existence long predates the enactment of compulsory education, attesting not only to the extent of voluntary education strategies, but also to their self-sufficiency and independence from state resources and administration. The combination of these three networks—the schools arising from the endowed track, the schools arising from the voluntary track, and the working-class private schools—produced a maze of schools that was decentralized to the point that counts of official school attendance and the population census rarely coincided. By the mid–nineteenth century, "the untidy mass of educational endowments seemed ripe for administrative rationalization and curricular reform" (Owen 1964: 249).[7] This complex of charity organizations and working-class schools established an institutional path of punitive benevolence centered on correctional and reformatory policies toward social deviance. This path would extend well into the twentieth century, culminating in the special education category of "social maladjustment." Indeed, today "emotional and social difficulties" is a widespread category of special educational need in developed countries (see OECD 2004: annex 2).

*The Path of Paternalistic Benevolence.* When we turn to France as a model of contrast to England, one of the most striking differences, which goes far to explain their different paths of institutional development, is the absence of anything comparable to the Poor Laws. The Poor Laws arose in England in the early part of the sixteenth century in large part because of the eradication of Catholic structures (principally monasteries) that cared for the indigent poor. As part of a political intent to form a unified state authority, those who enacted the Poor Laws struggled to develop them as an instrument of state centralization, yet were always blunted by local divisions and resistances. In France, the Catholic Church and its network of parishes and their clerics, maintaining their predominance, were far more effective. The French tradition of *bienfaisance,* sustained by Catholic doctrines of charity, was both a religious and social obligation.

Like England, eighteenth-century France witnessed the weakening of apprenticeships as the traditional barrier to inherited pauperism. Local communities of the old regime had their vagrants and indigent poor, but for the most part, they were cared for and protected by the "exchange" of piety for charity (see Viner 1968; Woloch 1986).[8] Throughout the French countryside, as well as in Paris, a network of "hospitals" grew where the poor, sick, aged, and infirm would be cared for—the local Hôpital Général (Jones 1989). This was guided more by the principle of confinement than medical treatment. Yet for the rising numbers of poor who could not be helped by relatives and who refused to work, charity turned to punitive measures, institutionalizing many in workhouses (*depots de mendicité*) that rid public spaces of the poorest and forced them to work.

The decline of a religiously sustained *bienfaisance* and the increasing reliance on secular forms of control was softened by the corporatist, paternalistic structure of work. French apprenticeship was much more than the practice of binding out youth to a master to learn a trade and gain rudimentary book learning. Far more than English apprenticeship, the relationship between apprentice and master was constrained by the "corporate idiom," the language of labor that referred to a moral community over instrumental exchanges. The master was the "core of the corporate community," and the community "was technically constituted by the masters alone" (Sewell 1980: 30). The corporate community was composed of a diverse number of smaller social entities, most notably the *compagnonnage* brotherhoods of journeymen. Much like the English associational philanthropy, such brotherhoods were forms of benevolent institutions, creating horizontal radial ties among apprentices and journeymen and structuring vertical hierarchies based on skill and status. With the nearly invisible erosion of the old regime, through incremental commercialization and centralization so keenly described by Alexis de Tocqueville (1955: 8, 23), cultural divisions emerged that intensified popular and governmental views of the poor. The turning point in French benevolence was the emergence of the *enfants trouvés*, the reality of "large numbers of innocent, abandoned foundlings" in hospitals (Forrest 1981: 117). The difference between illegitimate and neglected children whose parents were too poor to care for them and unwanted children who were deliberately abandoned because their parents feared losing employment became a focal point of popular, humanitarian opinion.

In contrast to English humanitarianism was the intellectual context of French Enlightenment. The humanitarianism of the 1770s and 1780s was actually a late manifestation, antedated by dramatic experiments and pedagogical breakthroughs in the treatment and education of the deaf, the blind, and the "idiotic." Nurtured by the climate of intellectual Enlightenment and the writing of the philosophes, the work of Edouard Seguin (1812–80) on the "physiological method" for curing "idiocy" (1866) contributed to work on the treatment of deaf mutes.[9] The pioneering work of Roch-Ambroise Sicard (1742–1822) and his teacher, Charles-Michel de l'Épée (1712–89), known as the "father of the deaf," led to the establishment of the National Institute for Deaf-Mutes in Paris, in 1750.[10]

For France, the transforming influence of the revolution in 1789 elevated the political above most other affairs. In contrast to England, France's institution for the deaf in 1750 was national in title and in purpose, as was its institution for the blind in 1785. Both were founded before the revolution, attesting to the influence of French Enlightenment thought on the conditions of blindness and deafness. The only legislation on child labor in France came in 1841, and it was largely ignored (Heywood 1988: 231; also Sewell 1980). Yet seven years earlier (1834), legislation established France's national commitment to asylums for the "moral treatment" of lunacy, promoting in turn the significance of psychiatry. The comparable event for England came thirty-three years later with the enactment of the Metropolitan Poor Act, which was less concerned with the treatment of the insane and more concerned with consolidating the administration of lunatic asylums at the district, not national, level.

Thus, for France, a key event in its sequence of institutional foundings was legislation that affirmed a national commitment to the treatment of physical and mental disabilities. Such a commitment inaugurated an institutional path of paternalistic benevolence, one that would diverge from the punitive treatment of the blind, the deaf, and the insane that was so entrenched in England and elsewhere throughout Europe. The establishment of national institutions for the deaf and blind signaled an "enlightened" view, as a national ideal and a national responsibility. For France, the infirmities of the body and mind were removed, by centralized authority, from economic constraints, and education as a response was elevated to a national ideal.[11]

## THE CIVILIZING PROCESS AS METANARRATIVE: A THEORETICAL SUMMARY

The many exchanges between the English descendents of Locke and the French philosophes represented a main axis of the remarkable intellectual revolution of the Enlightenment. Yet Enlightenment thought did not long remain the esoteric property of learned individuals and their elite networks. By way of the counter Enlightenment and the periphery Enlightenment, topics that may have begun as philosophical questions soon became issues with practical implications. The largest of these implications was addressed at length by Locke himself in his essay on education. If human understanding derives from experience, then individuals become that which is imprinted on their nature. By logical extension, the philosophical debate over the origins of human understanding becomes a debate over what they can and ought to become.

It is important to remember that Locke published *Some Thoughts Concerning Education* in 1693, just a few years after his *Essay Concerning Human Understanding*. Locke's focus on education was only partially an extension of his philosophical treatise in *Essay*. His work on education was, in fact, much more than some thoughts, for he advanced a theory of pedagogy decades before the topic of popular education would be broadly discussed. This emphasizes a key fact of historical timing: discussion of the potential and limitations of popular education long preceded its legislative implementation.

Locke's focus on education was not a personal peculiarity. On the contrary, the topic of education is evident across Enlightenment writings; it especially drew the attention of the French philosophes. The attention given to blindness, by no means confined to Diderot and Voltaire, suggests a national context that favored inquiry into human potential, or rather, human perfectibility. The French counterpart to Locke's *Thoughts* was Jean-Jacques Rousseau's *Émile ou de l'éducation* (Emile, or On Education), published in 1762 (2003). For both Locke and Rousseau, the topic of education was primarily the question of what the young should become and how to ensure that outcome. For Locke, the ideal outcome was becoming a gentleman and the ideal education was one that taught the social and civil restraints that were the necessary attributes for membership. For Rousseau, the ideal outcome was strikingly similar. Rousseau's celebrated sympathy toward the rural peasant belied his "smugness of superiority" that only a few were educable (Crocker 1976: 76). For both Locke and Rousseau, popular education never implied a democratic, national access. Their slim and practical works on popular education reflected an urgency to delimit education precisely as Enlightenment thought had expanded the inquiry into human potential (Kay 1868; Carpenter 1888?: 176; Mortier 1968).

If the official Enlightenment, the counter Enlightenment and the periphery Enlightenment constituted the trinary structure of thought, then human understanding, the senses, and popular education constituted its substantive structure, a marvelous internal coherence, never safe from external events and real circumstances.

Especially conspicuous was the social threat of vagabondage, a symbol of the dislocations brought on by the erosion of traditional institutions within and between communities. Yet the spread of vagabondage was a component of a broader event, the emergence of the *menu peuple*. From peasants now free to purchase and own land to the urban laboring classes, these groups did not participate in the Enlightenment; they "existed outside" it (Chisick 1981). The people encompassed a diverse number of groups previously distinguished from one another by feudal traditions and laws, as well as royal edicts. Yet by the mid–eighteenth century, the people were increasingly viewed in benign terms, as a mighty resource, national in scope and potential. With such a shift in view, the people took on admiring, indeed nobler attributes. It is here that Enlightenment thought met and fed the rise of institutions and specific organizations devoted to schooling.

There is, however, a crucial caveat: the "deserving" people played the lead role, and the "undeserving" played, at best, the understudy. Even for the deserving, incorporation into the "Nation" is problematic. As Philip Corrigan and Derek Sayer note about state formation, there is a key disjuncture between "society" and the "Society" (1985: chapter 6). The Nation signifies a level above and removed from the particularities of laboring, ethnic, and religious groups that inhabit "society." The formation of this level entails, without question, a coercive regulation of these groups, especially their rights to organize and be politically represented. This coercive regulation of collectivities that inhabit "society" is counter-balanced, as it were, by a moral regulation, exerted by improvement and religious organizations that represent "Society." The incorporation of collectivities via Society is a "*moral revolution*" that "culminates in a certain kind of admission—sponsored, protracted, conditional and profoundly disruptive—of [labor] into society" (Corrigan and Sayer 1985: 115, emphasis added). Although Corrigan and Sayer speak to the "working class question," one may insert equally marginal groups that inhabit society: the social deviancies of poverty, crime, and delinquency; physical and mental "abnormalities"; people with chronic illnesses and disabilities; and, with intensified affinity, indigent people with disabilities. Like the laboring classes, social deviants and those with differences of body and mind may inhabit society, but their inclusion in society has entailed a concerted moral revolution, where admission has been sponsored, protracted, conditional, and profoundly disruptive (Corrigan and Sayer 1985).

The distinction between the punitive benevolence in England and the paternalistic benevolence in France reflects different forms of sponsorship. It reflects the particular ways in which Enlightenment thought interacted with the founding of institutions, that is, how *the sequential order of institutions materialized ideas.*

This interaction resonates with the historical dynamic elaborated by Norbert Elias, the thesis that a "civilizing process" accompanied the rising material improvement that spread across Europe from the mid–eighteenth century on (Elias 2000). Where the conduct of the poor and laboring classes and the blind, deaf, and insane were the intellectual topic and target of practical interventions, this civilizing process turned to the institutions that were constructed to control, care for, and treat the troubling members of these classes. It is here that we may better understand Foucault's term "sensibilities" in describing the great confinement. For England, the extensive attention given to the education of pauper children, undeniable by the sheer volume of charity schools alone, combined a benevolent belief that "pauper children are dependent, not as a consequence of their errors, but of their misfortunes," with a punitive ideology asserting that "intellectual proficiency being an object of inferior value to the establishment of *good* habits" (Kay [1838] 1970: 2, 31, emphasis added). Charity, ragged, and pauper schools were at once evidence of benevolence toward poor children and sites for their socialization. The physical sites (schools) represented incorporation into society, yet exhibited the dominant pedagogy that was the means to sponsor that incorporation. As explicated above, the path of punitive benevolence reflects an amalgam of Enlightenment ideas: the moral benevolence of Shaftesbury with the critical irony of Mandeville and the conservatism of Defoe. And importantly, with institutions as the target of civilizing intentions, the disagreements and disputes between writers, as between Shaftesbury and Mandeville and Defoe, fade into irrelevance, usurped, as it were, by a higher purpose.

The rise of institutions appeared as the realization of Enlightenment ideas, as a culmination of the best of intentions. With such a founding purpose, institutions signaled the dawning of a new level of civilization. Within the confines of "protective" organizational forms, the education of the poor and laboring class would extend across generations as institutions joined technical instruction for admission to the trades with moral socialization enabling admission to society. Such a "pedagogical reach" (Richardson 2006) links the training of pauper children in the late eighteenth century to the reformation of hooligans in the late nineteenth century, and both to school "strikes" and protests by students with disabilities in prominent universities (see Edwards 1974; Humphries 1981; Barnartt and Scotch 2001).[12]

Similarly, the extensive attention given to blind and deaf people in France attests to a larger national sensibility. Although French Enlightenment thought played a significant role in the conceptual formation of the nation, the central ideas of the philosophes emphasized natural unity prior to political unity. The very intention of the *Encyclopédie* of Denis Diderot and Jean d'Alembert was in fact a unification of all knowledge. But the goal of such a project was grounded in the central belief that the universe "is in fact organized into a vast, rational, interconnected system," a system that, in its essential form, expressed "the geometric spirit" (Knight 1968: viii). Although the totality of this system is beyond the reach of observation, man can observe the parts of the system and comprehend how they are all interconnected. For the philosophes, such a theory of the physical world informed a theory of the social world. Benevolence toward the poor, paternalistic to be sure, nonetheless took the form of national ideals over local treatments. No doubt stimulated by a motivation to restrict church properties, major figures such as Diderot in particular "proposed nationalization of funds dedicated to the *hôpitaux* so that they might be distributed fairly according to the needs of institutions" (Payne 1976: 127). National institutions would be connected to more locally situated programs, each a part of an integrated whole. The geometric spirit of ideas would assume material form in a geometric distribution of institutions, the totality of which represented the nation.

For Elias, the civilizing process that transformed Western nations was characterized by an "extension of interdependence" propelled by an ever-advancing division of labor. Such an evolutionary theme has a long heritage, but Elias's emphasis is less on the evolutionary momentum than on the "chains" of interdependence and the "planes" of power. The civilizing process is not the result of rational intervention; on the contrary, it proceeds largely from its own cumulative momentum. Yet the result is broadly the same, the "long-term thinking and the active attunement of individual conduct to some larger entity remote in time and space"—a civilizing process that "spreads to ever-broader sections of society" (Elias 2000: 380).[13] As the civilizing of conduct spreads to lower strata and marginal groups, the groups rise, for their conduct is "forced increasingly in a direction originally confined to the upper strata" (Elias 2000: 381). Here, Elias joins an original historical force that is common to Western nations, to very different societal mechanisms, such as schooling, that have "forced" the behavior of lower and marginal groups.

We have sketched the process of the institutional development of benevolence—one primarily punitive, the other primarily paternalistic—in England and France, respectively. We have traced these different emphases back to the trinary structure of Enlightenment thought, the ways in which leading thinkers and legislators reacted to the social problems of the time, and the sequential order in which institutions and organizations were founded to deal with social, demographic, and economic challenges such as poverty, delinquency, and disability. These institutions and organizations were the realizations of key Enlightenment ideas that were assumed to have a civilizing influence, especially on poor people—mainly through social control, less so through education. The importance of education in compensating for differences in human sensing was the harbinger of what we now take for granted as "special education." Pedagogical innovations in France, from sign language to Braille, were crucial in facilitating the learning process as well as in revising the boundaries of human potential. These changes occurred first in national institutions within a centralized country. By contrast, in England, reformers established new forms of local organizations, such as prisons, representing original social control mechanisms. Although both pathways were viewed as necessary responses to social problems and on their own terms were innovative, they set their countries on contrasting developmental trajectories as education gradually began to rise as the central means for the nation-state to develop, socialize, and monitor *all* of its citizens.

## CHAPTER 2

# ECONOMIC CHANGE, STATE MAKING, AND CITIZENSHIP

INSTITUTIONALIZING RESPONSES TO SO-cial deviance and disability did not result only from En-lightenment thought or solely because of the engagement and activism of a few individuals, influential as these builders of myriad organizations were. Economic change, state-making activities, and broadened, more democratic conceptions of citizenship would also prove crucial as origins of special education. Much like the late eighteenth century marked the genesis of special education in terms of ideas and principles, the late nineteenth century marked its formal inauguration with the enactment of national compulsory education laws, which would vastly increase the diversity of learners in public schooling. This origin point may be found in Northern and Western Europe. For some countries, compulsory education was the logical next step in the process of breaking the inherited cycle of pauper-ism by incorporating youth in more beneficent and pedagogical ways—

providing an alternative to the dangers and drudgery of factory work. With European nations taking the lead, the idea of mass schooling gained legitimacy and has diffused throughout the world since (see Meyer, Ramirez, and Soysal 1992).

As mass schooling was coupled with economic development, a minimum education available to all was increasingly viewed as being among the best indications of a nation's strength and stature.[1] Yet "education for all" was far from being realized. The schooling of people with disadvantages and disabilities, now categorized as the "special classes," germinated gradually within mass schooling. This partial, selective integration, based largely on the nascent professions, gave rise to special classes and schools. These were considerably smaller in scale than state institutions, but similar in function nonetheless, and they relied most heavily on state resources, instead of the charity of churches, families, and individuals as they had in earlier eras.

Thus, to understand the origins of contemporary special education—and the beginning of its tremendous rise in differentiated education systems over the course of the twentieth century—important lessons can be drawn from theories of state making and the enactment of individual rights that came with expansive notions of citizenship. A substantial body of scholarship on the formation of nation-states has addressed both the timing of their emergence and their institutional form. Yet there is no clear relationship between timing and form. Although the European nation-states may be exemplary, they present a two-fold problem: what explains their emergence from the fifteenth century to the late seventeenth century, on the one hand, and what accounts for their external and internal variation, on the other? Answers have bearing on the institutionalization of special education and its contemporary organizational forms.

## EDUCATION SYSTEMS AS NATIONAL RECONFIGURATIONS

### Lessons from the Formation of Nation-States

Like national or state education systems that emerge in large part by supplanting voluntary and private arrangements, the Western nation-state overcame alternative models, namely, trans-local structures based on networks of commercial ties as well as religious dominance over secular affairs. Comprehensive historical works converge on the critical role that power struggles and wars played in generating "state-making processes." Thus, aside from some variation in timing, that is, whether a state emerged comparatively early or late, the formation of the nation-state was a triumph of sovereignty and constitutional representations that by the nineteenth century was largely induced by incessant competition and violent struggles (Poggi 1978: 86–116).

The pressures to secure the necessary resources to wage war led to alliances and compromises that contributed, in turn, to the concession of rights and the extension of protections. Such state-making processes blurred the distinction between external forces and internal adaptations (Tilly 1990: 185). The internal structure of class relations interacted with external pressures, determining the capacity to engage in profitable commerce and effective warfare. Yet most important is how the pressures of competition among nation-states shaped internal responses, including to schooling and other social welfare provisions, which have become distinguishing marks of Western nation-states. External pressures bound monarchies to landed elites and joined both to the potential resistance and demands of a peasantry, or commercial class. Internal relations became more interdependent, yet groups gained a heightened sense of their relative power. Political crises moved upward, enabling certain groups "to complement the 'public sphere' constructed from above with a 'public realm' formed by individual members of the civil society transcending their private concerns" (Poggi 1978: 82). Thus, although the combination of external pressures and internal political crises strengthened the coercive reach of states, this upward movement yielded quite the opposite result: the increasing reliance of states on local resources, from administrative personnel to soldiers, augmented internal activities that were once marginal to the state-making processes of war and competition. These lower-level activities, denoted by Charles Tilly as adjudication, distribution, and production, involved "more state intervention outside the realm of coercion and war" (Tilly 1990: 97). The lower-level process expanded the citizenry, albeit slowly, but most of all it began the shift from indirect to direct rule. The shift occurred during the period of nationalization, roughly between 1700 and 1850, when states created mass armies and assumed direct control over fiscal matters (Tilly 1990). This was also the period when states contemplated the idea of free, but compulsory primary education; in some nation-states, for example, Prussia, this was widely implemented (see Cummings 1999).

The period when state powers began the shift to direct rule is a reasonable indicator of the emergence of the nation-state, defined by sovereignty and representative politics. The question of timing might be assumed to be an issue of what hastened or slowed the transition from indirect to direct rule. Yet the augmented power of the state to penetrate into the lives of local communities was, as Michael Mann keenly notes, a "two-way street" (Mann 1993: 59). Distinguishing between despotic and infrastructural power, Mann sorts out the variations in the form of nation-states by focusing on what he calls the "radial development of institutions." Despotic power denotes the capacity of a central state authority to exert controls over local communities and representatives of civil society "without routine negotiation." Infrastructural power is the institutional capacity of a central state to implement its policies. Thus, the growth of despotic power enhances infrastructural power; however, this in turn enables collective institutions to restrain the actions of central authorities. By cross-classifying despotic and infrastructural power, Mann produces ideal types: the imperial-absolutist and the bureaucratic-democratic, which are distinguished by contrasting levels of each mode of power. Imperial-absolutist states are high in despotic power, but low in infrastructural power; bureaucratic-democratic states have the opposite combination. If France exemplified the imperial-absolutist state, then England would be classified as a bureaucratic-democratic state. As discussed in Chapter 1, the former led to a paternalistic form of benevolence focused on institutions and national organizations, and the latter developed a punitive form of benevolence focused on individuals and local organizations.

Encompassing such variations as judicial and legislative structures and property versus political franchise, Mann's definition of infrastructural power as "radial institutions" indicates how the development of such institutions may be formally tied to central state authority, yet nonetheless restrains the reach of this authority. Like Tilly's state-making processes, the development of radial institutions suggests a key intervening process that can explain the variable capacity of a nation's infrastructure to limit despotic power. But the importance of infrastructural power raises the question of the origins of

TABLE 2.1. Comparing thought, benevolence, and state in England and France

|  | England | France |
|---|---|---|
| Focus of Enlightenment thought | Rationality | Sensory ability |
| Benevolence type | Punitive | Paternalistic |
| Nation-state type | Bureaucratic-democratic | Imperial-absolutist |
| State infrastructure | Territorial-based assembly | Status-based assembly |

its own variation. Addressing this question directly, Thomas Ertman (1997: 26) notes the frustrations of prior theories to pinpoint more sharply the capacity of infrastructural institutions to resist central state authority. Like Mann's typology, Ertman cross-classifies state infrastructure by "character", whether patrimonial or bureaucratic, and by political regime, whether absolutist or constitutional. France typifies the combination of a patrimonial state infrastructure with an absolutist political regime, and England typifies the combination of a bureaucratic infrastructure with a constitutional regime. Such differences between England and France in Enlightenment thought, benevolence, and type of nation-state are compared in Table 2.1.

A critical variable in explaining differences in state infrastructures is the distinction between territorial-based and status-based assemblies. Territorial-based assemblies, typified by England, Poland, Hungary and the Scandinavian countries, were largely two-chamber representative structures, with the higher chamber representing the nobility and the lower representing the common people, in effect, the country. The status-based assemblies of the German territories and Latin Europe were tricurial in structure, with a separate chamber for each of the three "estates" of clergy, nobility, and burghers. Here, representation was not so linked to concrete territorial entities as to the symbolic powers of the Estates. As Thomas Ertman notes, the key to this categorical distinction was not so much the number of chambers as their "internal structure" (Ertman 1997: 21), specifically, the degree to which representation reached into the local level. Here, the territorial-based assemblies were far more embedded in local communities, and were, as a result, more structurally durable. The distinction, while broadly clarifying, is incomplete, for it does not by itself explain the persistently divergent forms of European states in spite of the common external pressures of competition and industrialization. The more clarifying aspect was *when* a country experienced these external pressures. According to Ertman, the nonsimultaneous experience of external pressures was key: "[D]ifferences in the timing of the onset of sustaining geopolitical competition go a long way towards explaining the character of state infrastructures found across the continent at the end of the 18th century" (Ertman 1997: 26). For example, the experience of an external pressure such as war may certainly induce a state to enhance its competitiveness. Thus, consistent with the distinction between territory and state-based assemblies, Ertman also demonstrates persuasively that the character of local government (state infrastructure) prior to 1450 is a strong "predictor" of the "actual distribution of absolutist and constitutional regimes found in the 18th century" (29). The strength of Ertman's thesis is the emphasis he gives to the interaction of a state's infrastructure and when it experienced external pressures.

A second lesson to draw from Ertman's thesis is that latecomers may not necessarily be able to catch up. Ertman demonstrates how state structures (forms) are "path dependent" and how the specific ways in which a state infrastructure interacted with external pressures at a particular time shaped the pace at which the state would subsequently develop. This suggests that wars and other forms of competition—especially the ever-increasing economic and, more recently, scientific and technological rivalries—are surface reflections of the long series of interactions between state infrastructures. These interactions are events that witness the expansion and contraction of social relations and their radial institutions.

State making, seen this way, is akin to how Philip Abrams suggested we view towns: ". . . as moments in a process of usurpation and defense, consolidation, appropriation and resistance; as battles rather than as monuments" (Abrams 1997: 31). Such a view concentrates on the dynamic sequences of change, a focus that inhibits the construction and intrusion of "spurious social entities." The town, in this instance, is not an entity with clearly demarcated boundaries; rather, it is a space and a time wherein the dynamics of power exchange occur. This dynamic sequence is akin to Max Weber's "nonlegitimate domination," wherein burghers, once freed from their dependence on feudal authority, in turn imposed themselves on the peasants and artisans. With equal applicability to towns and nations, the instrument of this nonlegitimate domination was "usurpation through an act of rational association"

(Weber 1978: 1212–1372). Whether the topic is the rise of towns, the formation of the nation-state, or the expansion of national education systems, we
shall see below that all are forms of confraternization, each, as it were, a "legal person." Viewing them as "moments in a process of usurpation and defense" relaxes the inclination to seek finer distinctions of type.[2]

A final lesson may be one that juxtaposes variation and similarity. In their
study of English state formation as a cultural revolution, Philip Corrigan and
Derek Sayer argue persuasively against viewing the state as a single and tangible entity. English state formation was a struggle—"material, categorical,
moral"—that was brought in by a "new theory of representation" (Corrigan
and Sayer 1985: 116). Principally, the linking of property possession with the
exercise of rights was the material; the boundary between inclusion and
exclusion—primarily the exclusion of the laboring classes, of women and of
people with disabilities—was the categorical; the legitimation of state intervention was the moral. In political interpretation, the legitimation of state
intervention permitted the market "on which laissez-faire theory depends,"
(Corrigan and Sayer 1985: 118) revealing "society" as a fictional entity composed of individuals now free to enter into a multitude of relations. Society
becomes an object in and of itself: the welfare of the poor and laboring
classes is transformed from a political to a national concern; factories are in-
spected as a means to secure this; the education of children becomes a moral
obligation and a practical imperative. With this new theory of representation, the radial institutions of union workhouses, reformatories, and asylums
become more public obligations than local possessions. All along, however,
the state and society operate at different levels. The former is the agent of the
moral transformation of old and now illegitimate collectivities; the latter is
now composed of new collectivities that are, nonetheless, as unequal and
stratified as their predecessors. As access to the nation expanded, the role of
the state to sponsor admission expanded.[3]

The foregoing lessons from theories of the nation-state suggest that it is
more profitable to view education systems not as culminations, but rather as
reconfigurations. Even if a state or national act legislates education as "free
and compulsory" and does so in a way that is markedly different from earlier
legislations, the details that specify how, when, and where the law will apply
reveal new levels of variation. Some details are positive elements, such as the

amount of schooling that is provided free, whereas others are negative, such as punishment for noncompliance. The former is a quantitative advance expressed as a sacred right to be universalized, and the latter is a quantitative constraint expressed as a profane obligation. Whether legislated in a centralized or a decentralized state, free and compulsory schooling reconfigures both elements. The analytical problem that remains is to explain both the origins of this reconfiguration and the particular form it assumes.

### Theoretical Consolidations

*T. H. Marshall and the Double Process of Social Change.* Whether the problem of state and national education systems is their origins or their institutional form, the distinctive beginning point is that schooling ceases to be predominantly voluntary. At the same time, who participates in which forms of schooling reveals vital information on the categorical boundaries of citizenship. Complete inclusion in public schooling has not been fully achieved, of course, for sectarian and other forms of private schooling persist, but the exclusion of categories of children and youth from schooling based on their perceived "educability" or disability becomes less and less legitimate. Private schools are maintained alongside the system of state, or public, schools, and in most instances, they are subordinate to state regulation. By stipulating some level of schooling to be an individual right, the formation of national education systems parallels the idea of citizenship and the political, civil, and social rights that have accompanied its elaboration.

Like the contrast in approaches to explaining education systems and nation-states, there is no shortage of contrasts in explanations for citizenship rights. Yet unlike the former, the lineage of theoretical approaches to citizenship may be said to originate with the seminal statement by T. H. Marshall (1964). Marshall's proposal was notably succinct: citizenship rights are inseparably linked to the dynamic relations of social classes, and their elaboration has proceeded sequentially, from civil to political to social rights. The widely acknowledged limitations in Marshall's thesis have been the inspiration for a number of different approaches to citizenship. At the very least, Marshall's early statement "crafted citizenship as an explanatory framework" (Janoski 1998: 3), and the contrasting intellectual paths taken since differ according to whether the concept is viewed as a dependent or an independent variable (Brubaker 1992: 21). For special education, the crucial element is that full citizenship for people with disabilities, even among the wealthiest Western countries, has been realized only in recent decades with the rise of human rights and disability movement activities (see Janoski 1998; Carey 2009 on disability and citizenship).

There is no intention and no need here to review the considerable literature that occupies the roads taken "since Marshall." Rather, the intent is to revive, but at the same time reconceptualize Marshall's central proposition—that citizenship comprises three elements, three sets of rights, that have "evolved" sequentially. The first element is composed of civil rights, the rights necessary for individual freedom. Marshall joins liberty of the person, freedom of speech, thought and faith, the right to own property and to conclude valid contracts, and the right to justice. The second element is composed of political rights, those that enable individuals to participate in the exercise of political power. The third element is the social element, which ranges from the right to a minimal level of economic welfare to the right to live a life commensurate with the prevailing standards of a community. Marshall further proposed that each set of rights had particular institutions attached to them. Thus, the courts of justice were associated with civil rights; parliament and councils of local government have been the institutional embodiments of political rights; the institutions "most closely connected [with social rights] are the educational system and the social services" (Marshall 1964: 8).

If for Marshall the manifest topic is citizenship rights, his latent topic is the institutions with which rights are associated. Yet it may be just as useful to reverse the order, viewing institutions as the manifest topic, and rights, the latent. Then it is the founding of institutions that moves at different rates of speed, and as they are established, their routine functions and administrative practices that regulate access and exclusion accumulate as a collective meaning system, the conceptual source of rights and obligations. The ideological shift to which Marshall refers becomes, then, a reflection of a more concrete generating process, that of legislating the founding of physical structures and social regulations that organize first around the "old assumption" and then around the "new assumption."

The view that confers a primary significance to the founding of concrete physical institutions—the array of organizational forms—was elaborated in

Chapter 1: the rise of asylums, poorhouses, workhouses, prisons, houses of refuge, industrial and reform schools, and state hospitals.[4] As individual case studies and as comparative investigations, studies suggest supportive evidence for Marshall's proposition that the development of these citizenship rights has followed a sequential path.[5] This process continues to unfold; for example, with the 2006 International Convention on the Rights of Persons with Disabilities (UN 2006; see Chapter 6). Now we return to economic change, which impacted nation-states' power and which would influence the quantity and quality of provisions in education and social welfare.

*Karl Polanyi and the Double Movement of Economic Change.* In his classic work, *The Great Transformation*, Karl Polanyi (1957) advanced a penetrating analysis and interpretation of the economic origins of the twentieth century and of the political outcomes that were so destructive to so many. At the center of these economic and political changes was a claim of immense scope: the collapse of "nineteenth-century civilization." For Polanyi, the civilization of the nineteenth century rested on four pillars: the balance-of-power system, the gold standard, the self-regulating market, and the liberal state. Although the collapse of the gold standard was the decisive blow, the "fount and matrix" of the system was the self-regulating market. Polanyi's explanation for this great transformation was centered on this pillar: "our thesis is that the idea of a self-adjusting market implied a stark utopia" that "could not exist for any length of time without annihilating the human and natural substance of society" (1957: 3). The response to the expanding industrial market system was certainly articulated and led by ideological forces, but it was far more general than what might be reduced to class interests. The response was inevitable, for "society took measures to protect itself," which, in turn, initiated further disruptions and intensified the overall collapse (Polanyi 1957: 3).

With striking parallels to Marshall's "double process," Polanyi condenses his considerable historical evidence around a single, dynamic process as well, what he terms the "double movement." In all modern nations, there are two organizing principles: the principle of economic liberalism that promotes the creed of laissez-faire and the principle of social protection that seeks to conserve man and his natural condition against the "threat to the human and natural components of the social fabric" (Polanyi 1957: 132, 150). The expansion of an industrial market economy, particularly when left unregulated, threatens the broader social solidarity of society, which extends its destructive effects not only into man's economic well-being, but also into his very nature. At the other end of a laissez-faire market economy were two forms of collective protection, which Polanyi termed reciprocity and redistribution (1957: 47), examples he drew primarily from anthropological literature. The example of reciprocity fits societies (such as the Trobriand Islanders) in which there is an effective system of exchange relating to sexual organization, one that balances marriage and kinship by way of the balanced exchange of women. This institutional pattern of symmetry, or dual organization, underlies the effectiveness of an economic reciprocity. The example of redistribution fits societies that have a common chief from whom produced goods are distributed according to need. This institutional pattern of centricity underlies the distribution of economic production. Centricity and symmetry are not mutually exclusive; rather, they are political structures that are mutually adjusted as a society changes in size and composition. For Polanyi, both reciprocity and redistribution illustrate that individual interest and material inequality are exceptions and not the rule. The principles of economic liberalism and collective protection have ideological faces that on the surface debate and struggle with each other. But here Polanyi's thesis becomes methodologically sophisticated.

Ideological and class struggles are real and influential and seemingly arise at common times armed with similar intentions. Yet it is precisely this temporal coincidence that Polanyi exploits, minimizing the long-term influence of class interests. Class-based explanations become, in effect, spurious:

The countermovement against economic liberalism . . . possessed all the unmistakable characteristics of a spontaneous reaction. At innumerable disconnected points it set in without any traceable links between the interests directly affected or any ideological conformity between them . . . . Moreover, we suggested that comparative history of governments might offer quasi-experimental support of our thesis if particular interests could be shown to be independent of the specific ideologies present in a number of different countries. For this also we could adduce striking evidence (Polanyi 1957: 149–150).

It was an *underlying process* that "set in," a double movement between a self-regulating market and society's self-protective response to its effects. As Polanyi notes, not even the staunchest of economic liberals argued for laissez-faire when faced with the social calamities of the market system. One of the most important responses to such negative consequences has become the tremendous investments in schooling and training by states and individuals alike.

Like Marshall's double process of fusion and separation, Polanyi's double movement was an underlying dynamic that best accounted for similar events occurring across nations that were otherwise quite dissimilar. England, Germany, Austria, and France were "poles apart," but in the same era, each passed legislation pertaining to public health, factory inspection, workmen's compensation, and social insurance. Thus, despite the "most varied slogans" and motivations, varied political parties and social strata, similar legislation was passed to establish principles to respond to social problems recognized as demanding of state intervention and (differing) measures of control.

Polanyi employed the concept of double movement with particular reference to the rise of politically reactionary movements and to the Great War that was among the factors in the "collapse" of civilization. Yet his conceptual argument is equally relevant to the form and content of working-class movements and other counter-movements. In this respect, his argument may reasonably be extended to the history of treatments, authoritarian and benign, toward people with disabilities.

The relation between "the laws of the market" and the "organic forms of existence" was inherently antagonistic (Polanyi 1957: 163). The organizations of "kinship, neighborhood, profession and creed" were examples of noncontractual social relations, distinct from the contractual relations of a laissez-faire market system. The principles of economic liberalism reached into these noncontractual relations and directly threatened both their survival and their legitimacy. Because their relations were organic, based on trust and affective reciprocity, they were seen as constraints on the freedom of the individual to engage in commercial exchange and thus to maximize economic gain. Because the ultimate unit was the individual, the principles of economic liberalism defined all intermediary groups as barriers to the freedoms achieved through unrestricted economic participation.

It is instructive that Polanyi noted the parallels between the economic liberalism of advanced Western nations and the ideology of colonial imperialism.

The natives of colonies controlled by Western nations "were to be forced to make a living by selling their labor." The traditional societies of colonial peoples were barriers to economic freedom much like the organic forms of modern societies. Traditional societies lacked the very idea of poverty, for the prospect of a single individual going hungry was inconceivable. The idea of poverty was Western, elaborated and exported from the sixteenth century on.

*Integrating Marshall and Polanyi: Social Mechanisms and the Origins of Special Education.*   Among the main implications of Marshall's thesis is the proposal that the development of rights that define citizenship has a directionality: a sequential progression. The struggles over civil rights generate the seeds of political struggles that, in turn, eventuate in legislation that enacts social rights. The generating force is an ever-widening mobilization, an accentuation of the democratic principle of common participation. Thus, accompanying the more horizontal character of citizenship rights is a vertical dimension of societal incorporation. Among the major implications of Polanyi's thesis is his insistence that the social defines the economic; that institutions structure all economic transactions and change.

Applied to our case of special education, the notion of directionality seen in these concepts need not imply a benign linearity—that special education has moved progressively from exclusion to inclusion. On the contrary, if the direction taken by special education began as one of support and service to those completely excluded from public schooling, it has now been overtaken by changing societal norms that emphasize the social right of participation. The structure of special education in a particular country, as we shall see in Part 2, is not easily transformed, especially given the incremental and path-dependent change typical of complex education systems. The accumulation of paths taken and not taken constitutes the "history" of special education. Nonetheless, the structure of existing institutions sets the parameters of change.

Although both Marshall and Polanyi identify the general dynamics of change, most often by the term "principle," they both also suggest very specific mechanisms that generate patterns of long-term change. For Marshall, the mechanism is a "double process," one of fusion, another of separation. These twin dynamics involved a contrast in the movement of rights, a downward movement from royal authority to local communities for civil and political rights and an upward movement from local communities to the national level for social rights. As these movements occurred, there was the assumption or fusion of authority by new agents as functions became separated from local communities, towns, and guilds. The consequence for the institutions "on which the three elements of citizenship depended" has been that they "parted company"; the consequence for the machinery "giving access to the institutions" has been that [they] "had to be shaped afresh" (Marshall 1964: 9). The larger result, as Marshall portrayed it, was that the three elements of citizenship became in effect "divorced," proceeding at such different speeds that it is possible "to assign the formative period in the life of each to a different century—civil rights to the eighteenth, political to the nineteenth, and social to the twentieth" (Marshall 1964: 10). During the course of this transformation, a crucial ideological shift occurred, from an "old assumption that local and group monopolies were in the public interest" to a "new assumption that such restrictions were an offence against the liberty of the subject and a menace to the prosperity of the nation" (Marshall 1964: 11). Marshall warned that this sequential process "must be treated with reasonable elasticity," for because the progress of each element occurred at different speeds, there was overlap, "especially between the last two" (Marshall 1964: 10). Yet this perspective is challenged by a minority group of people with disabilities, because their citizenship rights have been significantly compressed in time, since even within the first half of the twentieth century few rights were accorded this heterogeneous group (see Powell 2011). Only over the past several decades have disability equal rights laws been passed throughout the world (see Quinn and Degener 2002), in attempts to solidify and protect the rights of people with disabilities.

For Polanyi, the mechanism was the interplay of two broad principles: reciprocity and redistribution: "the two principles of behavior not primarily associated with economics" (Polanyi 1957: 47). Reciprocity relates primarily to the spheres of family and kinship, defining their relation between the sexual and reproductive sphere of society and the economic sphere, the self-regulating market system. Redistribution relates to the allocation of material, economic goods. Both principles are social mechanisms that have integration and orderliness as their central objectives. While both are social in their operation, they favor the continuity of the market system by immunizing the market from disturbances coming from the organic relations of family and community and by ensuring the orderliness and legitimacy of production and distribution. Polanyi notes, "As long as social organization runs in its ruts . . . no [individual] economic motives need come into play," for "man's economy is submerged in his social relationships" (Polanyi 1957: 47).

Yet social organization does not always "run in its ruts." The rise of rural pauperism and vagabondage, discussed in Chapter 1, altered the principles of reciprocity and redistribution. As effects of a spreading market system, both were deviancies that triggered protective reactions, no doubt inspired by genuine needs to preserve traditional behaviors. The breakdown of reciprocity and redistribution activated, as it were, Marshall's double process of fusion and separation. In this context, the middle and late eighteenth-century attention to blind, deaf, and mad people was a forced attention, akin to reactions to vagabondage and pauperism. The turn to institutions as a means to treat and educate was, in this context, a response motivated by the desire to control, as Foucault (1988) has argued; but also, simultaneously, it was a response motivated by the desire to preserve. Large-scale institutions were, in this light, expressions of the need for renewed reciprocity and redistribution. And more than the individual figures whose celebrated works and methods presumed to lead the way, the construction of institutions was a collective endeavor much like the construction of cathedrals. They were instrumental means that objectified the invention of the idea of society.[6]

More contemporary events, specifically the shift away from the "post-welfare" society of the 1960s and 1970s and back toward the more politically conservative decades of the 1980s and 1990s, suggests how recurring Polanyi's concept of double movement has been and how consequential it is for education. As Tomlinson (2001: 34) chronicles for England, the social optimism and egalitarian reforms that marked the postwar welfare years gave way to political strains over economic competitiveness, which in turn fed the anxieties of parental strategies to ensure their children's access to education and education-based mobility. The concerns and anxieties about the economic standing of the nation elevated the primacy of market forces and their exigencies—namely, the accentuation of the training of skills necessary to meet the perceived demands of a new global economy. As a consequence, controls over teaching and the curriculum and forms of school grouping moved upward, away from the historic partnership between the state and local authorities and toward a greater centralization of education. Polanyi's "laws of the market" swept over and dwarfed the authority of liberal principles and their noncontractual social relations. The competition of the market has seeped into family, neighborhood, and community relations, raising the anxieties between social classes (see Ball 1993: 12), even as education became increasingly privatized (see Tomlinson 2008), with the state retracting itself from sponsorship of higher education.

Returning to a finding of Chapter 1, there is no single origin of special education. There are multiple origins, recurring in patterned ways that vary in their amenability to prediction. These recurring origin points are triggered by Polanyi's double movement, and then set into motion Marshall's process of fusion and separation. Within these general processes, disability and education have been transformed, with tremendous consequence for individuals with disabilities and societies alike.

*De-Civilizing Disability and the Rationalization of Institutions.* In his *History of Disability*, Henri-Jacques Stiker (1999) concurs that the late eighteenth century was a turning point between old ideas and their institutions and new ideas and their institutions. As he notes:

The year 1770 may serve as reference point for this development—incredible in its effects, since it will dominate the two following centuries, that is, until the present day. In 1770 physicians paid by the royal administration begin to spread across the French countryside. This is the realization of the medical profession's great dream to care for the ill and in so doing to become the adjudicators of a social norm that is defined on the basis of norms of life and of health (Stiker 1999: 104).

The change in ideas was considerable. Throughout the Middle Ages, the infirmities of body and mind were viewed as "monstrosities," sinful and unalterable. The particularly monstrous conditions of deafness and blindness were minimized by the confluence of both with pauperism. Yet as Stiker reminds us, these prevalent images of disability did not entirely confine the deaf, blind, crippled, or insane to the margins of society. Rather, disability often played a central role in communities and alongside power: the madman could utter things to the populous that the king could not, and did so with the king's blessing. Thus there were "two kinds of marginality: that which challenges the social order and that, much deeper, which calls into question the organization of culture and ideology. To the former belong the robbers and rovers, to the second, the disabled or foreigners" (Stiker 1999: 85). The two, as Stiker notes, have long been "confused in the general mind." The differentiation of disability from pauperism was an empirical shift; but the "decivilizing" of disability was part of a different, albeit related, process of marginalization.

As we have argued, in the previous chapter, Enlightenment thought, particularly its peripheral form, articulated the intellectual rationale for the new marginalization of disability. The influence of French social thought in general and of Diderot's work in particular set the standard for a "completely new concern"—for *education* and *rehabilitation*: "Diderot's text inaugurates the period when aberrancy, monstrosity, diminished faculties, and deformity will be addressed as simple impairments" (Stiker 1999: 85). Diderot's benign intellectualization of blindness was certainly a revolt against monstrosity. Yet it was "perhaps not so far removed from the social space that is assigned to all marginality," for such a space *under the command of reason*, is the confines of the hospital" (Stiker 1999: 103, emphasis added).

Stiker's wording, "under the command of reason," provides considerable help in understanding the rise of institutions and organizations at the close of the Enlightenment. Organizations would be specialized according to the nascent professions of the day and founded on recognized instructional methods and their technologies; they could have avowed goals, to teach the deaf student to sign or to use rudimentary speech and the blind student to read Braille (Stiker 1999: 107). The construction of these new organizations profited by their contrast to the workhouse, for they believed discipline and punishment were neither necessary nor legitimate. State institutions for deaf and blind people and other organizations were entrepreneurial undertakings whose continuation largely rested on the reputation of the founding figure, and reputations were linked to the success of instructional methods. They were, in essence, cultural exhibits that rested on delicate financial grounds.

*Revaluing Disability: From Parasitic to Exchange Value.* The change in perceptions and beliefs about disability was simultaneously a process of differentiation—distinguishing disability from poverty—and a process of remarginalization, terminating both the silence of familial embrace and the socially and politically "special" roles of jester, sage, and conscience. By the late eighteenth century, disability became the topic of intellectual reflection, not only about particular conditions, but also about the general capacity to participate in and contribute to the nation. Again in Stiker's words: "It was no longer a question of simply gathering the disabled together, or even of putting them to work as less than able-bodied. The objective was rather to provide entry to the common cultural and social heritage of their fellow citizens" (Stiker 1999: 107). However, this shift in ideas about disability is not simply intellectual history, for it was accentuated by another process of change. By the mid–eighteenth century, the course of an intellectual history about disability encountered an institutional history, one that began in the early seventeenth century with the workhouse and the encompassing deviance of vagabondage. By the late eighteenth century, these two histories intersected, setting the context for the rise of "new" institutions and organizational forms.

The rise of new institutions and organizations for education and rehabilitation has been the subject of variable explanations. These explanations sort by vocabularies of motive, ranging from the restrictive machines of social control to the benign intentions of treatment and cure. The former highlight antagonistic relations, principally those of class and culture; the latter highlight the appeals to an orderly past or ride the optimism that accompanies new theories about human behavior. At the center of this division is disability on the one hand and deviance on the other. As new institutions arose "under the command of reason," new images of disability, disadvantage, and deviance emerged, and with them came new images of social order. The causal dynamics do not agree easily with either adherents of social control or believers in ideal reconstruction. Explanation requires elements of both, for the actual relationship between ideas and institutions was highly fluid and reciprocal. Even as new ideas led to the imagining of new institutions, as in the case of Bentham and his penitentiary, old beliefs and traditional structures retained their power, leading to gradual, path-dependent change instead of wholesale replacement. The logic of the workhouse carried over to the rationale for the asylum and hospital, and the latter influenced the design of reform and industrial schools.

To place the "deviance" of disability in the center of competing explanations for the rise of institutions is akin to Stiker's reminder that prior to the late eighteenth century, disabilities enjoyed a political and social centrality. To be sure, "centrality" overstates. A fruitful depiction is provided by Michel Serres and his concept of the parasite (Serres 1982). As Serres points out, the term "parasite" has three meanings in French: noise in a communication channel, an uninvited guest, and an organism that feeds off a host (Paulson 1988; Hayles 1990). The three meanings are conceptually similar, for they share two common properties. The first is the asymmetry of the relation: the "chain of parasitism is a simple relation or order, irreversible like the flow of a river . . . . One feeds on another and gives nothing in return" (Serres 1982: 182). The asymmetry of the relation extends upward, from the local to the global: "Asymmetry is local on a chain and is propagated globally the length of a series, through transitivity" (182). In the hierarchy of relations that dominated through the Middle Ages to the great transformation of industrial capitalism, the position of disabled people was profoundly parasitic, situated in a chain of dependency that reduced these persons to feed from the charity given. The parasitic relation is paradoxical; it is being and nonbeing, relation and nonrelation. Like the politician, the parasite "is always there in our relations," but can "instantaneously disappear" (Serres 1982: 179). The centrality of disability noted by Stiker attests to the ever-presence of parasitic relations; yet the removal from such a central place attests to its disappearance.

A second property is the central feature of the parasitic relation. The parasite, those who "feed on another," is a "third man" to dyadic exchanges and other interactions; the parasite is conceptually similar to *noise*. As contextual noise, parasites interrupt exchanges, forcing interactions to respond to the disturbance by intensifying their exclusion or accommodating their inclusion. Noise, as ambiguity prompted by a disturbance of established communication patterns, necessarily enters the ongoing communication or interaction of others; indeed, it is an integral part of interactions, for interactions as dialogue are "a sort of game played by two interlocutors considered as *united against the phenomena of interference and confusion*" (Serres 1983: 66–67, emphasis added). For Serres, noise is a form of chaos—it is the "fury" that upsets the equilibrium of established relations and communication. The fury of unstable, nonbounded interactions challenges the stability and boundedness of established groups and social classifications. Noise is the diffused energy unleashed during times of dislocation and transition. The rise of vagabondage in the latter half of the eighteenth century was a contextual change that challenged established beliefs and practices, destabilizing the hierarchy of relations. Like other times of contextual change, it was a time of diffuse noise. The parasitic relations that bound poor people and those with disabilities together, as well as to both economic and social dependence upon hosts, were exposed and vulnerable to reconception and reconstruction. When Stiker speaks of the differentiation of disability from poverty, Serres speaks of systemic responses to noise.

For Serres, the systemic response is a positive, and thus noise is a central generating force for change. Chaos and disorder are the antecedents, indeed preconditions for order and development. From these premises, Serres advances a core thesis. The parasite and parasitic chains have always been prior to established relations. The parasitic relation (and nonrelation) of feeding off another and giving little in return violates the common interpretation of exchange, particularly the interpretation of the gift. The parasitic relation is measured by its "abuse value," a calculation of the asymmetry that has always preceded use and exchange value. Thus, the change that accelerated during the late eighteenth century was certainly, as Stiker reveals, a change in ideas about disability, but at the core of this change was an underlying, decisive shift: disability entered the hierarchies of exchange value. Its abuse value moved from the parasitic dependence on charity to the vicissitudes of a market system founded on the asymmetric relations of class.

*Replicating Disability: Self-Similar Institutions.*    Among the implications of combining the perspectives of Stiker and Serres is the view of historical change as neither linear nor teleological. The belief that historical change proceeds in a cumulative, linear manner and is directed for a more benign or positive result is conceptually at odds with the dynamics of parasitic chains and adaptations to external noise. Yet for both authors, there is a discernible emphasis on the quality of change. For Stiker, the rise of new institutions committed to education and rehabilitation, however under the command of reason, was nonetheless a markedly positive direction. For Serres, although linear change is too facile and unsupported, change nonetheless has both a direction and a consistency. Disability has not enjoyed linear progress; rather, advances and setbacks share in weaving a complex tapestry of appeals to solidarity and abolition of human rights.

The metaphor of change, historical and scientific, is "neither a straight line nor a circle," but a "spiral" (Serres 1983: 99). The response and adaptation to external noise is a communication between the local and the global, that is, between the particularities and differences at the local level and the idealizations and similarities at the global level. As the global level expands, that is, as society expands, demographically, culturally, and juridically, the differences contained within local spaces are accentuated in contrast to the ideals and standards of the global. Indeed, attempts to mobilize and integrate historically marginalized groups into mainstream institutions, be they political parties or public education, can have the paradoxical effect of intensifying local group differences, enhancing modes of resistance that were adaptive responses to the legacy of exclusion (Mayhew 1968). Regardless of the cultural specifics, the general dynamic is broadly the same: intensifications of difference introduce noise, which inserts itself as a third force into the dialogues for reform and integration. According to Serres, space is especially problematic, for differences are unevenly distributed across geographic places. Physical spaces, racial-ethnic ghettos or barrios, and neighborhoods dominated by linguistic and cultural nationalities "are repressed because they are possibly, better yet, certainly, disorderly" (Hayles 1990: 200). Time, on the other hand, is identified with similarity and order. Administrative authorities can more easily manipulate time, inserting temporal distinctions in legislative acts as a means to manipulate spatial differences. Thus, the objective is to absorb local turbulences by way of a temporal orderliness. From the chaos of such disorder emerges a new order, at a higher level than before.

Critiques of Serres's spiral metaphor aside, the imagery of consistent replication is especially useful in highlighting a third comparative property of special education: the metaphor of the spiral parallels an empirical feature of historical and contemporary forms of special education—whether sectarian or state funded, structures for delinquent and disabled youth exhibit organizational similarities across time and across space, when such categorical boundaries can be drawn at all. The organizational similarities are not just mirror images, as in architectural designs or designated names. Empirically key is that historical forms—such as the workhouse, the asylum, and the reform and industrial schools—and contemporary forms—such as approved schools, day schools, and special classes—are what Andrew Abbott terms "self-similar social structures" (2001: 165). The quality of self-similarity "is based on a unit that repeats itself," such as a hierarchy of authority within (and across) bureaucratic organizations. The distinguishing feature of self-similar structures is this: units that are similar to structures parallel or horizontal to them are also similar to units hierarchically above them. This "nesting similarity" differentiates self-similarity from other examples that display commonalities. Such segmental structures abound, but do not exhibit the "theme of survival"— that is, the retention of "several 'layers' of such divisions into a single *coincident present*" (Abbott 2001: 165, 174, emphasis added).

Abbott's notion of a coincident present resonates with Serres's spiral. Both imageries fit well the genealogical histories of institutions and schools for youth who are poor, neglected, and delinquent and those with disabilities. Contemporary special education is, in this view, a population of self-similar institutions, the survival of which is rooted in historical structures that possessed similarities in strikingly coincident ways. Thus, although the *Rasphuis* of Holland predated the *Zuchthaus* in Germany, both were "corrective institutions aimed at disobedient and disruptive locals rather than vagrant beggars or other outsiders" (Harrington 1999: 324). The self-similarity here is horizontal, diffused across cities within a short duration of time. Self-similarity is also evident as a vertical genealogy, replicated through a process of institutional mimicry and merging. Thus, the unit of self-similarity that joined the workhouse to the prison by the late eighteenth century became, in turn, the common model for the hospital and subsequently the lunatic asylum (on the former, see Cobbe 1861; on the latter, see Rothman 1971; Scull 1981). The same continuity is exemplified by reformatory institutions: ". . . 'industrial' schools, which accommodated destitute children, and 'reformatory' schools, which contained criminal children, which were merged under the title of 'approved schools'" (Humphries 1981: 213). The process of merging erased the earlier distinction between destitution and criminality and formed, thereby, a similar grouping. This new grouping of youth in approved schools was, in turn, defined more by educational than by correctional terms, for approved schools became a legally acceptable placement option for "socially maladjusted" youth. Whether the self-similarity is horizontal or vertical, the various forms of institutions are all centered on a common unit that repeats itself. Whether a workhouse or an approved school, hospital or lunatic asylum, or the special schools and classes of today, the unit is the same: successful placement, occupational or otherwise, after "special" education—socialization, rehabilitation, or training.

The similarity across institutions and their survival need not be due to particular intentions or successfully implemented policies. Institutional similarity and survival are explained better by "bureaucratic momentum" (Humphries 1981: 318), the superior staying power of procedures over policies, rather than the effect of all-knowing omniscient policymakers and policies with only anticipated and intended consequences. Once established, practical routines have an economy that resists or absorbs periodic attempts to alter them. As these established procedures carry over to other institutions (Melosi and Pavarini, 1981: chapter 1), self-similarity extends across time and place. The continuity of work as a means to correction and skill acquisition as a preparation to vocational placement are common procedures, although policy intentions might be very different. As if obeying Serres's imagery of a spiral, this procedural continuity extended to nineteenth-century charity schools, pauper and ragged schools, reformatory and industrial schools, all exerting their organizational imprints on the construction of "special education" as compulsory education was enacted at the close of the century (as discussed in the following chapters).

### FROM IDEAS TO INSTITUTIONS AND BACK AGAIN: A RETROSPECTION ON THE ENLIGHTENMENTS AND DISABILITY

The ideas of Stiker, Serres, and Abbott have clear affinities; as means to understand social processes, they are linked dialectically. Merely gradual change in ideas about disability reinforces established institutional arrangements of exclusion, segregation, or separation. Transformative change in prevailing ideas threatens established patterns, presenting disability as "noise" that must be addressed. As the threat of challenges ascends outward from traditional arrangements, new institutional patterns are imagined and constructed. The continuity and self-similarity of institutions is the substance of temporal, historical change, not a teleological direction believed in or inferred. We discover these dynamics if, in Elias's terms, "one looks not from us to them, but from them to us." Stiker emphasized the *duality* of disability history as one of exclusion and poverty, certainly, but in various ways and in specific times, people with disabilities also enjoyed special powers, emanating in particular from the mysteries of blindness, deafness, and madness. They could be exempted from the maltreatment of secular and religious powers, at times even exerting magical forces. Well into the eighteenth century, such rites of exemption reinforced long-entrenched beliefs even as they led to routines of exclusion still prevalent today.

We can draw out such exclusions for closer view; as Serres points out, there is always a "third man," the excluded middle. The exclusion of this *noise* is given little critical attention because it is shrouded in naturalness, unseen because attention is given to the privileged, recognized parties engaged in dialogue. Yet Serres brings this external noise and the practice or exclusion to the forefront and reveals how the very content of the dialogue is shaped by the necessity of the privileged parties to address, even accommodate the noise, if only because it is annoying. The exclusion of people with disabilities was bounded by poverty and enforced by the systems of charity up to the late eighteenth century. Then at the end of the eighteenth century a decisive alteration occurred in the value of disability. Disability entered the economic and social systems of exchange value.

From Abbott we are able to discern and name the long and intertwined genealogy of institutions that have confined, mistreated, corrected, and educated people with disabilities. The concept of nested self-similarity demonstrates that the historical antecedents to contemporary special education and the language of "special educational needs" reach back to the seventeenth century. These antecedents comprise a linked series of forms that vary, but that embody enduring and common functions: the social and economic placement of the young and the reproduction of hierarchies in society.

The ideas of Stiker, Serres, and Abbott hearken back to the three Enlightenments. Returning to Serres, the official Enlightenment and the counter Enlightenment were the recognized participants. The writings of Locke were the preeminent texts of the official Enlightenment. The number of figures whose works—and recognition—were oriented toward Locke reached across to the continent and beyond. As Locke's French counterpart, Denis Diderot exerted a certain international influence as well. The two were, in essence, the core dialogue of the Enlightenment. Yet beyond their individual and combined influence, it is noteworthy that the human senses were the central subject of major philosophical texts. From a more editorial perspective, it is noteworthy that Molyneux's problem (recall the blind man gaining sight: can he distinguish the cube from the sphere by sight, a difference he had known only by touch?) found its way into Locke's *Essay* almost as a footnote. Whether as a central focus or late insertion, the human senses generally, and the blind and deaf in particular, were the long-excluded "third man." The sensory differences of seeing and hearing pressed upon official philosophical arguments not simply as convenient illustrations of sensory deprivations, but as social categories able to assume membership in the emerging political entity of the nation and to assume the rights of participation in its corollary, the public sphere—but at the margins. Molyneux's problem may not have been as much physiological as political. In the absence of substantial evidence to answer the question, on what grounds can it be answered? If one answers in the negative, as did both Locke and Diderot, a measure of "ineducability" is retained; if one answers in the positive, then a difference believed to be impenetrably deep is argued to be far less, and national membership and public participation are then reasonable and humane. The "noise" of blind and deaf people needed to be silenced, but on grounds that were similar to those of charity. It is not accidental that national institutions for them arose in Paris in the late eighteenth century. Such institutions were established as well in England, but they were *local* in scope and private in benefaction and not founded on a deep sense of *national* obligation.

In both countries, institutions were constructed, in large measure as responses to disruptions that challenged prevailing ideas and beliefs. Although each country began the construction of institutions from very different levels, the *system* dynamics remained the same. For England, the noise of the blind and the deaf and the mad was a local disturbance; for France, the noise was national. For decentralized England, the array of schools and institutions at the local, district, and municipal levels constituted a system of interlocking levels. For centralized France, the number of schools and institutions was far less numerous, and furthermore, they were interlocked with the national level, all based in the capital city of Paris. In terms of organizations established to serve people with disadvantages or disabilities, the national level in France was, in effect, the equivalent to the local level in England. Although we can say that the noise of the blind and deaf reverberated upward in England and downward in France, it would be more useful to relax such directionality and to speak of what level was most proximate to the noise. It is worth noting Serres in full:

Consider any level of an interlocking system. Locally, it operates like a series of chemical reactions at a certain temperature. Let us forget for the moment their precise equations and the unique elements at work here. Let us consider only the energy conditions at this one level. It mobilizes information and produces background noise. The next level in the interlocking series receives, manipulates, and generally integrates the information-background noise couple that was given off at the preceding level . . . . Indeed, if one writes the equation expressing the quantity of information exchanged between two stations through a given channel and the equation which provides this quantity for the whole unit (including the two stations and the channel) a change of sign occurs for a certain function entering into the computation . . . . In a certain sense, the next level functions as a rectifier, in particular, as a rectifier of noise. What was once an obstacle to all messages is reversed and added to the information. This discovery is all the more important since it is valid for all levels. *It is a law of the series which runs through the system of integration* (Serres 1983: 77–78, emphasis added).

The construction in the late eighteenth century of institutions and schools for the deaf, blind, and mad, despite the level at which it was begun, was a form of *integration*. The initial level from which this integration begins, which can be traceable to particular national differences, is very significant. Knowing this as a starting point, we may venture predictions as to directionality. For England, the only real direction was toward the national, whereas for France it was away from its historical legacy of centralization. We consider the implications of such long-term developments as we move on to survey and analyze cross-national data on special education systems and delve into the contemporary institutionalization processes of well-developed and expanding special education systems.

## PART TWO

# COMPARING SPECIAL EDUCATION

HOW HAVE THE IDEAS OF THE ENLIGHT-
enment influenced the institutionalization processes of
organizations that care for and control children and youth? Exported around
the world in a century of Western dominance, how have these processes
played out in Europe and beyond? As we have seen, the theoretical outline for
the evolution of citizenship rights given by Marshall and the double movement proposed by Polanyi are prominent examples of general processes of
state making and the interplay of social and economic dynamics, which significantly structured the expanding educational and social welfare institutions. Numerous works share the theoretical goal of identifying the significant causal forces that have contributed to nation-state formation and to civil
society and the public sphere. Yet in spite of differences in nations compared
or processes studied, they are vulnerable to a common critique: general, or
"universal," theories of nation-building and citizenship may more accurately

be viewed as narratives of the western European experience. The process of nation building and its legitimation—as centered on the successful constraint of absolutist power by the rise of an autonomous public sphere (Taylor 1990: 100; Held 1996: 314)—fits the historical path of most western European nations. It does not fit so well, if at all, the paths of most African, Asian, and Latin American nations.

The primacy of the Western form has, nonetheless, remained a model narrative about the origins of special education, the course of its development, and its central purpose and goals. This diffusion has been facilitated by international organizations and supranational governments, such as the United Nations and the European Union, as elements of a global culture and polity (Meyer 2005, 2010). Economically dominant western European nations have been tremendously influential in forging and defining special education as well as inclusive education. The tendency to extend this prominence through general theories unduly confounds specific historical circumstances with contexts significantly different in time and content.

The legitimacy of universal theories has been amplified not only by the dominance of Western nations, industrially and imperialistically, but also by the enhanced salience of cross-national comparisons arising with internationalization. Comparative methodologies have contributed to this, for example, in the power of multivariate techniques to yield general inferences, which has been well suited to the aims of general theories. The reliance on a large number of cases, such as countries or regions, and measurement of common structural properties constitute the foundation of comparative analyses designed to yield general inferences (Skocpol 1979; Ragin 1987, 1997; Sewell 1996). Such variable-based methods can powerfully detect general patterns of association and causal effects.

Central among the general patterns explored in Part 2 is the cross-national evidence for how the goals of special education and then inclusive education have become institutionalized around the world. By the middle of the twentieth century, student disability and special education were beginning to join other issues of global importance. Much like poverty and war, the undereducation of persons with disabilities and their social exclusion was deemed not only wasteful of human capital, but also immoral. An important measure of this global institutionalization was the first cross-national survey of global special education. Conducted by the United Nations in 1957, with a larger follow-up in 1970, the intent of these surveys was to assess the level of special education provisions, mainly by the number of students in schools and classes. This "Large N" comparative dataset provides a window into the global structure of special education.

Despite the inferential strength of variable-based methods, overreliance on them comes at a high cost, as important statistical assumptions are not easily met. Two assumptions can be especially burdensome: that the cases in the analysis are independent and that the meaning of variables is the same across cases (see Ebbinghaus 2005). Nations (as cases) are clearly not independent: their geographic proximity, trading histories, military conflicts, cultural, scientific, and diplomatic exchanges, linguistic similarities, and international organizational memberships make them interdependent. In addition, the meanings associated with such global phenomena as schooling, migration, and disablement varies considerably between nations and within regions. So, too, does special and inclusive education vary.

Lessons drawn from postcolonial histories pose especially forceful challenges to variable-based methods. The methodological challenge, among the more substantive ones, is the insistence that descriptions, claims, affirmations, and interpretations be contextualized—that is, be grounded in comparisons of contexts. Here the focus is not directly on explaining variance, but in explaining diverse outcomes despite similar conditions and similar outcomes despite diverse conditions. Because the focus is on a small number of cases, the appropriate methods are "logical methods": the method of difference and the method of agreement. The former compares cases that differ in some outcome, whereas the latter compares cases that agree. Thus, specific countries whose special education systems differ but that are otherwise similar are compared, and vice versa. The objective is to identify the factors or conditions that best account for these differences. The focus on diverse outcomes turns the tables on Large N comparisons, replacing the objective with detailed attention to diverse contexts, especially how such dynamic contexts shape the decisions or events that in turn shape the course of change. The goal may be to determine how outcomes depend on institutional changes and how institutions develop in a largely path-dependent fashion, not deterministically as a result of "original conditions" (see Goldstone 1998).[1] With comparisons of a limited number of cases, relevant combinations of factors (interactions in statistical methods) take center stage, for cases are viewed as configurations and not as the sum of variables.

Mindful of the strengths and limitations of Large and Small N comparisons, the chapters that comprise Part 2 move in two directions, methodologically and theoretically. The chapters shift from a cross-national, variable-oriented analysis of special education participation rates to a case-oriented focus on select Western and European nations. The move illustrates the previous discussion of the strengths and limitations of Large N comparisons and the importance of more specific analyses of a small number of cases to discuss in detail the institutionalization processes of special education systems. Theoretically, the following chapters step from the previous focus on general, underlying processes to a focus on the social logics of similar and different special education systems. This shift in focus seeks to complement general theories with the mechanisms that link underlying processes to predictable outcomes. In this respect, the benefits of these methodological strategies and theoretical aspects are joined, each guiding and strengthening the other.

Chapter 3, "The Global Institution of Special Education," presents cross-national analyses of the first international surveys of special education participation rates (UNESCO 1960–95, 1974). These multivariate analyses, of factors known to be determinants of placement rates, underscore the international dimension of raised awareness of disabilities and special educational needs and the subsequent increases in special education provisions worldwide. Building on earlier analyses (Putnam 1979), but finding other results, a significant factor is the influence of world culture, measured in memberships in nongovernmental organizations. The analysis follows T. H. Marshall's theory of citizenship, specifically the movement from civil to political to social rights that also reflects the increased diffusion of human rights discourse, international charters, and national legislation. At the cross-national level, the rise of these organizational memberships—ties to the global polity—suggests a specific source for the worldwide diffusion of special education and its varying levels across countries.

Picking up the variance in special education systems found on different continents, Chapter 4, "Historical Models and Social Logics of Special Education Systems," probes the modal types of special education systems. The major distinction across nations is the difference between the Western (largely European) model, which joins democratic principles with bureaucratic organization, and the non-Western (African, Asian, Latin American) model, which joins the historical influence of patrimonial authority with elements of democratic participation. The chapter integrates critiques of the Western model by a comparison of the social logics that are associated with the Western and non-Western models.

Delving deeper into the processes of twentieth-century special education institutionalization, Chapter 5, "Institutionalizing Special Education Systems and Their Divergence over the Twentieth Century," provides a case-based comparison of special education in two countries—the United States and Germany. These countries pioneered special education and are broadly similar in major institutional respects, but they maintain very different special education systems. These systems of special education are examined in order to contrast two types of special education system within the Western model: the separate class in the United States and the segregated school in Germany.

Focusing on the dramatic divergence of these cases over the twentieth century indicates that even within the Western model of providing significant special education support and services, major institutional and organizational differences remain. Structural and cultural differences question the notion that these countries' special education systems are on a path to convergence—or that one model exists that has become globally dominant. Indeed, given their decentralized education systems, neither country has successfully implemented inclusive education equally in all regions or localities. Inclusive education, although a globally acknowledged goal, poses deep challenges to both the multiple-track and dual-track special education systems prevalent around the world. Special education enrollments and inclusive education have risen in many countries, but segregation and separation persist, as do the outcomes of low certification and labor market marginalization, even in developed democracies. Among the results of prevalent stigmatization, lowered expectations for education, lesser learning opportunities, and social exclusion are dependence on social assistance and, worse, deviance and criminality. These empirical patterns contradict the ideal of democratic citizenship secured through schooling and human development. Some countries, such as the United States, emphasize investments in education and equalizing opportunities, paired with

marginal redistribution or rehabilitation as well as large criminal justice systems (the punitive model). Other countries, such as Germany, maintain class-
based education and elaborate segregated special education while focusing on
equalizing outcomes through generous social welfare provisions (the paternalistic model). Thus, (special) education, disability, and criminal justice
policy must be viewed together if we are to grasp the tremendous costs of the
systemic production of less-educated persons, the theme of Part 3.

## CHAPTER 3

# THE GLOBAL INSTITUTION
# OF SPECIAL EDUCATION

IN ITS CONTEMPORARY FORM, SPECIAL EDU-
cation appeared by the close of the nineteenth century, beginning in European countries as alternative or auxiliary organizational forms
to regular schooling. Often in parallel to compulsory education, parents were
obligated to send their disabled child to a state institution, an obligation that
for a time resembled that of general compulsory education laws. As a means to
accommodate children who did not easily master the curriculum or whose
circumstances rendered continuous or successful attendance difficult, special
schools or special classes within public primary schools arose as critical adaptations to broaden the reach of public education. Such legal and organizational modifications comprised the infrastructure of an instructional system,
but these systems existed on tenuous legal and formal grounds. They were
neither wholly outside the broad jurisdiction of general education, nor completely subsidiary to it.

For the first half of the twentieth century, the maturation of such organizational adjuncts to general education was incremental and largely unobtrusive. Its nascent global institutionalization may have been reflected by cross-national conferences attended by professionals, but its truly worldwide scope became most evident as of the mid-1950s. In 1957, the first survey of special education conducted by the United Nations revealed its presence in a diverse array of countries spanning all continents. Fifty-five nations responded to this survey, reporting total numbers of students in special education schools and classes by gender and by category.

Less than a decade and a half later, the United Nations conducted a second survey to which an additional 52 countries responded, yielding data on national systems of special education for a total of 107 countries. In 1969, the United Nations published the results of a survey of legislation on the education of "handicapped children and young people." Thirty countries responded, providing the first body of comparative information on the legal bases of special education and the existing provisions for students with special educational needs.[1]

In 1993–94, Seamus Hegarty carried out an updated review for the United Nations Educational, Scientific, and Cultural Organization (UNESCO). Sixty-three of ninety member states from Africa, Europe, Asia, Latin America and the Caribbean as well as Arab states participated. The updated review found two-thirds of those countries continued to exclude children with special educational needs from the public education system (UNESCO 1995: 11). The study of special education systems, from Australia to Zimbabwe, found that most countries had legislation pertaining to "integration" and simultaneously maintained an array of organizational forms: these forms included special boarding schools (55 countries), special day schools (49), special classes in regular schools (47), support teaching in regular classes (46), and resource rooms (45) (UNESCO 1995: 16–17).

In the first decade of the twenty-first century, large-scale cross-national surveys reappear as detailed international analyses of "policies, statistics, and indicators." These surveys were conducted by the Organisation for Economic Co-operation and Development (OECD), a member-country-sponsored think tank (for example, OECD 2004, 2005, 2007). For Europe, the European Agency for Development in Special Needs Education (EADSNE) carried out comparative analyses of up to two dozen countries (for example, EADSNE 2003, 2005). An independent research organization, the EADSNE was established by a large group of European member countries to facilitate collaboration in the field of special needs education and is supported by the European Commission and European Parliament. It is worth noting that from the UN surveys at mid-century to these most recent surveys, the trend has been from the world level (or as many nations that would respond) to developed nations, most of which are western European. In the 2000s, the developed countries, represented in the OECD, have systematically compared their (special) education systems more than ever, engaging in comparative reporting and research. As ever in comparative education research, the paramount goals are to learn from others and to diffuse good or best practices worldwide. The World Bank has also begun to estimate the tremendous costs of poverty and disablement, underscoring the significance of investments in human capital and thus joining the voices in favor of education for all and inclusive education (World Bank 2003).

This chapter explores the cross-national variation in special education classification and participation rates. We discuss the results of comparative analyses that examine the relative influence of variables that reflect a nation's economic and demographic conditions, those that are internal as well as those that reflect ties to world culture via international nongovernmental organizations and supranational governance. The principle focus of the analyses, and the chapter's central theme, is the structure of special education as a global institution.

## GLOBAL PATTERNS IN SPECIAL EDUCATION

The industrialized nations of Western Europe led the way in the institutionalization and organizational differentiation of special education. When modern special education is traced back to its eighteenth- and nineteenth-century predecessors, its origins are largely unambiguous. As long as schooling remained voluntary, disadvantaged children and those with recognized disabilities were largely excluded. Blind and deaf children and those with mental disabilities presented no threat to the prerogatives of public primary schools; they could be turned away as "uneducable" and were often transferred to state residential institutions. Networks of institutional predecessors that did exist remained in place and were often expanded to serve the growing group of children labeled as uneducable (Humphries and Gordon 1992). Their existence, geographically and administratively separate, provided assurance that a free and compulsory primary education could be implemented broadly with only minimal disruption to the routines of general schooling.

Yet to the extent that enacting compulsory education enlarges the number of children potentially willing and legally eligible to participate in primary education, organizational challenges arise. For nations that enacted compulsory education comparatively early, principally Western nations, the "special class" and the "special school" emerged as a means to lessen the organizational complications of compulsory education by providing schools and teachers with a way to circumvent the calls for the integration or inclusion of disabled children, thereby protecting the priority and intent of compulsory schooling (see Sarason and Doris 1979; Sutherland 1981, 1983; Potts 1982; Lazerson 1983; Armstrong 2002). Thus, the organizational infrastructure of special education originated not as a means to broaden participation, but rather as an instrument of restriction and (re)segregation.

Organizationally, the growth of special education follows the course of public education, which has expanded at all levels, gaining speed since World War II. The participation rate of children in special education should closely parallel the number enrolled in primary education *if* special educational needs are based on objective and diagnosable features of learners. Yet as emphasized here and in the following chapters, the variance within countries and across time is vast, casting significant doubt on clinical diagnosis of individuals as reliable and unbiased and demanding instead social and political explanations for these trends and patterns. The rise of special education provisions facilitates an on-going process of organizational differentiation. Yet the crucial causal question is where to locate and prioritize the sources of this institutional and organizational change.

### Conceptual Distinctions and Theoretical Considerations

Pressures leading to an expansion of special education may come from sources particular to a country. For England, the enactment of the Education Act of 1870 signaled that a free and compulsory education was a right, and it facilitated the enactment of the Elementary Education (Blind and Deaf) Act of 1893, a stimulus to expanding provisions and categories of special education. Similarly, in 1889 in France, the law led to a decisive decline in paternal authority relative to state powers and paved the way for the 1909 law for "national readaptation" of schools for socially disadvantaged and disabled children (Schafer 1997: 152–166; Armstrong 2002: 449). Moreover, shifts in public enrollments, fluctuation in private school enrollments, health epidemics, collateral troubles from wars, the immigration of peoples of diverse cultural, religious, and linguistic backgrounds, the type and density of urban areas, and increased juvenile crime and incarceration all may be factors that account for expansions and contractions in special education (see Tomlinson 1982, 1985; Richardson 1992; Gabel et al. 2009).

Yet the expansion of special education also derives from ideational diffusion and normative pressures owing to cross-national interconnections, exchanges that promote special education provision on pedagogical and ethical grounds, with rationales that are quite independent of monetary calculations (Dyson 1990; O'Hanlon 1993; Prokou 2003). The adoption of the Universal Declaration of Human Rights by the UN General Assembly in 1948 had reverberations, pressing for recognition parallel to the endogenous organizational growth of disability interest groups and political and social action. A global context that embraced, protected, and promoted human rights was articulated and legitimized, ultimately including and specifying the perspectives, rights, and needs of people with disabilities around the world (see Charlton 1998; Groce 2002). Both the 1981 International Year of Disabled Persons and the UN Decade of Disabled Persons that followed (1983–92) emphasized the need for increased awareness of and commitment to address the living conditions and life chances of Persons with disabilities worldwide.

In 1981, the key goal was to affirm and implement the principle "full participation and equality" contained in the UN General Assembly's 1975 Declaration on the Rights of Disabled Persons. Disabled people should participate fully in communities, self-identify their needs, and share in their societies' wealth. However, to fully realize these ambitious goals, continued social and political action, advocacy, and awareness raising is needed everywhere. Over time, 1981 has come to symbolize the paradigm shift from deficits and charity to civil rights, accessibility, and participation.[2] Further steps toward awareness and action have included the 1989 UN Convention on the Right of the Child, the 1990 World Conference on Education for All, and the United Nations' adoption in 1993 of the Standard Rules on the Equalization of Opportunities for Persons with Disabilities, all of which led up to the UN International Convention on the Rights of Persons with Disabilities treaty in 2006 (UN 2006; see Chapter 6). More specifically attuned to education issues, the Salamanca Statement and Framework for Action on Special Needs Education, adopted by the World Conference on Special Needs Education in June 1994, emphasized the importance of access, equity, and inclusion (UNESCO 1994). Like key tenets of Enlightenment thought, the institution of special education became an object of international focus and concern, a contextual effect in its own right, exerting an influence on nations above and beyond within-country institutionalization processes at the nexus of parental and professional knowledge, interests, and responsibilities.

The construction of formalized special education systems, redoubled in the mid-1900s, has been accelerating ever since.[3] The elements of special education analyzed here reach beyond national differences and peculiarities, for they are replicated within and affected by a transnational context that supersedes the histories of individual countries. This context has developed considerably, with international charters, policy statements, touted good practices, and specific recommendations for the implementation of education for all, for special education programs, and, lastly, for inclusive education.

### Measuring the Growth of Special Education

In a pioneering cross-national study of special education, Rosemary Werner Putnam (1979) alluded to the "stage theory" in the structuring of special education provisions, beginning with those for children with sensory impairments and ending with additions for children with speech impairment and learning disabilities. She noted that ". . . the 'menu' of services offered by each country should not be randomly composed. Relatively 'advanced' services should be offered only by countries that also provide more 'basic' services. *Skipping of steps on this 'staircase' of special educational services should be relatively rare*" (1979: 85, emphasis added). Such a view ties the growth of special education to economic capacity and educational investment. Special education should be "built up" from basic services, because that is what limited economic means can afford. From such an economic deterministic point of view, Putnam proposed a *need* hypothesis, which predicted that countries "have more special education" because they "have a higher proportion of handicapped children." Alternatively, the construction of even rudimentary special education may reflect a greater *demand* for provisions from an informed public or a greater *effort* that reflects a heightened focus on education generally and a higher allocation of resources to this effort particularly. Finally, a *resource* hypothesis predicts that "richer countries will spend more on special education," in part because they can afford it.

Putnam analyzed a number of variables that were argued to be direct or indirect indicators of these competing hypotheses, examining correlations for the 1970 UNESCO survey. The essential findings were clear: more special education is found in wealthier, urban countries that have better health care—resulting in a lower infant mortality rate—and more developed general education systems. In brief, the strength of measures such as the gross domestic product and education expenditures (as a proportion of the GDP), confirmed all hypotheses to some degree. If not inhibited by low literacy rates, countries have more children in special education because they can afford to establish and extend provisions to the population of children with disabilities.

The thrust of such an interpretation, however seemingly definitive, confers a preponderance of influence upon structural properties of countries that are "internal" possessions. The gross domestic product is akin to a commodity, possessed by individual nations. The will or effort to extend provisions to children with special educational needs is, intuitively, an extension of this resource. If possessed at an adequate level, provisions are extended at an expected level, one that corresponds to this resource capacity. If this resource is in limited supply, special education provisions reflect this. Despite its rationality, there are important limitations to such a crisp interpretation, restricted by the source or location of the factors presumed to generate special education—and by the level at which these factors operate. Each country's level of economic development is an attribute that reflects its particular economic and political history, and this history will be of consequence for educational provisions; however, such longitudinal developmental processes are often ignored in cross-sectional analysis.

The presumption that individual countries act independently of one another and that they remain relatively independent is problematic, even if the emphasis on nations as independent units goes well with an emphasis on certain structural properties as causes generating the phenomenon of special education. With favor given to such characteristics, interpretations are inclined to be more homogeneous, to view structural properties as having similar meanings and similar effects across quite different national contexts. Yet thus is set a circular trap: if the central organizational elements of special education have affinities with central structural properties of nations, it is a plausible interpretation that such organizational elements originate and expand from these structural properties. As we shall see below, such explanations are inadequate.

Although demand, effort, and resources may well reflect economic and social conditions within each country, they also may reflect—and may even primarily refer to—external circumstances such as more central or peripheral location in the global economy and processes of nation-state building and democratization. Effort may be correlated with economic capacity, but its true source may be more external, ideational, and normative than material— owing to ongoing developments in the global culture of schooling (see Baker and LeTendre 2005). A less developed country may establish special education as a symbolic expression of its commitment to the ideals of educational access and social welfare, as a measure of its membership in the international community, or as a reflection of its ambition to match, or even surpass, the policies and programs of developed nations. In defiance of its economic limitations, such developing countries report on special education as they comply with surveys requested or required by central international agencies.

The sketched dynamic turns the tables of causation. Ties to international organizations are a form of participation in the increasingly global institution of (special) education. As acts of global citizenship, ties to international organizations and compliance with supranational governance and data-gathering activities can result in positive feedback on the domestic organizational structures of (special) education. Thus, although a "country may *choose* to devote a greater share of its resources to education,"[4] it would do so less because it can and more because of policymaking priorities. Moreover, the desire may be more authentic than instrumental, for it signifies a cultural resource that may be of more value than economic resources, even when the promise of financial assistance upon meeting certain criteria obviously also has an impact. After all, to extend special education in the face of limited economic means can bring a higher return, in such a measure as cultural stature. In short, the causal effect and the meaning of economic, demographic, and educational factors vary across nations in magnitude and over time.

In contrast to the presumptions that nations are independent and attributes are functions of internal properties, this analysis rejects the independence of countries, especially given the impact of such factors as supranational governance and cross-national studies that distinguish and rank countries. It relocates causal forces, acknowledging the power of cultural hegemony and global isomorphic pressures, and emphasizes the interrelations, even interdependence, among nations. Thus, international relations are significant sources of effects. As a consequence, the meaning of structural attributes varies, as does their effect. For example, the centralization of education governance may well have meanings in Latin American, Asian, and African contexts that is quite different from European contexts, where centralization also varies.

The conditions that have contributed to the origins and expansion of special education differ, even during similar time periods. The historical sensitivity of economic, political, and demographic conditions may be even more of a factor when considering the education of children with disabilities. Just as the French philosophes were more attentive to the senses than were other national thinkers of the Enlightenment, the genesis and expansion of special education across countries reflects a variation in social and education policy responses contingent on historical time and place. Thus, a country may devote more to special education not simply because a higher GDP enables it to do so, but because the particular time and place accentuates the necessity of educating children with special educational needs and providing resources to accomplish this goal. Indeed, nations that have higher levels of resources may strengthen overall schooling, indirectly promoting a decline in need for special education expenditures, or they may favor inclusive education with a corresponding decline in special education participation. Special education in a "rich" nation may not expand further because it has already grown to its limits. For developing nations, economically able to provide schooling for all or not, their call to develop some form of special education came, at the latest, with the UNESCO surveys.

*Cross-National Variation in Special Education: 1957 and 1970*

The 1957 and 1970 surveys of special education participation rates by the United Nations present an opportunity to assess the merit of competing *conceptualizations* for the variation in numbers of children enrolled in special schools and classes. The reporting nations differ markedly in the number of students with special educational needs as a proportion of the number enrolled in (primary) schools (see Table 3.1). The range in the numbers of students in special education reported by the 55 nations in the earlier survey is considerable, from a low of .01 percent of the total primary enrollment (for example, India, Turkey) to a maximum of 3.61 percent (Sweden); and for the 107 nations in 1970, the range was from a minimum of .01 percent (for example, Lesotho), to a maximum of 5.62 percent (United States). The retention of a low minimum is explained by the entrance of new states into the 1970 survey, and the increase of the maximum is attributable to expanding levels among highly developed nations. As a result of the inclusion of new states in the analysis, the overall variation nearly doubled.

Guided by the conceptual issues and implications discussed, four potential explanations for the variation across nations are examined, labeled as: Population Health, Resource Capacity, Educational Formalization, and World Culture. The first, akin to Putnam's need hypothesis, explains the level of special education as a reflection of population health and social and

TABLE 3.1. Number of countries reporting in UN surveys, by world region, 1957, 1970

|  | 1957 | | 1970 | |
|---|---|---|---|---|
|  | N | % | N | % |
| Europe | 28 | 51 | 37 | 31 |
| North and South America | 13 | 24 | 30 | 29 |
| Asia | 10 | 18 | 23 | 23 |
| Africa | 4 | 7 | 17 | 17 |
| Total | 55 | | 107 | |

*Source*: UNESCO Statistical Yearbooks (1960, 1974).
*Note*: Although the number of countries reporting on special education for the 1970 survey is 107, in subsequent analyses eight cases are eliminated because they are not legitimate independent sovereign nations but rather territories (e.g., Netherland Antilles, French Guiana, French Polynesia) or collectivities (San Marino, Naura). The working total of cases for which there are numbers of students in special education reported is 97. Complete data for variables in subsequent analyses reduces the N to between 74 and 81.

demographic conditions that would measure in some degree the prevalence of children with disabilities. Consistent with Putnam, we measure the infant mortality rate from 1965 and add the number of inhabitants per physician. The latter is an attempt to capture the availability of medical resources that would facilitate the maintenance and growth of institutional provisions. The second set, akin to Putnam's effort and resource hypothesis, captures the capacity to maintain classes that derives from demographic contexts and economic resources seemingly conducive to special education. From this perspective, the number of students in special education is a direct result of available economic means: nations that are higher in economic development would have more students enrolled in special education, whether schools or classes. Three measures from 1965 are utilized that are more direct indicators of this resource capacity: the gross domestic product, expenditures on education as a percentage of the GDP, and urban concentration. In addition to these three, a fourth variable is included that is a control on resource capacity: the degree of ethnic and linguistic fractionalization. This measure is included as a contextual influence that may promote or inhibit special education. A higher degree of fractionalization may promote special education placement as a means to control—or divert—student diversity, an outcome that would be consistent with contemporary evidence of racial/ethnic overrepresentation in special education around the world (see Gabel et al. 2009). Alternatively, when measured across nations with quite different cultural histories, ethnic/linguistic fractionalization may represent significant divisions that inhibit the extension of compulsory education to children in general and to children with special educational needs in particular.

A third variable set, educational formalization, focuses on a different form of capacity, the institutional capacity of a nation's education system to establish and expand special education. Central to this is the date at which a country enacted a law mandating primary schooling as free and compulsory, predicting that earlier enactments would lead to higher levels of special education by the middle of the twentieth century. In addition to this measure, the set includes a dummy variable as to whether a nation's education system is centralized or decentralized. Two measures tap the educational maturity or reach of mass schooling: the enrollment ratio for secondary education and the per-capita enrollment number for higher education. Secondary enrollment captures not only pressure stemming from an expanded population base, but also pressure stemming from the heightened stratification of students. Akin to Putnam's reasoning and interpretation, with increased higher education enrollments, "one would expect an increasing awareness of and sensitivity to the needs of the handicapped" (Putnam 1979: 86): on sheer quantitative grounds, as compulsory schooling is universalized and thus nearly all young adults are enrolled in schools, "more disabled children will be 'discovered' and will have to be educated."

A fourth set of variables captures the conception of special education as a global institution. This set challenges the assumption that nations are independent, doing so with measures that capture the structure of the world culture. The world culture denotes the global level that transcends national boundaries; it is constituted by the participation of nations in an array of international nongovernmental organizations (INGOs/NGOs) and agencies that identify and promote international issues and concerns. Since 1870, world culture has grown in composition and influence (Meyer 1987; Boli 1989; Boli and Thomas 1997; Boli and Thomas 1999: chapter 2; Lechner and Boli 2005). Compositionally, the expansion in the number of international organizations—such as the United Nations, the OECD, and the World Bank—has brought with it the influence of world culture into social sectors. One such sector consists of organizations concerned with individual rights and welfare, rights advanced as universal and thus transnational in scope. The expansion of global organizations that condemn abuses and advance human rights has paralleled closely the advancement of the educational rights of children with disabilities. Participation in such global arenas ought to be a source of influence on a nation's level of special education, both on its will and on its capacity to provide support and services. This argument parallels the theory of global integration and ethnic mobilization as well as the empirical findings that "the number of connections to INGOs" heightens a country's connectedness to the global human rights ideology, increasing protest movements that press for greater extension of rights (Olzak 2006: 14). In addition to the measure of membership in international organizations, the world culture variable set includes a measure of the year countries qualified as a state and a measure of the exchange of diplomats between nations. The former captures the timing of formal entrance into the world culture; the latter captures a degree of connectedness.

## ANALYSES AND FINDINGS

Noteworthy initially is the strength of the correlations between special education and all the independent variables except that of ethnic / linguistic diversity. (The bivariate correlations for all variables are given in Table 3.2.) Moreover, the intercorrelations among the independent variables are modest

TABLE 3.2. Predictor variables and levels of special education placements, 1970 (bivariate correlations)

|    | 1 | 2 | 3 | 4 | 5 | 6 | 7 | 8 | 9 | 10 | 11 | 12 | 13 | 14 | 15 |
|----|---|---|---|---|---|---|---|---|---|----|----|----|----|----|----|
| 1  | — |   |   |   |   |   |   |   |   |    |    |    |    |    |    |
| 2  | 36**<br>(96) | — |   |   |   |   |   |   |   |    |    |    |    |    |    |
| 3  | 40**<br>(78) | 19<br>(78) | — |   |   |   |   |   |   |    |    |    |    |    |    |
| 4  | 56**<br>(78) | 29**<br>(84) | 28*<br>(80) | — |   |   |   |   |   |    |    |    |    |    |    |
| 5  | −16<br>(77) | 12<br>(77) | 14<br>(72) | 27**<br>(71) | — |   |   |   |   |    |    |    |    |    |    |
| 6  | 61**<br>(80) | 48**<br>(80) | 67**<br>(72) | 64**<br>(72) | 01<br>(70) | — |   |   |   |    |    |    |    |    |    |
| 7  | 72**<br>(87) | 36**<br>(87) | 49**<br>(78) | 65**<br>(77) | −11<br>(77) | 63**<br>(79) | — |   |   |    |    |    |    |    |    |
| 8  | −59**<br>(81) | −40**<br>(81) | −38**<br>(72) | −47**<br>(73) | 09<br>(72) | −62**<br>(76) | −60**<br>(81) | — |   |    |    |    |    |    |    |
| 9  | 68**<br>(84) | 47**<br>(83) | 33**<br>(72) | 67**<br>(77) | −23<br>(74) | 66**<br>(75) | 74**<br>(81) | −64**<br>(76) | — |    |    |    |    |    |    |
| 10 | −28*<br>(70) | −18<br>(70) | −24<br>(62) | −31*<br>(63) | 03<br>(63) | 34**<br>(70) | 34**<br>(70) | .15<br>(69) | 34**<br>(66) | — |    |    |    |    |    |
| 11 | 33**<br>(81) | 51**<br>(81) | −23<br>(71) | −20<br>(72) | 11<br>(72) | 30**<br>(75) | 30**<br>(80) | 43**<br>(78) | 38**<br>(76) | 19<br>(68) | — |    |    |    |    |
| 12 | 58**<br>(95) | 57**<br>(94) | 19<br>(77) | 44**<br>(82) | −06<br>(76) | 54**<br>(79) | 59**<br>(86) | −54**<br>(81) | 65**<br>(83) | −13<br>(69) | 47**<br>(81) | — |    |    |    |
| 13 | 44**<br>(77) | 31**<br>(77) | 90**<br>(72) | 39**<br>(74) | 16<br>(69) | 67**<br>(73) | 54**<br>(77) | −46**<br>(75) | −42**<br>(73) | 26*<br>(64) | 34**<br>(74) | 30**<br>(77) | — |    |    |
| 14 | 50**<br>(42) | −13<br>(42) | −13<br>(41) | 49**<br>(42) | 34*<br>(41) | −34*<br>(41) | 59**<br>(42) | 43**<br>(42) | 67**<br>(39) | 07<br>(38) | 18<br>(41) | −24<br>(42) | −15<br>(42) | — |    |
| 15 | −25*<br>(75) | −29*<br>(75) | −09<br>(71) | 45**<br>(76) | 39**<br>(68) | 33**<br>(70) | 30**<br>(75) | 21<br>(71) | 45**<br>(71) | 02<br>(62) | 32**<br>(70) | 33**<br>(74) | −16<br>(72) | 63**<br>(41) | — |

\* p=<.05; ** p=<.01; ( )=N of cases.

(continued)

TABLE 3.2. *(continued)*

|    |                                                    | Mean  | SD    |
|----|----------------------------------------------------|-------|-------|
| 1  | Special education placements (1970)                | .98   | 1.42  |
| 2  | Special education placements reported (1957)       | .54   | .50   |
| 3  | Gross domestic product (1957)                      | 13073 | 49810 |
| 4  | Urban concentration (1965)                         | 25.7  | 15.71 |
| 5  | Ethnic and linguistic diversity (1965)             | .28   | .24   |
| 6  | Higher education enrollment (1965)                 | 316.5 | 314.6 |
| 7  | Education expenditures / GDP (1965)                | 31.05 | 40.03 |
| 8  | Compulsory education law passed                    | 1938  | 33    |
| 9  | Secondary level enrollment (1970)                  | 39.48 | 26.96 |
| 10 | Centralization of education system (1965)          | n/a   |       |
| 11 | Date qualified as a state                          | 1892  | 60    |
| 12 | International organization membership (1965)       | 45.81 | 18.68 |
| 13 | Diplomats sent (1965)                              | 244   | 375   |
| 14 | Infant deaths (1965)                               | 51.2  | 37.2  |
| 15 | Inhabitants per physician (1965)                   | 7776  | 17352 |

*Data sources for variables*: World Survey of Educational Statistics (1952); Statistical Yearbooks (1960–95); Russett (1964); Union of International Organizations (1965); World Survey of Education (1971a, 1971b).

to strong, affirming their historical relevance and underscoring their theoretical affinities to one another. For example, when a country qualified as a state and when it enacted compulsory education are related. Both of these are linked to levels of special education, as later dates are associated with lower levels. Additionally, the later a country qualified as a state, the lower its participation in international organizations, a relation that influences, in turn, the development of special education provisions—and on special education reporting in 1957. These patterns emphasize that comparisons of special education systems must address such systems as *historically structured*. The dates of key historical events across states are systematically related to the possession of resources and to the participation in activities tied to the education of children with disabilities. With this in mind, we turn now to multivariate analyses of these patterns of influence and patterns of change.

There are two dimensions of the cross-national variation in 1957 and 1970 that are interconnected and amenable to comparative analysis: first, the factors that distinguish the nations that reported special education in 1957 from the nations that did not report in 1957 but did report in 1970; second, the factors that best explain the variation in special education enrollments at the two reporting dates and thus explain the expansion from 1957 to 1970. Each dimension is explored in turn.

### Reporting / Not Reporting Special Education in 1957

The first dimension is addressed with discriminant analysis, a means to identify the cluster of factors that distinguish the two populations, or that best predict group membership. Table 3.3 shows the results of the analysis, which reveals a decisive fact: neither Population Health nor Resource Capacity measures fully distinguish those nations that reported special education in 1957 from those that did not. Rather, the variable sets for Educational Formalization and World Culture better distinguish the two populations. For the Educational Formalization variables, secondary education enrollment contributes strongly to distinguishing the two populations, with higher education enrollment not far behind. This suggests that reporting to an international body is influenced by the maturity of a nation's educational system, over and above the nation's economic resource level. The final variable set of World Culture shows the greatest predictive strength. All three variables, but especially when a country qualifies as a state and its memberships in INGOs, significantly contribute to distinguishing nations that reported from those that did not.

If the results of the discriminant analysis give cautious support to factors internal to nations, they lend stronger support to factors that link nations to the global community. The more a nation participates in the world polity, the more it is able and willing to participate in the reporting of its provisions for the education of children with special educational needs. The earlier a country qualifies as a state and the more international nongovernmental organizations it joins are two conditions that significantly predict reporting special education provisions to the United Nations.

This pattern conveys how national citizenship precedes and encourages global citizenship, for "transnational identity and national identity [are] complementary," and thus "national citizenship is a requisite part of the defini-

TABLE 3.3. Countries reporting/not reporting special education data (results of discriminant analysis), 1957/1970

| Variable sets | | Discriminant coefficients (standardized) |
|---|---|---|
| Population health | | |
| | Infant mortality (1965) | −.04 |
| | Inhabitants per physician (1965) | 1.33 |
| | Canonical correlation $x^2 = 1.33$; p = .54 | .18 |
| Resource capacity | | |
| | Gross domestic product (1957) | .09 |
| | Urban % > 20K (1960) | .35 |
| | Education expenditures, % GDP (1965) | .62 |
| | Ethnic/linguistic diversity (1960) | .59 |
| | Canonical correlation $x^2 = 5.94$; p = .20 | .29 |
| Educational formalization | | |
| | Date of compulsory education | .16 |
| | Secondary education enrollment (1970) | .71 |
| | Higher education enrollment per capita (1960) | .49 |
| | Centralization (1960) | −.01 |
| | Canonical correlation $x^2 = 11.31$; p = .02 | .41 |
| World culture | | |
| | INGO memberships (1966) | .83 |
| | Date qualified as a state | −.73 |
| | Diplomats sent (1965) | .48 |
| | Canonical correlation $x^2 = 23.43$; p = .00 | .53 |

*Data sources*: World Survey of Educational Statistics (1952); Statistical Yearbooks (1960–95); Russett (1965); World Survey of Education (1971a, 1971b); John Boli, personal communication.

tion of the modern, active individual, with respect to world-level action as much as national or local action" (Boli and Thomas 1997: 61). To be sure, the reporting of special education implies the existence of such provisions. However, the reporting itself is an expression of a nation's globally understood and validated citizenship rights. The *act* of reporting affirms this right, which can be exercised even with the lowest of economic resources; however, aggregate data such as these do not allow us to infer differences in quality of services and quantity of supports provided.

*Two Paths to Special Education:*
*State Making and Formalization of Education*

From the results of this analyses, specific factors emerge as significantly related to special education—at least to the reporting of provisions and numbers of students. Five emerge as most prominent: (1) the date at which countries achieved statehood; (2) the date at which countries enacted a free and
compulsory system of education; (3) the level of education expenditures as a
percentage of the gross domestic product; (4) the level of secondary school
enrollments; and (5) the number of nongovernmental organizations in which
a country is a member. The significance of each of these variables to the level
of students in special education for 1970 is confirmed by simple correlations.
They are also, as expected, correlated among themselves. Yet beyond their
statistical interrelation, they are substantively related in a way that makes
good sense historically and intuitively.

The five variables suggest two main paths to the cross-national levels of
special education as reported in 1970. One path is that of *state making*, detailed in the previous chapter, in particular the course of events that lead
from the formation of nationhood to an increasing participation in the system of international relations. Two variables capture this: the year that a
country qualified as state and the number of INGOs to which it belonged in
1970. The second path is *educational formalization*, the course of events that
lead from the enactment of compulsory education to an increasing maturation of the national education system. Two variables capture this path: the
date nations enacted compulsory education and the level of secondary education enrollment. The two paths join, or intersect, at the fifth measure: national expenditures on education relative to the gross domestic product. This
variable is a mix of both paths, for it certainly reflects the increased obligation to fund mass schooling as statehood becomes more established, that is,
as state authority enlarges; yet this obligation is itself shaped by the national
commitment to compulsory primary, and later secondary, education. The
timing of this commitment is important, as the enactment of compulsory
education sets into motion the obligation to fund free primary schooling.
Thus, comparative differences in the timing of enactment have bearing on
the pace of educational development and the institutionalization of special

education, which responds to expanding and differentiating student bodies due to compulsory schooling (see Richardson 1999). National expenditures for education is an intervening variable; it translates the elements of state authority downward that are pertinent to national education and, in turn, reflects upward to the state level the exigencies needed to sustain the growth of education as an institution.

Figure 3.1 displays the interrelations of these key variables and their relation to the variation in special education placements in 1970. The path model suggests that the cross-national variation in special education was structured by the variety of direct and indirect influences discussed above. These factors in special education development derive from education expenditures, an internal resource of nations, as well as from memberships in nongovernmental organizations, an external property of nations. Both statehood and compulsory education exert their imprint on special education at mid-century, but do so through more proximate factors. Of the two, compulsory education has exerted its influence through secondary education enrollment levels and through education expenditures. Statehood's influence has run through participation in nongovernmental organizations, or, in other terms, its participation in the world culture.

The statistical significance of nongovernmental organizations affirms the theoretical importance of external ties as a source of international pressure on nations to establish special education provisions. It suggests that this pressure constitutes a sort of global queue, insofar as membership level is associated with incremental increases in the numbers of students participating in special

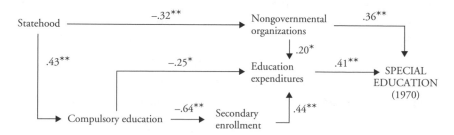

FIGURE 3.1. Paths to special education levels in 1970
*Note*: Standardized regression coefficients (betas) are shown.
* p = < .05; ** p = < .01

education. Yet the measure is a crude one, capturing little beyond the total number of organizations to which nations belong. The statistical significance of this measure begs a closer look, one that asks the question: to which specific organizations do nations belong that are the specific conduits of world culture that facilitate the transfer of ideas into national educational policy and practice?

### A Closer Look at International Nongovernmental Organizations: Operationalizing Marshall's Sequence

The concept of policy transfer addresses the specific sources of international influences, principally the network of foundations, think tanks and nongovernmental organizations that are the fora and medium for the generation of ideas that assume the form of policy statements and recommendations (see Stone 2000). The processes of policy transfers, of "policy band-wagoning," is especially germane to examples of patterned international differences, and to analyses of policy similarities despite significant national differences.

To address the question of the specific organizations to which nations belong requires theoretical refinement. The Yearbook of International Organizations for 1965 classified nongovernmental organizations into eighteen categories, ranging from politics to science to law to trade unions. Such a categorization is consistent for earlier and later years. Yet a more theoretically meaningful categorization is needed, one that not only addresses the question of specific membership, but also does so in a way that helps to explain the variation in special education placements in a statistically significant, but plausible way. To this end, we return to T. H. Marshall's theory of the sequential development of rights (Marshall 1964; see chapter 2).

To recapitulate: Marshall proposed that rights, individual and collective, have historically developed in a sequential manner: moving from civil to political to social. Civil rights constituted the struggles of the eighteenth century and centered on the achievement and protection of such rights as a free press and free speech. The nineteenth-century struggles were over political rights, the right to vote and otherwise participate in the political arena. The twentieth century saw the struggle for social rights, those that pertain to employment and health insurance and participation in education. Special education is a particularly strong illustration of social rights, for it symbolizes the right of disadvantaged and disabled children and youth to free and compulsory schooling, which has increasingly been viewed as central to individual human development as well as to national economic stability and growth.

To adapt the range of nongovernmental organizations to Marshall's thesis, organizations that specified civil, political, or social objectives as their principle *aims* were identified. From the Yearbook of International Organizations for 1965, organizations that best met this criterion were selected and then further delimited by having at least 35 nations as members. The result was a considerable reduction in the number of organizations, yielding a total of five civil, three political, and five social nongovernmental organizations (see Table 3.4).

Marshall's thesis of sequential rights suggests at least two relevant hypotheses to the variation in levels of special education. If we replace centuries with world regions, we may explore the hypothesis that the economic, political, and cultural conditions that distinguish Asian, Latin American, African, and western European nations could be reasonable proxies. That is, we would expect that European nations would predominate in all three categories of organizations, but most of all in those that have social rights as their major aim. Nations that are least economically developed as well as politically and culturally distinct from Western nations, would be underrepresented in these organizations in general and most often so in organizations that have social rights as their major aim. A second hypothesis is more like a guide to locate the specific source of the policy transfer from nongovernmental organizational membership to national contexts that affect education policymaking and thus the provision of special education. It is hypothesized that social organizations more than civil and political ones, and *particular* social organizations at that, are the information connections that link global participation to national systems of (special) education.

To address the first hypothesis, we examine the relationship between world regions and the thirteen selected organizations. Immediately evident are the consistently strong correlations between the European nations and all organizations save for two. More importantly, European nations show the strongest correlations with all of the *social* organizations. In stark contrast, African nations are the reverse, with all but one correlation inverse. This pat-

TABLE 3.4. Civil, political, and social nongovernmental organizations with levels of special education, 1970 (bivariate correlations)

| NGO | Special education 1970 | Western Europe | Eastern Europe | Latin America | Asia | Africa |
|---|---|---|---|---|---|---|
| C1: International Press Institute | .28 | .30 | −.15 | −.21 | .09 | −.12 |
| C2: International Organization of Journalists | −.12 | −.12 | −.06 | −.13 | .01 | .34 |
| C3: International Institute for the Unification of Public Law | .21* | .34** | −.04 | .19 | −.11 | −.42** |
| C4: International Bar Association | .30* | .39** | −.12 | −.19 | .11 | −.31** |
| C5: Institute of International Law | **.45*** | **.34*** | **.05** | **−.04** | **−.09** | **−.31*** |
| P1: International Association of Women | .32** | .42** | −.07 | −.36** | .23* | −.25* |
| P2: International Conference of Free Trade Unions | .26* | .27** | −.26* | .07 | .03 | .17 |
| P3: World Federation of Trade Unions | .07 | −.01 | .30** | .11 | −.09 | −.18 |
| S1: International Society for the Rehabilitation of the Disabled | .27** | .33** | −.06 | −.01 | .02 | −.41** |
| S2: International Union of Child Welfare | .29** | .39** | −.17 | −.04 | .07 | −.39** |
| S3: World Council for the Welfare of the Blind | .46** | .43** | .13 | −.25* | −.05 | −.31 |
| S4: World Federation of the Deaf | .39* | .29** | .39** | −.24* | −.09 | −.25* |
| S5: International Association of Workers for Maladjusted Children | **.50*** | **.52*** | **.01** | **−.16** | **−.23*** | **−.26*** |

*Source*: Union of International Organization (1965).
* p < .05; ** p < .01.

tern suggests some evidence for a sequential movement across international organizations that differ along the lines proposed by Marshall. European nations are members of all organizations, but predominate in civil and social nongovernmental organizations. European nations decline in the representation across all three segments, Latin America remains stable, while Asian and especially African nations indicate growth across all types of organizations, as Table 3.5 shows.

TABLE 3.5. Percent membership in non-governmental organizations by world regions, 1958/1965

| Organizational type | World regions | | | |
| --- | --- | --- | --- | --- |
| | Europe | Latin America | Asia | Africa |
| Civil | 44 / 37 | 25 / 24 | 23 / 24 | 9 / 13 |
| Political | 26 / 24 | 28 / 26 | 21 / 23 | 15 / 24 |
| Social | 51 / 45 | 23 / 22 | 18 / 23 | 8 / 10 |

The second hypothesis concerns the specific organizations that link the global culture to national policies and practices in special education. This question reaches deeper than the sequential movement from civil to political to social organizations. And short of evidence at the level of individual actors and their network ties, it cannot be addressed directly with survey data. Within these limitations, however, the statistical significance of the number of nongovernmental organizations can be given a more precise interpretation.

To explore this, the effects of specific organizations on special education levels for 1970 are examined. Two significant organizations, the Institute for International Law (Civil) and the International Association of Workers for Maladjusted Children, are discussed. As shown in Table 3.6, they have equal explanatory power. This suggests that memberships in these specific organizations may be of more import than overall membership. Whereas the aims of the first organization pertain to global civil rights, the other's aims pertain to global social practices in relation to "maladjusted" children.[5]

The significance of these two organizations, one whose objectives pertain to civil rights, the other's, social rights, lies initially in their strength to explain levels of special education after controlling for education expenditures and the GDP. They both contain information about special education levels that is given by the gross number of NGOs in 1966. This finer specification of the effects of global organizations is given by particular aims of each organization.

The Institute of International Law (IIL) is one of the oldest of all nongovernmental organizations. It was founded in 1873—in the aftermath of the Franco-Prussian War of 1870–71—in Ghent, Belgium, with the primary intent of coalescing a body of internationally renowned jurists committed to

TABLE 3.6. Effects of specific nongovernmental organizations on levels of special education, 1970

| Variable | B | Beta | B | Beta |
|---|---|---|---|---|
| NGOs, 1966 | −.06 (.17) | .36** | | |
| Education expenditures | .01 (.00) | .41 | .01 (.00) | .41** |
| C5: Institute for International Law | | | .55 (.28) | .19* |
| S5: International Association of Workers for Maladjusted Children | | | .77 (.32) | .25** |
| Adj. $R^2$ | .47 | | .47 | |
| F (N) | 36.5 (81) | | 24.9 (82) | |

Source: Union of International Associations, Yearbook of International Organizations, 10th ed., 1964–65 (Brussels, Belgium, 1965).
  * $p < .05$; ** $p < .01$.

world peace through international law (Abrams 1957). The longevity of the IIL attests to its capacity to harness the ideal of world peace to practical strategies for international cooperation. The strategies of the IIL, such as the codification of national statutes and regulations, were guided by scientific evidence and scholarly knowledge. Yet the vision of global peace and international legal justice remained the overarching aim of the organization. To this end, the IIL is ideologically and procedurally akin to the international human rights movement. It has long sought to create a balance across nations by the broadest possible participation, consistent with the scientific and scholarly methods of achieving global cooperation.

Whereas the IIL is an indirect channel of issues of international human rights to national special education, the International Association of Workers for Maladjusted Children (IAWMC) provides a direct link between the two. The organization was founded in 1951 in Freiburg im Breisgau, Germany. Its principle aim is to assist workers for "maladjusted" children—"those children who suffer from inner and/or outward maladjustment." The IAWMC was founded with a mandate to improve the quality of services to "delinquent" children through the initiative of *educateurs* in France in 1942. Like the IIL, which was established in the aftermath of war, the IAWMC was founded after the nadir of World War II, within the context of thousands of displaced children (Ness and Mitchell 1990: 199). The model of the *educateur* was in sharp contrast to traditional treatments that isolated an aspect of the child for special attention. This model addressed the whole child, particularly in relation to the social environment in which she or he lived. The French model strongly resembled the model of child guidance clinics in the United States, a movement for the direct treatment of youth deemed maladjusted to their home, community, and school environments.

The post–World War II years of the 1950s and 1960s witnessed a dramatic expansion and transformation of secondary education, particularly across western European nations and the United States (see, for example, Trow 1963). Secondary education was no longer viewed as the terminal point of compulsory schooling; it increasingly became organized as a transition to higher education. With social dislocations of the war, such as food rationing and mass migration, came problems of "maladjusted" youth. As these mounted, demands were put on schools that could not readily be absorbed. The Report of the Committee on Maladjusted Children, issued in 1955 by the Ministry of Education in England, sounded the warning of maladjustment, framing the problem in terms of space: "Despite the gradual growth in the number of special schools, local education authorities found that it was impossible to obtain places in them for all the maladjusted children in their areas who needed to attend a boarding school" (Ministry of Education 1955: 13). The maladjusted child was soon aggregated into the special category of "socially maladjusted." The socially maladjusted category grew at a faster pace than many other categories of special education. The roots of the category can be traced to the "backward child," invented in the 1920s (Franklin 1980). The significance of the category is more organizational than pedagogical, as it signified a nonscientific category that by virtue of its ambiguity could expand to include a wider and wider diversity of problem behaviors (Tomlinson 1982; Richardson 1999: chapter 4; see also chapter 6).

The postwar combination of a global human rights movement with the reorganization and expansion of secondary schooling was a context especially favorable to the rise of special education. Exemplars of this growth were two international organizations, one that was central to the principles of human rights, the other situated to address the practical adaptation of schools to "problem youth." The evolution of both agendas would become increasingly intertwined. As the right to education became codified as a global mandate, nations that differed along economic and political dimensions could align around the common problem of "at risk" children, the contemporary succes-sor of the "backward" and "socially maladjusted" child.

CONCLUSIONS

From these cross-national analyses of special education levels, the most promi-nent findings are the overall rise of schooling and the consistently significant effect of participation in world culture, which emphasizes ever-expanding educational participation—from primary to secondary to tertiary and special educaton—as central to achieving political, economic, and social goals. The weakness of economic measures per se points to external forces that define and legitimize particular types of educational provision. Normatively or even regulatively, countries were encouraged or coerced to enforce a global queue that regulates the pace at which special education enrollments expand. In the case of special education participation, disability classifications and provi-sions are legitimized by international bodies, from the World Health Organi-zation and the United Nations to the OECD and the EADSNE, and dif-fused across nations that become engaged in constructing special education systems. Once begun, such isomorphism accelerated across countries, even if convergence, where it can be identified, largely consists of rhetoric and labels, rather than in the size of special education populations or the organizational forms in which they are schooled (topics to which we return in the following chapters).

The effects of world culture through the diffusion of ideas, such as the international charters in special and inclusive education, are evident in the shifting legitimacy of institutions that provide contrasting educational envi-ronments in which students with special educational needs are schooled, and on educational and social policies that determine the services and supports available to children and youth with special educational needs. The effects on institutions can be compatible with existing historical and cultural differ-ences: given the tremendous diversity in policy and practice across even the developed democracies, noted in every OECD publication that identifies benchmarks and ranks members states, there exist legitimate models that fa-vor the entire range or continuum of educational settings, from segregation and separation to integration and inclusion. Yet however uniform global articulations of special or inclusive education may seem and however similar national declarations or policy statements may appear, such indicators of consensus and convergence can be deceptive. Below the level of international declarations that proclaim universal rights to education, national differences endure. Such differences are not restricted to individual countries, but can also coalesce as regional patterns. In contrast to countries in Latin America, Asia, and Africa, the countries of western Europe—in particular, some of the Nordic countries—have led in the expansion of special education and, more recently, the advancement of inclusive education. However, although they may lag "behind" western European countries in some indicators, the countries of Latin America, Asia, and Africa exemplify alternative strategies in educational integration as well as alternative images of inclusion that hearken back to different values regarding independence, the formation and guarantee of capabilities, and strategies to secure well-being in local contexts. This is the topic taken up in the next chapter.

## CHAPTER 4

# HISTORICAL MODELS AND SOCIAL LOGICS OF SPECIAL EDUCATION SYSTEMS

A s (SPECIAL) EDUCATION BECAME INCREAS-
ingly aligned with human rights efforts and the global
proclamations arising from such efforts, the mode of commitment to international ideals and principles became a metric that gave some measure of movement toward the comparative advancement of special needs education and,
in turn, inclusive education. UN surveys gathered national summaries as to
goals and objectives and the legislative bases of special education (Brine
2001). Over the past decade, the European Union, World Bank, and especially the OECD have expanded their efforts to compare developments in
special and inclusive education around the world. As explored in the previous
chapter, the variation in special education participation is matched by the
increase in the number of countries reporting enrollments in classes and
schools as well as achievement and attainment data. Global pressures to insti-
tutionalize "education for all," increasingly include provisions for children

and youth with special educational needs. This trend is, presumptively, toward a common goal, which increasing numbers of countries avow as a national commitment: the integration of children with special educational needs into general education and the elimination of discriminatory barriers, whether they be in political participation, employment, or community life.

The more recent global goal of inclusive education, as codified in international charters, has facilitated special education's cross-national connectedness as well as engendered criticism of its programs. The declaration that children with disabilities, difficulties, and disadvantages ought to be given an education that best fits their capabilities and potential is sufficiently general as to incite few, if any, detractors—at least in most contemporary Western societies. At the level of goals and objectives, national declarations are notable more for their similarities than their differences. Moreover, this rhetorical similarity is increasing, in part because it can be politically rewarding as an avowed national project that helps countries meet international proclamations, if not actually implement "best practices" or even meet minimal standards. Developing countries may write legislation and implement policy with the same language as developed countries. Yet, as John Boli and Michael Elliott (2008: 546) note, the "enactment" of "world-cultural models and scripts" can be costly, for it requires resources that many nations lack. Not only because of a lack of resources, but also because of vested interests, these global prescriptions and actual practices by nations are "loosely coupled" (see Weick 1976), just as within each country the wishes of centralized policymakers often do not transform the state or local routines (see Tyack and Cuban 1995). Thus, we must be wary about taking rhetorical compliance at face value; successful cross-national emulation and compliance indicate "achieved isomorphism," yet true convergence is quite rare (Powell and Solga 2008: 12).

One can be deceived by the rhetorical similarity manufactured by global ideals that are not seriously contested, at least among policy elites that build bridges between countries and translate attractive models into national reform agendas (see Steiner-Khamsi 2004). Moreover, such foreign ideals may be seriously challenged within the realm of national and local politics and decision making about schooling, which often pits education professionals and administrators against parents and students. The potential deception from assuming similarity across nations or regions can be grave. Given the growing strength of the supranational level, be it through governance structures like the European Union and the United Nations or international non-governmental organizations such as the OECD, one may presume that countries are on similar paths with respect to (special) education policy, provisions, and practices. We argue that such conclusions about convergence are premature and potentially misleading, despite their being especially attractive when particular elements of special education are isolated, removed from context, and compared in cross-sectional benchmarking exercises and league tables. Quantitative features are more amenable to isolation, as explored earlier. Comparisons of such indicators as classification rates and inclusive education legislation do not exhaust the complex range of features that compose the education of children who receive special education services. The process of identifying, assessing, and diagnosing children, the state administrative powers and the distribution of authority to local and regional levels, the social policies and regulations for hearings and appeals, curricula and instruction—all are salient features of special education as a *system*. Such features of special education are interlocked. Thus, in-depth comparisons of special education systems are crucial, and become ever more important as policies are translated across linguistic and transferred beyond national boundaries.

The decades since World War II have seen the global rise of special education as part of the larger massive expansion of education (as shown in Chapter 3). And special education *predated* compulsory schooling, which led to the expansion of general education (as shown in Chapter 1). Thus, we argue that the education of children with special educational needs is more than a mere subsystem of general education, even if it is organizationally and legally placed in an auxiliary position. We assert that the content of policies and their procedural stipulations, the types of classifications and the number and meanings of categories, the organizational forms and educational environments and their respective instructional methods, and the modes of administration and regulation must all be taken as a systemic whole that is greater than the sum of its parts and is not merely subsidiary to general education.[1]

Special education systems may be viewed as forms of control or domination over children with disabilities to be sure, but over culturally and socially disadvantaged or disruptive children as well. Western nations have extended this domination beyond their boundaries by defining the terms and rules of global debates over special and inclusive education. The discourse of inclusive education may be thought of as similar to a populist or labor movement and as a component of general education or social welfare. When the diversity of nations is the universe of cases, countries outside Western Europe suggest very different terms and conditions with reference to special education. These are neither underdeveloped nor merely intriguing variants of Western models; they are historically different models.

Often hidden by the abstract transnational discourse of inclusion, the tremendous diversity of special education systems lies below the surface. This chapter develops a framework that systematizes this diversity while avoiding a reification of the particular historical experience of western European nations.[2] Informed by the "ideal type" approach of Max Weber (see Kalberg 1994; Ringer 1997), the strategy engages in comparative-historical analysis in which outcomes of interest, such as levels and forms of special education participation and placement, reflect similar *combinations* of variables, not just similar levels of individual variables. Mauro Guillén states it well:

A comparative institutional approach . . . argues that there are multiple viable paths [to development] . . . . Countries embark on different trajectories depending on a complex set of variables . . . [that] make certain development policies and paths more feasible than others. The dynamic unfolding of development policies over time interacts [with variables] to produce different combinations of organizational forms (Guillén 2001: 13, 15).

Central to this approach is society, not simply as a theoretical concept, but as an actor. Society "acts" insofar as it presents "preexisting institutional arrangements" that pose "a path-dependent context of action, guiding and enabling socially embedded action" (Guillén 2001: 15). As Guillén notes further, "different combinations of organizational form" reflect certain "organizing logics" that differ qualitatively from one set of countries to another, as well as within each country (as analyzed in Chapter 5). The *logics* "are the product of historical development, are deeply rooted in collective understandings and cultural practice, and resilient in the face of changing circumstance" (Guillén 2001: 15; also Biggart and Guillén 1999).[3] Education policy in general and programs and provisions for the education of children with special educational needs in particular are good examples of "developmental policies" that are shaped by the particular combination of organizational forms. They indeed *unfold over time*, but not necessarily in the same direction. As stressed before, the origins of special education are not uniform and the development of special education shows no linear trajectory. On the contrary, there are several trajectories, with some paths more feasible than others. Finally, these paths have led to a number of paradoxes, which we discuss in Part 3.

## THE WESTERN NARRATIVE: MERITS AND LIMITATIONS

The dominant theory of historical change in the education of people with disabilities is a narrative of progress, a linear development of ever more and better provisions. The standard tale goes something like this: national education policies toward people with disabilities have moved from broad philanthropic care to state assistance through separate, institutional residency to models of integration, "normalization," and, finally, inclusive education (see, for example, Wolfensberger 1976; Hegarty, Pocklington, and Lucas 1981; Dahl, Tangerud, and Vislie 1982; Gartner and Lipsky 1987; Peters 1993; UNESCO 1995: 9; UNESCO 1996: 43–44; Barton and Armstrong 2001). This evolutionary model rests on three premises: (1) special education was the stepchild of the organizational dilemma that arose when Western nations faced the specter of an expanded and diverse population of school-age children who now could seek and indeed must participate in primary education as a result of free and compulsory education laws; (2) this "illegitimate" origin persists to define special education as marginal and subsidiary or dependent on mass education; and (3) contemporary special education reforms reflect this legacy. Research is often deeply skeptical and thrives, in various ways, on the gap between the good intentions of teachers and other professionals and poor outcomes of students schooled in special education (Barton 1986: 283; Skrtic 1995). Such an interpretation is conceptually organized around a critical sequence that is often glossed over: legislation of compulsory education comes only *after* separate institutions and myriad organizational forms for people with a variety of disabilities are established and only *after* a substantial base of popular schooling was in place. The dominance of this interpretation derives from the dominance of articulations on the experience of western

European nations, for after all, the key sequence largely fits their institutional histories—as generally told or even well known in the research community at large.

For many developing nations, special education is seen as a criterion of mature nationhood (Miles 1988: 44). Yet the historical sequence of institution building and the expansion toward mass education on the basis of compulsory schooling fits developing countries less well. In national contexts outside the West, the determinants of special needs education can be qualitatively different from those in the western European model, even, in fact, reversed. In their analysis of schooling in Nigeria, Festus Obiakor and others are most frank: "The borderline or at-risk cases are not easily identifiable, which *makes the whole idea of special education to be nonexistent* in Nigeria. Most exceptional students are indiscriminately integrated into mainstream classes. It becomes a matter of 'survival of the fittest' for these individuals" (Obiakor et al. 1991: 347, emphasis added). The barriers against special education in Nigeria go beyond economic conditions, for the majority of Nigerians "view disability, and disabled people as a whole, as a retribution or a curse from God who repays everyone according to his or her deeds" (Abang 1988: 72). The consequences are pervasive educational and social discrimination: The integration of children with disabilities in regular classes is "indiscriminate," neither meeting individual needs nor providing a basis for a *rights* discourse that seeks to equalize opportunities outcomes.

The resilience of traditional social groups, be they tribes, clans, linguistic minorities, or castes, may inhibit mass education and individualization and may thus negate special education with particular virulence. Primary loyalty to tribe or caste has been seen, in Western terms, as a social impediment to the bureaucratic mode of special education so prevalent among developed countries.[4] Indeed, in many non-Western societies compulsory education was enacted not only significantly later than in Western nations, but in the midst of or before economic "takeoff" and often after struggles for independence from colonial rule. Yet enacting compulsory education is not so much an achievement of internal politics as the result of an ambition to enhance the nation's international standing as it conforms to the "world education revolution" (see Meyer et al. 1977).[5] For developing nations, the coupling of democratic principles and bureaucratic organization is unstable at best, forged more as a rhetorical compliance than as a timely and solid integration of ideas and institutions.

The different sequence of events that led to compulsory education is a significant historical divide for Western and non-Western countries. This historical contrast imprints itself onto contemporary educational structures and education policies. A nation's definition of education, how it conceives and states the "objectives" and "principles" of education, is a reflection to some degree of its historical sequence. A most discernible contrast is between objectives of education that have *collective* goals and objectives that have primarily *individual* goals. For collective goals, national education is seen as a means to enhance not only solidarity and equality but also economic growth through the dissemination of scientific knowledge. For individual goals, the national education policy is a means to promote knowledge and skills as well as moral and ethical responsibility. To people with disabilities, who have routinely faced a tenuous commitment to their education and employment as well as to their social and political participation, it matters a great deal whether a society tends in the collectivist or individualist direction. Along the significant divide of collectivist and individualist societies, such differences for select countries still exhibit national particularities (see Table 4.1).

The Western nations avow both collective and individual objectives. The sample of Western nations displayed in Table 4.1 refers directly to the individual, citing as the goal of education to expand knowledge and human capital, mental and physical health, and the sense of ethical and civic responsibility. The positive effects on the nation are secondary mentions in educational acts, if mentioned at all, although this seems to be changing in some "post-welfare" countries as they embrace market principles that emphasize the role of education in a country's global competitiveness (see Stronach 1990; Tomlinson 2005). The emphasis for non-Western countries is, in contrast, almost exclusively on collective objectives. For developing nations, the central focus is the nation itself. Individuals are the vehicles through which the nation is made visible and strong, and thus competitive in the modern world. Equal access to education and the promotion of knowledge and skills, as well as the promotion of tolerance for other human beings, are properties of the society as a collective entity. A reverse logic characterizes developed nations: the

TABLE 4.1. Collective and individual objectives of education (illustrative evidence, select countries)

| Nation | Collective | | | | | Individual | | | | |
|---|---|---|---|---|---|---|---|---|---|---|
| | Provide equal access | Promote equality | Promote nation | Promote modern-int'l world | Promote scientific knowledge | Promote mental/physical health | Promote moral/ethical responsibility | Promote knowledge and skills | Promote exercise of citizenship | Promote tolerance |
| | 1 | 2 | 3 | 4 | 5 | 1 | 2 | 3 | 4 | 5 |
| **Africa** | | | | | | | | | | |
| Sierra Leone | • | | • | • | | | | • | | |
| Tanzania | | | | | | | | | | |
| Zimbabwe | • | • | | | | | | | | |
| **Asia** | | | | | | | | | | |
| Afghanistan | • | • | • | | | • | | | | |
| China | • | • | • | | • | | | | • | |
| Malaysia | | • | • | • | | | | | | |
| Thailand | | | • | | | | | | | |

| | 1 | 2 | 3 | 4 | 5 | | 1 | 2 | 3 | 4 | 5 |
|---|---|---|---|---|---|---|---|---|---|---|---|
| **Europe** | | | | | | | | | | | |
| Bulgaria | • | • | | | | | • | • | | | |
| Czech Rep. | • | • | • | • | | | • | • | | | • |
| Finland | | | • | • | | | | | • | • | |
| France | | | | | | | • | | • | • | • |
| Lithuania | • | | • | • | • | | | • | | • | • |
| Norway | • | | • | • | | | | • | | • | • |
| Spain | • | • | • | | | | | | | • | |
| Sweden | • | • | | • | • | | | • | • | • | • |
| **Latin America** | | | | | | | | | | | |
| Argentina | • | • | • | | | | | | | | |
| Colombia | • | • | • | | • | | | | | | |
| Guatemala | • | | | | • | | | | | | • |
| Paraguay | • | | | | | | | | | | |

*Sources:* The World Law Guide: www.lexadin.nl/wlg/; "Legislation" (last accessed 27 April 2010).

nation is the beneficiary of that which individuals attain, for that which lies within each individual is prior and superior to aggregate effects of education (see Greif 1994; Hofstede 2001).

On one level, the collectivist-individualist dimension is too condensed to capture the considerable variation across national cultures. On another level, the contrast cannot adequately capture the changes that rearrange the variation across cultures. The contrast between collectivism and individualism can quickly become a false dichotomy if the variation within each group exceeds the variation between them. The latter is more likely and clearly more plausible. The dimension does, nonetheless, reflect an influential force that can permeate downward from centralized political authority and upward from the decentralized worlds of local communities. A collectivist or an individualist emphasis can diffuse further or remain entrenched to the extent political and economic structures are reinforced by cultural beliefs and practices. It is more theoretically profitable to conceive of such an emphasis as one feature among others. It is more historically accurate to examine how this feature is intricately intertwined with others—and so varies with them.

## SPECIAL EDUCATION SYSTEMS AS IDEAL TYPES: A THEORETICAL FRAMEWORK

When special education is examined across a wide array of countries, patterns of similarity are conspicuous at the level of general goals and objectives, which reflect the more general goals of schooling that have spread around the world, such as access to education, achievement, and attainment (see Baker and LeTendre 2005). To some degree, these similarities can be rhetorical artifacts of structured survey questions from international bodies with considerable influence and the responsibility for translating results into policy-relevant documents. When details are examined, however, it becomes evident that systems are far more complex than general policy goals and legislative mandates can convey. Such details include the locus of authority and administrative procedures, parental duties and familial responsibilities relative to national obligations, institutions and organizational types and their legacies, and teacher training and instructional goals. However strong in their ability to discern general patterns, statistical analyses stretch assumptions that are difficult to maintain when the specific context and history of education systems in individual nations are the focus.[6]

The comparative-historical work of Max Weber (1978) exemplifies an alternative, but complementary approach to multivariate statistical techniques. Rejecting the claim that concepts can, or seek to, capture social reality, Weber employed the *ideal type* as both a theoretical construct and a methodological yardstick for comparison and interpretation. The ideal type was a purposeful exaggeration of empirical features, formulated not as an objective measure but as a hypothesized, ideal configuration of "action-orientations" (Kalberg 1994; Ringer 1997). Action-orientations specify a delimited and interrelated number of behaviors that can tend increasingly toward stability or toward dissolution.[7] Although factors might be structurally similar, they nonetheless can have very dissimilar meanings. In his comparison of the Occidental world with the Orient, each had cities, intellectual strata, money economies, systems of rule, and dominant religions. Yet the meaning of each differed significantly, and thus their comparison can be interpreted only as the result of their particular configuration, that is, their multicausality.

From his historical-comparative studies of what distinguished the West and the East, Weber outlined two modal ideal types. The model that distinguished the West was the combination of democracy and bureaucracy, whereas the model that distinguished the East was patrimonialism. The features of these two ideal types parallel the contrast between individualist and collectivist societies. The individualist pattern for developed, western European nations is founded on an institutional base long acquainted with the principles of democracy and the organizational neutrality of bureaucracy. In contrast, the institutional base for many non-Western societies derives from structures of rulership in which power emanates from the household of the king or emperor and is antagonistic to principles of democracy and bureaucratic neutrality. Each type delineates how political, organizational, and cultural elements are intertwined, constituting a *system of domination* that is resilient over time. A nation's image of its education system is a key element of this structure of domination, for struggles to expand access to schooling may best be viewed as continuations of the long, unfolding process of political incorporation. The (special) education of people with disabilities must be seen as part of this long-term political struggle.

While Weber identified pure examples of historical models, he repeatedly returned to core themes: that real historical dynamics are ones of interaction between and among types, a premise that rejects the search for an independent influence by factors considered separately; and that the yardstick by which we can measure the emergence and persistence of social institutions is how they *sustain* action-orientation as regular and enduring. Weber's multi-causal approach examines interactions within and between two dimensions: societal domains and domain-specific ideal types. The former is composed of six domains: religion, law, the economy, rulership, universal organizations, and status groups. Corresponding to each of these are particular ideal types: specific paths to salvation, types of law, stages of economic development, types of authority, types of universal organizations, and major forms of status groups. The focus of comparison is the interaction of specific ideal types with the societal domains. Thus, a particular path to salvation can coexist with a particular form of rulership, as do magical forms with personalized rule. But shifts in stages of the economy, from an agricultural stage to an industrial stage and the prominence of market systems, are affected because their affinities are now jeopardized. The possible antagonisms and affinities that arise, or fail to arise, follow certain logics that prescribe forms of interaction between societal domains and specific ideal types.

The sources of interactions, in Stephen Kalberg's terms, are synchronic and diachronic (Kalberg 1994: 155). The former denotes the combinations at specific historical times, as how regular action-orientation in the domain of religion penetrates families and households as forms of universal organizations. Weber's interest was the "penetration range" of interactions. Weber observed how the Indian caste system, accentuating status stratification in the extreme, penetrated remote areas of Indian life. As a consequence, and with particular relevance to education in general and special education in particular, the caste system would be intensely antagonistic to notions of natural law or human rights (157). The natural affinity between a caste system and traditional forms of law would pose a considerable barrier to the introduction of ideas that all children have a right to an education and, more intensely, a barrier to education for all regardless of disability, disadvantage or difficulty.

The second source of interactions, the diachronic, illustrates more emphatically Weber's rejection of static formulations and ahistorical explanations. The penetration range of previous historical events, or conditions, can be considerable, and is often overlooked. The causal influence of past historical conditions, again in Kalberg's terms, takes the form of "legacies" and "antecedent conditions" (1994: 159, footnote 24). Both intradomain and interdomain interactions "cast their shadows" across many subsequent time periods and do so against economic and political (and technological) changes that would logically undo their affinities. The influence of legacies is especially strong. The "strain" of certain ideas, such as a monotheistic God, or a practice, such as an oath, can be seen as passing from Judaism to Catholicism to Protestantism, doing so even as forms of rulership and economic organization change significantly. Weber paid special attention to the tenacious staying power of ideas and practices that originate within universal forms of organization: those of family, household, and community. As with the caste system, ideas of exclusion—in marriage, residency, and descent—can persist for extensive periods of time and, more importantly, can be reinforced by external interactions that threaten their affinity. Against the contemporary notions of access to education as an individual right and equal participation in social, political, and economic spheres, ideas and practices of marital, descent, and residential exclusion are formidable sources of resistance.

The models of democracy-bureaucracy and patrimonialism are not to be taken as static or as snapshots of the past. Rather, they are the means to *expand* empirical analyses. As dynamic configurations, they have lines of antagonism within them as well as between them. These "analytic antinomies" are the specific combinations that may originally have had an elective affinity, but over time, or from pressures emanating from other domains, these affinities may become antagonisms. Weber's description of "passive democratization" is instructive, as he notes how reliance on abstract rules and procedural decision making tend bureaucratic strata toward enclosing around their specific jurisdiction of power. A result is a progressive antagonism toward democratic principles—that of equality of access in particular. Weber gives numerous examples of tension within patrimonialism, noting the natural antagonism between feudal and patriarchal modes of rule.

Yet the logics that distinguish democracy-bureaucracy and patrimonialism may be less consequential than conditions that mix the two. Compound types, as for example "patrimonial bureaucracy," arise when a feature of

rulership founded on personal attributes is combined with impersonal exami-
nations, a bureaucratic feature that can enhance patrimonial rule. Contemporary examples are numerous and bear directly on debates over special and
inclusive education. When dictatorial regimes take hold in previously democratic polities or vice versa, as in Latin America and eastern Europe, or when
the economies of specific Asian countries with long histories of patrimonial
rule undergo dramatic expansion through ties to global capitalism, they must
now integrate the demands of a market system with the traditional beliefs and
practices of religion and its intricate penetration of families and households.
For compound formulations, Weber's objective remained consistent: to generate hypotheses that fit the range of empirical possibilities predicted by the
particular historical model. In more specific terms, Weber's focus was on the
effects of interactions, whether the new "penetration range" enhances economic growth or social reforms, or is antagonistic to such changes.

### The Western Model: Democracy-Bureaucracy

One of the more consequential achievements of the Western model was the
separation of the office and the person. This form of "nonlegitimate domination" was nurtured by the coincident emergence of democratic movements,
espousing principles of equality and challenging monarchical power. Weber's
analysis and interpretation of democracy and bureaucracy as a distinctly
Western "historical model" was strengthened by a parallel analysis and interpretation of its diminished presence in the East.[8] Many countries had elements of democratic movements and bureaucratic organization that were
necessary for the emergence of institutions noted in the West, yet they lacked
the critical elements that were sufficient for the emergence of the individual as
an abstract idea and the attachment to it of rights, freedoms, and potential.

The Western model of mass, compulsory schooling, citizenship rights, and
an expanded, but relatively benign, state authority has aligned each of these
components not only to democratic principles but also to the bureaucratic
structures that have carried each. The democratic principle of free and compulsory primary education was propelled by similar principles that expanded
the rights of assembly, free speech, and the franchise. The neutrality of bureaucratic organization, nominally free of the sectarian influences of religion,
ethnicity, and socioeconomic privilege, was a context that could be expanded
as "comprehensive." In terms of education, such comprehensivity enabled the

accommodation of diverse populations by means of common pedagogical objectives and methods. Despite struggles over public schooling, strikingly similar for both the nineteenth and twentieth centuries, the bureaucratic neutrality of public schools has been the favored site of education reforms pressing for expanded access (see, for example, Tyack 1974; Silver 1983; Tyack and Cuban 1995). And in spite of the persistence of religious and ethnic differences and socioeconomic inequalities, if measured by the expansion of secondary and tertiary enrollments alone, the success of reforms has been considerable. As noted earlier, much of the politics over special education is a reflection of such struggles ultimately leading to successes. In general terms, as the democratic boundaries of public schooling expand, becoming more comprehensive, the measures and procedures that regulate selection and transitions to higher levels of education are subject to new political contests. Throughout this process, an expanded base that allows for new contests remains important.

It is commonly observed, as it must be, that special education is a "nested" system, not only within general education, but also within itself. As Claes Nilholm aptly notes, the reduction of special education issues to two perspectives, a "deficit perspective" that locates problems within the child and a "curriculum-based perspective" that instead finds problems within the school and classroom, is misplaced, for they are "interactive" (Nilholm 2006: 433). Because of this interaction, "dilemmas appear at different levels in the school system"—and "a view of special education as a response to fundamental dilemmas could be 'combined' with different views of society" (Nilholm 2006: 434–435, emphasis added; see also Allan 2008: 27). From the classroom to society, any dilemma that arises and that is enacted as such is specific to a given social level. Moreover, the designated level is structured in advance; it is the combination of culture and history that prescribes a given education level as the site of dilemmas, such as the "distributive dilemma of disability" (see Stone 1984) or the more specific "resource-labeling dilemma" (Füssel and Kretschmann 1993) in special education: to accept the provision of resources as well as the stigma that so often accompanies the labels associated with special educational needs categories (see Powell 2010, 2011).

The combination of conditions that is especially conducive to the generation of educational dilemmas is the coupling of democratic principles and bureaucratic organization (Roth 1971). For Weber, this coupling was the model of Western institutions, arising from the particular structure and meaning of the Occidental city. From this urban context, rights as individual attributes emerged from their corporate origins, one of several consequences that followed the delegitimation of kinship (Alexander 1983: 51–52). The delegitimation of intermediary groups promoted the legitimacy of civil society below and autonomous from the state. Most importantly, it promoted "a web of autonomous associations, independent of the state" (Taylor 1990: 96; also Roniger 1994: 209).

The coupling of democracy and bureaucracy, to update Weber's ideal type, encompasses three crucial elements: civility, social trust, and civil society (on the tripartite composition of the modern state, see Pye 1999). The element of civility denotes the "rules" of acceptable conduct, the norms of proper behavior that are widely understood as basic to the functioning and stability of society as a whole. Civility is a property of the highest level, above the many cultural subgroups and communities that otherwise distinguish people by lifestyle and behavior. To Edward Shils (1997), civility is essential in a democracy, where opposing views can become highly combative and potentially corrosive. Civility is an expression of the "collective consciousness," a measure of the bonds integrating individuals into the wider society. The crucial division in civility is between the norms of conduct that regulate intimate relations and the norms that regulate "intermediate" groupings and the range of "status gradations" of superior-inferior relationships (Pye 1999: 766). Often for people with disabilities, these norms seem not to obtain, as relationships must acknowledge differences in social standing and the all-too-prevalent stigmatization and fear deriving from lack of contact resulting from architectural barriers and residential segregation. At the same time, for democracy and its coupling with bureaucratic organization, the norms of civility greatly enable participation in a diversity of *public* interactions and relations. Respect, good manners, and politeness can be a double-edged sword when it comes to visible disability, as staring—a natural response to curiosity about those who differ from us—may be forbidden, and people like to stare, but don't like to be stared at (see Garland-Thomson 2009).

The foundation to civility is a civil society and its corollary of social trust. As noted earlier, a civil society is the sphere of autonomous associations that individuals can join freely and that collectively stand as a check on the power of the state. The latter is most crucial. The power of autonomous associations to restrain state power presumes that associations are outside the state, neither subordinate to it nor too deeply integrated into it. The autonomy of civil society mirrors the distinction between the sphere of personal relations and public interactions. Public conduct is civil and reasonable, independent of the social obligations that bind kinship and community relations. Finally, both civility and civil society are joined by and function through social trust, what Lucien Pye denotes as social capital, or "the accumulation of binding sentiments of trust and reciprocity" (Pye 1999: 769). For a vibrant democracy, sustained by the neutrality of bureaucratic organization, the sentiments that accumulate and bind are those that cut across social levels, permitting movement between the personal, local, and traditional and the impersonal and public. The line between personal and public relations is often marked by sentiments of distrust. Members of outside groups can be as "foreign" as persons from another society. For example, Deaf people emphasize that their community maintains an independent culture built around sign language (e.g., Groce 1985; Sainsbury 1986). Yet as Pye keenly notes, trust and distrust are found in all societies, for they provide "theories" of "unseen worlds." Not only in developed democracies is education—especially primary schooling, in which most children living in a community spend the better part of each weekday interacting with each other—a central mechanism that shapes the sentiments of trust and distrust, thus regulating both civil society and civility. In such a context, behavior norms are crucial; therefore, special education, which so often determines the range of opportunities that children and youth who challenge such conventions have in school life, is particularly relevant. Thus, a key argument for inclusive education emphasizes that learning while in school about the tremendous diversity inherent in all human groups will facilitate social inclusion in other contexts (see, for example, Sapon-Shevin 2007).

*The Logics of Democracy-Bureaucracy*

The Western model that couples democracy and bureaucracy accentuates the relation between state power and educational policies. It situates education as a mediating institution between state power and parental authority. Education laws (and court rulings adjudicating their boundaries) are linked to the

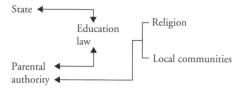

FIGURE 4.1. The Western model: Democracy-bureaucracy

state in a reciprocal, almost dialectical manner. Through legislative enactments, the state exerts an influence on education law, and in return, the professional interests of teachers and the commonly acknowledged and legally entrusted rights of parents can exert an influence on the local interpretation and implementation of education law. These parties are interlocked in a system of influence, at the center of which is the linkage between education law and parental authority. The model of democracy-bureaucracy is portrayed in Figure 4.1.

The whole passage of students into special education, from initial identification, through assessment, diagnosis, and classification, to placement, is based on the presumption of bureaucratic neutrality toward the interests of parents and the state. The multistage process of classification into special education is adjudicated by powerful clinical professions—foremost, those of psychology and medicine—that seem to be neutral and objective. Yet they are anything but independent, as the tremendous spatial variance in classification rates will show. The sequential steps of the bureaucratic process of transfer from general to special education that is designed to balance competing interests magnify due process procedures as the central instrument that mediates the relation between state powers and parental authority. As a result, a focal dynamic of this system, with consequences for special education, centers on the relation between state power and parental authority. Specifically, as the boundaries of education expand, rhetorically through a discourse of inclusion and demographically through internal and external pressures, the nexus of state power and parental authority tightens, and the pedagogical reach of special education narrows, for the stratification of parental authority becomes more salient. Thus, whereas the proportion of students participating in special education may expand, the system of special education contracts around established processes, solidifying and preserving itself as a semiclosed, reproductive structure (Kontopoulos 1993: 119). Parents lacking cultural, social, and economic capital—which includes being unable to speak the dominant language—are at a serious disadvantage in the negotiations with school gate-keepers and professionals as they seek the best for their child.

A semiclosed system is akin to the family of social processes that are, as Thomas Schelling keenly noted, reproductive "in the aggregate," for they persist "no matter how people behave" (Schelling 1978: 50).[9] Like the home thermostat that "controls the temperature by responding to the temperature," there is an internal regulation of the processes that compose the Western model. Special education systems control the inclusion or exclusion of disabled children *by responding to them*, deciding where and when they enter, how long they remain, when they exit, and where they go. These pathways are known in advance, as they have been the subject of self-referential education policymaking and court decisions accumulated over decades of feedback dynamics. The sequences of decisions that lead to classification and placement in special education environments constitute a *process structure*, and the pace of these linked decisions is the *parameter structure*. The result, or *output structure*, depends on both; it is predetermined by whether each changes or remains constant. When each remains essentially unchanged, the outcome is "reproduced" (Hernes 1976); in the aggregate, the results approximate a semiclosed system. As Clark et al. acknowledge (1997: 176): "In reconstructing itself, special education has frequently simply replicated itself." A particularly significant example: even after the denouement of the Second World War, the profession and practice of special education in both West and East Germany experienced a nearly complete "restoration," with continuity despite the attempts by the Western Allied occupation forces to "democratize" the education system (see Ellger-Rüttgardt 1997a, 1997b; Powell 2011).[10]

The composition of this output structure, measured in such indicators as classification rates and the proportional placements in segregative or more inclusive settings, and disparities along socioeconomic status, race, and gender lines are also to a certain extent predetermined and independent of individual behavior and characteristics. In short, the outcomes that are often the subject of "dilemmas" in the special education systems of dominant Western nations are largely reproduced, unintended, and difficult to modify. They are dilemmas insofar as they remain more or less immune to incremental reforms, producing a number of paradoxes in contemporary special education (to which we return in Part 3).

The norms of democracy act as a force on the diverse array of individuals and groups who regulate, administer and teach in special education organizations as well as those who receive the support and services provided. Increasing over time, there has been a positive inclination to incorporate children with disabilities, difficulties, and disadvantages in some educational setting, along the continuum from segregation to inclusion; however, this expansion has *not* led to a linear progression to more integrated schooling or inclusive education everywhere. These differences persist in international and regional comparisons (see Chapter 6).

If the act of incorporation as public recognition and validation of difference is most relevant, there is, in essence, collusion between the norms of democracy and the practices of bureaucratic implementation. In less accusatory terms, there seems to be "institutional isomorphism" (see DiMaggio and Powell 1983, 1991) between the two, as special education's sense of self is one of benevolence for those who must be helped to join the community of learners. This requires, however, the identification of those needing support to do so. This similarity through copying the ideals, norms, and regulations of general education is especially germane to the Western systems of special education (as argued in Chapter 5). For Western systems, the democratic ideal of inclusion is an "institutionalized rule"—as "classifications built into society as reciprocated typifications or interpretations" that should be "distinguished from prevailing social behavior" (Meyer and Rowan 1977: 341). The goal of inclusion as a democratic ideal does not imply reclassification so much as it demands the end of classification as a necessary precondition for services: such bureaucratically driven, official, and immutable boundaries between groups of learners should no longer be necessary (e.g., Skrtic 1995).

The goal implies normative obligations that assume a rule-like status. Yet in the process whereby democratic ideals are transposed into rule-like facts, the ideal assumes mythic proportions, becoming an external force that is impressed on organizations that inhabit a common institutional environment. First, education for all diffused worldwide, followed closely by inclusive education as internationally recognized ideals. Under such conditions, the discrepancy between rhetoric at a highly aggregated level and local school realities is destined to widen. Education goals often remain aloft of schools and residential institutions. This can result because the bureaucratic imperative is anathema to the idealized goal, such as inclusive schooling that values diversity without requiring the reification of categorical boundaries and the labeling of students. Alternatively, it can result precisely because the bureaucratic mechanisms for diffusion and implementation of educational reforms are lacking, especially in many non-Western societies. In numerous societies, as the earlier example of Nigeria demonstrated, the fundamental goal of offering any kind of "special" education or the provision of additional educational resources remains unresolved, notwithstanding that elites and even local schoolteachers may recognize the need to offer something called special education to comply with international norms.

For developed Western nations, these democratic ideals are not to remain aloft, but instead are constraining forces to which schools seek to comply, as the rise of inclusive education attests. This introduces a key element to the logics of the Western model. A noticeable feature of special education in advanced Western nations is the prominence of categories that pertain to misbehavior in school. From the mid-twentieth-century category of "social maladjustment" to "social and emotional disturbance" and "learning disability" as more contemporary descendants,[11] assessments have also been based on "inappropriate" conduct, acting out, or simply displays that are seen as "naughty, difficult or disruptive" by teachers (see Her Majesty's Inspectorate 1978; Francis 1980: 12–14; Lloyd-Smith 1984; Mongon 1988). The recent rise of disruptive or inappropriate behavior, frequently specified as "attention deficit hyperactivity disorder" (ADHD) as a signal of "special education need" is a reflection of a shift in political climate. This postwelfare era is defined by references to market forces and economic competition and continuous standardized testing and psychological measurements of school progress and educational success. In Polanyi's terms, the shift is a return to the principles of economic liberalism and the reinvigoration of beliefs in the self-regulating market system (1957). The rise of psychometric testing in the United States (see Lemann 1999; Bradley and Richardson 2009) facilitates market-based education reforms, such as the No Child Left Behind Act of 2001, which requires the monitoring of "Adequate Yearly Progress" via the National Assessment of Educational Progress. In such a context, judgments about academic capability and promise "favour actions such as paying attention to teachers, to classroom rules and to the task in hand with in-seat, on-task behaviour" (Adams 2008: 114). Teacher perceptions of inappropriate behavior are made against a standard of civility that is now defined within a context that subordinates schools to market forces, subjecting student performance to cultural expectations "which do not *necessarily* reflect impairment, but rather socio-cultural and political actions" (Adams 2008: 114, emphasis added).

Education policy, and education law in its concrete form, reflects this shift in political climate—this *double movement*. The categories of special needs education, such as ADHD (coupled with the increasingly widespread usage of pharmaceuticals like Ritalin to control behavior), become a means to explain and direct the treatment of diagnosed low school performance or underachievement, which has become threatening as education's economic potential and impact has increased. Behavioral categories "provide the digestible benchmark" with which parents, students, teachers, and administrators can interpret school progress, or more accurately, lack of school progress. The benchmark of learning disability provides a "label of forgiveness" that complements and absolves parental authority while reinforcing professional authority. This dynamic, however, runs against inclusion, for now "education enters into a contract that seeks to distinguish and support the 'disabled' as opposed to the 'disadvantaged'" (Adams 2008: 121). Yet middle-class parents will continue to find ways of getting the most out of special education, which provides additional resources to access the curriculum. The "classification threshold" (Powell 2010) will most likely decline further as the negative consequences of "having a special educational need" such as stigmatization and segregation are reduced and the value of schooling, achievement, and attainment continues to increase (which we discuss in Chapter 6).

The dynamic that links perceptions of education performance and categories of special educational need to external market forces requires a set of circumstances defined by the major features of education systems in developed Western nations. Central among them is a high level—nearing universality—of school participation through the secondary level. Disruptive classroom behavior may best be understood as a disruption of a bureaucratic organization that is charged with preparing for the transition of a substantial student population from secondary schooling to postsecondary education and a variety of labor market contexts. Within these constraints, the perception and diagnosis of disruptive behavior as *impairment* is defined often by transgressions against the "physical school," the complex of behaviors defined by space, time, movement, and sound/voice (see Mehan et al. 1984: 85; Armstrong 1999: 81, 2003: 162; Imrie 2000). As the education system matures organizationally and encompasses ever more and diverse students for longer durations, the "physical school" becomes more prominent. Students who are *not* in the right place at the right time can be "at risk"[12] of being perceived and diagnosed as having special education needs.

For the Western system of special education, in sum, dilemmas, conflicts, and politics are endemic and predetermined. They may best be seen as expressions of the ceremonial and ritualistic activities that are "logical" responses to institutionalized myths. As an example of such a myth, inclusive education is often more celebrated than calibrated, despite genuine attempts to do the latter (Booth and Ainscow 2002). Yet all the while, the system reproduces outcomes in a remarkably consistent and predetermined manner. It has become a common observation that inclusive education is often diverted from its initial ideal. As Roger Slee and Julie Allan (2001: 174) put it: "We maintain that the subversion of inclusion from an emancipative to a conservative project is ineluctable given the application of traditional epistemologies of special education to new times." This is certainly true. Yet, as suggested here, inclusion can be subverted less by adherence to traditional epistemologies than from adherence to contemporary ones, that is, from the deliberate pursuit of inclusion as an institutionalized myth. Inclusion is subverted by the decoupling of policies designed to facilitate it from processes that compose the formal structure of schools. Some of these processes will likely retain practices that produce, in the aggregate, segregative results (see also Carrington 1999: 260; Graham and Slee 2008: 279). Like Zeno's paradox, the more schools seek inclusion, the further away it can appear, for it is never quite fulfilled. Roger Slee captures this succinctly: "Inclusive education is an ambitious project given that we seem to be commencing with an oxymoron as our organizing concept. Schools were never really meant for everyone. The more they have been called upon to include the masses, the more they have

developed the technologies of exclusion and containment" (2001: 172). However, this judgment refers primarily to the Western model. Whether the non-
Western model suffers similar endemic paradoxes is an open question, to
which we now turn.

### The Non-Western Model: Neo-Patrimonialism

From his comparison of the West with the East, principally China and India,
Max Weber constructed an alternative ideal type that would capture the dis-
tinctiveness of the East. The critical element retained in the East but eroded
in the West was patrimonialism, the fusing of patterns of rule with the
household of the king or emperor. Under patrimonialism, the mode of domination was traditionalism, in which rule making was an expression and extension of the emperor's household as the political center. Territorial and
popular domination was anchored to sacred texts, where interpretation did
not follow from rational principles that could be accessed through sufficient
"education," but from sacred teachings accessible to only a privileged few
who were steeped in the classic texts.

Many of the features of the patrimonialism that Weber described at the
close of the nineteenth century have persisted in shaping developing societies
in the majority of the world today. The developing nations and the new states
that emerged from colonial rule continue to diverge sharply from the developed Western nations on economic and political dimensions. The burden of
economic underdevelopment is aggravated by political systems that are often
dominated by single rulers and their appointees. Political contests are frequently permeated with corruption and are resistant to democratic challenges.
Yet economic and political barriers are often rooted in deeper divisions. In
Western nations, civil society and the public sphere developed as concepts
and places separate from private and sectarian influences. Both are fragile at
best in many other societies. The elements of civility and social trust seem, as
a result, to be the sole property of Western institutions, and the coupling of
democracy and bureaucracy, to be unattainable.

Many African nations exemplify this neo-patrimonialism, noted for their
"two publics": a "civic public" that has a nominal similarity to the Western
civil society and a "primordial public" that comprises kinship and tribal relations. The divide between the two is their asymmetry, for "their relationship to

the primordial public is moral, while that to the civic public is amoral" (Ekeh 1975: 108). This is in contrast to the direction of sentiments and obligations in Western nations. As a consequence, the public or civil society is not protected from political influences, nor does it enjoy autonomy from private interests.

The weakness of developing and postcolonial nations is most evident in the state. Lacking the institutional infrastructure for empirical statehood, they are quasi-states in which corruption pervades both politics and bureaucratic organization. These nations have emphatically asserted their sovereignty within the international system and have received protections and assistance (Clapham 1999: 524). Yet their sovereignty is mainly "negative," defined as a freedom *from* constraints, rather than as a positive sovereignty that reflects a capability to control their own resources and destiny (Jackson 1987: 527; Jackson 1990: 22).

*The Logics of Neo-Patrimonialism.* In contrast to the elements of civility, civil society, and social trust that mark the Western model, many non-Western nations retain historical influences that mirror patrimonial rule. In neo-patrimonial societies, the feature that can structure politics and determine participation in public institutions is the persistence of *clientelism.* This is a mode of structuring social interactions that is, at least in practice, antithetical to the principles of democracy and the neutrality of bureaucratic organization. Clientelism has a distinct logic of its own, centering on social exchange. Although it can take variable forms, clientelism shares a "set of core analytical characteristics" that are constructed around "asymmetric but mutually beneficial and open-ended transactions and predicated on the differential control of social actors over the access and flow of resources in stratified societies" (Roniger 1994: 3). The control over access is in the hands of family and friendship relations, connections of social exchange that become ones of patron and client. Control over the flow of resources is based on extra-legal grounds, those of personal loyalty, family honor, and reputation. The asymmetrical structure can extend both outwardly, linking local communities to broader public matters, and upwardly, linking local communities to state powers. From its strength as an arrangement of interpersonal solidarity, it is portable as a system of interdependencies. As such, it embodies a contradiction between social solidarity founded on vertical inequalities and the potential for coercive measures taken to ensure voluntary compliance with social exchanges.

Like the principles of democracy, clientelism promotes access to valued resources. Shmuel Eisenstadt and Luis Roniger denote the key linkages: the relations that link local communities to the "centers of society . . . the bases of production . . . to the major institutional markets . . . the setting up of most public goods . . . and to the public distribution of private goods" (1980: 59). Yet more than democratic and bureaucratic principles, the very asymmetric structure of clientelism restricts access to resources, largely through the "broker" that mediates the relations between patrons and clients. Brokers constitute a third party that is crucial in facilitating the indirect relations of patrons and clients as they bridge the distances that separate them. The broker "does not control what is transferred," but can nonetheless influence the "quality of the exchange." Brokers have resources of their own "that [they] can add to the exchange" and thus influence them through manipulation and lobbying (Kettering 1988: 425).

An irony of many non-Western nations is that clientelism coexists with an organic view of society. The elevation of the collective good above private interests inserts a tension into the rule by elites. Yet an organic conception links state power to the social welfare of society. Within this tradition, a central linkage in the non-Western model is the relation between parental authority and the state. Centralized states in Africa, Latin America, and Asia promote education as a means to affect the collective solidarity of the nation, but for many, this is done by affirming the natural primacy of the family and its obligation to care for and educate children. For many Latin American nations, where family particularism has been long entrenched, education law details a partnership between the natural obligations of the family and the political obligations of the state. The mutual responsibilities of families and the state constitute a social contract that is projected as a critical foundation to national solidarity, health, and advancement (see Figure 4.2).

In contrast to the Western model of democracy-bureaucracy, historical sequences that are at odds with or the reverse of T. H. Marshall's outline of citizenship—combined with comparatively recent enactment of compulsory education and the expansion of secondary schooling—define the special education systems of many non-Western nations as more open than closed.

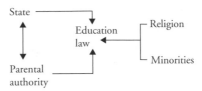

FIGURE 4.2. The non-Western model: Neo-patrimonialism

Lacking the relative autonomy achieved by (special) education in Western nations, (special) education in developing nations is more deeply embedded in the social hierarchies of local communities. The decision points that identify, assess, and place children with disabilities are more sporadic and discontinuous in non-Western nations. Yet these are not, to use Weber's term, rationalized, for they are not highly bureaucratic decisions. The decisions that regulate entry into special schools or classes or even less formal arrangements are made by families and communities, who are guided by traditional obligations; therefore, in many non-Western nations, long-standing cultural beliefs and customary practices determine entry into special education. In effect, the process structure does not change. With reform efforts that seek to extend education provisions to local communities and insulated groups, the pace of parental / kinship decisions can change abruptly. Hence, the parameter structure changes. As a result, in developing countries, the aggregate patterns of special needs education, their output structures, change. The systems of special education in these countries show similarities to demographic transitions wherein the processes that generate the outcome undergo little or no change, but changes in the pace (parameter) of such processes result, over time, in a very different system.

For the open systems of non-Western societies, the institutionalized myth of inclusion is an exogenous pressure that has an added effect because compliance can signal positive sovereignty. Yet from daily routines the decoupling of formal structures that typifies the special education systems of Western nations cannot easily occur, largely because formal structures—and the resources necessary to maintain such organizational features—are few and feeble, but also because aggregate patterns of special education are not, as a result, so easily determined.

### Special Education as Social Exchange

In the previous discussions of the Western model, the elements of civility and social trust are seen as endemic properties of the logics that underlie the coupling of democracy and bureaucracy. Civility, in particular, is a behavioral rule that is rooted in this coupling. The rule diffuses vertically and horizontally, emanating from culturally understood principles that reach across social divisions of class and ethnicity, but penetrate within strata as well. In patrimonial societies, clientelism is the counterpart to civility in democratic-bureaucratic societies. It also diffuses vertically and horizontally, emanating from historically established practices that reach across divisions of caste, clan, or tribe. Of particular interest is how such rules permeate education, from organizational levels to student conduct within classrooms. Both civility and clientelism can be conceptually refined as manifestations of different systems of social exchange. More concretely, special education may be conceptually refined by considering different systems as different modes of social exchange. From the behavioral indicators that trigger evaluation and assessment to the diagnostic conclusions that result in classification and placement, the sequential steps into special education are elements of a broader structuring, as *modes* of social exchange.

Modes of social exchange may be conceptualized as the intervening mechanisms that relate Weber's societal domains, that is, *how* family relations interact with economic transactions or political behavior. The contrasts between the norms of democracy and bureaucracy and the norms of patrimonialism mirror the differences in the two major systems of social exchange: between specific and general, or in more contemporary terms, between *negotiated* and *reciprocal* exchange. The former entails relations that have specific utilitarian, economic returns. Negotiated exchange denotes impersonal transactions conducted "at arm's length" and in which the actors "jointly negotiate the terms of contractual agreements (as in market exchanges)" (Molm, Schaefer, and Collett 2009: 2). Negotiated exchange relations are bounded by utilitarian interests and contractual stipulations, primarily because they are direct interactions between parties that know what is to be received in exchange for what is given. Generalized, or reciprocal, exchange denotes more personal interactions wherein individuals give and reciprocate not presumably with utilitarian intentions or specified contractual outcomes in mind. In contrast to negotiated exchange, the more general range of outcomes of reciprocal exchange relies more on trust that extends beyond the particular interests of the parties, lay and professional, that are engaged in exchanges. Both forms of exchange are evident across a range of social contexts, from families and households, to work places, to political participation. A particularly important outcome beyond the specific returns to an exchange is how negotiated or reciprocal exchange systems contribute to individual affect and, by extension, to collective solidarity. Thus, the broader cultural environment defines the form of exchange and the form of exchange in turn defines the cultural environment.

To the extent that education systems reflect political, social, and economic structures, it is instructive to explore how education systems replicate modes of social exchange. The relations between the Western model coupling democracy and bureaucracy and the non-Western model of neo-patrimonialism exemplify different forms of exchange (see Figure 4.3). A key intervening property of both is the dimension of centralization / decentralization found in structures of education governance that identifies the level at which broad decisionmaking occurs. This division runs across both models, but has quite different meanings within the institutional context of each.

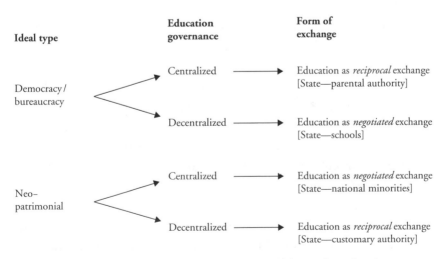

FIGURE 4.3. Ideal types, educational governance, and forms of social exchange

For centralized state and educational structures within the ideal type of democracy-bureaucracy, education is conceived as a reciprocal exchange, in which the critical relation is between the state and parental authority. In the French law on special education of 1975 (loi no. 75-534), for example, the centralized state contributed to parental authority by way of the "special education allowance" that symbolized the moral obligation of the state in concert with parental authority. As a generalized, reciprocal exchange, special education "structures the flow of social trust." In contrast, for decentralized state and educational structures within democracy-bureaucracy, education is conceived as a negotiated exchange, in which the locus is the relation between the state and local schools. As exemplified by the Warnock Report in England (1976) and the Education for All Handicapped Children Act (Public Law 94-142) in the United States (1975), the central theme is individual rights, and the procedural safeguards are designed to implement special education and facilitate integration at the school level. From the discourse of rights at the national level, the implementation of education narrows to the specific contributions of the state and local schools that more or less assist parents in attaining the education or training that they desire and is appropriate for their children.

For decentralized systems within the democracy-bureaucracy model, a paradox emerges from the negotiated exchanges that structure special education. The exchanges that structure the sequence from referral to assessment to placement heighten the difference and conflict between the parent / child and professional agents. Precisely because investments and returns are more apparent, as they are specified in contractual terms, "the relative salience of the competitive, conflictual aspects of exchange [become] more pronounced for actors in negotiated than in reciprocal exchange" (Molm 2003: 13). The "at arm's length" structure of negotiated exchange expands the network of "weak ties" (Granovetter 1973) that link parental and school authority. As a result, from referral to placement, the system of special education is less burdened by the obligations that accumulate from more personal and emotional interactions. Such objectivity at the very moments, such as school-leaving and transition planning, when individual capabilities and aspirations require honest, pragmatic attention, may be helpful, but direct knowledge and understanding of an individual personality is also crucial for successful planning, beyond mere compliance, to ensure accommodation and adaptation.

The contrasts between the two forms of exchange extend to the locus of authority over diagnosis and placement. In centralized France in 1975, a hierarchy of committees, with parental representation equal to political appointees, monitored assessment and placement. The majority of children with disabilities (56.2 percent) attended organizations in the "health" sector, funded by the Ministry for Social Affairs. These associations "are bodies with their own statutes and management structures, which in the case of the major national associations, resemble large benevolent companies" (Armstrong 2003: 148). In Germany's *Länder*, most schools are not fully accessible and if educational organizations do provide health-related services or therapy, they are most likely to be special schools; considered by many to be part of the health care sector (see Pfahl in press). In decentralized England and the United States, there is no clear dividing line between the societal domains of education and health, especially in schools that offer a range of health-related services. Assessment and placements are extensions of legislative mandates and court decisions and are implemented by professionals (McLaughlin and Rouse 2002).[13] (Figure 4.3 displays the configurations discussed.) The meaning of a "right" to education—and the supports and services required to realize that right—is significantly influenced by the degree of centralization / decentralization of the educational structure.

The conception of comparative differences as alternative paths or trajectories emphasizes the contingent nature of institutional change. Yet change is not contingent on single measures of development, but on the logics of the preexisting institutional arrangements that constrain action toward some paths and away from others (see Chapter 5). Institutional logics are "sense-making constructs"; they are the "product of historical development, are deeply rooted in collective understandings and cultural practices, and are resilient in the face of changing circumstances" (Biggart and Guillén 1999: 725; see also Friedland and Alford 1991).

The logics of Western nations, centered on the coupling of democracy and bureaucracy, have dominated the discourse about modernity and thus about notions of a civil society and its public sphere. A central theme of these logics is one of participation. Yet, paradoxically, the path between education and modernity is mediated by "gross, classificatory categories" of (in)competence that "have been developed as part and parcel of the institutional practices of categorization that are bound up in bureaucratic government, and have consequences in the lives of people with respect to the allocation of resources and penalties" (Jenkins 1998: 224). This approaches contradiction: although the development of categories in official classifications derives from the norms of democracy, such as providing additional resources to support the goal of equality, their institutional implementation relies on bureaucratic practice that reifies difference. Policies and the resulting bureaucratic practices can divorce categories from local knowledge and experience, insulating them further by anchoring them in public institutions.[14] Yet the resource-labeling dilemma ensures that these categories will reflect local ascriptions of meaning and conflicts between those who label and those who are labeled. Regardless of often-negative consequences of classification, special education resources are mostly bureaucratically allocated due to funding models that require categories to be filled instead of decided locally on an ad hoc basis.

Such dilemmas reflect Polanyi's double movement. The Western systems oscillate between decentralization and centralization. Movement from one toward the other is "activated" by the change in the market system, that is, when the economy no longer "runs in its ruts." Whether the change is toward economic liberalization or social protectionism, movement is activated. Yet the character of education policy as social exchange depends on which pole is the target. If change is away from decentralization, resulting centralization will subordinate local differences and autonomy. The upward ascension of decisions would be less reliant on specific diagnoses of individuals' learning needs. As a consequence, classification can become more continuous and flexible. For example, in England, an umbrella term of "special educational needs" is used instead of the fifteen categories of impairments or disabilities used in the United States and the nine categories of educational support used in Germany. As education policy becomes more general and potentially serves more people, the "classification threshold" (Powell 2003b, 2010) should decline, increasing participation rates in special education.

If the change is away from centralization, as exemplified by France, local differences would gain more authority and autonomy. Education policy would reflect more intentions of negotiated exchange because educational outcomes would become more tightly coupled to market outcomes. Classification would be more categorical and delimited by more quantitative criteria. On the other hand, as noted above, the greater role for professional agents from referral to the construction of individual educational programs that minimizes the intrusion of personal and emotional elements, by identifying specific services and transition planning, can enlarge the range of vocational options. The greater density of weak ties in decentralized systems generates an output structure that includes a higher range of options, regardless of category.[15]

For neo-patrimonial regimes, the combination of a centralized state and educational structure contributes to a view of special education as a negotiated exchange, yet for different reasons and with different meaning compared with Western examples. The articulation of educational principles that promote collectivist values underlies this political vision of education. The key actors behind a centralization of state authority are national minorities, ethnic and indigenous, that retain their local identities and resist participation in the civil society of the nation. African, Latin American and Asian nations, such as Kenya, Tanzania, Bolivia, Colombia, and Uruguay as well as Indonesia, Malaysia, and the Philippines, exemplify this pattern best. Common to these countries is a *historical tension*: indigenous minorities long antedate a national identity and modernization reforms. As a result, the ideal of the nation is reified above internal differences and divisions. For example, the Indonesian Education for All Act (2002) affirms that "basic education is made available to . . . socially marginalized groups, and those living in remote areas." For Mexico, where indigenous minorities impede national integration, the public sphere is highly segmented—controlled, to use Claudio Lomnitz's apt phrase, "through a geography of mediations" (Lomnitz 2000: 240). Such cultural fragmentation leads to an exaggerated celebration of the nation focused on the persona of the president. As an "elusive ideal," the self-celebration of the nation accentuates the centralization of state power. Yet as Karen Barkey has shown, for the "Ottoman route to state centralization" (1994: 191, 230) the patrimonial regime secured political stability through brokerage with minorities, not through repressive techniques or acquiescence. As with the state-bandit relation in the Ottoman Empire, the state-national minority relation in neo-patrimonial regimes is a central axis. This axis defines very different meanings than Western notions of civil society and public sphere and uses different terms for inclusion in them. Inclusion is not predicated on the Western universal theory of participation, but rather, as

Stephen Cornell (1988) argues, on the political terms that define the logics of *incorporation*. It is worth noting his point in full:

In the conventional academic view of political development, groups are incorporated politically into a society insofar as they participate in the institutionalized political arrangements by which the society is governed. . . . Political incorporation can be measured 'by the degree of responsiveness of the political system to the grievance of the group . . . The emphasis here is different. Political incorporation refers not to the degree of group participation in larger political structures or the responsiveness of those structures to group concerns, but more generally to the political relationships that link the group to the larger system, whether those relationships are responsive to group concerns or not. *There are not so much degrees of political incorporation as types*; groups are not more or less incorporated, but are differentially incorporated on terms that provide different degrees of political opportunity and thereby facilitate or inhibit collective political action of various kinds (Cornell 1988: 88, emphasis added).

For cases that combine neo-patrimonialism with decentralized state and educational structures, the form of exchange is reciprocal—again, the opposite of Western decentralized examples. Yet this pattern has particular affinities with the combination of democracy and centralized structures. The strongest affinity is a common structural tension: the norms of democracy constrain centralized structures, and decentralized structures constrain patrimonial rule. In contrast to the need to broker the relation between state and indigenous minorities, the pattern of neo-patrimonialism and decentralized structures amplifies a conception of education as a specific exchange centered on the link between state and parental authority. As affirmed in the national education law for Argentina, education action is the responsibility of the family as a natural agent and primary provider of education (Law 24,195.29/4/93: Federal Law of Education, Article 4). Countries that are otherwise different in economic development share this pattern, such as Argentina, Brazil, Chile, Barbados, India, Japan, and Togo.

### Contemporary Change and Compound Types: Market Economies vs. Economies of Affection

Intended to distinguish the West and the East, Weber's ideal types highlighted the importance of central features present in one but absent in the other. As noted earlier, Weber was keenly aware of the overlap of ideal types, of "mixed" or "compound" types. The strategy of interpreting comparative differences by means of typological groupings does not end with the sorting or classifying of cases as members of a particular ideal type. The objective of such a strategy is twofold: to first use the ideal type as a guide to distinguish major traits and thus to denote membership, and to then develop "secular theories" around the combination of traits (Roth 1971: 119).

Democracy-bureaucracy and neo-patrimonialism constitute institutional arrangements that define a nation's trajectory of development. They do so, as Guillén (2001) notes, by shaping the policies and actions that are more or less feasible. They are, however, not the trajectory itself. The course of development, or institutional change, is subject to both internal and external pressures that combine with existing institutional structures in particular ways. Far from subordinating or delegitimizing intermediate groups, the combination of economic development and political independence strengthened such groups. Patrimonialism did not erode; rather, it remained and gained new forms and was accordingly renamed "neo-patrimonialism." Most instructive, however, is the contrast to Western experiences. Different to the consociational sequence of Western states, social, cultural, linguistic, and geographic divisions "were not especially oriented towards the access to universalistic frameworks, but rather to the establishment of closed segregated particularistic units or sectors" (Eisenstadt 1973: 23). The mixture of traditional patrimonialism with accelerated economic growth brought with it an accelerated social mobilization as a variety of groups sought access to the political center. The reconfigured patrimonialism was a model of political and organizational structures that developed with some reference to the West, yet more importantly with reference to structures and patterns in existence long before Western or international influences.

In transitions from patrimonialism to democracy-bureaucracy, the course of institutional change is shaped by the *logics* of the preexisting institutional structures. Thus, democratic and bureaucratic elements that are introduced or adopted are likely to be configured to accommodate the antecedent condition of entrenched patrimonial routines, and the legacy of democratic-bureaucratic institutions may constrain the ascendancy of dictatorial rule and shape the decline of such rule. This accommodation may proceed in one of two directions: toward a consolidation of state power and thus the *central-ization* of institutional arrangements; or toward a distributed power and thus the *decentralization* of institutional arrangements. If inertia can be overcome, the path taken is partially determined: centralized systems may move toward decentralization; decentralized systems may move toward centralization. The intervening process is the orientation of ascriptive groups toward (a) public goods and (b) the public distribution of private goods (Eisenstadt and Roniger 1980: 53; Roniger 1989: 223).[16] Persons with disabilities will figure in this process in ways that depend to some extent on the gains (or losses) secured by the other major ascriptive categories, such as class, sex, and race (see Gordon and Rosenblum 2001). Disabled people benefited more or less from attempts to reform "backward classes" in India (Galanter 1972); or from the end of apartheid in South Africa (Sayed, Soudien and Carrim 2003).[17]

Returning to the level of interactions, the distinction between negotiated and reciprocal exchange is traceable to Claude Lévi-Strauss's work on the elementary structures of kinship (1969).[18] Much of the focus since has been largely on marital-kinship exchanges and their implications for the distribution of economic resources and collective solidarity. The addition of social solidarity as an outcome likened to an economic return broadens the comparison of exchange beyond negotiated and reciprocal systems. It introduces a third form of exchange that contains elements of both negotiation and reciprocity. Drawing principally on the classic work of Marcel Mauss (1954), the form accentuates "gift exchange" and the role of affection over instrumental, utilitarian motivations.

Whereas negotiated exchange may be closer to the market economy, the economy of affection, and thus gift exchange, has more affinities with reciprocal exchange. In contrast to contractual relations that originate from a market economy, reciprocal exchange is linked to the relations that are ostensibly non-contractual, exempt from economic accountings. Here, exchange transactions—for example, a small loan—are conducted between or regulated by extended family relations. In Goran Hyden's definition: "the economy of affection . . . denotes a network of support, communications and interaction among structurally defined groups connected by blood, kin, community or other affinities . . . it links together in a systematic fashion a variety of discrete economic and social units which in other regards may be autonomous" (Hyden 1983:

8).[19] The economy of affection presents a marked contrast to the market economies of Western nations. As Hyden notes, such networks of blood, kin, community, and other affinities turn the conception of market systems on their heads: "the economy of affection argument implies that economic decisions are embedded in social and other non-economic conditions, *along the lines originally suggested by Polanyi*" (Hyden 1983: 9, emphasis added). In the economy of affection, transactions function much like gifts, for the gain is not an accumulated monetary return, but the reinforcement of the collectively held principles that sustain trust and mutual solidarity. Negotiated and reciprocal exchange may be said to reflect Polanyi's *double movement*—between the principle of a self-regulating market and the principle of social protection. Early forms of charity, as extensions of church doctrine and of local parishes, may be thought of as forms of an economy of affection. The recurring *origins* of special education, as discussed in Chapter 2, are then a part of a long historical evolution of economies of affection. Such economies, paralleling market systems, have their own genealogies.

Economies of affection, wherein gift exchanges are crucial to the very initiation of social and economic interactions, are especially pronounced in non-Western societies where patrimonialism is the antecedent condition and clientelism is its legacy. Such a gift economy reflects the persistence of patrimonial structures and can function as an instrument that mediates the combination of patrimonial antecedents with contemporary economic or political institutions. China illustrates Weber's compound types—new pressures from the economic domain impinge not only on the political domain, but also on the domain-specific arena of family and household. The exchange system of *guanxi* translates as a relationship that involves "the cultivation of personal relationships and networks of mutual dependence; and the manufacturing of obligation and indebtedness" (Yang 1994: 6). The role of guanxi is highlighted in the context of a centralized state distributive economy that purports to maximize the allocation of material resources on the basis of need. The practice (or "art") of guanxi flourishes in the interstices between political ideals and economic realities, challenging both official power and the more modern conception of a market economy (Yang 1994: 189). The source of this challenge is its antagonism to the very notion of social categories. As Yang notes:

Rather than creating discrete and unified ontological categories of persons, each having the same equality of rights, the Chinese subscribe to a relational construction of persons. That is to say, the autonomy and rights of persons and the sense of personal identity are based on differences in moral and social status and on the moral claims and judgments of others. Chinese personhood and personal identity are not given in the abstract as something intrinsic to and fixed in human nature, but are constantly being created, altered, and dismantled in particular social relationships. (Yang 1994: 192).

The relational construction of persons enforces boundaries that distinguish those who are "inside" from those who are "outside"—from kinship groups to places of residence. As a consequence, the sphere of obligation is circumscribed by an ever moving dynamic, expanding and contracting who is inside or outside. As Yang summarizes: "Therefore, in the art of guanxi the pull of obligation must be introduced or strengthened by encompassing the outside within an expanding sphere of the inside" (193). Although the line between guanxi and official (bureaucratic) corruption is often thin (Yang 1994: 108), its popular definition is positive and, of course, widely and routinely practiced. For China, the interaction between guanxi and the societal domains of the economy and government is more conducive than antagonistic.

In contrast to China, many countries of eastern Europe, Latin America and Africa exemplify the extension of negative features of clientelism, from the endemic corruption in some African and Latin American states to the "second economies" of eastern European states. One common pattern is the resurgence of the patron-client relation as the core unit of economic, political, and social exchange —with the rise of dictatorial regimes that have a legacy of democracy and bureaucracy, the collapse of democratic institutions under the weight of protracted civil violence, both official and indigenous, or the destructive imposition of European models through colonial oppression in Africa. For Africa and Latin America, a perverse effect is the strengthening of corruption[20] and clientelism as principles of democracy and bureaucratic rule are extended. Because both corruption and clientelism are grounded in kinship lines, they promote hierarchical structures that are only partially attributable to elites. The belief and participation in either practice is diffuse, for they are "driven by vertical ties of patronage in which power is maintained by redistributing resources accumulated through 'corruption' to clientelistic networks according to rules of reciprocity that have their origin in a kinship-based social organization and morality" (Smith 2001: 347).

The affinities between Chinese guanxi, African corruption, Latin American clientelism, and eastern European second economies are considerable. What distinguishes one as protagonistic from others that are antagonistic are the specific interactions between societal domains and domain-specific ideal types of conduct. The interactions between the antecedent condition, political change, economic form, and hypothesized system of educational exchange can be traced (see Table 4.2). There seems to be an implicit association between these combinations and the dimension of (de)centralization. For cases in Eastern Europe, with a legacy of democracy-bureaucracy, the return of democratic structures after postwar authoritarian regimes is constrained by second economies. These shadow economies see production and trade as being for private gain, whether legal or illegal (Wellisz and Findlay 1986). As a form of corruption, second economies coexist in an interdependent manner with official, or primary, economies. Such a deep division in a central domain permeates other domains, evident in expressions of student misconduct in schools. As Leino and Lahelma (2002: 82) note for Estonia: "To perform as an individual has become almost a new norm after the socialist norms disintegrated. This change has its impact on students' conduct. While major behavioural problems did not exist in schools before the 1990s, teachers today are under increasing pressure in situations where more and more young people behave in new ways, lack motivation and express difficulties in learning." A

TABLE 4.2. Compound types and modes of educational exchange

| Antecedent type | Political change | Economic form | Mode of educational exchange/benevolence |
|---|---|---|---|
| Democracy-bureaucracy | Authoritarian regime [Eastern Europe] | Redistributive (second economy) ⟶ | Reciprocal |
| | Indigenous resistance [Latin America] | Reciprocal (clientelism) ⟶ | Negotiated |
| Patrimonial | Democratization [Africa] | Reciprocal (corruption) ⟶ | Negotiated |
| | Capitalist expansion [Asia] | Market/redistributive (gift economy) ⟶ | Reciprocal |

central task of education, in this new context, is to forge a new vision of national civility, a task that favors a centralization of educational goals.

In Latin American cases, the decentralization of power as a result of protracted civil conflicts reinforces clientelism and, in turn, a negotiated system of exchange. Where patrimonialism is the antecedent condition, the dimension of (de)centralization is highly contingent on the specific form of political change. In African cases, the introduction of democratization, as in the fall of apartheid in South Africa (Muller 1998), can strengthen initiatives that are formulated at a centralized level and implemented downward; yet this is impeded by a strengthening of corruption embedded in kinship and tribal structures. In the case of China—a prime example of an explosive market economy derived from its ties to global capital and international demand for its unparalleled labor force—political centralization is strengthened as well, but is challenged by the gift economy of guanxi. The resulting mode of educational exchange is reciprocal, exhibiting affinities to Western centralized states founded on democracy and bureaucracy.

## DISCUSSION AND CONCLUSIONS

The merit of conceptualizing national differences in special education as Weberian ideal types lies in how it forces attention to historical details. It allows for countries that are different by a single measure of relative development, but are similar by more deeply structured dimensions. The strategy of sorting national differences as ideal types takes seriously the conception that there are different paths to similar outcomes and there are similar paths to different outcomes.

When the logics of non-Western nations are addressed as equally feasible, as deeply rooted in collective understandings and cultural practices, the tables are turned on the Western model. Not only are conceptions of dis/ability different, but also the visions and practices of education vary. There are now several public spheres and a multiple images of appropriate behavior. This variation arises from the margins, from orientations strategically adopted by indigenous, ethnic, local groups toward the dominant public sphere. The patrimonialism of many non-Western societies, combining an economy of affection with the instrumental role of clientelism, presents a distinctly different logic of providing education for children and youth with disabilities.

The logics of the Western model, with its democratic, bureaucratic, and individualistic principles and its recent focus on education for all and inclusive education, contrast with the logics of the non-Western model, with its patrimonialism and clientelism. Although countries may seem to be converging at the global level of discourse, the two models are followed at the national level, maintaining divergent paths of institutionalization. The distance between the two reflects the most pressing and fundamental tensions: between state authority and individual autonomy, between public participation and the survival of corporate entities.

For non-Western societies, multiple identities coexist alongside multiple publics (Herzog and Roniger 2000: 301; Roniger and Waisman 2002). As a consequence, multiple special education systems coexist alongside these identities and publics. Schools as separate places into which children with disabilities are to be integrated can be viewed as distant and threatening to the natural authority of parents and tribe. So it is for many Latin American societies, where the family is the natural agent, not the school. The link between state and parental authority is a central axis in many non-Western nations, as it is in many Western nations. The meaning of this link, however, varies in consequential ways. For Western nations, the relation is forged through a discourse of educational rights that is only viable given the preexisting institutions of democracy and bureaucracy that define and adjudicate *individual* rights and responsibilities; for non-Western nations, the relation is forged through a discourse of societal welfare and familial responsibility. In the former context, special education shares the fate of highly developed and differentiated general education. Inclusion into general education is a gift of hospitality, yet the price is high, for both general and special education are vulnerable to the fluctuations of labor markets. In the latter context, special education must grow without a developed general education system as role model and without a steady source of students who can be classified in the currently relevant special educational needs categories. Although certainly subject to economic fluctuations, the path of special education in this context extends from a primary, moral obligation. It is vulnerable to state power, to which it is inextricably joined. Both Western and non-Western systems of special education are, in Serres's term, variant forms of the parasite, remaining subject to larger systems of domination.

# THE INSTITUTIONALIZATION OF SPECIAL EDUCATION SYSTEMS AND THEIR DIVERGENCE OVER THE TWENTIETH CENTURY

SPECIAL EDUCATION SYSTEMS HAVE BEEN institutionalized worldwide to facilitate access to learning opportunities for children with disabilities, difficulties, and disadvantages. Originally heralded as innovative, the positive views of these mainly separate organizations have been increasingly challenged. Owing to frequent stigmatization of participants and the negative effects of segregation, such as social marginalization, calls for special education expansion and reform have been joined by international charters that instead make the case for individualized learning supports provided in general schools and classrooms. These state that schoolchildren should not be forced to adapt to educational structures; rather, school organizations should be reformed to accept and acknowledge the diversity of student bodies and support each individual learner. Although the rhetoric of inclusive education is increasing globally, national and local resistance to it is evident. This has led to debates and conflicts about the role of special educators, professional practices and standards, the relationship between special and general education, and the status of inclusion. The debate is likely to continue, indeed needs to continue if change is to go beyond superficial or rhetorical similarity to transform the principles of schooling.

This chapter comparatively examines the United States and Germany to show that even within the so-called Western model there are important structural and cultural differences. Both countries were at the forefront of institutionalizing special education, as they were in realizing compulsory schooling. Yet they have diverged, especially since the 1950s. The ongoing expansion of special education has not facilitated inclusive education, although participation rates in such programs are also rising (as we discuss in Chapter 6). Despite a multitude of local, national, and international reform initiatives, Germany continues to serve the vast majority of children who have special educational needs in segregated special schools, whereas in the United States nearly all children with special educational needs are integrated in general schools, though most spend part of their school day outside the general classroom. This institutional analysis compares the genesis, expansion, and persistence of special education as a multitrack separating system in the United States and as a dual-track segregating system in Germany. It is these highly institutionalized systems that pose perhaps the most significant barrier to inclusive education.

The ongoing diffusion of special education, both as a discipline and in terms of its professional practices, has increased access and available services for students. Special education's institutionalized organizational forms now range from individualized support provisions in separate classrooms to spatially segregated settings, such as residential schools, hospitals, detention centers, training schools, rehabilitation centers, and correctional facilities. Regardless of the quality of the services and support they provide, these organizations constrain the opportunities of contemporary decision makers, interest groups, and individual gatekeepers and participants to realize school integration. Even if integration and its more ambitious sibling, inclusive education, have become increasingly discussed and implemented, they are not universally accepted goals. Moreover, in countries with decentralized educational governance, dialogue and outright battles over the appropriate forms of special and inclusive education play out not only at the national level, but also in every state and local educational authority; indeed, in each community.

Both important similarities and considerable differences in the institutionalization of special education will be emphasized here. Since World War II, there has been not only an extraordinary expansion of educational systems, but also a convergence of their ideological charters worldwide (Ramirez and Boli-Bennett 1982), with compulsory schooling joined by education for all and inclusive education. Nevertheless, "cultural forces for educational convergence are working against the structural forces which condition the endurance of different systems of education" (Archer 1984: 203). In exploring the growth and persistence of special education systems in the United States and Germany, the analysis concentrates on these factors: societal values, educational ideologies, and disability paradigms; interests of professionals, parents, and advocates; federal polities and decision-making structures; individual rights and resources; and gatekeepers and authorized selection processes. The cross-national and historical comparison of these factors facilitates an understanding of institutional change and persistence as educational systems have reduced exclusion but struggle to become more inclusive.

Since the beginnings of special education, the merits of various settings in which to provide support to learners have been debated. Influencing such ongoing local and national discourses, international governmental and non-governmental organizations—such as the United Nations (Muñoz 2007), the European Union (2008), the OECD (2004, 2005), and the World Bank (2003)—emphasize education for all as a human rights issue; they accentuate the important contributions that inclusive education can make to enhance learning opportunities, produce skilled workers, and foster social inclusion. Inclusive education does not imply a continuation of mainstreaming or integration policies of prior decades. Rather, it broadens the focus of educational reform to include the restructuring of schooling in order to embrace learners across diverse categorical boundaries—disability, social class, gender, ethnicity, national origin, sexual orientation, and religion—and to celebrate that diversity (Booth and Ainscow 2002).

In international comparison, the United States and Germany have neither the most inclusive nor the most segregative education systems. Among developed democracies, the range extends from nearly all students receiving additional resources to access the curriculum in segregated settings to nearly all students being served in inclusive classrooms (OECD 2004). Although the trend toward more school integration and inclusive education is unmistakable, the developments to reach this goal remain far more gradual in Germany than in the United States. In this chapter, we aim to understand the origins and development of two national special education systems that were originally quite similar but have diverged over time in response to broad social changes transforming disability, education, and human rights.

## SPECIAL EDUCATION CLASSIFICATION RATES

In absolute numbers and in proportion, Germany and the United States witnessed dramatic growth in their special education populations as special education programs and practices diffused. Around 1900, both countries reported approximately 12,000 "abnormal" children being served with additional or specialized attention, either in special classes or in special schools. In Germany, special education growth was particularly rapid during the late 1950s and early 1960s—a period characterized by the expansion of general education—and again following reunification in 1990. The special education population has risen to around 6 percent of the student population in general schools, representing nearly half a million children and youth (KMK 2008). In the United States, growth has been continuously upward. Passage in 1975 of the Education for All Handicapped Children Act (since 1990, the Individuals with Disabilities Education Act [IDEA]), which guaranteed all children and youth with disabilities in the United States access to their local public schools as a civil right, led the population to reach 8.3 percent in 1976–77. By 2006, six million public school students received special education services under the IDEA (approximately 13 percent of all students). These figures signal the increased access to public schooling for children with special educational needs as well as elaborated classification systems that facilitate growth in the proportion of students labeled and thus receiving services.

As special education was institutionalized, its programs developed to serve a heterogeneous group, including those with physical and intellectual difficulties or disabilities as well as those with social, economic, ethnic, and linguistic disadvantages. Although special education organizations in both societies have served a population of students continuously changing in size and composition, they have disproportionately served children with lower socioeconomic status, and those belonging to ethnic, racial, migrant, and linguistic minority groups. They have also increasingly integrated children with disabilities. Responding to the challenge of increased heterogeneity, classifications and their categories were differentiated, as were school systems themselves, informed by growing disciplinary knowledge and power. Categories applied since the early 1990s underscore the considerable national differences: in the United States, categories refer to individual student disabilities, whereas in Germany, categories represent educational supports that are still mostly provided in segregated settings. Current U.S. categories of individual impairments, disabilities, or special needs are: autism; deaf-blindness; developmental delay; gifted and talented; hearing impairments; mental retardation; multiple disabilities; orthopedic and other health impairments; serious emotional disturbance; specific learning disabilities; speech or language impairments; traumatic brain injury; and visual impairments (U.S. Department of Education 2005). By contrast, in Germany there are nine "categories of educational support" (*Förderschwerpunkte*): bodily and motor development (*Körperliche und motorische Entwicklung*); illness (*Kranke*); emotional and social development (*Emotionale und soziale Entwicklung*); hearing (*Hören*); learning (*Lernen*); mental development (*Geistige Entwicklung*); multiple/unclassified (*Mehrfach/nicht klassifiziert*); seeing (*Sehen*); and speech (*Sprache*) (KMK 2008). Despite their differences in meaning, shifts in categorical boundaries over time, and the resulting associated services provided by specialized professionals, these categories are all used to group students and organize special education support. Classification as having special educational needs requires extensive mediation between its many consequences, both positive—provision of rights and additional resources—and negative— prevalent stigmatization, even institutionalized discrimination. Such consequences frequently last throughout the life course; a major reason for the ambivalence and conflict surrounding special education (see Powell 2003a, 2003b).

## SPECIAL EDUCATION LEARNING
## OPPORTUNITY STRUCTURES

Turning from classification to allocation among available learning opportunity structures, the contrast between the U.S. and German national education systems becomes even clearer. Despite a growing diversity of organizational forms in the German states (*Länder*), there is as yet no significant continuum of settings as in the United States, but rather the institutionally constituted either-or of special or general school (see Figure 5.1). In the United States in 2005, more than half of all special education students spent almost the whole school day in general classrooms (inclusion), a quarter spent a majority of the day in regular education (integration), 17 percent were schooled mainly in special classrooms (separation), and only 4 percent attended separate facilities (segregation). German schools generally do not have the more flexible and often temporary supports offered within American schools, and in Germany, almost all children diagnosed as having special educational needs attend special schools. In 2005, 83 percent of all special education students in Germany were segregated. With few categorical exceptions, such as speech, they rarely return to general education (Preuss-Lausitz 2001). However, of the special education students who attended general schools, the majority spent most, if not all, of their school day in the general classroom, since few general schools in Germany provide special education teachers and classrooms.

Four decades of integration attempts have failed to transform the rigid, segregative system of school types. The American model's comprehensive schools are outwardly democratic and egalitarian, but many continue to stratify internally via tracking, the aim of which is to produce more homogeneous classes (Lucas 1999). Nevertheless, such schools allow more flexibility in curricular planning and permeability in allocation to courses or tracks, whereas German schools do not (Hamilton and Hurrelmann 1994). Germany's primary schools are the most inclusive school type in Germany, but after children receive only four to six years of primary schooling, the stratified and selective education systems of the *Länder* differentiate students of all dis/ability categories into separate secondary and special schools, with these organizational forms differing considerably by *Land* (see Below 2002). During extended schooling, organized learning processes in schools are crucial to support learning, even as students exhibit various abilities, resources, and identities as well as particular ways of dealing with the requirements and challenges of attaining culturally valued knowledge and skills.

Looking at the consequences of these differently structured education systems for individual outcomes, four-fifths of those youth leaving Germany's

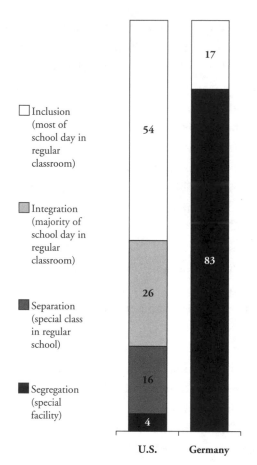

FIGURE 5.1. Distribution of students among special education organizational forms, United States and Germany, 2005
*Sources*: U.S. DOE (2007); KMK (2008); authors' calculations.

segregated special schools do not attain the lowest qualified certificate (*Hauptschulabschluss*) (KMK 2008). Without this minimal certification, vocational training opportunities and hence opportunities in the labor market are seriously limited (see Solga 2008). By contrast, nearly half of American special education students graduate from high school with a regular diploma, the credential necessary (but not sufficient) for entry to postsecondary education and most entry-level jobs. Research on school-to-work transitions, including the National Longitudinal Transition Study, shows only modest participation in job training and work-related activities by secondary students with disabilities, even though more students with disabilities go on to post-secondary education, especially community colleges, as well as vocational and technical schools, adult education, and life skill centers than ever before (Florian and Rafal 2008). The German *Hauptschulabschluss* and the American high school certificate (where offered) have especially declined in value with the expansion of education. In fact, expansion has led to the increasing exclusion of less-educated youth, whose group size has declined, from vocational training and from many occupations (Solga 2002). Despite the access to education that special education students have won, they suffer a vicious cycle of cumulative disadvantage. In the United States they represent a growing proportion of the working poor, and in Germany, a growing proportion of the long-term unemployed and receivers of social assistance (Daly 1997).

### EXPLAINING SPECIAL EDUCATION SYSTEM DIVERGENCE

Why did these originally similar systems diverge over time? Institutional theory offers a useful approach to find the answer. In modern societies, institutionalized rules act as powerful myths built into society to interpret the world. These rules influence both the original formal structure of organizations and their ability to survive and retain their legitimacy (Meyer and Rowan [1977] 1992). If institutions are social patterns that have achieved a certain state or property (Jepperson 1991), then institutionalization represents the process by which structures evolve. Further, the concept of institutional logic reaches beyond the symbolic to specific organizational structures that are politically defended and technically and materially constrained and as such are historically specific (Friedland and Alford 1991). Thus, there is not just one institution or institutionalization of special education, there are many, as the resulting nation- and region-specific continua of organizational forms and the diversity of corporate and individual actors involved attest. As David Baker and Gerald LeTendre (2005: xii) have shown, "schooling is shaped and changed by a world culture of values about education . . . producing remarkable similarities. . . . Yet there are striking differences from nation to nation, and from place to place within nations." Here, the case of special education is examined by comparing two countries with different institutional logics in schooling and different institutionalization trajectories of separating (American) and segregating (German) education systems.

We focus on three key institutionalization processes (isomorphism, expansion, and persistence) in examining how special education organizations were institutionally embedded in national education systems. We explain why the German and American special education systems have increasingly diverged—in classification rates and in organizational structures. If in these decentralized systems the regional variance reflects the origins and developmental paths of specific state / *Länder* educational systems (see Hofsäss 1993 for Germany; Richardson 1999 for the United States), here the cross-national comparison emphasizes the persistent and legitimated division of special and general education—and the challenge of inclusive education both countries struggle to implement.

*Institutional Genesis, Expansion, and Persistence:*
*Embedding Special Education Within General Education Systems*

Reflecting societal values and dis/ability paradigms, special education has imitated general education in each country. Although special education preceded compulsory schooling laws (as discussed in previous chapters), its diffusion and expansion have increased relatively recently. Nevertheless, as both systems reduced the (widespread) outright exclusion of children with disabilities, especially since the 1960s, they did so without departing from the path established on the eve of the twentieth century: the independent, segregated *Hilfsschule* in Germany and the separate class within the comprehensive school in the United States. Special education, dependent on transfers and serving those barred from or selected out of general education, assumed the institutional logic of each expanding, differentiated national education system.

Special education expansion derives from two sources, one largely exogenous, the other significantly endogenous. The first wave of growth followed universalized compulsory schooling mandated by laws in Germany and the United States that greatly increased the heterogeneity of student bodies in existing public schools. Schools and teachers responded to the challenge diverse students pose for schooling "efficiency" by establishing new organizational forms, justified by the nascent academic and professional field of special education and related fields. In particular, the category of learning disability reflects deviance from the norms defined by teachers as they taught classes that were increasingly heterogeneous in terms of such characteristics as social background, languages spoken, and migration experiences. The emerging tools of psychometrics in the United States around World War I were then used in widespread IQ testing programs within schools (see Lemann 1999). Developing class-based secondary school forms in Germany required teacher recommendations at the transition from primary schooling. Such recommendations provided a method to respond to differences and to organize and legitimate sorting practices, including referral to special education.

The expansion of education facilitated affirmation of schooling for all children as a goal, yet growing diversity led to official differentiation and standardization, attempts to resolve the tension between expanded access and organizational constraints: rules of *access* and of *passage* governed the exemption of those deemed "ineducable" or "disabled" (Richardson 1999). The second wave of expansion was self-generating and self-reinforcing—path dependent—as special educators responded to the supply of students provided by general educators by elaborating the categories to identify these students and by increasing the organizational options to provide them with opportunities to learn.

In the case of Germany, this led to more than a dozen types of special schools. In contrast, special educators in the United States defined individual "exceptionalities" (later, "disabilities" and "special educational needs"), eventually including fourteen categories of students attending special classes, from "developmentally delayed" to "gifted and talented" (discussed above). Furthermore, the contemporary developments of Germany's stable segregated special school system and the United States' ever-larger special education programs, mostly located within comprehensive schools, develop in path dependent fashion. U.S. states, much more so than Germany's *Länder*, have increased the permeability between these two branches of education (Table 5.1).

TABLE 5.1. The institutionalization process: Special education genesis

| Phase | Germany | United States |
|-------|---------|---------------|
| *Genesis, ca. 1900–1950* | Segregated special schools within an hierarchical educational system (interschool differentiation) | Separate special classes within comprehensive schools (intraschool differentiation) |

*Isomorphism in Educational Structures.*   To explain isomorphic institutional change—structures becoming more similar over time—it is useful to distinguish three types of homogenizing pressures: coercive, from political influence, policymaking, and legitimacy needs; mimetic, learning from others as a response to uncertainty; and normative, through standard-setting and professionalization (see DiMaggio and Powell 1983, 1991; Scott 2003). All three help to distinguish the complex, dynamic relationship between general and special education. As rationalized states gain dominance over (public) schooling, schools increasingly reflect rules, laws, and organizational forms legitimated and institutionalized by the state (Meyer 1992). Directly imposed or not, standardization, compatibility, and coordination demands apply pressure on organizations that are dependent on the state for resources, authority, and legitimacy. Despite such *coercive* pressure, special education professional associations successfully mediated the myriad demands of governments, schools, members, and advocates to advance the interests of the profession.

While a special class was inaugurated in Halle, Saxony, in 1859, it was Prussian civil servants who created an entire administrative division within the central state bureaucracy for "support schools" or *Hilfsschulen*, around the turn of the century. American local school boards instead set up special classes in city school districts. In selecting these organizational solutions, each country followed the institutional logic of the education system—class-based segregation in Prussia and ability-based separation in the United States (with race-based segregation in the American South). These early choices had considerable effects on the institutionalization of special education. The resulting education administrations emphasize formal, ritual compliance, of which these special schools and classrooms are testaments. Their efficacy and, even more so, their equity have been continuously questioned and debated since the very beginnings of special education. Especially since the human rights revolution after World War II, which accentuated personhood (Skrentny 2002), governments have been keen to ensure that local school systems include children with disabilities, mandating the provision of services for them.

*Mimetic* processes can be found in new special education organizations being modeled on successful ones already operating in the field. With the demystification of disability, mainly in conjunction with the clinical professions of medicine and psychology, asylums and "state institutions" as alternatives to special schools and classes have lost their legitimacy.

Their process of professionalization represents the third isomorphic pressure, *normative*. Professionals guard their occupational autonomy, attempting to control how and where they work. The establishment of specialized training programs, research to legitimate particular treatments or teaching methods, and professional associations to network the people and disseminate the results are another primary source of isomorphic change. For these reasons, the organizational forms established in special education programs—expanding beyond, but remaining dependent on general education for most of its students—were institutionally isomorphic to those of general education systems.

The "institutionalization" paths[1] of special education differ between Germany and the United States. In Germany, the segregated "support school" (*Hilfsschule*) that provided support for "abnormal," mainly poor, children served as the model for later differentiation. In the United States, these children may have remained in general schools, but in lower curricular tracks, with special education offering a further option (often in conjunction with grade retention) below the academic, general, and vocational (see Entwisle, Alexander, and Olson 1997). In both cases, special educators sought to care for and control children with disabilities, substituting for asylums, families, and general education. The German competition between school types in a hierarchical education system (interschool) contrasts with the American competition within individual comprehensive schools (intraschool) and between districts (which, owing to residential patterns, produce considerable resource inequalities). In Germany, welfare state redistribution ensures that school resources do not so much vary between schools as between school types, whereas in the United States, property taxes determine in large measure the available resources for schooling.

*Expansion of Special Education.* In both Germany and the United States, functional differentiation—responding to increasingly heterogeneous student bodies originally resulting from compulsory schooling and child labor laws—was later reinforced by changing pedagogical assumptions about individuals as learners with complex, special needs (Garnier 1980: 91). Special education's dependence on transfers from general education (representing demand) was complemented by its elaboration of classification systems (categories), lobbying activities, and offers of support (representing supply). The

TABLE 5.2. The institutionalization process: Special education expansion

| Phase | Germany | United States |
|---|---|---|
| *Expansion, 1950 to present* | First wave: Universalized special education (growing, heterogeneous student bodies) | |
| | Second wave: Organizational differentiation (10 school types) | Second wave: Individual differentiation (14 impairment categories) |
| | Relief for general educators, legitimacy for special educators | |
| | Legitimate selection into high-resource, lowest expectation/status school types | Legitimate selection into high-resource, lowest expectation/status track |

first expansion phase was driven by policymakers' decisions (such as passage of compulsory schooling laws), industrialization, demographic changes (immigration, urbanization, increased longevity), and nascent disciplines (for example, statistics, psychometrics). The second expansion phase resulted from educators strengthening their profession through specializations they elaborated. Systemic growth such as this clearly will affect the distribution of educational opportunities provided (Walters 2000: 242).

Although these developments affected population size and composition, special education expansion from the mid-1950s onward was driven by the conflation of two distinct student groups, associated with pedagogies and professional divisions: those with low-incidence or "hard" impairments or disabilities (such as blindness) and those with high-incidence or "soft" disabilities relating to learning or behavior standards (see Table 5.2). The history of special education testifies to the dramatic changes in definitions of dis/ability, intelligence, and ab/normality as classification systems were tinkered with to match the euphemisms of the day (Powell 2010). As the profession developed, a wide array of special knowledge and treatments were devised for each category. However, despite the affinity between certain types of schooling and disability category (for example, separate schools for deaf children), both across and within these countries, classification into a certain category did not and does not always lead to the same school setting or provisions.

In Germany, the number of special schools (*Sonderschulen*) peaked more than a quarter century after the Education Council (*Bildungsrat*), in 1973, declared inclusion to be preferable to segregation. Although some *Länder* have begun to consolidate or transform *Sonderschulen* into resource centers, others continue to build them anew, often touted as infrastructure investments, producing yet more supply. Effectively, education systems are stratified in five dis/ability tiers. Yet some *Länder* serve a large minority of students in inclusive education, resource centers, or with ambulatory services, demonstrating that even in Germany, special schools are not the only method to provide individualized support. Model programs, many proven effective, have encouraged some *Länder* to pass laws extending and even prioritizing inclusive education, even if adverse fiscal conditions and political priorities hinder their expansion throughout Germany (Heyl 1998).

In the United States, inclusive education is a goal to which many teachers and administrators, school systems, and educational authorities subscribe. However, innumerable court cases have been necessary since the original IDEA law was passed in 1975 to provide children with disabilities access to their local public school, which must be more accurately described as school integration. Even as half of all students in special education remain in the general classroom for most of their school day, considerable differences between states remain. Nationally, still a quarter of all special education students are separated for most of their school day or for the entire day. In some local districts in the United States, expansive definitions of special educational needs or educational risk, along with extensive "child find" activities (see Baker 2002), have led to such low classification thresholds for special education that up to a third of all students spend some portion of their school day in special education classrooms. The expansion, especially since the mid-1960s and with a recent surge since the No Child Left Behind Act of 2001, resulted in special educational services being offered within nearly every school. But districts also must maintain, or fund, a continuum of placement options, often ranging from segregated residential facilities to full-time inclusion in general classrooms, providing the least restrictive environment for particular students at a wide range of costs.

As national and state / *Länder* education systems expanded, special education experienced both exogenous and endogenous growth as it became embedded within local schools and systems. Simultaneously, the American and German education systems have witnessed struggles to reduce the outright exclusion, segregation, or separation of children and youth with disabilities.

Increasingly over the twentieth century, children considered disabled participated in public schooling, but only since the 1970s (not 1870, as some claim) has truly universalized primary and secondary schooling been achieved (see Meyer, Ramirez, and Soysal 1992). The contemporary challenge for proponents of inclusion is to restructure institutions once again to educate all children together full-time. But this goal contradicts the logic not only of Germany's vertically differentiated, segregating system, but also of the American comprehensive, separating system. Although some localities and states have realized this fundamental change, opportunities for such transformation are constrained by the legitimacy of the respective segregating and separating structures of special education, by the specialized, additional resources that special education provides, and by the authority of and vested interests in special education.

*Persistent Separation in the United States and Segregation in Germany.* School systems and individual schools are deeply embedded in the ideologies and institutional arrangements of state / *Länder* education systems. Specific historical structures in these education systems exhibit considerable institutional inertia. As an indicator of the institutional age of a state education system, the enactment dates of compulsory schooling laws, among other factors, shaped the development of special education programs (Richardson 1999). Early establishment of particular asylums and special education facilities pioneered not only disciplinary ontologies and methodologies, but also organizational strategies and structures. Owing to their legitimated selection processes and vested interests in the status quo, these persist to the present day (Table 5.3), despite strengthened initiatives in both countries since the mid-1980s toward inclusive education.

TABLE 5.3. The institutionalization process: Special education persistence

| Phase | Germany | United States |
|---|---|---|
| *Persistence, mid–1980s to present* | Special educators' professional interests (resources, authority); bureaucratization | |
| | Legitimate selection into high-resource, lowest expectation/status school types | Legitimate selection into high-resource, lowest expectation/status track |

Yet innovative programs that challenge the status quo have been continuously realized, usually with extraordinary effort. National and regional differences not only in institutional embeddedness but also in vested interests and in the extent of centralization are common cleavages found in comparing education systems (Archer 1979). The influence of these origins and historical paths on later development and persistence is heightened in the German and U.S. decentralized systems because subnational policies provide the frameworks and the conditions within which local school systems operate. Further, the loosely coupled structure of schools restricts the impact that top-down reforms have on state and local education administrations and local schools: "Decoupling enables organizations to maintain standardized, legitimating, formal structures while their activities vary in response to practical considerations" (Meyer and Rowan [1977] 1992: 57–58). In both countries, the reality in schools wholly reflects neither the law nor the restructuring that social movements and educational researchers have underscored as key to realizing inclusive education. This gap between the conditions necessary for inclusive education and the standard operating procedures has raised doubts about the feasibility of countrywide implementation of inclusive education (Kavale and Forness 2002). However, reform processes in a wide range of schools have enabled them to uncover taken-for-granted assumptions, move beyond bureaucratic compliance, and become fundamentally transformed into inclusive schools (for example, Ware 2004; Thousand and Villa 2005; Sapon-Shevin 2007). Special and inclusive education debates persist, although a settlement may be found in melding the systemic focus on necessary conditions for educational restructuring with attention to reformed local practices that serve each child's individual needs (Andrews et al. 2000).

Growth in existing organizations proceeds in education systems along paths chosen long ago and influenced by the dynamics of which student bodies attend which schools and which teachers instruct them. Specialization and accessibility costs are traditional functional arguments brought routinely to justify separate organizational structures and to counter proposals for the shift to integration and inclusive education. However, educational access, elimination of physical and communication barriers, and technological advances as well as antidiscrimination laws that emphasize individual rights reduce the legitimacy of separation and segregation. Yet, as we discussed in Part 1, these have been features of special education since the beginning.

In Germany, integration has been exceedingly difficult to achieve against the legitimated selective system and its vested interests, exemplified by the only modest success of comprehensive school reform, as such *Gesamtschulen* were an addition to, not a replacement, for the traditional "sponsored mobility system" (Leschinsky and Mayer 1999; Turner 1960). Higher-status groups hindered these reforms, primarily through the mechanism of party politics, but they also supported inclusive education program models in some *Länder*. Although this lost battle reduced the overall potential for integration, the comprehensive schools had themselves also often refrained from including students with disabilities in their integrative vision.

In the United States, internal differentiation is by track, with interests and ability paramount in the decision to take college preparatory, general, or vocational courses. Although the opponents of tracking have been vocal, it continues to occur more or less informally. But even the American comprehensive system has yet to implement fully inclusive educational programs for half of those students classified as having special educational needs. In these contrasting institutional arrangements, segregation and separation are difficult to overcome owing to institutional inertia and to each system's legitimated processes of differentiation and allocation (see Carrier 1984, 1986a for a comparison of the United States and Great Britain). Institutionalized in path dependent fashion, these contrasting special education programs within expanding national education systems reflect societal values, educational ideologies, and dis/ability paradigms.

## SOCIETAL VALUES, EDUCATIONAL IDEOLOGIES, AND DIS/ABILITY PARADIGMS

Societal values and educational ideologies as well as societal and school-specific conceptions of dis/ability frame German and U.S. general and special education systems. These values legitimate the symbolic and social boundaries drawn around categories of students that receive different opportunities and resources to access the school curriculum. At the nexus of individual dis/abilities, schooling, and social reproduction, special education remains a contentious, ambivalent institution because it simultaneously offers additional or specialized resources and (usually) confers stigma and an official status of abnormality (Powell 2003a, 2010). As nation-states, policies, and science have developed, ab/normality and dis/ability have been continuously elaborated in statistical classification systems. These systems reflect shifts in educational values, goals, and interests; they also mirror the state and society in which they guide the process of sorting students. Thus, understanding the institutionalization of special education requires attention to the ideals and values manifest in the boundaries drawn around those who have been considered "ineducable," "abnormal," "exceptional," "disabled," or "special."

Germany's conservative welfare state regime places primacy on the family, on social insurance and redistribution, and on integration through state provision. Education and social policies remain separate, even in special education, where provisions of personal assistance, therapy, and technical aids may be key to accessing curricula. Citizens are integrated into the German nation from above, as the state frames society, with rules, public laws, and administrations addressing each stage of the life course (Mayer 2005; Mayer and Muller [1986] 2009). Although both countries have highly bureaucratized and state-regulated school systems, Germany has not only provided quantitatively less schooling than the United States, but also has been more highly stratified. The learning opportunities provided in more integrated schools in the United States, traceable to what is often noted as "American exceptionalism" with regard to class formation and political processes (see Rubinson 1986), contrasts with the highly stratified, class-based education systems in Germany.

If German schooling serves to enhance individual life chances, it also maintains status differences and produces order by building homogeneous groups. School placement rests on measured past academic achievement, which determines appropriate support for each individual to develop his or her "natural aptitude" or "given talent" (*Begabung*), an ideology affecting all levels of education, including higher education, in Germany (Lenhardt 2005: 27). The corporate institutional logic of selection leads to students being sorted into groups defined by secondary school types; however, individuals with exceptional talents are not separated out to receive individualized, additional support. By contrast, in many U.S. states, special classes for "exceptional," "gifted," or "talented" children have long constituted a part of public education. In Germany, students are defined less by their unique individual personality than by the school type they attend, which is determined by grades and teacher evaluations and school recommendations. Distinctions between school types remain strict, despite increases in comprehensive-school attendance and rising stigmatization and fewer vocational training opportunities associated with attending the lower-status school types.

Whereas Germany imported a liberal democratic order after World War II that is now thoroughly supported, the individualistic and meritocratic values of the "American ethos" have resisted change over two hundred years (Fuchs 2000: 67). As a liberal-individualist state, the United States offers scarcely more than basic income programs. In the value system of competitive individualism, success or failure is attributed to individual performance. The American obsession with individual opportunities and competition, educational and otherwise, leads to one of the best-funded school systems in the world. After providing primary and secondary schooling, however, the state's duties toward citizens are circumscribed; except programs for tertiary education for members of the military and especially veterans of foreign wars (for example, the G.I. Bills). Unlike Germany, the United States invests more in education than in redistributive antipoverty or basic income schemes (Heidenheimer 1984). Free public education and, since the 1960s, the increasing number of categorical programs, such as special and compensatory education, are taken to be among the most important social provisions the federal government can mandate. Since the beginning of "common schooling" and the enactment of compulsory schooling laws between 1850 and 1920, American public schools have been among the most inclusive in the Western world, responsible for integrating children from different classes, religions, and national origins (Tyack and Cuban 1995). However, complete access to public schooling enabling full participation still is not a reality for children with special educational needs, and people with disabilities, adults and children alike, are in the throes of the "last civil rights movement" (Driedger 1989; see also Charlton 1998; Barnartt and Scotch 2001; Fleischer and Zames 2001).

Education policymakers have based their decisions on moral-religious values reflecting an integration ideology that emphasizes individual and political freedom, equal opportunity, achievement, and civic engagement through personal equality and independence, as a "good society" derives from society itself, not through state action (Bellah et al. 1985). The crucial exception was the inegalitarian system of racial segregation in the American South (see Myrdal 1944), which would lead to societal conflict, struggle, and eventually the force of the federal government to ensure school integration on the basis of race, a significant precursor for integrating students with disabilities in local public schools.

To maintain democratic values and to enhance individual life chances are the most important goals of American public schooling, affirmed in such landmark court decisions as *Brown v. Board of Education* in 1954 and, in 1972, *Pennsylvania Association for Retarded Children (PARC) v. Commonwealth of Pennsylvania* or *Mills v. Board of Education*, which stipulated "consent decrees" as constitutional support for integrated schooling (see Minow 1990). These goals are to be realized, respectively, by (1) integration through participation in comprehensive schools that reflect the pluralism of the places in which they serve as community centers and (2) individual aptitude and achievement, continuously measured by standardized tests. The tensions between these precepts continues to be at the center of education debates, as education practices often focus on either individual learning goals or meeting collective standards. Especially important in an immigrant nation, the purpose of public comprehensive schools in the United States was to create a unified society out of myriad cultural, linguistic, and religious groups (*e pluribus unum*). Even if equal opportunity in education is not always forthcoming or practiced, it is idealized. Meritocratic myths, such as "equality of educational opportunity" (see Coleman 1990 on the evolution and usage of this concept), are among the most powerful of American beliefs. Large investments in education focus to a certain extent on leveling the playing field for all individuals. This is of the utmost importance for students with special educational needs, who require support to compensate for their disadvantage. Yet unequal education outputs and outcomes are not only tolerated, but celebrated: individual students are ranked by and publicly rewarded for their outstanding academic, aesthetic, or athletic achievements. Gifted and talented programs, where they exist, indicate that school performances not only on the left tail of the bell or normal curve but also on the right tail are deserving of additional support and services. In both cases, the extent of the support depends on local resources and established practices of the schools in question.

Orientation toward the future emphasizes aptitude, effort, and, most especially, personality development. This prospective view encourages belief in each person's unique potential. Within this logic, individual exceptionalities are to be acknowledged, compensated for, or further developed to ensure the best possible performance. Tracking and other forms of grouping students often counter or even contradict this logic, which taken to its extreme might lead to all children being individually tutored. (In Finland, about a third of all students receive some form of additional support to access the curriculum and this is often provided ad hoc within each school.) The federally mandated Individualized Education Program (IEP)—under which every school must develop an IEP for each of its special education students—can be understood as a thoroughly American individualist solution that expresses this ideology in legal terms. Nevertheless, in distinct contrast to the multitude of German special schools, based on particular categories of special need, American special education classrooms are often as diverse as those found in general education.

Both societies share meritocratic values typical of Western capitalism: individual achievement and performance are most important, but social justice—providing for needs, compensating for disadvantages—is also crucial (Roller 2000). But the balance of these values is dynamic and relative, as often-conflicting historical and contemporary education ideals, such as integration and segregation, are reflected throughout these education systems. On the whole, American schooling has aimed for common schooling to provide equal educational opportunities that facilitate meritocratic competition, but with accepted wide disparities in outcomes. German schooling, an aspect of the state's benevolent paternalism, historically has aimed for appropriate status (and its maintenance), elaborate vocational training, and occupational careers: the organizational fields of higher education and vocational training are divided and impermeable, allowing little transfer between them (Powell and Solga 2010). Whereas in the United States there is a "contest mobility system" of education in which all compete throughout their school careers, Germany operates a "sponsored mobility system" in which children are sorted very early in their school careers, with those children of certain backgrounds enjoying additional support and hence better trajectories and smoother transitions later in life (Turner 1960). Moreover, this individual ranking vs. status group logic extends to each school and its students. That some students will deviate from the norm emphasizes the importance of culturally specific definitions of "special educational needs."

Although people with disabilities are frequently stigmatized in both societies, the responses of education vary considerably within the countries and over time, which suggests that additional factors are necessary to explain the divergent institutionalization of special education as well as tenacious regional variance. Major institutional differences that produce stigma include instruction in separate classrooms or in segregated schools as well as negatively valued categorical membership (for example, "mental retardation"). One of the key responses to such stigmatizing labels has been the phenomenon of changing categorical boundaries to effect a shift toward less negatively valued categories of special educational needs—in short, of the use of politically correct euphemisms (Powell 2010). The dominant German classification system over the postwar period reified disabilities in many generously staffed, but segregated special school types; the American system maintained medical-model impairment and disability categories to specify legitimate functional needs for which to compensate, even as society moved beyond the clinical deficit paradigm to include economic and more positive socio-political, minority, and human variation models of dis/ability (Schriner and Scotch 2001). Indeed, inclusive education reforms must explicitly engage broader societal attitudes toward disability, especially as they shift from a clinical model to one that understands disability as an ascriptive category similar to race, gender, and class (Ware 2004: 185; see also Gordon and Rosenblum 2001).

The direction of change these systems will take depends not only on institutionalized ideologies and values, but also on interest groups' current political influence and protest activities. Disability activists and advocates in the United States facilitated enactment and implementation of progressive policies. In Germany, the special education profession was most effective at lobbying for further differentiation and expansion of special school systems (see Pfahl in press). Whether path dependence or departure is most probable depends on the organizational structures—the interests that succeed in producing or shifting local or regional ideological consensus—that dominate the decision-making process and, ultimately, on shifting gatekeepers' range of options.

INTEREST GROUPS IN SPECIAL EDUCATION:
PROFESSIONALS, PARENTS, AND ADVOCATES

Certain groups interested in maintaining or changing special and inclusive education have been more successful in setting the political agenda and reforming special education organizations than others. The diverse beliefs and interests of advocates for students with disabilities, professionals, parents, and policymakers have often led to conflicts with clear winners and losers. In the United States, parents and other activists—often working through the courts, advocating via associations, and lobbying policymakers—have prevailed in implementing school integration (though less so inclusive education). In Germany, special school teachers were more successful in defining the goals in political decision making, and this led to a mainly segregative special education system. Parents largely conformed to the given educational structure, namely, school forms based on dis/ability groups. In each country, there now seem to be considerable majorities for maintaining the status quo, which reflects the education system as a whole.

Which groups mobilized to change schools to reduce the exclusion of children and youth with disabilities? How much did they influence policymakers in controlling the agenda and to what extent did they affect teachers and other gatekeepers working within schools? An understanding of interest groups and their victories and defeats is necessary in order to explain not only the (divergent) institutionalization of special education in these two countries, but also the considerable regional variation within each country.

Political parties have played a less significant role in disability policy than in education generally and in representing certain perspectives on fiscal priorities and on values and ideologies such as equality and social justice. More importantly, professional interests of special educators, physicians, and psychologists have influenced the expansion and persistence of special education's organizational structures. The classification systems and categories constructed and legitimated by these professional fields influence research agendas, teacher training, and, more generally, knowledge and awareness; exemplified in recently booming categories such as autism spectrum disorders or attention deficit hyperactivity disorder (ADHD). Powerful membership associations have continuously lobbied national, state, and local policymakers and the various branches of government, in some cases providing the texts used to model policy.

Although coalitions of parents and disability advocacy organizations have effectively used pressure and protest to limit the power or shift the goals of professional associations, they have done so most often according to the institutional logic of the education system, in Germany favoring segregation and in the United States favoring separation. Nevertheless, both the American disability rights movement and the German disability rights movement, which followed the U.S. model with some delay, have successfully utilized a rights-based strategy, with lobbying, protests, and court cases being crucial factors in achieving passage of educational access and antidiscrimination legislation. Whereas the U.S. judiciary has treated children with disabilities as a minority group in need of protection, in Germany, the interests of children with disabilities have consistently been weighed against those of the majority, in effect applying cost benefit analysis to the aim of school integration (Degener 2001: 45). German public opinion, dominated by large neocorporatist organizations, is far more rigid than American public opinion, in which innumerable flexible interest groups arise continuously to champion new issues and causes (Savelsberg 1994). In the arena of disability in Germany, many key players are large membership organizations founded by war veterans; until recently, advocacy groups active in promoting inclusive education have been locally based.

In Germany, the most influential group was and continues to be the special education schoolteachers and administrators, organized in a highly successful membership association. Since 1898, the *Verband deutscher Sonderpädagogik* (VDS) and its precursors have provided a strong voice and professional legitimation for the special school system. In 1954, the VDS distributed a white paper to *Länder* cultural ministers that led to profession-inspired, rather than empirically validated, differentiation of school types. Since that critical juncture, special educators have established, controlled, and defended about a dozen discrete school types based on disability categories.

By contrast, in the United States a multitude of advocacy organizations, the disability rights movement, and parent-activists gained access to schooling and ensured that special education would be offered in comprehensive schools, reducing segregation. At the national level, the Council for Exceptional

Children, founded in 1922, coordinated the lobbying effort needed for Congress to pass, in 1975, the IDEA, which guarantees all disabled children a "free, appropriate public education" in the "least restrictive environment." Special educators in a comprehensive school system did not so much argue for their own school type, although special schools existed, as for mainstreaming, which would potentially provide access to every comprehensive school in which they could serve students. Special educators recognized their interests in this new policy, and an unusual coalition of political actors created the necessary consensus to pass it (Melnick 1995). To guarantee both that this categorical program would not be abused and that public schools would no longer shirk their duty to this vulnerable class of students, an extensive, heavily bureaucratic program developed within each district, including "child find" recruitment requirements codified in law (Baker 2002).

The specific resources and rights demanded by the disability movements, parental groups, and advocacy organizations in Germany and the United States vary, as does the strength of the various groups. Professionals in the fields of special education, medicine (rehabilitation), and psychology, together with administrators at all levels, advanced their interests in both institutional expansion and continuity. Professional associations have played particularly salient lobbying roles in national and state contexts as well as local contexts. The resulting social, political, and economic conflicts between levels of government and between special and general education led to increased legal oversight and bureaucratization of public schools (Neal and Kirp 1996).

Increasingly, advocacy organizations of and for people with disabilities and the disability rights movement influence politics and reform in both countries; however, here again there are important differences that reflect particular historical experiences, legal traditions, and welfare state programs. The American disability rights movement in particular followed the civil rights movement in demanding rights, with legislation and litigation resulting from often vague policy guidelines (for example, the words *integration* and *inclusion* are nowhere to be found in special education law). The laws have required lengthy processes of judicial review and interpretation. Unified in arguing for enhanced services, parents and advocates have found no consensus as to the most appropriate educational environments. The debate about organizational placement has been a constant on both sides of the Atlantic.

## DECENTRALIZED DECISION-MAKING IN FEDERAL POLITIES

Despite both being federal democratic polities, the German and American decentralized decision-making structures determine differently the opportunities available for interest groups to affect existing policies, particularly in education (Münch 2000). Especially the degrees of centralization, relevant educational regulations, and types of federal legislative and judicial action have structured the opportunities for change. Whereas in Germany each *Land* retains control over education, in the United States the local districts and schools exercise far more autonomy vis-à-vis both the state governments and the national government. However, national decision-making bodies in both countries have had considerable impact on schooling—in different directions. German consensus building among the *Länder* hinders departure from the national path and favors incremental change. In the United States, the federal government mandated individual civil rights relating to schooling, securing such rights coercively when necessary. Distributed differently among governmental levels in each country, laws, regulations, and funding formulas produce particular incentive structures. In Germany, school laws determine placement; in the United States, laws guarantee choice.

Germany's intrastate, interlocking federalism divides powers exclusively by policy field with clear constitutional mandates. Although the federal parliament is responsible for civil rights legislation, *Länder* must codify and implement these laws. Policies have successfully reduced regional disparities through considerable redistribution. Because education belongs to a *Land*'s cultural sovereignty (*Kulturhoheit*), developments in special education are not a federal prerogative, whereas social policy programs (such as transfer payments to individuals with disabilities) are. Because of "euthanasia" and how schools were used during the National Socialist regime from 1933 to 1945 (see Burleigh 1994; Poore 2007), education has been purposefully, carefully protected against national government control.

By contrast, U.S. interstate federalism emphasizes the vertical division of power and competition between the executive, legislative, and judicial branches that provide checks and balances. The American division of competencies with clear constitutional mandates is by function (federal lawmaking, state administration), not by policy field. States delegate educational responsibility to local districts. With a desire for a strong society, not state, centralization tendencies are rejected—except to guarantee civil rights, integration, and equality of opportunity. Yet these key aspects affect general and special education and have led to increasing centralization at the levels of discourse and policymaking, although less so in the finance and control of school districts and schools. Yet ever-more ambitious and highly prescriptive special education policies passed without generating much controversy or opposition, largely due to the judicial action and the framing in terms of individual rights that united a diverse reform coalition (Melnick 1995). The federal government has achieved increased authority over special education, with greater power to support inclusive education and reduce school segregation.

Civil rights relating to public education and integration have been protected by innumerable affirmative federal court decisions, resulting in extensive judicial regulation of American education, of which special education is a paradigmatic case. With the bureaucratic mechanism of the IEP, the U.S. Congress created a right for disabled children through a special categorical program and imposed this right by court decree when lower-level bureaucrats were unwilling to provide "free, appropriate public education" of their own accord (Neal and Kirp 1996). Yet the mainstreaming law did not have only positive effects, as it institutionalized highly bureaucratic systems and categorical programs that reduced much informal, autonomously organized general-class attendance for children with special educational needs (Weatherly and Lipsky 1977). Since the mid-twentieth century, children with special educational needs have been considered a "suspect class"—a group deserving of such high protection that any discriminating state action must survive a court's strict scrutiny—and the federal and state courts have repeatedly protected this group (see Turnbull and Turnbull 2000). Thousands of court cases are testimony to the need for litigation in order to ensure not only participation in public school systems, but also school integration and inclusion in general classrooms when appropriate.

This is less so in Germany, where parents must bear the costs of litigation, first seeking decisions from administrative, and then constitutional, courts. In the few school integration cases the Federal Constitutional Court has heard, it has hesitated to force *Länder* to change their school laws to be more inclusive, arguing that although preferable and an individual right, inclusive education is contingent on *Länder* finances (Graser 2004). The Constitutional Court has taken into account the interests of the other students, fiscal concerns, and political decision-making structures (see Degener 2001; Graser 2004). Gradually, decisions carry over into federal parliament deliberations and *Land* policymaking. Notwithstanding European Union (2008) policies and international charters supporting inclusive education, Germany's Culture Ministers' Conference, which coordinates *Länder* consensus-based policymaking, offers only recommendations. The wide range of legal statements and organizational solutions throughout Germany was bolstered by the 2006 Federalism Reform, which further increased *Länder* autonomy regarding matters related to education, especially schooling.

## RESOURCES IN SPECIAL EDUCATION AND INDIVIDUAL RIGHTS

Groups that mobilized to win rights and resources were often satisfied with legislative and judicial advance without following through on state and local implementation and enforcement. American and German advocates share the necessity to ensure that the formalities of legislative policymaking, commissioned accountability reports, and legal decisions are carried out locally— and enforced. Decentralized decision-making supports the regionally specific status quo, forcing interest groups that demand equal treatment or additional resources to fight these battles at the local or state level, even if national framework legislation constrains the space in which such groups operate and advocate. Rights without resources, as admonished in the International Convention of the Rights of Disabled Persons, are insufficient (United Nations 2006).

Multiple levels of government provide fiscal support for special education, producing incentive structures that encourage teachers and other gatekeepers to classify or segregate students: funding systems may reward or discourage classification, the provision of certain services, or particular placements, or all three. The German separation of special and general school systems has a corresponding barrier in the separation of social and educational policy. The division between policy arenas hides the actual costs—especially in terms of reduced life chances and social exclusion—from policymakers'

decision-making processes. Yet vested interests and lobbies resist the calculation of segregation's actual costs: very few studies comparatively document
the costs of various educational environments, including teacher salaries, infrastructure, services, and transport (but see Preuss-Lausitz 2002; Klemm
and Preuss-Lausitz 2008). Comparing the welfare state provisions, Germany
focuses on compensatory social policy that is oriented to old age, with a ret-
rospective view, and reacts to poor labor market outcomes via monetary
transfers, whereas the United States invests in preventive educational policy
that is oriented to youth, with a prospective view, and influences future
market processes via the production of qualifications (Allmendinger and
Leibfried 2003). Such emphases disadvantage certain groups more than
others.

Resource levels, limits, and incentives are crucial contextual variables
that affect special education classification and participation rates. It is within
these institutional constraints that resources are provided in special and inclusive education classrooms and decisions are made about individual students. Whatever the supply of support and services, however, these are mainly
delivered in the contrasting institutionalized organizational forms that dominate each special education system. In Germany, the organizational provision (attending a special school) supersedes individual needs as the basis for
allocation within the system. In the United States, individual needs as codified in the individualized education plan have primacy over the setting. Indeed, in the United States, a free, appropriate education can be provided in a
tremendous range of settings, from schooling at home to the entire day spent
in an inclusive classroom to innumerable combinations of settings. The basis
for resource allocation in the United States is an individual's diagnosed need;
organizational provision follows from that. By contrast, in Germany, organizational provisions are maintained, then individuals are allocated to those
organizations according to diagnosed need.

In Germany, school integration continues to be subject to *Länder* fiscal
conditions (*Finanzierungsvorbehalte*); American schools face unfunded federal mandates, which constrain the provision of special education services and
support, even if special education programs enjoy funding priority. In the
United States, costs have not been the main consideration in judicial decision
making. Nevertheless, the continuously rising special education population

has reached fiscal limits since the 1990s, with many states responding to the fiscal drain by reforming their special education finance laws to reduce incentives to classify and separate or segregate students (Parrish 2001). Limits on the proportion of students who may receive special educational services and on how many students may participate in inclusive education programs have long led many interest groups to call for federal, state, and local policy reform. Since the No Child Left Behind Act of 2001, the debate has grown over the unfunded, yet federally mandated standards and the costs of realizing those standards.

Special education finance may inhibit integration and inclusion, especially if funds and service provision are linked with particular settings, rather than with students (Meijer, Pijl, and Hegarty 1994). German special education finance allocation rewards segregation, especially given infrastructure investments in small-scale special schools, whereas the U.S. system rewards classification. Although provision of special education services is determined largely independently from settings, mostly within the comprehensive school building, the "least restrictive environment" for an individual student may well be another (more or less costly) setting. Increasingly in the United States, rights have come before resources, with decisions on individual cases favoring students with special educational needs. Congress-commissioned education research and numerous precedent-setting cases have encouraged legislators to generalize innovations in required Congressional reauthorizations of special education policies, as American spending on general and special education is high—and rising. Meanwhile, both the United States and Germany face an increased emphasis on standards—on schools' outputs as measured by students' performance, achievement, or attainment.

## SPECIAL EDUCATION SELECTION MECHANISMS

Beyond the elimination of outright exclusion, German and American reforms to shift the allocation of students among learning opportunity structures have succeeded only partially. Whereas guarantees of state and / or local autonomy in public schooling are designed to enhance discretion and choice, institutional inertia and path dependence shape and constrain those choices and opportunities for change. Yet the values and preferences of policymakers, educators, and parents are often at odds, resulting in conflicts about future developments.

Individual educational trajectories result from school-specific opportunity structures and decision making that depend heavily on institutionalized characteristics of education systems. Especially teachers' values and beliefs, their training, their personal and practical experiences with diverse student bodies and special educational needs, and the resources and support made available to them influence whether and how they will react to students' diverse range of abilities and other characteristics. Among the tenacious barriers to inclusive education in Germany, which in 2009 ratified the International Convention on the Rights of Persons with Disabilities whose Article 24 calls for inclusive education, is the almost complete lack of teacher training relating to the needs of special education students in general education courses of study. Without changes at the stage of professional socialization, the implementation of inclusive education programs proposed or demanded by international charters will be much more difficult to achieve. The educational system's early selectivity continues to operate, and despite limited longitudinal data, regional research shows that the achievement gap between special-school students and *Hauptschule* (lower secondary school) students with similar original performance levels increases steadily over time, limiting the special-school students' probability of returning to general education (Wocken 2000). Furthermore, the limited diffusion of knowledge about beneficial pedagogical strategies in inclusive education poses a serious barrier to the provision of high-quality and equitable services. International and national databases and further longitudinal studies would be beneficial for educational practices and policies alike. For example, Germany began conducting the National Education Panel Study (NEPS) in 2009 (Leuze 2008), which will be vital to answering questions about education and employment careers, such as: How do the competencies of students with special educational needs develop in different types of schooling? Why do some students with special educational needs do better in school than others? What are the life course consequences of different types of schooling and training (such as special schools or classrooms and inclusive education)?

Even with better data, the continuing challenge will be to weigh the supposed benefits of additional resources and the supposed costs of low status, lower expectations, and stigmatization: the resource-labeling dilemma (Füssel and Kretschmann 1993). Teachers' normative expectations differ according to the category into which they sort students, who respond accordingly (Mehan, Hertwick, and Meihls 1986). This is particularly important because special education, despite its good intentions, often reduces learning opportunities instead of increasing them (Tomlinson 1982). The classification of a student as having special educational needs becomes a self-fulfilling or self-sustaining prophecy (Powell 2011: 100–102). As long as resources for special education services are bound to stigmatizing labels that provide bureaucratic accountability to justify compensatory provision, the distributive dilemma of disability—inherent in social and education policies of all kinds—will remain operative (Stone 1984).

Despite Germany's new classification system of "educational supports" (*Förderschwerpunkte*), the organizational structures have changed only marginally. The change reflects the effects of human and civil rights challenges to the legitimacy of segregation since the late 1960s and continuous pressure by the disability rights movement and parent-advocates for inclusion and equality. Yet solely primary schools have substantially reduced segregation, due in large measure to their inclusive design since the *Reichsgrundschulgesetz* (primary school law) of 1920 (see Heyer 2000). The institutionalization of a new classification system highlighted (1) intractable difficulties of defining disability and special educational needs, (2) considerable *Länder* and local variability beyond any biodemographically explainable variance, and (3) the desire of *Länder* culture ministries to appear as if they were pro-integration when few have approved broad-based integration even after successful inclusive pilot projects (Cloerkes 2003b). In a textbook case of loose coupling, school systems have met exogenous demands without transforming the main organizational forms except for a few additions to existing arrangements as well as in some *Länder*, such as Bremen, Berlin, and Saarland. Ideologies of equality and integration, extended to students with special educational needs, challenge ministry bureaucrats, individual teachers, and other school gatekeepers, yet not enough for them to abandon the ideologies of homogeneity and status-appropriate education. Despite international pressure to support integration and inclusive education, Germany's *Länder* continue to support interests of those who operate the special school system, viewed by many as the most appropriate school type for students with special educational needs. Policymakers, teachers, and other gatekeepers have changed categories and labels, which is easily done, while reacting to local or regional demands for more integration idiosyncratically.

In the United States, integration and equality as ideals facilitated the victory of the special class over the special school early in the twentieth century. Since the 1960s, despite the broad diffusion of minority or sociopolitical paradigms of disability, medical model categories in special education have been maintained, even new ones added (for example, autism, traumatic brain injury). Such new specializations and categories are professionally legitimated and are used to justify the increasing resources required for an expanding population, a self-reinforcing process. Integration is the raison d'être of American public schooling, despite the reality of residentially based socioeconomic and racial segregation. Options for support or transfer to special classes favor individualized classification, then separation along a continuum of general and special class time distributions. Importantly, group diversity is also reflected in special education programs. This American strategy of accepting heterogeneity is antithetical to Germany's process of homogenization, elaborate differentiation, and allocation to segregated school types.

More so than the U.S. education system, Germany's education system can resist change through the legitimation that results from the congruence between societal *and* educational idealization of homogeneity within status groups. Teachers well know that referral for diagnosis nearly always leads to classification. Until 1994, it implied immediate allocation to one of the low-status special school types, with a correspondingly high "classification threshold". This has led to retention as the preferred solution: options for support or transfer to special schools favor retention first, then segregation, as an option of last resort.

Whereas German schools rely on overall grades and teacher referrals, schools in the United States frequently use psychometric testing as a screening device for special education and retention while maintaining subject-based flexibility in placement. Although tests can also be used to declassify students, this is not commonplace. Nevertheless, the continuum of special education settings contributes to the permeability of tracks within comprehensive schools and a low "classification threshold." Unlimited as long as resources are available, special education is viewed by gatekeepers as a viable alternative for a large group of students having difficulties or those with challenging behaviors, and parents, rather than resisting, actually demand the additional services. In both societies, however, disadvantaged groups are overrepresented in special education (Powell 2011). General education teachers' difficulties in teaching these students lead the educators to transfer such students out of their classes using legitimated organizational responses to learning or behavioral issues—mainly, retention and special education. As in many other countries, this affects an ever-larger proportion of students.

## CONCLUSIONS

This chapter has shown that the development of special education systems reflects a complex of cultural and structural factors operating at multiple levels in federal polities. Although this cross-national comparison has identified an array of similarities and differences in American and German education systems, questions remain as to the relative importance of each factor, especially at state / *Land* and local levels, for the past and future institutionalization of special and inclusive education. Differentiated school structures, bureaucratic divisions, and professional interests resist the reform and restructuring of the existing segregating (Germany) or separating (United States) special education systems. These have borrowed from and rely on the legitimated institutional logic of each country's national education system. They reflect fundamental societal values and educational ideologies of earlier eras, in which special education was institutionalized. And they frame the interests that have successfully fought for special education's diffusion and differentiation. Over the twentieth century and into the first decade of the twenty-first century, special education expanded and was embedded within existing educational institutions, whether in class-based school systems (Germany) or tracked comprehensive schools (United States).

Although some schools, districts, and even states / *Länder* have changed special education's organizational structures considerably over the past few decades, others have been unable or unwilling to overcome the barriers delineated herein. Regional variation shows that path departure toward inclusive education is possible, albeit incrementally—measured in hundreds or thousands of students—that is, single-digit, not double-digit percentages. Changes in financing could reduce the need to classify by providing additional resources for services directly to schools for them to allocate when and where necessary. Alternative models provide ways to modify bureaucratic procedures that foster collaboration, problem-solving, and flexibility in meeting individual needs instead of focusing attention mainly on diagnosis and procedural compliance (Skrtic 1991a). Shifting professional interests from the maintenance of special schools and classrooms by modifying state/*Länder* policies that have built-in incentives to classify and separate or segregate students is a necessary, but not sufficient condition to facilitate inclusive education.

The cross-national divergence shown here in indicators like participation rates, learning opportunity structures, and educational achievements and attainments cannot be explained solely by reference to individuals' disabilities and disadvantages. Rather, we can understand this divergence by analyzing the long-term institutional developments in the educational systems that brought forth highly differentiated special education organizations to serve a plethora of interests, guided by powerful ideas about abnormality, disability, and special educational needs. Along with rising rates of inclusive schooling, special education's path-dependent, self-reinforcing expansion continues—enabled primarily by general educators' authorized continual supply of students—as many parents value the additional resources and specialized, professional services of special education more than they worry about the potential stigma of such schooling. Such cleavages emphasize that neither in the United States nor in Germany has a national consensus in public and professional discourse or in educational and social policies been achieved. Individual actors make these often-difficult choices interpreting individual needs within local contexts. In Germany and the United States, respectively, the persistence of institutionalized special education systems that segregate and separate poses a considerable challenge to the restructuring of schools to become more inclusive.

## PART THREE

# CONTEMPORARY PARADOXES

CONTEMPORARY PARADOXES EMPHASIZE the challenging position that contemporary special education faces—and has faced since the very beginning. Debates about how best to organize schooling, to deal with deviant behavior, and to address social disadvantage represent a constant from the Enlightenment to the present day. The prevalent idea that special schooling can lead to societal inclusion has been called into question. Regardless of the diversity of current special education programs, most countries are under increasing global pressure to achieve "education for all" and to help facilitate inclusive education, which is often viewed as more equitable. These worldwide calls for change occur at the same time that standards and output measures increase the pressure on general education to increase aggregate performance and question special education's long taken-for-granted effectiveness and efficiency. Consensus exists neither within nor surrounding special education as to whether its expertise is required to achieve inclusive education for all. While some argue for its necessity, others suggest that special education itself poses the greatest barrier to inclusive education.

The first of three paradoxes explored in Part 3 refers to education expansion writ large: ever-longer educational careers and the vastly larger proportion of persons attaining secondary and tertiary education have actually increased the visibility and simultaneously the marginality of those who attain less education. The second—and related—paradox refers to the simultaneous rise of special education segregation rates and inclusive education programs. These coexist, despite the ongoing delegitimation of the former as global discourse and international human rights laws favor the latter. The third paradox, found in the United States, relates to the education rights guarantees in special education compared with those in the juvenile justice system. In the former, rights restrictions have recently been placed on youth for behavior infractions, whereas in the latter, the right to education has been extended within its formerly impermeable boundaries of punitive measures. It seems that the sequences of rights developments have moved in opposite directions. All three paradoxes result from particular institutionalization processes and from the relationship of special education to such neighboring institutions as general education, vocational training and professional education, labor markets, and the juvenile justice system.

Thus, as emphasized in the preface, a central feature of special education is its *interconnectedness*. As a field, special education is situated largely, but not entirely within general education. Although, as we have shown, forms of special education predate compulsory schooling, it continues to be viewed as marginal by many, despite its considerable expansion over the postwar period. Special education's interconnectedness stretches organizationally beyond general education, as its organizational field includes health care systems, vocational training programs and transition planning, and labor markets, among others. Further, special education serves many of the most disadvantaged youth, and in so doing, it shares an organizational community with the juvenile justice system. For these reasons, special education is intricately embedded in the institutional arrangements and the social and education policies that regulate education and training as well as juvenile justice. Although special education often has been and remains confined to a subordinate and marginal

position by way of its functions and its clients, by virtue of its multitude of
ties, special education attains an institutional centrality. Here, then, is another
paradox we address in this third part of the book.

As noted earlier, it is not uncommon for practitioners and theorists to
interpret the processes and outcomes of special education as "dilemmas."
Whether they be conflicting decisions faced by practitioners or the intransi-
gence of unwanted outcomes that seem unexplainable by current theories,
such examples may better be described as paradoxes than as dilemmas. Gatekeeping decisions made by teachers, parents, nurses, counselors, and school
officials may not have the desired outcomes. Despite how small such decisions may be in scale, they nonetheless reverberate through the whole education system and can, paradoxically, result in large-scale disturbances or
alternations. At the very least, the structural interconnectedness of special
education needs to be incorporated into any interpretation, whether of decisions made or of the aggregate outcomes from those decisions. In the other
direction, special education too often remains ignored in both research and
policy, despite its importance in serving among the most disadvantaged children and youth, clearly a priority in equalizing opportunities to learn and
ensuring successful transitions to adulthood.

Paradoxes abound in special education; they are recurrent and patterned.
In this light, special education is akin to chaotic systems whose central property is nonlinearity. As many have noted, far from being a negative property,
chaos is a source of order and is deeply structured; it is "a presence rather
than an absence" (Hayles 1990: 6). The study of chaotic systems, as the study
of complex systems, may take one of two paths. One may study the emergence of order or organization *from* chaos; another studies the order *within*
chaotic systems. The latter is especially analogous to special education. The
order within chaotic systems is evident as deep structures that are not easily
discernible. Such structures can "generate new information . . . and patterns
of extreme complexity, in which *areas of symmetry are intermixed with asymmetry* down through all scales of magnification" (Hayles 1990: 10, emphasis
added). The key that unlocked this view of chaotic systems was the separation of information from meaning. The generation of new information and
more complexity can arise from the structure of the information itself and be
quite independent of what the information might mean to those who receive

it. This dynamic was broached previously, in Chapter 4, as a property of western European systems of special education. As semiclosed structures, many of the processes and outcomes recur, and they do so independent of the ideas and attitudes of individuals within the systems. The social reproduction of outcomes, largely unforeseen and unwanted, appear as paradoxes. Such a dynamic may be extended to encompass social organizations, particularly special education, in which areas of symmetry are intermixed with asymmetry. Thus, patterns of segregation developed over centuries can be intermixed with patterns of educational and social inclusion. Patterns of centralization on a higher level intermix with patterns of decentralization on lower levels. Yet it is the interconnectedness of these patterns that generates their particular country-specific fusion, and in so doing, their interconnectedness produces new information, new meanings, and, indeed, new forms of special education that, even within Europe, dramatically range from nearly total segregation to almost complete inclusion. The manner in which this structural interdependence generates these mixed patterns provides insights into the construction of dis/ability as well as the variable institutionalization of special education.

The interconnectedness and mixing of patterns is not the product of structures that are politically and socially neutral. Segregated schools and residential institutions for deaf and blind people, for children and youth with other disadvantages, and for children and youth considered delinquent exist *in relation to* integrated schools and inclusive classrooms as they make up a broad continuum. Moreover, the different valuation of different organizational forms, such as special schools or classrooms, reinforces contemporary norms regarding dis/ability and ab/normality. Ideologies that ignore disabling contexts and conditions, school failure, and alternative learning modes strengthen institutional hierarchies as "purposeful" (Brantlinger 2006: 200). The purpose of general education is different from the purpose of segregated residential institutions. Although general education is equated with rights and expectations of education access, achievement, and ascent, many residential institutions are synonymous with limitations, exclusion, and immobility, coupled with conditions of treatment. When the boundaries that define such distinctions are transgressed, the cultural rules that have constituted them as systems are jeopardized; what were "normal" routines, distinctions, and outcomes now diverge. In contemporary Western societies, we are witnessing a number of resulting paradoxes, which affect not only special education. These paradoxes deeply challenge the status quo, as elaborated in educational, economic, and criminal justice institutions.

Yet institutional distinctions are always changing to some extent, with incremental changes keeping institutions always in motion. Shifting boundaries and disturbed rules contribute to the instability of distinctions and consensual rules. Thus, it is wise to consider the predominance of a pattern as temporary at best. Empirically, we ask not only why segregation is present, but also why its alternative, inclusion, is absent. The paradox of the simultaneous rise in segregated schooling and inclusive education cannot be explained solely by interrogating or deconstructing inclusion. It can be explained only in relation to the segregative structures of which they are the antithesis.

The chapters in Part 3 explore such paradoxes in education systems. With affinities to the study of chaotic systems, the chapters concur that nonlinearity is a more reliable guide than is the ideal of linear development or a narrative of progress that can withstand neither the heterogeneity within the developed democracies nor a broader international comparison. Addressing the simultaneous rise and coexistence of segregation and inclusive education, Chapter 6 presents an overview of participation rates in Europe and the United States. It explores the relationship between classification rates (and hence the size of the population receiving additional resources to access the curriculum) and allocation to certain learning opportunity structures and organizational forms in schooling. Finally, we analyze the association between inclusive education and particular types of education system structures and forms of education governance.

Comparing the two institutional arenas of special education and correctional institutions, Chapter 7 contrasts the right to education in public education and in the criminal justice system. The specific focus is on the content of court challenges that reveal measures of the divergent paths traveled by special education as the traditional arena in which "least restrictive environments" have been discussed and by correctional institutions whose system purposely maintains the "most restrictive environments," limiting liberty with the goal of modifying behavior or curtailing deviance. Focusing on legalization and educational rights in the United States, we examine court challenges from the 1970s to the present and explore a provocative hypothesis:

public education and correctional institutions are moving in opposite directions, with special education retreating from the right to education as state
correctional facilities embrace the right to education. The divergent directions with respect to the right to education reflect a paradox: a discourse of
rights evolves within confinement, whereas a discourse of confinement evolves
from an initiation of rights. The analysis of special education from the angle
of correctional facilities provides an especially revealing perspective on the
directions that special education and juvenile justice are moving in law. From
such a comparison, the implications for a rights discourse in special education are at once broadened and sharpened.

Finally, in the concluding chapter, the themes and threads of the book are
tied together in a discussion of the development of special education since
the Enlightenment in Europe and around the world. Comparative data on
the enactment of compulsory schooling laws and those relating to special education, understood as programs within the education system proper, manifest
the recent transformation of special education into a central concern for
countries around the world, despite its origins several centuries ago. We also
return to the nascent institutions and organizations devoted to persons with
disabilities in Europe, discussed at the outset, which long preceded the contemporary expansion of education that has—with special and inclusive
education—truly universalized compulsory schooling to include all children.

In this summary and outlook, we discuss the gap between the global
rhetoric of inclusive education and the empirically demonstrated realities of
institutionalized organizational forms in special education that continue to
vary tremendously across countries. As we argue throughout, the inertia in
special education and the persistence of particular forms has much to do with
its interconnections with other institutions, ranging from the justice system
to labor markets. Thorny deliberations and decision making occur in both
decentralized and centralized systems, but the latter seem more likely to broadly
implement inclusive education. Such comparisons of national systems of special education provide distinctive perspectives on the battles between older
and newer paradigms—multiple modernities indeed—that influence *whether*
and *when* countries around the world will achieve their shared goal of inclusive education for all.

# SPECIAL EDUCATION PARTICIPATION AND THE SIMULTANEOUS RISE OF SEGREGATION AND INCLUSION

A S ITS DIVERSE ORGANIZATIONAL FORMS developed over the twentieth century, special education offered assistance not only to children with a range of impairments and disadvantages, but, increasingly, also to those with a variety of newly defined student disabilities, or "special educational needs." Especially over the past several decades, international calls for inclusive education and the national and local movements needed to advocate for and implement such restructured schooling have led to increases in the proportion of students schooled in inclusive classrooms. Yet paradoxically the proportion of all students who learn in segregated settings has also increased. Around the world, special education has diffused, like other types of education, from primary and secondary to tertiary and lifelong learning.

On the one hand, raised awareness, disciplinary diagnostics, and professional knowledge increased the proportion of children and youth with disadvantages or disabilities and are schooled in the traditional, often segregated, settings. On the other hand, individualized education programming and the recognition that each and every student demands and deserves support to reach his or her own learning goals have strengthened inclusive education. With an ever-larger proportion of children being diagnosed as having special educational needs in many countries, we have witnessed the *simultaneous rise* and *coexistence* of segregation and inclusion, two contrasting organizational forms in which children with recognized special educational needs are supported.

In contrast to abundant good intentions and compensatory investments, special education settings—authorized to offer *different* educational opportunities—seem to legitimately *reduce* individual access to opportunities to learn, especially due to lesser expectations and peer interactions. This reduction in opportunities, combined with regulations regarding certification, limit educational attainment. Individuals' risk of low (or no) attainment usually increases in special education, with its students significantly overrepresented in the group of less-educated youth. Paradoxically, expansion of education has *increased* stigmatization of less-educated youth because they constitute the lowest educational category—which has become smaller and more socially selective over time—while ever more of their peers have earned certificates (Solga 2002: 164, 2005).

Indeed, not only does education influence political and economic allocation, but also having credentials has become the "primary mechanism by which individuals are defined as full and legitimate societal members" (Ramirez and Rubinson 1979: 80). Thus, education is seen as a global human right that states must provide, and nearly everyone supports the norm of universal access to education and equal opportunity, despite interindividual variations in ability (Meyer 2001). Yet the institutionalization—regulative, but often residential as well—of these individuals' life courses had been steady until advocates of "normalization" and "deinstitutionalization" challenged this status quo in recent decades (Braddock and Parish 2001; see also Zola 1982). Despite massive general expansion of education and the disability rights movement's successful activism for increased access to integrated or even inclusive schooling, more than ever before, being disabled remains linked to being less educated than one's peers. Conversely, being less educated leads to an increased risk of becoming disabled, of experiencing poverty, and of suffering social exclusion (OECD 2003a). Responding to these principles and global trends, states and nongovernmental organizations around the world have committed themselves to "education for all"—and to inclusive education (for example, UNESCO 1994; World Bank 2003; UN 2006).

Exploring the above-delineated paradoxes, this chapter reveals three significant patterns. Firstly, the differentiation of students through the application of elaborate classification systems—measured in the number of categories—has no definitive impact on the type of (special) education system to which these students are then allocated. Secondly, the population sizes, as measured in classification rates, and institutionalized special education organizations are only weakly correlated. Contrary to a popular hypothesis, having a larger proportion of students with special educational needs neither necessarily facilitates inclusive education nor reduces segregation rates. Thirdly, decentralized education systems often maintain a *dual* structure of special and general education sectors—and thus tend to segregate. In contrast, the centralization of educational governance seems to strengthen inclusive education. Movement along the spectrum of (de)centralization is of significance in meeting this internationally codified goal. Far from being an easily achieved set of goals and changes, inclusive education challenges the long-ago developed structures of educational systems, which sort and group students in different ways. As shown in the previous chapter, the institutionalization of inclusive education requires at least partial *deinstitutionalization* of special education, a process that has been accomplished in very few countries, owing to myriad barriers to inclusion (see also Powell 2011).

Despite the rising importance accorded educational participation, performance, and certification, some students still leave schooling without qualifications. Formal schooling shapes the life courses not only of the highly educated, as educational expectations have risen considerably, but also of all young adults. A consequence of these higher expectations is a rapidly growing proportion of students who, because they are not performing in school adequately or quickly enough, are referred to special education programs that are designed to compensate for disadvantages and disabilities. As we will show, this has much to do with the structure of the education system and less to do with the measured characteristics of individual students. This finding stands in contrast to clinical models of disability that have focused almost exclusively on individuals and not on the resources and interactions within variable schooling contexts.

Nevertheless, knowing which types of students are most likely to participate in the expanding special education systems demonstrates which children and youth are most likely to grow up less educated. To investigate these issues empirically, we analyze students' classification into special education and their allocation to schooling structures that provide or constrain opportunities, along a continuum from segregation and separation to integration and inclusion. The cross-national differences in constructions of and organizational responses to special educational needs investigated here emphasize the need for institutional explanations in place of those that focus solely or mainly on individual special educational needs. Similarly, the multidisciplinary field of disability studies, developing over the past several decades, suggests that attention to attitudinal and environmental barriers will provide important explanations for the rise of special education and its consequences. These lessons do not require or even call into question the relevance of the ongoing search for the elusive etiologies of particular impairments or special educational needs, emphasizing instead the social factors that produce special educational needs varying considerably across time and space.

Embedded in a broader cross-national comparison, examples from England, France, Germany, and the United States presented here accentuate national patterns of association between classification rates that measure selection processes, structures that provide differing opportunities to learn, and educational governance. After a comparison of classification and segregation rates and educational system structures, we turn to a discussion of recent patterns in inclusive education and de/centralization, arguing for more attention to these factors in explaining the pathways made available to students with disadvantages and disabilities.

## INTERNATIONAL ORGANIZATIONS, DISABILITY RIGHTS, AND INCLUSIVE EDUCATION

International organizations, especially the United Nations, have been influential in the establishment of human rights, including education rights, and also in calling for equality for hundreds of millions of people with disabilities worldwide. To emphasize the need for increased awareness of and commitment to addressing the living conditions of people with disabilities globally, the United Nations proclaimed 1981 the International Year of Disabled Persons (IYDP) and proclaimed the period of 1983 to 1992 the UN Decade of Disabled Persons. The IYDP's key goal was to affirm and implement the principle of "full participation and equality" contained in the UN General Assembly's 1975 Declaration on the Rights of Disabled Persons. Despite these early calls for awareness and action, the situation for most disabled people worldwide continues to be dire. Thus, an international convention was conceived to emphasize the need to extend, reinforce, and intensify efforts to secure equality. To reach this overarching goal, education is assumed to be absolutely vital.

In the international codification first of "education for all" and then of inclusive education, a range of international organizations has provided ideas, standards, and legal texts. Yet the most potent statement thus far came from the UN General Assembly on December 13, 2006, when it adopted the International Convention on the Rights of Persons with Disabilities, which has since been ratified by dozens of countries.[1]

As the first human rights treaty signed in the twenty-first century, which was largely crafted and carried through by the increasingly networked global disability rights movement, the Convention is unequivocal about the centrality of education for all and inclusive education for the goals of equality and participation. Equal access to education and inclusive education are included in the Convention as tenets of education as a human right. Because of its importance as a summation of what has been learned over the past decades about schooling and disability as well as of the contemporary perspective, it merits a close look.

### International Convention on the Rights of Persons with Disabilities

The text of Article 24 of the Convention, on education, states clearly the conditions needed and the extent to which different levels of access to education are to be guaranteed. In the first paragraph, unmistakably, the full development of individuals and societies is viewed as fundamentally based on education systems that are inclusive at all levels. Without such systems, persons will neither be enabled to become citizens who participate fully nor be individuals who reach their potential and freely develop their personality in order to maximize their capabilities (see Nussbaum 2006).

1. States Parties recognize the right of persons with disabilities to education. With a view to realizing this right without discrimination and on the basis of equal opportunity, States Parties shall ensure an inclusive education system at all levels and lifelong learning directed to: (a) The full development of human potential and sense of dignity and self-worth, and the strengthening of respect for human rights, fundamental freedoms and human diversity; (b) The development by persons with disabilities of their personality, talents and creativity, as well as their mental and physical abilities, to their fullest potential; (c) Enabling persons with disabilities to participate effectively in a free society (UN 2006: Article 24, Section 1).

To reach such significant goals, certain conditions must be met—conditions that have continuously challenged governments, the professions responsible for teaching and care, and communities. The widespread exclusion from education of people with disabilities has been overcome in developed democracies with much struggle over the past several decades. Yet some developing countries make no distinctions while providing only limited additional supports and services. Given the strength of this ideal of inclusive education, there may be a compression—or even the skipping—of the stage of development so characteristic of many Western countries, that of establishing asylums and segregated schooling. Indeed, the institutionalization of segregated organizational forms contributed much to defining some children, youth, and adults as "uneducable" within general schooling in the first place. Witnessed repeatedly, the risk of bureaucratic compliance substituting for meaningful participation is great. Nevertheless, the knowledge base on special and inclusive education as on disability has grown considerably (see, for example, Albrecht, Seelman, and Bury 2001; Albrecht 2005; Reynolds and Fletcher-Janzen 2007). Building upon the knowledge that many decades of successful inclusive education programs in myriad countries have brought, the next paragraph in Article 24 states in unambiguous language how the right to inclusive education can and must be realized, with accommodations and individualized support:

2. In realizing this right, States Parties shall ensure that: (a) Persons with disabilities are not excluded from the general education system on the basis of disability, and that children with disabilities are not excluded from free and compulsory primary

education, or from secondary education, on the basis of disability; (b) Persons with disabilities can access an inclusive, quality and free primary education and secondary education on an equal basis with others in the communities in which they live; (c) Reasonable accommodation of the individual's requirements is provided; (d) Persons with disabilities receive the support required, within the general education system, to facilitate their effective education; (e) Effective individualized support measures are provided in environments that maximize academic and social development, consistent with the goal of full inclusion (UN 2006: Article 24, Section 2).

Further, specifying communicative access, Article 24 emphasizes that alternative modes of communication, orientation, and mobility must be facilitated, especially if community identities are to be maintained, promoted, and developed. This calls for taking a policy approach of accessibility and universal design prior to the "treatment" of individuals. Disabling structures can be modified, reducing the incidence of disablement, without clinical intervention.

3. States Parties shall enable persons with disabilities to learn life and social development skills to facilitate their full and equal participation in education and as members of the community. To this end, States Parties shall take appropriate measures, including: (a) Facilitating the learning of Braille, alternative script, augmentative and alternative modes, means and formats of communication and orientation and mobility skills, and facilitating peer support and mentoring; (b) Facilitating the learning of sign language and the promotion of the linguistic identity of the deaf community; (c) Ensuring that the education of persons, and in particular children, who are blind, deaf or deafblind is delivered in the most appropriate languages and modes and means of communication for the individual, and in environments which maximize academic and social development (UN 2006: Article 24, Section 3).

The importance of teacher training and careers in schooling of students with special educational needs—as those optimally qualified to raise awareness, to increase diversity, and to transmit disability culture—is underscored in the next paragraph:

4. In order to help ensure the realization of this right, States Parties shall take appropriate measures to employ teachers, including teachers with disabilities, who are qualified in sign language and/or Braille, and to train professionals and staff who work at all levels of education. Such training shall incorporate disability awareness

and the use of appropriate augmentative and alternative modes, means and formats of communication, educational techniques and materials to support persons with disabilities (UN 2006: Article 24, Section 4).

In line with other global discourses, such as lifelong learning and human capital, the Convention emphasizes not only primary and secondary schooling but also accommodations to ensure equality in terms of vocational training as well as higher and adult education. Ongoing expansion of education has resulted in enhanced access as well as higher standards. Ever more educational certificates, as positional goods, will be required for all who wish to maintain their educational advantage. Without accommodations, the playing field will not be even for all, yet even in the wealthiest Western countries, education and training opportunities beyond primary and secondary schooling are still seriously lacking (see, for example, Powell, Felkendorff, and Hollenweger 2008 on Austria, Germany, and Switzerland).

5. States Parties shall ensure that persons with disabilities are able to access general tertiary education, vocational training, adult education and lifelong learning without discrimination and on an equal basis with others. To this end, States Parties shall ensure that reasonable accommodation is provided to persons with disabilities (UN 2006: Article 24, Section 5).

However, without prior schooling and credentials, such accommodations will likely be insufficient to compensate for "cumulative disadvantage" (see Mayer 2005). Despite ongoing debates at national and local levels about how to ensure democratic participation by citizens and how to achieve highly qualified workforces, at the international level the Convention codifies a progressive and ambitious vision of learning throughout the life course. However, the steps necessary to achieve lifelong learning for more than a highly-educated few depend on concrete reform processes that must engage the ideas, norms, and policies of highly institutionalized education systems. Comparative research can help to uncover the factors that hinder or facilitate such goals. Attention must be paid to the danger of mere rhetorical upgrading or euphemism, especially in the stigmatized domain of disability.

Along with the United Nations, the European Union has called for the transformative restructuring of education systems to be more inclusive, meaning that all children should learn together in the same classrooms. In the case of special education placements, disability classifications are legitimized by international bodies, in particular by the World Health Organization (WHO 2001) with its International Classification of Functioning, Disability, and Health (see Üstün et al. 2001). The Organisation for Economic Co-operation and Development (OECD 2004, 2007), in defining prominent cross-national disability categories for use in evaluating education systems, has emphasized the different supply of support and services individual students receive. The European Agency for Development in Special Needs Education (EADSNE 2005) offers a range of quantitative and qualitative data to chart persistence and change in special education across Europe. The World Bank (2003) has also shown interest in education provisions as preventive social policy in order to reduce the long-term costs of disablement and low education. All of these international nongovernmental organizations (IN-GOs) have participated in diffusing knowledge and practices across nations that have become increasingly engaged in constructing special education as well as responding to inclusive education principles.

In the case of inclusive education legislation, as in the case of special education decades ago, specific language again emanates from international agencies and is adopted as legitimate and necessary. Such language—affirming the right to education and to the development of one's potential, prohibiting discrimination against disabled persons, and obligating authorities to extend provisions to disabled children—has become a policy paradigm of international scope. International conventions, constitutional amendments, and national legislative acts enjoin nations to comply with world principles, classifications, and procedures and to do so aligned with world time.

The effect of world culture is on ideas, such as the above-mentioned international charters in inclusive education, and on national education institutions and organizations that provide contrasting educational environments in which students with special educational needs may be schooled. The effect on institutions may or may not be compatible with existing historical and cultural differences. Such frequent discordance is a key source of the discrepancy between discursive commitments of inclusive education and the persistence of segregated schools and separate classrooms. Segregated organizational forms, which grow as extensions of special education and as complementary adjuncts to the universalization of compulsory education, contrast with contemporary models of inclusive classrooms. As we have seen, for centuries the rights and needs of disabled children were met in "special," most often segregated, organizations. With the principle of integration, the precursor to inclusion, the schism of general and special education institutions was challenged, and much more so with inclusive education, which calls taken-for-granted boundaries, labels, and classifications into question, making these appear arbitrary and illegitimate. As a principle backed with global authority, the idea of inclusion becomes a new social imaginary that exerts its own normative influence on institutions as it inspires and demands reform efforts, some rhetorical, some structural. Although external forces have defined, legitimized, and attempted to coerce nations to increase inclusive education and as these isomorphic pressures have accelerated across nations, the question remains: how much impact has this actually had on national education systems?

Indeed, although global articulations of inclusive education may appear uniform and national declarations often seem similar, such indicators of consensus and convergence can be deceptive, as they often remain merely rhetorical and far removed from the reality of schooling in localities. Nevertheless, the way educational goals and settings are discussed provides insights into ideologies and norms that differ significantly across societies. The official translation of the above-discussed International Convention from English into German revised some of the basic precepts beyond recognition, as the term "inclusive education" was replaced with "integrative education." This exemplifies conceptual misunderstanding of distinctions—crucial elsewhere— that have little basis in the everyday practice of schooling in Germany and where the struggle centers on how to overcome persistent school segregation. While the disability rights organization Netzwerk Artikel 3 challenged the official government version with a "shadow" translation, the international understanding of inclusive education is only now entering the national policy-making realm. Policymakers and judges seek to defend the traditional, and recently affirmed, authority of the *Länder* over education, which has bolstered the disparities found throughout Germany (see Below 2002).

As revealed here, below the level of international declarations that proclaim a universal right to education, national differences endure. These differences are not restricted to individual countries; they can also coalesce as regional patterns. Thus, the countries of western Europe—in particular some of the Nordic countries—have led not only in the expansion of special education, but also in the advancement of inclusion, especially when compared with eastern Europe, Central and South America, Asia, and Africa. These other world regions lag behind even as they often exemplify alternative strategies in educational integration. Furthermore, images of and values regarding inclusion may be contrary with regard to independence—indeed, some collectivist societies value this not at all (Komardjaja 2004). As revealed above, comparisons of collectivist and individualist societies question the existence of a singular global norm of individual independence (see Table 4.1).

Over the long term, participation in international organizations does capture an orderliness to the growth of special education and the adoption of inclusive education, yet it also masks the substantial national and regional differences in the meanings assigned to educability and student disability as well as the contrasting learning opportunity structures, such as segregation, separation, integration, and inclusion, that constitute the continuum of prevalent educational environments. Within European countries, the variation in special education systems reflects several centuries of disability and special education history (discussed in Chapters 1 and 2). Yet the contemporary relative dominance of segregation or inclusion in Europe and the United States seems to depend heavily on the institutionalization of education systems and especially the centralization of education governance, a topic we return to below.

## COMPARING CLASSIFICATION, PLACEMENT, AND ATTAINMENT INDICATORS CROSS-NATIONALLY

Here, we present empirical indicators to reveal relationships and patterns of special and inclusive education. The classification rate—the percentage of all students classified into special education—underscores cultural differences in the interpretation of student disabilities and the resources provided for special education. The segregation and inclusion rates—which indicate, respectively, the percentage of all students that are segregated (defined as attending separate facilities or nearly full-time separate classes) and the percentage of all special education students that are in general education full time—show the distribution of students with special educational needs on the two ends of the spectrum of educational environments. The segregation index calculates the percentage of those students with special educational needs who spend most of their day outside the general classroom or school. Further, the type of special education system identifies whether all students are schooled in the same school and same track, divided between two tracks, or allocated to a wide variety of tracks. The last significant dimension discussed here is a dichotomous (de)centralization indicator, which reflects the importance of national governmental intervention to reform or even restructure education systems, especially in attempts to guarantee rights to education, school integration, or inclusive education.

### Classification and Categories

Before comparing nations' varying accomplishments in achieving their goal of inclusive education, we define "special educational needs" as referring to institutionalized cultural value judgments about behavior, intellectual functioning, and health that result in particular human differences being recognized as deserving of support or professional services. In her pioneering analyses, Sally Tomlinson (1981, 1982) discussed these complex and varied accounts of special educational needs as behavioral, bodily, functional, intuitive, linguistic, organizational, psychological, social, statistical, statutory— even tautological (as in: "a child with special educational needs has special educational needs").

Ambivalent and often contentious, classification as having special educational needs requires extensive mediation between its many positive and negative consequences—the former being provision of additional resources and rights and the latter being prevalent stigmatization, even institutionalized discrimination—which frequently shows its effects throughout the life course (Powell 2011). Analyzing special educational needs or student dis/abilities requires close attention not only to the relationships between individuals embedded in social situations, but also to cultural contexts, professional perspectives, disciplinary approaches, and translations of concepts into empirical measures that guide classification processes. Education administrations distinguish student disabilities and regulate access to special education services and settings according to culturally specific social norms and professional practices.

Applied by school gatekeepers—such as teachers, administrators, and school psychologists—at the individual level in response to particular behaviors, special educational needs categories imply deviance from social norms, or, in the language of INGOs today, education standards. Analyses of gatekeeping processes and concepts such as self-fulfilling and self-sustaining prophecies underscore differentials in students' learning within and between schools owing to expectation levels: ethnographic studies have explored how decision making in students' careers creates stratification within schools (Mehan, Hertweck, and Meihls 1986) and between school types (Gomolla and Radtke 2002; Kottmann 2006). Official classification furnishes students with specific rights, but simultaneously provides the bureaucratic legitimacy and accountability needed to justify compensatory provision of additional expenditures and specialized services (Powell 2011). This process is charged with resolving the "distributive dilemma of disability" (Stone 1984) in particular times and places. Special educational needs categories are continuously revised, yet the professionally authorized and bureaucratically organized processes of classification in schools, once implemented, resist change—as do the organizations established to serve classified students. Examining special education classification and school segregation, separation, integration, and inclusion rates emphasizes the contingent development of special education classification systems and school structures.

The dominance of medical models of disability and the clinical professions that define disability and special educational needs mainly in terms of individual deficits has been seriously challenged for decades. Nevertheless, we might expect that rates of special educational needs would be roughly similar across highly developed countries, and especially among the European democracies. Yet across Europe, the rates of all children classified and receiving services vary considerably, from less than 1 percent to more than a third of all students (Eurydice 2005).

Although some European countries utilize only one or two special educational needs categories and others more than a dozen, most nations have implemented six to ten such categories (Eurydice 2002: B-12), depending on extant official disability classifications, assessment procedures, finance regulations, allocated resources, and education system differentiation. Differences among the OECD countries exist, in the range of categories, in the meanings associated with them, and in the proportion among all categories (OECD 2004). Twenty categories are currently used to identify students with disabilities, difficulties, and disadvantages: aboriginal, autism, blind, deaf, disadvantaged, emotional and behavioral difficulties, gifted and talented, hospital (illness), learning difficulties (severe, moderate, light), learning disabilities, multiple disabilities (combinatorial), partially hearing, partially sighted, physical disabilities, remedial, second-language / mother-tongue teaching, speech and language disabilities, traveling child, young offender, other.

Despite this array, recent cross-national studies of inclusive and special education and social exclusion utilize just three broad groups of students who receive additional resources to access the curriculum: A – children with disabilities; B – children with learning difficulties; C – children with disadvantages (Evans et al. 2002; OECD 2004, 2007). That typology, which implements a supply-side approach based upon provided services and supports, highlights key differences between the main groups served by special education programs and policies. The substance of these additional resources and where they are provided requires more detailed analyses than can be presented here, but the classification rates reflect major differences in national policies and the variable institutionalization of special education, including organizational differentiation, service provision and curricular models, teacher training, and finance.

By any measure, the percentage of all students of compulsory school-age who have special educational needs varies greatly (see Table 6.1). In Europe, the proportions range from less than 1.5 percent in Greece and Italy, to 5 percent in Germany, to almost 18 percent in Finland (EADSNE 1998, 2003). The proportion in the United States was 12 percent. Indeed, significant differences between and within countries are found not only when including disadvantaged students or those with learning disabilities, but also in the seemingly "objective" categories such as visual and hearing impairments (Powell 2011).

Children and youth participating in special education are at the nexus of multiple social differences and ascriptive attributes, including disability, gender, and ethnicity. But the effects of social, economic, and cultural disadvantages are evidently hardly separable from impairments, disabilities, and / or

TABLE 6.1. Students with special educational needs (SEN) and segregated (%), select countries, 1999–2001 (ranked by segregation index)

| | Total classification rate* | Number of categories | Total segregation rate** | SEN group segregation index*** | Type of special education system |
|---|---|---|---|---|---|
| Switzerland | 6.0 | 14 | 6.0 | ~100 | Dual |
| Belgium (French) | 4.0 | n/a | 4.0 | ~100 | Dual |
| Belgium (Flemish) | 5.0 | 17 | 4.9 | 98 | Dual |
| Germany | 5.3 | 15 | 4.6 | 87 | Dual |
| Netherlands | 2.1 | 15 | 1.8 | 86 | Dual |
| France | 3.1 | 13 | 2.6 | 84 | Multiple |
| Sweden | 2.0 | 9 | 1.3 | 65 | Unitary |
| Austria | 3.2 | n/a | 1.6 | 50 | Multiple |
| England and Wales | 3.2 | 1 | 1.1 | 34 | Multiple |
| Finland | 17.8 | 14 | 3.7 | 21 | Multiple |
| United States | 12.0 | 15 | 2.1 | 18 | Multiple |
| Denmark | 11.9 | 1 | 1.5 | 13 | Multiple |
| Spain | 3.7 | 14 | 0.4 | 11 | Unitary |
| Portugal | 5.8 | n/a | 0.5 | 9 | Unitary |
| Norway | 5.6 | 1 | 0.5 | 9 | Unitary |
| Iceland | 15.0 | n/a | 0.9 | 6 | Unitary |
| Italy | 1.5 | 10 | <0.5 | n/a | Unitary |
| Greece | 0.9 | 15 | <0.5 | n/a | Unitary |

*Sources*: Eurydice (2002); U.S. DOE (2002); EADSNE (2003: 7); OECD (2004: annex 2); authors' calculations.

*Note*: n/a = not available or applicable.

*Classification rate = students that have been classified with SEN, in percent of all students. Note that some countries have classified students only if they attend special schools, therefore classification and segregation rates may appear equal (for example, Switzerland); however, some integrated students may receive services or support without being counted separately in official statistics. Conversely, special educational needs statistics are not a full census of children with impairments or disabilities. As the organizational forms change, so too must the bureaucratic counting procedures (for example, whereas in Germany inclusive education has been developed since the 1980s, not until 2000 were students with SEN who are schooled in general schools identified in official statistics); thus, these data should be interpreted with caution.

**Segregation rate = students in special schools or most of the day in separate classes, in percent of all students.

***SEN group segregation index = students in special schools or most of the day in separate classes, in percent of students with SEN.

special educational needs that are identified during a child's school career. Contextual factors include the diffusion of special education programs, variance in poverty rates, and ethnic diversity. Developments in dis/ability concepts, definitions, and labels exhibit the shifting boundaries between special and general education students. As shown in the previous chapter, in absolute numbers and proportion, Germany and the United States have witnessed dramatic growth in their special education populations, especially since World War II. Yet only since the 1999 school year, have official German national statistics included data on students with special educational needs attending general schools (*Integrationsschüler*). Thus, integration and inclusion developments across Germany's *Länder* could only be monitored and compared with official statistics for the past decade. The overall classification rate has increased to 5.6 percent of the student population in general schools, representing nearly half a million children and youth (KMK 2005: ix). In the United States, growth has been continuously upward, at a much faster rate: by 2001, more than 5.8 million students aged six through twenty-one received special education services, about 12 percent of public school enrollment (U.S. DOE 2005: 21).

The contrast is not only in classification rates, but also in categories. For four decades up to 1994 in Germany, students identified as having special educational needs were classified into one of ten or so categories of "having to attend a special school type" (*Sonderschulbedürftigkeit*). Thus, in one of the world's most highly differentiated special education systems, students were sorted according to the type of school they attended, with those administrative-organizational distinctions primary and individual needs secondary. In fact, with these categories, differentiation and allocation were unified, as the classification was supply-driven. The key questions seemed to be which type of existing school would be appropriate, rather than asking how best to serve individual needs. By contrast, following a paradigm shift a few years after reunification, the main classification system in use has been the individual-based, pedagogical "categories of educational support" (*Förderschwerpunkte*). Officially defined by the Conference of *Länder* Culture Ministers (*Kultusministerkonferenz*, KMK), the umbrella organization of state education ministers, the classification system continues to identify individual deficits as it refers to children and youth who "are so impaired in their educational, developmental, or learning potentials that they cannot be sufficiently supported in instruction within the general school without special educational support" (KMK 1994: 6, translation JP).[2] In contrast, the U.S. classification system has maintained a basically clinical approach from the beginning, which discusses "developmental" issues but continues to focus on impairments and illnesses—from speech impairments to traumatic brain injury—that are clinically diagnosed for the Individualized Education Programs by multiple disciplinary experts. Since disabilities do not necessarily have consequences for learning, classification systems produce a selective group that does not equal the population of all children and youth with disabilities who are of compulsory school-age, who may receive rehabilitation or other services provided by a variety of programs funded by health-care policies or social security (see Maschke 2008 for European comparisons). Traditional and standardized categories persist in both the U.S. and German federal classification systems, even if the newer German categories of educational support show a primarily pedagogical understanding of learning differences or difficulties.

Special educational needs are met within categories of educational support and are increasingly individualized, as they no longer explicitly require attendance in a special school, even if that setting remains most prevalent. New procedures exist for identification, referral, assessment, diagnosis, and classification, and new understandings of disability and the tools to measure its complex interrelation of personal, social, and environmental factors continue to evolve. Yet such changes in categorical labels have not transformed the organizations and settings in which students so classified spend their school days. The result of the differentiation of children through application of categories and labels is allocation to learning opportunity structures, but does the differentiation of a classification system and the size of the population have any effect on the allocation of students among segregated and inclusive settings or on the type of special education system? This organizational source of special education stigmatization continues in the range of educational environments and the differential opportunities to learn they provide.

*Educational Environments*

Special education programs serve a highly heterogeneous group of children with social, ethnic, linguistic, physical, and intellectual disadvantages. Although the group participating in special education includes children with similar disadvantages and disabilities in all countries, we find substantial differences not only in the size of the group and its demographics, but also in organizational structures (OECD 2004). Across Europe, a remarkable array of organizations provides special education in special schools or classes in more mainstream settings (Eurydice 2005: 129). Furthermore, every European country has been implementing reforms toward more school integration or inclusive education for some time, but at very different paces (EAD-SNE 1998). Among OECD countries (as within the European Union), not only do the rates of all children classified as having special educational needs vary considerably by nation and region, but the proportion of those who are integrated in general school settings ranges from almost none to almost all (OECD 1999, 2004; Eurydice 2000, 2005).

Across Europe, three models of special education arrangements are prevalent: dual, multiple, and unitary. These models exhibit substantial differences in segregation and inclusion rates, with the latter also reflecting the extent of centralization of education governance. These structural factors shape population sizes, learning opportunities provided, and the resulting inequalities in education qualification. The proportion of students in separate schools or classes ranges from less than 1 percent to more than 6 percent of all students (Table 6.1). By contrast, in the United States, although the proportion of all students not attending a general school full time is very low—0.4 percent of all students—factoring in the relatively large group of "separated" students who spend more than 60 percent of their school day in separate classrooms places the United States in the mid-range, at 2.1 percent. Such large cross-national differences—often matched or exceeded by regional variance within countries—demonstrate that the proportion of children classified and their learning opportunities depend not solely on individual characteristics, but largely on special education systems' institutional development and the classification systems in use, associated with particular cultural meanings ascribed to categories of student disability and the provision of additional resources.[3]

Unitary education systems, such as those in Italy and Norway, aim for full inclusion, educating nearly all students in general classrooms. Some OECD countries, including the United States, maintain a continuum of settings, from inclusive classrooms to segregated special schools, representing the opposite, multitrack, system. In between, but with the highest segregation rates, are those systems, such as in the German-speaking countries, Belgium, and the Netherlands, in which many types of special and general schools occupy parallel worlds. Gradually, these dual-track systems have witnessed some differentiation, with these segmented education systems moving toward a "continuum," or multitrack, model as in the United States. Over the twentieth century, many asylums and special schools were closed in favor of students sharing in the mainstream of school life, yet segregating or separating students with special educational needs remains part of policy and practice in most countries. This is so despite the aforementioned international charters and innumerable national laws that aim to increase school integration and / or inclusive education.

Education systems, as argued in Part I, exhibit institutionalization processes begun several hundred years ago, long before compulsory schooling was enacted and universalized. The principles and structures elaborated over time continue to exert their considerable influence on the pathways available to students today. Based on these structures, the countries have been grouped into a tripartite typology of dual, multiple, and unitary: (1) *dual* involves parallel development of general schools and legally and organizationally separate special schools; (2) *multiple* offers a continuum of settings and services, from special schools to schooling partially in separate schools or classrooms to full-time participation in general classrooms; (3) *unitary* has a goal of inclusion for all children so that almost all students are educated in general classrooms (EADSNE 1998: 178–179, 2003). In many of these countries, as the authors of the EADSNE study argue, debate has centered on legislative advances prioritizing an increase in institutional flexibility (movement toward a continuum of settings and services), growing awareness of funding system consequences—such as incentives to classify, segregate, or separate—and the importance of parental choice.

Sorting the results by segregation index value (the percentage of only those students with special educational needs who spend most or all of their school day in segregated or separated settings; see Table 6.1) shows that, in this sample of countries, the dual-structure systems—evident in Switzerland, both parts of Belgium, Germany, and the Netherlands—had the highest values. The first three countries also had the highest segregation rates (the percentage of all students of compulsory school-age that are schooled in segregated settings: all above 4.5 percent). By contrast, this dataset shows that the unitary education systems of Spain, Portugal, Norway, Iceland, Italy, and Greece had the lowest segregation index values (all below 11 percent). However, in some southern European countries, as in many developing countries, the segregation index value may coincide with fewer support provisions of any kind, making a mockery of the ideals of individualized support and inclusive education as well as reflecting contradictions between stated and implemented policies (see, for example, Vlachou-Balafouti 1999 on Greece). Even when most special education students do attend a general school, the crucial goal of individualized support for accessing the curriculum cannot always be met.

If the first group of countries is dual and the later group is unitary, the middle group has had a broad range of segregation index values that reflect the multitrack system, in which children are distributed among a plethora of educational environments. This group has segregation index values ranging from 13 percent to 84 percent and includes Denmark, the United States, Finland, England and Wales, Austria, Sweden (which has a unitary education system), and France, which has a segregation index nearly as high as the dual education system countries. These figures reflect an association between dual structures and segregation and between unitary structures and inclusion. Furthermore, dual systems are found in countries with decentralized education governance, whereas most unitary systems are found in countries with centralized education governance, which suggests that centralization facilitates inclusive education (a topic we return to below). Although countries throughout Europe and indeed around the world have agreed that inclusion of students with special educational needs in compulsory general education is desirable, such models have yet to be universally accepted as appropriate for *all* children and youth with special educational needs, owing especially to issues of quality (Eurydice 2005: 129) and institutional and organizational barriers that hinder flexible, ad hoc provision of supports within general school settings without requiring lengthy and costly classification processes to legitimate resource provision (Skrtic 1991a, 1991b).

### Education System Outputs

Across Europe and the OECD countries, remarkable differences were found in (1) special educational needs classification rates and (2) learning opportunities provided in settings ranging from special schools to inclusive classrooms. Cross-national studies of disparities in achievement and attainment concur that even among the wealthiest nations, some education systems protect disadvantaged students from experiencing inequality far more than others (Baker, LeTendre, and Goesling 2005: 84). Although the impact of such national institutional differences is increasingly recognized, results from the OECD's Program of International Student Assessment and the United States' National Assessment of Educational Progress demonstrate that nations, states, and localities not only have highly variable rates of providing additional resources to access curricula, but also have highly variable rates of including students with special educational needs in assessments. Such exclusions from data collection and analysis render problematic aggregate comparisons of student performance, though these are increasingly required by law (for example, the United States' No Child Left Behind Act) and directly influence students, teachers, and schools. Pressures to perform provide multiple incentives for increased special educational needs classification and thwart attempts to account for all students' learning, especially according to their own goals, plans, and developmental trajectory.

The educational attainments of students in general and special education students in particular are vital to a full understanding and evaluation of national education systems. However, despite the quantification and comparison of every aspect of schooling, comparable data on educational outcomes are almost completely lacking for students with special educational needs, thus "future data gathering exercises will focus on collecting outcome data" (OECD 2004: 131). The availability of comparative disability data is limited; in many areas, it is seriously limited. The major data sources—social surveys (opinion surveys and socioeconomic surveys) with disability data and statistical databases—need considerable attention paid to gathering data on such topics as education, work, income, cultural and political participation, discrimination, mobility, and communication (van Oorschot 2008). From a life course perspective, early experiences and selection processes in schools are crucial to the types of transitions that are available to youth as they leave school, move on to postsecondary education, or enter the labor market; thus, longitudinal studies—such as the U.S. National Longitudinal Transition Studies (Wagner et al. 2003, 2005, 2006)—are needed in order to chart the accumulation of disadvantages over entire careers and to understand the impact of disablement on personal, social, and economic outcomes (see Wells, Sandefur, and

Hogan 2003). In 2007, Germany's Conference of Culture Ministers acknowledged that education researchers require linked data for an individual's entire education biography, from kindergarten to continuing education in adulthood and admitted that this will likely remain an unrealized vision (KMK 2007), not the least because of the federalism that has promoted considerable disparities in education opportunities and outcomes across the *Länder*. Notwithstanding, a rich new source of data in Germany will be provided in the large-scale National Education Panel Study (see Leuze 2008).

Special education's growth—and its students' disparate participation rates, internationally and domestically, in large-scale assessments—indicate its increasing, but not uniform authority. To emphasize the challenge of effecting the reforms needed in order to make education systems more equitable and excellent, we turn now to an analysis of the global shift toward inclusion rhetoric and patterns of special and inclusive education throughout Europe and the United States.

## THE SIGNIFICANCE OF EDUCATIONAL STRUCTURE FOR SCHOOL INTEGRATION AND INCLUSIVE EDUCATION

As discussed earlier, education for all and inclusive education have become global norms, although the empirical data presented accentuate how far most education systems are from reaching these ambitious goals. We analyze the classification rates in comparison to the rates of inclusive education (roughly measured as participation in general classrooms). Although such aggregated data can be used as an important quantitative measure to compare many countries, like most benchmarks or league tables, these data cannot tell us much about the quality of support and services provided. Nevertheless, more recent data collected by the EADSNE for a larger sample of countries show that there is no strong relationship between the size of the group classified as "having special educational needs" and the proportion of those students who remain in general classrooms (see Figure 6.1).

Further, the variance even among the developed countries of Europe is considerable: from 2.4 percent in the Netherlands to 36.6 percent of all students in Finland received some form of additional support. According to these aggregate data, there is also remarkable variance in school integration and

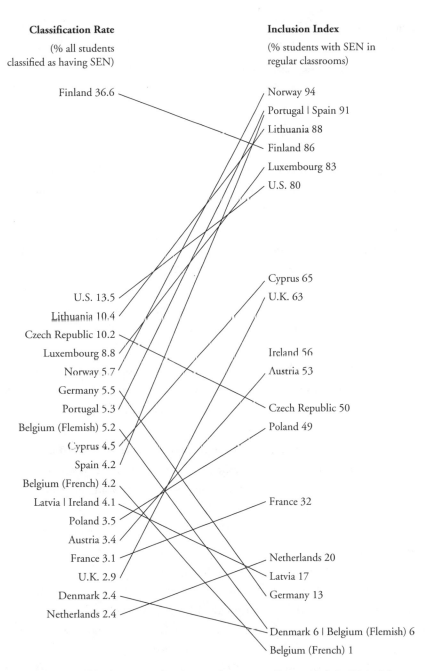

**Classification Rate**

(% all students
classified as having SEN)

**Inclusion Index**

(% students with SEN in
regular classrooms)

Finland 36.6

Norway 94

Portugal | Spain 91

Lithuania 88

Finland 86

Luxembourg 83

U.S. 80

Cyprus 65

U.S. 13.5

U.K. 63

Lithuania 10.4

Czech Republic 10.2

Luxembourg 8.8

Ireland 56

Norway 5.7

Austria 53

Germany 5.5

Portugal 5.3

Czech Republic 50

Belgium (Flemish) 5.2

Poland 49

Cyprus 4.5

Spain 4.2

Belgium (French) 4.2

Latvia | Ireland 4.1

France 32

Poland 3.5

Austria 3.4

France 3.1

Netherlands 20

U.K. 2.9

Latvia 17

Denmark 2.4

Germany 13

Netherlands 2.4

Denmark 6 | Belgium (Flemish) 6

Belgium (French) 1

FIGURE 6.1. Classification and inclusive education in Europe and the United States
*Sources*: EADSNE (2005); U.S. DOE (2007); authors' calculations.

inclusive education: between just 1 percent in French-speaking Belgium and 94 percent in Norway receive special education services and support within general classrooms. The United States occupies a spot in the middle of the range on both indicators. Its high inclusion rate derives from the generous definition used here, of spending at least a minority of the school day in a regular classroom, not requiring a qualitative shift toward well-implemented, high-quality inclusive pedagogy. Although Germany, too, has witnessed increases in the proportion of all students classified as having special educational needs (5.5 percent) and thus also falls in the middle of the range, in terms of inclusive education, its 13 percent places it near the bottom in this sample of countries. Such disparities underscore that even within a global context of the growth of special and inclusive education, more attention must be paid to the development of education systems themselves—and to cross-nationally comparative analysis (see Archer 1979, 1982, 1984, 1989). A key factor in these systemic differences analyzed by Margaret Archer was the (de)centralization of education governance, which we discuss next.

It is useful to recall that differences in level of economic development alone did not determine the timing of legislative enunciation of the integration of children with disabilities as a national commitment (see Chapter 4). The variation in dates of legislation, however restricted, is also a reflection of ties to world culture, measured by way of membership in international nongovernmental organizations and other factors. The general pressure to become more similar (isomorphic) derives not only from organizational memberships. Singular events that affirm the human rights of disabled people and of children in particular, such as the aforementioned International Year of People with Disabilities (1981) or the International Convention no doubt generate a global desire to comply with tenets of inclusion, although the tangible impact is difficult to measure. However forcefully these visions may be communicated, the economic, political, and historical differences that played a role in prior legislative events are considerable sources of resistance, as shown in the cases of the United States and Germany (see Chapter 5).

In addition to the influence of factors reflecting global membership and state legitimacy, the structure of a nation's education system and the degree of its (de)centralization in terms of education governance exerted some influence on the legislation of special and inclusive education. In the realm of education policy, nations with a centralized structure enacted school integration and legislation earlier than did nations with decentralized systems. There are a number of reasons for this influence on policy and practice. Centralized systems define state authority as superior or antecedent to local authority; elites' decisions have implications throughout the country, especially through resource allocation and coercively enforced regulations. Decentralized systems tend toward heterogeneity as regional and local decisionmaking processes require debate and consideration of conditions that can be ignored at higher level. Differences in centralization of educational structure bear on the prevalence of segregated, separated, integrative, or inclusive settings. Decentralized systems reinforce existing social structures, arrangements that have long histories sustained by voluntary admissions or state placements. For example, New York City has long maintained a separate special education school district, Number 75, in flagrant disregard of national laws emphasizing school integration but acknowledging the challenges faced by a school district in a tremendously diverse urban environment (Connor 2009). In contrast, by elevating, but not removing powers above local communities, centralized systems modify the degree to which social and demographic patterns could intrude into the decision making. Despite their historical legacy, segregated placements are the last intention and resort of state authority, in large part because such placements would be counter to the general and abstract principles that define centralized authority.

The association between educational structure, as viewed through placements of students with special educational needs in integrative settings, and the measure of centralization in education governance is displayed in Table 6.2. With data from the EADSNE (2006) for nearly two dozen countries, the focus is mainly on western and eastern European countries, which we might expect to be relatively advanced in school integration and inclusive education, given the international and European Union charters calling for such reforms, the normative influence of powerful think tanks like the OECD, and coordinating agencies such as the EADSNE. The data offer an important perspective on contemporary patterns of learning opportunities, particularly

TABLE 6.2.  Students with special educational needs in inclusive education and measures of centralization

| Country | % SEN inclusive* | Centralization / decentralization | |
|---|---|---|---|
| | | 1955 | 2003 |
| Italy | 99 | C | C |
| Portugal | 97 | C | C |
| Norway | 94 | C | C |
| England | 93 | D | C |
| Cyprus | 92 | C | C |
| Malta | 92 | C | C |
| Lithuania | 91 | C | C |
| Iceland | 83 | C | C |
| Spain | 83 | D | C |
| Greece | 77 | C | C |
| Estonia | 74 | — | C |
| Ireland | 60 | D | D |
| Austria | 55 | D | C |
| Poland | 49 | D | D |
| Czech Republic | 48 | D | C |
| Hungary | 47 | C | D |
| Luxembourg | 47 | C | C |
| U.S. | 45 | D | D |
| Finland | 42 | C | D |
| Slovak Republic | 32 | — | D |
| France | 30 | C | D |
| Netherlands | 29 | D | D |
| Germany | 13 | D | D |
| Belgium (Fl) | 9 | D | D |
| Sweden | 4 | D | D |
| Denmark | 5 | D | D |
| Belgium (Fr) | 1 | D | D |
| Switzerland | 1 | D | D |

Sources: *World Survey of Education, Handbook of Organization and Statistics*, Paris: UNESCO (1955, 1971); EADSNE (2003, 2006); U.S. DOE (2005); Reviews of National Policies for Education, Paris: OECD, 1994, 2000, 2002, 2004.

*Percent of all students officially classified as having SEN in inclusive education, for the public sector. Designation of education system as centralized/decentralized based on the legal basis and administrative structure.

on the division between integrative and segregative settings among the developed democracies, which also have long traditions of special and inclusive education.

The data on the proportion of schoolchildren with special educational needs who attend general schools reveal a tremendous range—from 1 percent to 99 percent—suggesting that thus far, no international convention or global trend has had the force necessary to lead to convergence, even within Europe. Neither has school integration or inclusive education been achieved everywhere within the United States, although the continuum of educational environments has shifted toward a more inclusive education system, especially in Vermont and a few other states.

The relationship between educational structure and special educational needs placements is strong, and the extent of centralization is a crucial factor in the type of education system (unitary, dual, or multiple) and the reformability of the educational environments the system provides. We find that majority integrative placements are found in more centralized systems, whereas majority segregative placements are found in decentralized systems (see Table 6.2). This pattern is evident for contemporary indicators of de/centralization in schooling. Utilizing data collected by UNESCO in five volumes of the *World Survey of Education*, the degree of centralization in the governance of education is reported for a year (1955) prior to the massive expansion of general and special education in many of these countries and for a recent year (2003), after the widespread enactment of laws supporting school integration, such as the United States' Individuals with Disabilities Education Act of 1990, and international charters inclusive education (UNESCO 1994).

Upon closer analysis, this association is strengthened by a "pattern within the pattern" in terms of institutional change and reformed educational structures from 1955 to 2005. The cases of England, France, Germany, and the United States exemplify the persistence of institutionalized special educational structures, yet they also show that the distinction between decentralized and centralized is not a sharp divide. Rather, they represent opposite ends of a continuum, with mixed forms abounding in between. As David Baker and Gerald LeTendre (2005) note, it is important to distinguish between an *official* and an *operational* form of centralization. Many nations officially avow a central role of the state in defining education, yet operationally delegate actual administrative discretion to local and regional authorities. If "in the trenches of managing schools there is considerable global movement among nations toward some form of decentralization" (Baker and LeTendre 2005: 138; see also Slater 1993), how has this global trend played out in these four cases?

As ends of a continuum, centralization and decentralization require definition as differing modes of governance. The degree of flexibility between them reflects both historical constraints and contemporary pressures. The former designates the "starting point" from which movement proceeds; the latter determines the pace at which the movement actually occurs. Indeed, "past reforms often have been guided by a false juxtaposition of centralization and decentralization. Both theory and recent experience show that the relationship between decentralization and centralization is complementary as well as conflicting, and centralization can be constructive and enable decentralization rather than oppose and suppress it" (Meyer 2009: 457). Modes of education governance shift between centralization and decentralization, producing varieties in between. This is most conspicuous for England and France, historically prominent examples of decentralized and centralized systems, respectively; but even for other decentralized systems, such as exist in the United States and Germany, the past decades have seen significant changes in education governance. Furthermore, de/centralization of general education governance need not apply to special education to the same extent.

In the U.S., judiciary and legislative advance together have protected minority rights, such as a nationally mandated "free appropriate public education." Special education policy is one field that has seen significant national intervention and facilitated legalization in education. The national Department of Education has funded research on special education and funded lawsuits to enforce its policy priorities when necessary to coerce school districts to comply. Within an otherwise decentralized education system, special and inclusive education reforms have facilitated centralization.

In England, the turn toward centralization was accelerated by the adoption of the National Curriculum in the late 1980s and the corresponding elevation of central authorities. As Stephen Ball (1990: 185, 213) noted, the struggles over a National Curriculum are struggles over the "idea of policy as a discourse," specifically as "refractions" of broader tensions and contradictions. The legislation of a National Curriculum (the Educational Reform Act, 1988) reflected a compromise of ideological orientations, one to the future and modernization, another to the past and traditional values. With the intention of raising the standards of schooling, core subjects and the time devoted to them became prescriptive, removed from the more flexible judgments of local authorities. The once-shared authority between central powers and local education authorities tipped toward the former, away from a "content-led thrust for change to an assessment-led one" (Ball 1990: 157).

In France, the turn has been toward decentralization. In contrast to England, the reversal of France's long history of centralization was less inspired by a conservative restoration than by the bureaucratic constraints inherent in centralized authority itself. The prominence of republican ideals can exaggerate the superiority of exceptional achievement and diminish the importance of responses to the problem of underachievement. The conflicting ideals of meritocracy and equality seem to generate an unintended dynamic that "inevitably produces a gradual elimination of students encountering difficulties as they move through the education system," which, in turn, heightens the need to "promote decentralized decisions" (Plaisance 2007). Equality is embodied in the "Rule of Law" where rules "have to be limited, precise, general, universal, predictable and fixed" but "quite indifferent to its consequences" (Bélanger 2001: 339). However, with a democratic pressure to extend rights, to articulate an "equality *in* the law," a new jurisprudence "allows interpretations sensitive to particular situations," resulting in the antinomy in which "an attempt to change the generality of the law [through] similar treatment of different cases results in unfairness" (Bélanger 2001: 340). The turn to a bureaucratic differentiation, with legislative amendments intended to curtail provisions to the particular needs of children, becomes the new republican ideal. The consequences, unintended but predictable, can be excesses in labeling and a resurgence of segregative placements.

Changes in degree of centralization have also affected the extent of school integration (mainstreaming) and inclusive education in Germany and the United States, but in opposite directions. These countries, having continuously borrowed each other's educational ideas and concepts (Drewek 2002), also unite the unusual mixture of federal democracies with decentralized control over education content and financing with more centralized rules for special, often unequal, groups of students, such as disabled, disadvantaged, and immigrant children (Meyer 1992: 236). These countries' special education institutions were originally quite similarly exclusionary and reform efforts have thus strived to implement inclusive education. Yet the German and American systems have diverged considerably over time as they continue to conform to the institutional logic of the education system, becoming less similar over the twentieth century as each developed isomorphically to the general education system (see Chapter 5).

The United States moved toward a more centralized, coercive federalism, especially regarding the school integration of minority groups, first and foremost the forcible racial desegregation of the American South. For special education, this turn was based on national legislation, such as Public Law 94-142, the Education for All Handicapped Children Act (EAHCA) passed in 1975, which we discuss in more depth in the next chapter. That watershed law facilitated innumerable lawsuits as parents and advocates sought to realize the right to school integration. The principle "separate is not equal"—powerfully argued in *Brown v. Board of Education* (1954) several decades prior to enactment of the EAHCA—ultimately also guaranteed school integration as a civil right for children with disabilities.

In distinct contrast, Germany's national government has had reduced influence over all matters relating to schooling. This was not just a response to the denouement of Hitler's totalitarian state. The power of smaller states in German history and identification with regional culture have led to a wariness toward national efforts. The Standing Conference of *Länder* Culture Ministers (*Kultusministerkonferenz*, KMK), made up of representatives of the sixteen *Länder*, struggles to come to a consensus regarding matters of education. Often, extended deliberations are oriented toward minimal concensus that maintains the status quo or allow at most incremental change. The limits on the national government regarding school policies were further intensified by the federalism reform of 2006. Although disability policies and advocacy coalitions are national in scope, special and inclusive education policies and their finance remain resolutely the prerogative of the *Länder*. Furthermore, unlike in the United States where the right to education integration has been adjudicated in thousands of court cases, Germany's courts have not worked in concert with legislative advances, which are the prerogative of the *Länder*, to protect this minority group's interests.

For these countries, we can define a sociological commonality: the direction each moves is away from its starting point. In England, the movement was toward centralization. In France, it was toward decentralization. Germany also moved toward further decentralization. The United States became more centralized. Thus, it remains to be seen how much influence international charters, such as the International Convention discussed at the outset, will have on the continuing legalization and standardization of education. The convention, once ratified, must then be interpreted into national and regional laws. Court decisions are required to adjudicate appropriate placements among the broad range of educational environments and thus different learning opportunities offered.

## CONCLUSIONS

To evaluate the impact of the recent, at times contradictory, international forces of achieving education for all, high standards of education performance, and inclusive education—and to uncover the extent and effect of the expansion of education more broadly—we compared an array of countries. To better understand the broader international patterns, we discussed special education systems and education governance. The broad European comparison manifests the tremendous range of responses to culturally specific definitions and categories within "special educational needs." The findings accentuate national differences in the definition of special educational needs, in ideologies of education, and in institutionalized (special and inclusive) educational structures. Despite these considerable differences, countries around the world have signed the International Convention on the Rights of Persons with Disabilities, which calls unequivocally for inclusive education for all.

Although attempts to realize the goal of education for all may have been (recently) achieved in developed countries, the aim of inclusive education remains significantly challenged—especially for secondary and tertiary levels of education—nearly everywhere. In Europe, few countries have fully embraced the unitary model of educating all students together in general classrooms.

Some countries, such as Italy and Norway, long ago reached consensus and moved quickly in that direction, but most continue to struggle to commit to the realization of inclusive education, which requires considerable restructuring. The type of education system—unitary, dual, or multiple—along with de/centralization of education governance that structures the possibilities for change, have undergone fundamental change in very few countries.

Special education organizations have served a population of students continuously changing in size and composition, but especially representing poor boys, children belonging to racial, ethnic, migrant, or linguistic minority groups, and increasingly integrated children with disabilities. It is these diverse student bodies that most challenge rationalized, standardized organizational structures of special education systems. Which disadvantages should be compensated, how much the compensation should be, in which school settings the compensation should take place, and what level of school certification should result remains a matter of continued debate.

Ambivalence toward special education highlights the tension between equality of opportunity and merit measured in school performance and by standardized testing. Resistance to the reforms and restructuring necessary to successfully realize inclusive education relies on the legitimated institutional logic of each national education system, whether focused on segregation (dual track) or separation (multitrack) or inclusion (unitary). These reflect societal values and ideologies of education as they frame the interests that successfully fought for special education's diffusion and differentiation. The institutionalization of special education and the myriad vested interests in the status quo pose barriers to inclusive education as a paradigm that has gathered force over the past several decades.

Within Europe, special education continues to be organized in a tremendous variety of ways, despite (gradual) movement toward more school integration and inclusive education. Holding national education systems accountable for *all* students' educational performance and adequate qualification requires recognition of persistent segregation or separation and stigmatization of children and youth with special educational needs, who more often than not are already among the disadvantaged. However, the resulting additional disadvantages in learning opportunities, educational attainments, and life chances are something that few societies, despite egalitarian rhetoric, have eagerly confronted.

Significant differences exist between and within these societies in the ways in which groups of disabled students are socially defined and sorted into education programs, the degree to which they are integrated into general school systems or inclusive classrooms, and the certification level to which they are allowed to aspire. Considerable inequalities in learning opportunities persist; in many countries, segregation is still the dominant organizational mode of providing special education support and services. Internationally, inclusive education has risen as a goal, as it promises to more fully utilize the diversity of interests and abilities found among all groups of children to develop each individual's intellectual and social competencies. However, inertia throughout education systems has hindered the reforms that would do most to enable inclusive schooling.

International comparisons emphasize that to explain why particular students have special educational needs and to understand their educational careers demands further in-depth analyses of education systems themselves. We have shown that special and inclusive education systems provide these children and youth with differential educational environments in which to learn. Special education participation rates are dramatically affected by contextual factors, analyzed here via classifications and categories, through the institutionalized organizational forms, and with respect to education governance. The simultaneous rise of segregation and inclusion likewise emphasizes not the individual characteristics, but rather institutionalized organizations that provide education and training. The seemingly paradoxical rise—indeed, the coexistence—of both school segregation and inclusion depends on continued expansion in the group of children and youth who receive additional resources to access the curriculum. However, the logic of segregation that posits separation as necessary to provide such individualized learning supports contradicts the powerful idea codified in international charters that to strengthen democracy and enable active citizenship requires nothing less than inclusive education for all.

# RIGHTS, LIBERTIES, AND EDUCATION IN "LEAST" AND "MOST" RESTRICTIVE ENVIRONMENTS

*Contrasting Futures of Public Education and Juvenile Justice*

with Doug Judge

INVESTIGATING A FURTHER PARADOX FOUND in special education, this chapter compares institutional change, especially owing to ongoing legalization in American education, in two arenas: public (special) education and state correctional institutions. We identify the different rights, liberties, and access to education that youth in the United States have been provided in these contrasting environments since 1970. The analysis begins before special education expansion reached every public school and before rights-based initiatives joined traditional concerns about conditions of confinement within state correctional facilities and the rise of juvenile crime and incarceration.

Over the past four decades, we argue, public education and correctional institutions have moved in opposite directions in terms of education rights. Whereas special education has withdrawn somewhat from the primary concern of the right to education (and school integration), state correctional facilities have adopted the right to education as a key concern. Paradoxically, the discourse of confinement joins the prior initiation and long-term solidification of rights, whereas a discourse of rights evolves within confinement, which previously did little to justify its limitation of education and treatment rights. These divergent paths accentuate the necessity to acknowledge and engage the interconnectedness of special education with other systems and institutions that serve disadvantaged children and youth, those who are deemed "abnormal" or "deviant," and those with recognized special educational needs.

The passage of Public Law 94-142, the Education for All Handicapped Children Act (EAHCA), in 1975, is without dispute among the few federal-level actions that have fundamentally altered the structure and practice of American education. It was preceded by numerous attempts at federal coercion, such as the Smith-Hughes National Vocational Education Act of 1917, which secured vocational education within public schools by providing financial support and guidelines and deterred the construction of a dual system of education and in-firm training. The Supreme Court decision *Brown v. Board of Education* in 1954 inaugurated attempts to desegregate public schools, which process required federal troops. For its part, the EAHCA affirmed that *all* children, regardless of "handicapping condition," have a right to a free and appropriate education (FAPE) in the "least restrictive environment" (LRE). The "mainstreaming" law, as it was known in the parlance of the day, was reauthorized and renamed the Individuals with Disabilities Education Act (IDEA) in 1990. The IDEA, together with the mandatory provisions of Section 504 of the Vocational Rehabilitation Act (1973), prohibits discrimination against individuals with disabilities by any agency or program receiving federal funding (Turnbull and Turnbull 2000), which includes all public schools. The IDEA assigns policy priority to the LRE, making this law a legislative foundation for inclusive education, at the same time that a continuum of educational environments and services must be available in order to guarantee a free and appropriate education (FAPE) chosen by parents and professionals. In distinct contrast to both the Smith-Hughes Act and *Brown*, the core intention of the EAHCA/IDEA—to guarantee school integration as a right of all children regardless of their dis/ability—was passed with surprisingly little resistance owing to a unique coalition (see Melnick 1995; Chapter 5). However, as with the Smith-Hughes Act and *Brown*, attempts to implement its rules and regulations and reform education systems can reveal barriers and activate reactionary forces that are often not anticipated.

Although the conditions of commitment and confinement in detention centers or prisons obviously and purposefully present circumstances unlike other institutionalized settings, the broad implications inherent in claims that institutionalized persons have a constitutional right to appropriate *treatment* and incarcerated youth have a constitutional right to *education* may not have been so clearly anticipated. Although the initial intention of the EAHCA was designed largely around the restructuring of public schools to provide enhanced access through accommodations and participatory rights for children with disabilities, the full breadth of this intention has expanded. Now education rights are being deliberated even in settings of confinement, ones that by definition are far from being a "least restrictive" environment. If their purpose is to restrict by sanctioning freedom of interactions and limiting social participation, the Juvenile Justice and Delinquency Prevention Act of 1974 actually called for "deinstitutionalization," as this system has faced many similar criticisms that special education has. A further similarity is that both systems—special education and those designed to address juvenile delinquency—exhibit conflicting paradigms that continue to be discussed controversially. Although the punitive approach has been challenged by a model of human development that relies on neurological, psychological, and social research (see Scott and Steinberg 2008), the United States remains the country with the highest incarceration rate in the world.[1]

Both special education and juvenile justice systems have faced continuous reform pressures, not the least owing to the dramatic rise in costs (Parrish 2001; Pew 2008). We focus our review on the legal developments in both systems, which testify to the ongoing evaluation of paternalistic and punitive approaches to disability and deviance among children and youth that have evolved since the Enlightenment (see Chapter 1).

Although these systems seem to have diametrically opposite foundational principles, they overlap in regard to the societal ambivalence toward them and in terms of the main groups they serve. Males, certain racial and ethnic minorities, and children and youth who live in poverty are overrepresented in both special education and juvenile justice. The number of youth in public and private correctional facilities is upward of 125,000, and of this population the predominant number are males from poor households and of African American heritage (Snyder and Sickmund 1999: 192). Surveys of administrators of state correctional facilities yield mean estimations of disabilities that range from 28 percent to 42 percent in their population (Rutherford, Nelson, and Wolford 1985). In their meta-analysis of studies on the prevalence of officially recognized disabilities in correctional settings, Casey and Keilitz (1990) reported a weighted average prevalence estimate of 35.6 percent for "learning disabled" juvenile offenders and 12.6 percent for "mentally retarded" offenders. In spite of the usual methological problems that complicate such meta-analyses, such as variations in definitions, diagnostic instruments, absence of controls, and political constraints in reporting, the authors found "penetration into the legal system" to be the only variable to correlate with reported prevalence rates of learning disabilities (Casey and Keilitz 1990: 95). Thus, estimations of prevalence rates increase as juveniles progress through the legal system. Likewise, the prevalence of student disabilities—in contrast to congenital impairments—that develop during educational careers and are based on relative school performance increases in each cohort as it passes through primary and makes the transition to secondary schooling. Thus, the "risk" of disability diagnosis in both systems increases with age and duration in the system.

The magnitude of prevalence figures, coupled with the evidence that they increase the further juvenile offenders pass through the legal system, are facts that are reminiscent of the problem of "racial overrepresentation" in special education classes revealed in the late 1960s—and that has bedeviled special education since (see, for example, Mercer 1971, 1973; Kirp 1973; Losen and Orfield 2002). Yet the issues of treatment and special education in correctional and residential institutions are more specific to their settings (Smith, Ramirez, and Rutherford 1983), and this has informed debates and judicial claims in ways that distinguish them from public education. These claims have defined legal jurisdictions with their own judicial case law and momentum.

The basis of the paradox discussed here is that from conditions of restriction and confinement, legal arguments and judicial decisions to guarantee treatments and education rights have expanded the most, with a greater potential to reach further into a variety of circumstances compared with arguments and judicial decisions from conditions of voluntary participation that govern education, which have become circumscribed. Analyzing this paradox, the case-law evidence examined here addresses its empirical merits and suggests implications for social and education policies that must address the increasing overlap—in terms of rights and legal situations—of youth with disadvantages and disabilities within public schools, in residential institutions, and in juvenile correctional facilities.

We first review the twin claims of the right to *treatment* and to *education* in the restricted settings of state residential institutions and in juvenile correctional facilities, respectively. Here, we focus on the crucial common roots of these twin claims and offer specific citations to show how they have both "traveled" to public education and yet have their own developmental paths within state institutions. From this review, we turn to the conceptualization of the case law and the analytical strategies that will be employed.

## RIGHTS TO TREATMENT AND EDUCATION IN RESTRICTED SETTINGS

### Residential Institutions and the Right to Treatment

Theoretical and legal consideration of the right to treatment arose first in matters of involuntary commitment, including cases of tuberculosis, alcoholism, and mental illness. In likely the first statement on the "new right" to treatment, Birnbaum (1960) proposed that the courts consider that persons institutionalized for mental illness be given adequate medical treatment so that they may regain their health and therewith their liberty. Moreover, he proposed that the courts consider this right "as a necessary and overdue development of our present concept of due process of law" (Birnbaum 1960: 503; also Murdock 1972) and do so independent of any action of whichever legislature.

The first decisive court case for residential commitments was *Rouse v. Cameron* (1966). Filed in Washington, DC, in 1966, the claim was made that the hospital in which Charles Rouse had been involuntarily committed had been transformed into a penitentiary because it lacked the appropriate treatment for Rouse. Most importantly, the court declared that mere availability did not fulfill the legal responsibility. Rather, the standard was "adequacy in light of present knowledge." That is, the state must demonstrate that it sought to find and make available adequate treatment given Rouse's particular condition. Failing to do so would be a violation of procedural due process rights, for confinement without treatment is punishment, thereby requiring criminal procedural safeguards (Renn 1973: 480). Indeed, shortly thereafter the right to treatment was joined to the constitutional due process level in *Nason v. Superintendent of Bridgewater State Hospital* (1968) (Birnbaum and Twerski 1972: 554).

The major focus of right to treatment claims was certainly the care of persons with mental disabilities and illnesses in private and state hospitals and institutions. *Wyatt v. Stickney* (1971) was the most significant initial decision articulating the constitutional rights of institutionalized "retarded" persons. In *Wyatt*, the Alabama federal court appeared to vindicate the constitutional rights of residents to appropriate treatment and required the implementation of service standards at the Partlow home for "retarded" children. But *Wyatt* was decided by a greater reliance on a reference to involuntary commitment than on the affirmation of a constitutional right to treatment, for "[by] fortuity, at Partlow most of the retarded children had been involuntarily committed under Alabama law" (Burt 1975: 299). By fortuity, *Wyatt* could rely on the precedent set in *Rouse*. But its real impact may have derived from how it opened for questioning the real difference between involuntary and voluntary placement, for "in many state retarded institutions, children are not formally committed but rather are 'voluntarily' placed by their parents" (Burt 1975: 299). Equally reasonable would be the claim that (exceptional) children are "involuntarily" placed in separate, special education classes or segregated, special schools, with or without the acquiescence of their parents. The dominance of professionals and official gatekeepers, inflexibility in the delivery of resources, lack of transparency, and even misunderstanding of the differences and consequences of different educational environments among parents and guardians all question the in/voluntary divide. At minimum, in this early case, a path of deliberation was formed from the state institution to public education. This connection would strengthen over time, as we show below.

The relevance of *Rouse* and *Wyatt* to the education rights of children with disabilities became evident in the key cases that set the stage for the EAHCA.

Building on the landmark 1954 *Brown v. Board of Education* decision, judicial and legislative answers to the questions of access to special education and other service provisions and concerning integration came in the form of *PARC v. Pennsylvania* (1972) and *Mills v. Board of Education* (1972). These two cases stipulated "consent decrees," or orders, as constitutional support for integrated schooling: as a result of the court cases, school systems agreed to provide appropriate services and programs for disabled children while including them within general school classrooms to the maximum extent possible (Minow 1990: 30). In *Mills*, the right to a publicly supported education was extended to children previously excluded as "uneducable"; in *PARC*, the right to a free and publicly supported education to all "retarded" school children was mandated, as well as a host of procedural due process rights. In contrast to *Wyatt*, however, *Mills* and *PARC* rested their claims on more concrete grounds: exclusion of "retarded" children from public schools on the assumption they were "uneducable" amounted to an unconstitutionally invidious discrimination. As a consequence, the right to treatment "traveled" to public schooling (see *Diana v. State Board of Education* [1970]; *Spangler v. Pasadena City Board of Education* [1970]; *Covarrubias v. San Diego* [1971]; *Guadalupe v. Tempe* [1972]). This process gave strength to the judicial language of a "free appropriate public education," which would take thousands of court cases to adjudicate in the decades following passage of the EAHCA (see, e.g., Turnbull and Turnbull 2000).

As the lessons of the court decisions on the "right to treatment" were applied to public education, it began to assume some differences in meaning and application in the myriad of residential institutions. One important outcome of *Wyatt* was the passage of the Civil Rights of Institutionalized Persons Act in 1980, which significantly broadened the jurisdictional powers of the Attorney General to act on behalf of institutionalized persons by monitoring state policies or, more actively, by intervening against practices in state-operated facilities. This expanded role at the federal level is best exemplified by the Supreme Court case of *Youngberg v. Romeo* (1982). Although *Youngberg* is the Supreme Court's first decision on the constitutional rights of institutionalized "retarded" persons, it set forth a number of "liberty interests" that were argued to be protected by the due process clause of the Fourteenth

Amendment to the Constitution. These included the right to reasonable care and safety, freedom from bodily restraint, adequate food, shelter, clothing and medical care, and adequate training and habilitation to ensure safety and freedom from bodily restraint (Cornwell 1988: 845).

In public education, the course taken in the sequence from *PARC* and *Mills* to the EAHCA and beyond becomes more contested. The connection between "right to treatment" and "appropriate education" was most visibly evident in the first special education case decided by the U.S. Supreme Court. In *Board of Education v. Rowley* (1982), the Court reversed the court of appeals by arguing that a school district did not have to provide a sign language interpreter as a "related service" to comply with the intent of the EAHCA. The Court held that the intent of FAPE was met to the extent that a school district made available an education opportunity that was *comparable* to that received by nondisabled children and to the extent the district engaged a professional team in the construction of an Individualized Education Program. In essence, *Rowley* stopped at the question of *how* a meaningful education would or could be achieved, addressing only the right to *pursue* it.

The right to treatment has been invoked in claims seeking the fulfillment of procedural rights intended by statutory and legislative acts. In *Frederick L. v. Thomas* (1977), the argument was made that failure to conduct comprehensive assessment resulted in the de facto exclusion of a significant number of students from special provisions for those with learning disabilities. It is noteworthy here that *Frederick L.* reversed the arguments in minority overrepresentation claims, for it sought expanded testing, contending that without such assessments it could not be known if placement in regular classes was appropriate. Such testing also reflects the tenet of the EAHCA that stipulates "child find" activities: the initial search for children illegitimately excluded from public schooling (Baker 2002). Indeed, national assessments of school performance are significant as a source of referrals to special education and are crucial in distinguishing learning disabilities according to the most prevalent "discrepancy" model that relies on measuring the gap between tested IQ and actual school performance in attempts to quantify underachievement.

The decisions in such cases as *Rowley* and *Frederick L.* suggest that the relationship between LRE and a free and appropriate education contains antinomous features that could lead away from mainstreaming, actually reducing the potential for school integration, depending on controversial interpretations. In *Irving Independent School District v. Tatro* (1984), the school district and the U.S. District Court agreed that Amber Tatro's need for catheterization may be needed for life support, but that it was not related to her ability to learn. The Supreme Court reversed this interpretation, affirming that the medical service was required to fulfill the intent of FAPE, thus blurring significantly the lines between treatment and education. Accordingly, Amber could stay in her local school, and the district had to pay for the service. The potential for a somewhat different consequence was suggested in *Honig v. Doe* (1988). Although affirming that the intent of Congress was to strip schools of their traditional unilateral authority to exclude students with disabilities, *Honig* nonetheless sought to balance the interests of parents, students, and school officials. In doing so, the Court upheld the "stay put" provision of the EAHCA. The provision could be invoked to keep children with disabilities in their school placement, even if disciplinary behaviors prompted school officials to seek to remove them. However, if their current placement is in private or partially segregated settings, the provision could be invoked to sustain these arrangements.

Likewise, mainsteaming was and is subject to a range of interpretations. Emphasizing the danger of schools' failure to provide accommodations, increase accessibility, and train teachers, Lane's (1995) metaphor of "drowning in the mainstream" is compelling, for mainstreaming without adequate provisions could be interpreted as injurious to learning. Whereas from one perspective mainstreaming would be placement in a "least restrictive setting" and thus fulfilling the intent of the EAHCA, from another it would not be fulfilling a deaf child's constitutional right to treatment. The achievement of education for all is a relatively recent success even in the United States, and the debate rages on about the subjective interpretation of what a "free appropriate public education" consists of, which can only be decided on a case-by-case basis. Nevertheless, the rights and needs of individual students are primary here, not the preferences and prerogatives of the system. By contrast, in the juvenile justice system—by its very nature punitive—such deliberations as to appropriate treatments and education rights might well come to very different conclusions.

*Juvenile Correctional Institutions and the Right to Education*

Two paths have led to the affirmation of the right to education within juvenile correctional settings. The first path is rooted in the language of state and territorial constitutions that declare the right to an education to be an extension of a general and uniform public school system. Such language is typically followed by the assertion that race, color, or caste cannot be the basis or reason for discriminatory preference. An original constitutional declaration that all children residing within the borders of the state have a fundamental right to an education was argued to impose a "paramount duty" on the state or territory to provide education to youth—whether in prison or not (Tyack, James, and Benavot 1987: 145). Moreover, the burden of this duty falls on the system of school districts and cannot be diminished by alternative providers. To discriminate because of incarceration is no different than to discriminate on the basis of race, color, or caste.

A second path arose independently of these original assertions and in distinct contrast to the first path. As the racial, cultural, and economic diversity of the larger population is reflected in the institutionalized population, the prevalence and incidence of physical or mental disabilities overlap with circumstances of juvenile correctional incarceration.[2] In *Creek v. Stone* (1967), the District of Columbia recognized that juveniles had a right to effective treatment "promised" by juvenile law. In the case of *Creek*, the federal district court stopped short of requiring that the juvenile court determine the adequacy of treatment, declaring only that the court should determine its jurisdiction over such an issue. Nonetheless, *Creek* signaled a shift away from the historical reliance on *parens patria*—the power of the government to substitute for the parent of any individual in need of protection from abuse or negligence by a parent, legal guardian, or informal caregiver—as the rationale for the absence of due process rights. Indeed, in *Morales v. Texas* (1974), the theory of *parens patria* was invoked as grounds for requiring proper assessment that might in turn require special education.

Symbolizing the difficulty of separating treatment from education, with the decision of *In re Harris* (1967), the right to treatment reached beyond the juvenile court by explicitly identifying *education* provisions as the necessary and effective treatment. Harris, a deaf-mute person, was found to be a neglected minor and held as a ward of the state (Illinois) in a facility that had no provisions for profoundly deaf and mute persons. In the judgment of *Harris*, the juvenile court judge affirmed that authorities were constitutionally obliged to provide appropriate treatment for Harris's impairment, specifically "to arrange forthwith for the daily transportation . . . to the . . . high school . . . in order that he may *attend the special classes* offered in said school for the deaf and mute" (*Criminal Law Reporter* 1968: 2412, emphasis added). Beyond the importance of basing the right to treatment on constitutional grounds, *Harris* exemplified how special education could be defined as appropriate treatment for the adjudication of delinquency. The profession of special education is viewed as the most legitimate provider of support and services for those with special educational needs, its focus for centuries.

For a number of states and territories, an original affirmation that education is a right enjoyed by all children residing within the borders of the state can and has been interpreted as *absolute*, one that cannot be disabled by some compelling state interest or invaded by legislative action (*Seattle School District vs. State* 1978; *Sunsirae Tunstall et al. v. Teresa Bergeson* 1998). Even if the right to education is not seen as absolute, the intent of legislative action or of state correctional authorities to limit or restrict the delivery of education to incarcerated or disabled youth often fails strict scrutiny reviews. Possibly the greatest test is balancing the educational intent of federal legislation with the task and responsibility of maintaining a secure and safe correctional facility. In *Willie M. v. Hunt* (1979), the consent decree upheld the right to appropriate education for seriously violent (juvenile) offenders, despite the greater disciplinary measures that must be taken and the greater financial cost to the state. In response, the North Carolina legislature took measures to establish a reserve fund to meet anticipated costs (Wood 1987: 90).

An even broader outcome is *Johnson v. Upchurch*, filed in 1986 and settled in 1993. Beginning with the individual complaint of Matthew Johnson against conditions of confinement he experienced at a juvenile justice facility near Tucson, it soon became a class action suit charging the Arizona Department of Juvenile Corrections with failing to provide special education services. The settlement in 1993 was sweeping, requiring an outside committee of consultants to oversee the implementation of the consent decree—in effect extending the challenge to Arizona juvenile corrections in its entirety (Leone and Meisel 1997).

As these diverse cases demonstrate, the boundaries between corrections and special education are not being made firm, rather, they are becoming more fluid over time. Indeed, these court decisions reach far beyond one organization to affect entire organizational fields. This calls into question the distinction between social and education policies. It also makes the boundaries between juvenile justice and special education—those systems that serve children with disadvantages and disabilities and delinquent youth—more permeable.

## JUDICIAL CHALLENGES TO THE RIGHT TO EDUCATION AND CONDITIONS OF CONFINEMENT AND THE DIVERGENCE OF PUBLIC EDUCATION AND JUVENILE JUSTICE

The comparison of public schools and correctional facilities or residential institutions suggests a divergence in the *sequential progression* of judicial challenges that have sought in various ways to implement the rights to treatment and / or education. In public education, we find a discernible progression that has traveled from an argument founded on constitutional rights of equal protection and procedural due process, minimizing alternative strategies that focused on individual grievances, involuntary servitude, exclusionary language of state education statutes, and even the right to treatment (Lippman and Goldberg 1973: 20–22). The progression has led to debates over particulars that contest and unintentionally limit the scope of the EAHCA/IDEA (Kauffman and Hallahan 1995; Richardson 1999: 165). One consequence has been the renewed rise of historically separated populations, such as deaf children (Bina 1995; Lane 1995). As we saw in the previous chapter, expanding inclusive education does not necessary require a decline in segregation rates, as the overall school-age population with diagnosed special educational needs continues to rise. In contrast, for restrictive settings, we discern a trend from particular challenges against conditions of confinement to the declaration that even institutionalized persons and incarcerated youth maintain their constitutional right not only to an education, but also to an education that matches the specific services and support that are provided in general or special public schools. In sum, we argue that in struggles between conditions of confinement, treatments, and education rights, public education and state institutions are moving in opposite directions.

Claims against the conditions of confinement address such matters as physical space and modes of discipline. Such claims are primarily corrective, for they call for modification of conditions more than their elimination (Parent et al. 1994). Often embedded in such challenges are claims for liberty interests that raise issues of health, freedom from bodily restraint, medical care, and personal safety. The reference to liberty interests expands the scope of a challenge, implying the addition of rights that may go beyond the immediate circumstances of physical space and discipline.

Here we explore the sequential progression of these forms of court challenge in the body of case law for (1) special education in public schools and (2) juvenile correctional facilities. The comparative examination of the two bodies of law is guided by the following propositions:

> P1: Public Education has been moving from a general Right to Education toward specific challenges of Conditions of Confinement; while

> P2: Correctional institutions have been moving from specific challenges of Conditions of Confinement toward a general Right to Education.

Certainly the challenges are not wholly distinct from each other. Rather, claims against the conditions of confinement may be expected to overlap with right to treatment claims. And challenges against the conditions of confinement will "anticipate," as it were, the right to treatment. This dialectical relation in turn promotes claims for liberty interests, out of which arise constitutional claims for a right to education. Within the development of case law, the right to education is, therefore, a consequence of this prior temporal sequence.

For special education within public education, three categories of cases are compared: qualification, due process, and related services (for overviews of the cases, see Thomas and Denzinger 1993; Murdick, Gartin, and Crabtree 2002).[3] "Qualification" refers to the category of cases that encompass challenges seeking FAPE and challenges against improper diagnosis and placement. Whereas the former instances seek access to provisions, the latter seek redress from improperly applied provisions. Both invoke rights as the basis for their claims and share affinities in their common reference to constitutional standards. Thus, *Mills* and *PARC*, as the celebrated cases that extended provisions to children with mental disabilities, share affinities with equally celebrated cases of *Larry P. v. Riles* (1972) and *Diana vs. State Board of Education* (1970) in California that challenged the use of intelligence tests on grounds that they were inherently biased and resulted in a restriction of access to a free appropriate public education. Qualification cases represent the category designated as the right to education.

In contrast, "due process" cases encompass challenges that address procedural issues, such as failure to inform parents of their rights to counsel or professional consultation and failure to conduct impartial hearings or mediations with all necessary parties involved. Due process cases encompass issues of education rights as well as matters of liberty interests. These cases are identified as the category of due process, signifying liberty interests that are intermediate between the right to education and conditions of confinement.

The "conditions of confinement" category encompasses cases that address specific issues of the immediate treatment or education of a disabled child. Involving issues that are akin to conditions of confinement, the category "related services" refers to matters of physical access to facilities, of access to medical treatments to enable participation in classroom instruction, of measures of discipline for disruptive behavior, and of the length of the school year. In the context of public education, however, the conditions of confinement category relates to the availability of resources within the physical context of the classroom or the instructional setting. Cases involving related services in public education are identified as signifying conditions of confinement in juvenile corrections.

For correctional facilities, similar categories have been distinguished, yet the sequential progression is reversed. The initial court challenges against incarceration addressed conditions of confinement. Following these challenges, cases that combined issues of confinement with inferences to constitutional rights were identified as the intermediary category of liberty interests. Finally, cases that invoked the right of incarcerated youth to an education equivalent to public schooling constitute the category of right to education.

*The Sequences in Special Education and Juvenile Corrections*

The cases brought against public schools show a sequential progression in the categories of qualification, due process, and related services (see Figure 7.1). Although the three categories display a common trend, rising from the mid-1970s to a peak in the late 1980s, and then descending, there is a sequential order. The qualification category is the largest category of cases at the beginning of the period of observation, quickly advancing to the peak before the others. Most notable is its disappearance by the middle of the 1990s. Following qualification is the category of cases pertaining to due process. This lags behind qualification, yet also nearly disappears by the late 1990s. The category of cases involving related services, interpreted as signifying conditions of confinement, lags behind both qualification and due process, yet evidences the strongest presence in the last time period. These results offer some support for a *sequence* of progression for public education. The direction appears to be from the right to education, which implies a historical movement toward expansion and access, to liberty interests, to related services / conditions of confinement.

In analyzing case law for juvenile justice and correctional facilities, we find the reverse sequence (see Table 7.1). Examining the cases in special education from 1970 to 2006 that involve juvenile correctional facilities, the

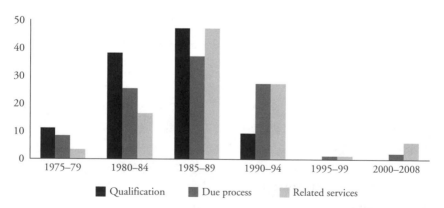

FIGURE 7.1. Sequential progression of case categories in U.S. special education, 1975–2008
*Sources*: Thomas and Denzinger (1993); Murdick, Gartin, and Crabtree (2002).

TABLE 7.1. Sequential progression of case categories in U.S. juvenile corrections, 1970–2006

| Years | 1970–73 | 1974–76 | 1977–79 | 1980–82 | 1983–85 | 1986–38 | 1989–1991 | 1992–94 | 1995–97 | 1998–2000 | 2001–3 | 2004–6 |
|---|---|---|---|---|---|---|---|---|---|---|---|---|
| Rights to education only | | | | | | | 11 | | | 30, 31 | | 37, 38 |
| Rights to education and conditions of confinement (liberty interests) | | 2 | 3 | | 5, 6, 7 | 8, 9, 10 | 12, 13, 14, 15 | 17, 18, 19, 20, 21 | 23, 24, 25, 26, 27, 28, 29 | 32, 33 | 34, 35, 36 | 39, 40, 41, 42 |
| Conditions of confinement only | 1 | | | 4 | | | 16 | 22 | | | | |

*Notes:* Total number of cases: 42.
Cases coded by the Center on Education, Disability, and Juvenile Justice (EDJJ) = 31; see www.edjj.org/Litigation/litchartOct05.pdf.
Cases coded by the authors = 11.
For cases not coded by the EDJJ, rights cases are defined as those in which the right to an education is clearly the primary focus of the complaint, and confinement cases are defined as those cases in which the educational issue is not the primary concern in the complaint, but rather one of a long list of conditions presented to the court.

most intense development occurred in the eight-year period from 1989 through 1997, during which both rights and confinement were of concern. Whereas the prior period witnessed only two cases that dealt with conditions of confinement and no cases dealing exclusively with rights, the later period produces the opposite trend. In the latest period, a number of cases focused solely on the definition and defense of rights, without addressing conditions of confinement. As noted by the diagonal arrow, the direction is especially clear for correctional facilities: court challenges have progressed from conditions of confinement to liberty interests to the right to education.


## DISCUSSION AND CONCLUSIONS

Public education and correctional institutions, representing the least and most restrictive environments, have moved in opposite directions since the early 1970s. This dynamic was found in the process of accumulation of decisions in case law. It could be expected that special education law would become increasingly enmeshed in procedural issues as special education programs diffused throughout the United States into all school districts and thus developed organizationally within public schooling. In this respect, due process and related services are measures of its maturation. Bolstered by many hundreds of cases, special education has indeed come a long way since the EAHCA was passed in 1975.[4]

Especially in the American context of substantial legalization of (special) education (see Neal and Kirp 1986), there are good reasons to explain the progression in public education as related to the way case law develops. Logically, the move from confinement issues to liberty interests is a change from corrective to expansionary claims. As such, it reflects a move from internal to external influences. The discourse on rights exemplifies references to legal doctrines and the rights they purportedly ensure, which greatly expand the depth and scope of claims (Tushnet 1984; Unger 1986; Fischl 1987; Black 1989: 5). The constitutional legal referents involve the standards of scrutiny, the level of legal test that underlies the topic of challenge in each case. The expansionary effect of liberty interests may be especially so in cases that challenge state institutions, for here the "object of litigation is the vindication of constitutional or statutory policies, not a resolution to a contest between private parties about private rights" (Chayes 1976: 1284). Moreover, decisions by courts rendered on claims against public institutions involve "structural injunctions" (Diver 1979; Resnick 1982; Horowitz 1983: 1266). Such injunctions can range from continued judicial reviews to the formal displacement of institutional officers. At minimum, the authority of such officers to manage institutions is in some manner challenged. Cognizant of their impact, judges will be guided by the principle of interest balancing. Yet this guide is itself shaped by the way existing institutional rules and practices interact with the changing ideological positions adopted by judges and lawyers: "The structure of legal constraints and modes of proceeding have evolved in a way that is congenial to the new conceptions, but the new conceptions could not have been put into effect without the preexisting structure of rules and traditions" (Horowitz 1983: 1269).

Such inherent dynamics notwithstanding, the sequential progression away from rights and toward conditions of confinement is not sufficiently explained by such immanent workings of the law. When compared with court challenges in correctional institutions, the pattern of divergence suggests that such immanent explanations are misplaced. In place of such ontogenetic explanations, the pattern of divergence is better explained as a reflection of two institutions that have been deeply interconnected, both historically and sociologically.

Historically, special education originated at a time when the deviance of delinquency was mainly confined to reform schools as distinct and separate institutions. A broader sequential progression defined this organic interconnection, which was laid out, in Chapter 1 for England and France: compulsory education laws were enacted only *after* states had established lunatic asylums, reform schools, and an array of other organizational forms. With this preselection of the school-age population, and hence the exclusion of children and youth with disadvantages and disabilities, public education could presume to be a public institution, situated within the public sphere and accessible to all deemed "educable." Yet, the rules defining access to public education were fashioned in negative terms. Admission to public education was a residual right, contingent on possessing a "normal" mind and body as well as on maintaining "appropriate" conduct. This was strengthened by conferring upon schools the power to exclude, via dichotomous categories of ab/normality, dis/ability, and in/educability that were, however, without objective guidelines given the relationality of every statistical norm, which produce deviations. Thus, public education and other public institutions for people with disabilities and those who behaved deviantly were joined at the "juridical hip" through the enactment of a free and compulsory education.

Sociologically, the most critical joint was the connection between public education and juvenile delinquency. The reform school provided a model for organizational management. The classification of delinquents confined in reformatories had its counterpart in ability grouping and tracking in public education. As public education developed from a mass primary system to one oriented to ever higher education, behavioral etiologies became the dominant frame of reference for underachievement, misconduct, and failure. The forces that linked "backwardness" to "social maladjustment" to "learning disability" in special education originated from outside public schooling, as they were originally mainly the attributes of delinquency; however, they were elaborated and applied within public education and have become increasingly legitimated by diagnostics and science. In the United States of the twenty-first century, having a learning disability no longer precludes having a successful educational career, even beyond secondary schooling.

The institutional dynamic that is the background to the categorical progression is the increasing interconnection between delinquency and public education. As we found in the German-American comparison (Chapter 5), in which special education developed isomorphically to general education and thus took on its structures, here the facilities built for the juvenile justice system have grown closer to public education. These policies have grown more alike, in language, design, and practice. Treatment in a correctional institution corresponded to instruction in public education. Rehabilitation in corrections corresponded to educational achievement in public schooling. The range of linguistic similarities has been narrowing over the past several decades, converging on theories and practices that seem applicable to any setting, be it in the least or the most restrictive settings.

At the center of this theorized convergence has been special education, and at the core of special education's common practices is the Individual Education Program (IEP), which attempts to provide services and supports to fit *individual* learning needs. As the mechanism that links delinquency and public education, the IEP has a long genealogy; conceptually and practically it helps to explain their growing isomorphism over time. The long-term goal of both institutions is to facilitate the transition to adulthood, to prepare and place their populations in occupational positions, and ideally to ensure future employment and social and political participation. The development of public education is neither separate from nor unaffected by the changing modes and rates of delinquent behavior.[5] Conversely, as the contours of delinquency change, they press upon public education, redefining misconduct in classroom behavior and redefining policies toward school discipline (Slee 1995).

The divergence in the progression of case law reflects the logic of expanded inclusion in mass public schooling and the expansion of education at every level. As participation rates expand, delinquency and public education are brought closer together, and the organizational mediation of this growing isomorphism falls increasingly to special education. The divergent progression of case law in these two systems reflects that for each, the only direction to go is toward the other, as they serve similar clients who are at the margins of schooling and society, yet who are participating in extended school careers, especially as transition services become increasingly important in the development of IEPs and service delivery until the twenty-second birthday.

As we found for decentralized education systems that often move toward centralization, special education's beginning from a right to education proceeds toward its antithesis and juvenile justice takes a turn from conditions of confinement toward liberty interests and education rights. Much like Alexis de Tocqueville's (1945) antinomy between equality and freedom so keenly observed in *Democracy in America*, the more inclusion is emphasized, the more liberty interests are specified, restricted to the conditions of confinement in public schooling. The paradox of growing education rights with a punitive system and resurgent confinement within an education system poses a challenge to all who reify the boundaries between these isomorphic—and, at least in the United States, convergent—systems. Interconnected, special education and juvenile justice have grown closer, but paradoxically in directions that lead away from their foundational principles of schooling and therapy and confinement, respectively. All the while, those children and youth, variously classified as disadvantaged, deviant, or disabled, remain largely the same, regardless of the institutions and organizations charged with their development or rehabilitation.

## CHAPTER 8

# BETWEEN GLOBAL INTENTIONS AND NATIONAL PERSISTENCE

## *From Special Education to Inclusive Education?*

I N   T H I S   F I N A L   C H A P T E R ,   W E   D I S C U S S   T H E
language of special education, addressing again the classification systems and categories that forcefully reveal both continuity and change
in education systems. We review the links between historical sequences and
the relationships between punitive and paternalist benevolence in countries
influential in establishing preeminent models of special education. Then, we
broaden the perspective toward global dynamics and national persistence.
We chart responses, even resistance, toward this mainly Western model of
special and inclusive education that has diffused around the world—to be
embraced, adapted, or rejected in countries of Africa and Asia. Only rarely
has special education research, even the explicitly comparative, gone beyond
its own cultural boundaries, yet a major goal of comparative and historical
analysis is to call into question cultures and structures of special education
that are taken for granted. Extending explicit comparisons with a perspective

beyond the West can facilitate that goal. Cultural conceptions of inclusion often focus on community life instead of schooling, underscoring the diversity of approaches and traditions regarding the human universal of disablement. Looking toward the future of special education in the countries examined most in-depth here, we identify ongoing reforms at the nexus of special and inclusive education. As influential exporters of ideas, standards, and policies in education, the countries analyzed in this book will continue to affect institutional change elsewhere—even as these countries have much to learn from others in the majority world.

## MACRO-COMPARATIVE SPECIAL EDUCATION

In research on special education, macro-level comparisons have been relatively neglected, especially the explicit comparison of the development of education systems over time. As noted at the outset, the considerable variability has, more often than not, been displayed with the chief intention to affirm cultural variation itself. The methodology of cultural display proceeds horizontally and synchronically, arranging cases one after another with minimal sorting by factors. Lacking are systematic analyzes of similarities and differences, especially the principles and the relationships to general education and other neighboring institutions. The picture frequently also remains static, thereby ignoring or tarnishing the crucial developmental features of each case. Often passing for comparative are so-called cross-cultural studies that have too often stopped at the doorstep of explicit comparative analysis and explanation. Analysis is interrupted by an abundance of descriptive features of single cases, such as a school or locality, which are in turn given exaggerated importance. We have argued that despite the challenges that explicitly comparative research on special education systems poses, such research offers important and critical insights that unmask our own assumptions.

From a macro-comparative perspective, the studies in this volume have situated the position of special and inclusive education between global dynamics and national persistence, sometimes even active resistance. The great range in the characteristics of special education institutions and organizations emphasizes that a diversity of models exists and that choices and reforms are possible. Nevertheless, important commonalities are also evident. In contrast to the few fully inclusive education systems, most special education systems group children with disabilities by categories that pertain to their physical or mental challenge—or, more recently, according to more or less learning-oriented, instead of clinical, categories of special educational need. Regardless of variation in economic level and political system across and within nations, there seems, at least in the West, to be a fairly common set of categories, which bear similar titles: twenty categories were counted among member states of the OECD (2004). In spite of geographic dispersion, nations seem to employ these titles while interpreting them differently. For example, whereas "learning disability" in the United States relies on the measured discrepancy between tested IQ and school performance to identify "underachievement," in Germany the term is a more legitimate moniker for social disadvantages—and Japan knows no such category. Different terms may signify similar concepts, but the meaning of what is signified will differ from one system to another and across levels within each system. That *handicapé* in French "has none of the negative connotations of the word 'handicapped' in English" (Armstrong 2003: 58) and "*Handicap*" has recently become common in Germany is just one among countless examples of nonequivalence and borrowing from abroad to suggest advance or political correctness. Cross-cultural analyses are challenged by shifts in invariably normatively charged meanings of dis/ability and the danger of euphemism. This is especially so since the human rights revolution, beginning after the Second World War, facilitated the social inclusion of people with disabilities and delegitimated stigmatizing terminology inherited from the preceding era of eugenics (see Snyder and Mitchell 2006). If we hope to more fully understand other systems of special and inclusive education, we must carry out such in-depth comparative analyses, a project only just begun here.

### Elementary Structures and Linguistic Planes of Special Education

The coexistence of similar national categories with differing local meanings suggests a further theoretical pathway through which we may explain the great range of differences in special education without trivializing or subordinating the differences, which are of great significance for identity construction and life chances alike. To borrow from the title of Claude Lévi-Strauss's classic study of kinship (1969), some findings of our comparisons may be summarized by proposing "elementary structures" of special education. The dis/abilities of children and youth or their "special educational needs," as analyses of participation rates clearly show, are mainly discovered in the interactions within classrooms and schools; the labels applied to student groups are given meaning by the participants, often guided by the official bureaucratic categories and professional knowledge at hand (see, for example, Hacking 1999; Pfahl in press). The social and pedagogical responses to students within schools and beyond often rely heavily on the categories and labels ascribed. The categories made available in education systems and the process of classification are crucial objects of study, as are the ways in which these categories are received and the corresponding labels used in everyday interactions.

The presumption that objects are separate from the observer and independent of others must be rejected. This was an influential change not only in linguistics. A good portion of this paradigmatic shift in linguistics can arguably be traced to the work of Ferdinand Saussure and his *Course in General Linguistics*, first published, posthumously, in 1916 (Saussure 1966). In *Course*, Saussure posed very basic questions about the structure of language itself, but did so with the objective of reducing the seemingly endless range of differences by rendering the structure of language amenable to scientific study and explanation. At the crux of his work was the distinction made between *langue* and *parole*. *Langue* refers to the formal structure of language, the body of terms and phrases that individuals can draw upon in their everyday speech, such as the official categories of special education. It is the system of forms that are learned and assimilated, mostly as social rules that shape their usage. In contrast, *parole* consists of speech acts that are enacted by individuals in concrete, living situations, such as the terms groups of students use to talk with and about each other. *Parole* can be wholly individual, an idiosyncratic verbal act that suggests little beyond what is spoken. However, for Saussure, the speech acts of real significance are social, for they suggest ideas or concepts that are external to individuals.

The distinction between *langue* and *parole* "separates the essential from the contingent, the social from the purely individual, and the psychological from the material" (Culler 1976: 85). *Langue* is a system of signs that is constituted by the relations between a speech act and the concept it signifies. As a wholly abstract and formal system, it determines what can and cannot be combined to form the functionally useful units of a language system. Especially crucial to the distinction is Saussure's emphasis on the "arbitrariness" of the relation between speech act and concept. The relation between a speech act as a signifier and the concept or idea that it signifies is not forged by any inherent, essential properties, whether it be phonetic sounds or phonological requirements. The speech act can thus be combined with any number of concepts. Conferring the meaning given to *parole* is the relation(s) between the speech act and the concept, and forging this relation is the external constraints of a collective community. It is the social community and broader collective society that defines and redefines the forms of language that compose *langue*, which in turn shapes the events of speaking. The rise of special education as a profession, along with the clinical professions such as medicine and psychology, has had tremendous influence in establishing and differentiating the language of special educational needs and "student disability." Interpretations of difference, when it comes to school performance and behavior, now have a defined range and diverse authorized categories into which students are sorted. The life course effects of these choices are rarely fully understood, but this does not diminish the impact of the bureaucratic categories on collective and individual identities.

Saussure's essential argument is that language cannot be reduced to a nomenclature or be made comparable by replacing one term with a foreign equivalent. For example, "learning disability" in common usage in the United Kingdom refers to a group that, in the United States, would in part be classified as belonging to the even now used official special education category "mental retardation." Distinguishing British "learning difficulties" from American "learning disabilities" and other boundaries of special education categories is contested terrain. Thus, even within the English-speaking world, studies must attend to culture-specific usage and connotations. This contrast exemplifies the divergence in linguistic usage within the same field of expertise and professional service in even relatively similar societies.

The distinction between *langue* and *parole* is complemented by the idea of paradigmatic relations. As Saussure insisted, *langue* is a system of oppositions, wherein the meaning of a word or phrase derives from its contrast to others, not from its presumed positive content. When words with similar meanings are joined, associative relations are formed, and an associative plane of discourse becomes a broadly constraining force. Thus, types of valued education can be associated with upbringing, training, and particular physical or mental attributes (Barthes 1977: 58). For example, intelligence may be associated with height, creativity, and friendliness even as low intelligence may be associated with smaller stature and unfriendliness (Bradley and Richardson 2010). Such semiotic chains of association are constructed out of contrasts and exclusions, for education does *not* refer to one certain upbringing or mode of training, manifest in the variability of forms and contents understood as "special education" shown in the previous chapters. This contrastive property constitutes the paradigmatic dimension of language. Each level of the linguistic system has contrastive and combinatorial properties, and this "basic structural principle . . . operates at every level of language" (Saussure [1916] 1966: 48). Nonetheless, the consequences or content of both differ by linguistic level.

Paralleling this plane of discourse is a combinatorial property wherein a term's meaning (or value) depends on its relations with the terms that precede and follow it *in a sequence*. In the United States, for example, "backwardness" preceded "mental deficiency," which preceded "educable mentally retarded," which preceded "learning disability" (Franklin 1980; see also Hobbs 1975; Trent 1994). The ongoing differentiation of categories, the elaboration of their labels, and shifts in connotations have long been a crucial method for analyzing the development of education systems and the boundaries of dis/ability (see, for example, Tomlinson 1982; Hofsäss 1993; Powell 2011).

The broader applicability of Saussure's principles was captured by Roland Barthes in the phrase "how the semiologic 'overflows' the linguistic" (1977: xi). Barthes, more than anyone, has explored this general applicability, doing so in his now classic study of fashion, in which dress is equivalent to *langue* and dressing is equivalent to *parole*. Barthes revealed the limitations of psychological studies that reduce clothing to tastes, preferences, or other like motivations. The proper object of study is the vestimentary system, which, like *langue*, has its own logic of development. Proposing that any institution that is large enough to exert social consequences is amenable to semiological analysis, Barthes went beyond the fashion industry, with its seasonal adjustments within the system of dress, to add the food system, the car system, the furniture system, and mixtures of institutions that produce "complex systems." Consistent with Barthes's methodological criteria and theoretical objectives, we can add special education—most especially the categories in its elaborate classification systems—as a complex system amenable to semiological analysis and explanation. In many countries, categories come into and go out of fashion as awareness-raising and ascription processes through the media, in education itself, and in related fields lead to their rise and fall (on dyslexia, see Bühler-Niederberger 1991; on attention deficit/hyperactivity disorder, see Malacrida 2003). Especially the professions of medicine, psychology, and education have constructed and defended particular classifications of student disabilities, difficulties, and disadvantages, which are rising in importance due to demands for increased accountability and higher standards, evidence-based practices and policies, and equitable resource allocation (Florian et al. 2006). Symbolizing the recognition of the complexity and context contingency of disability, the World Health Organization (WHO 2001) has completely revised its classification of impairment and disability, with its 2001 *International Classification of Functioning, Disability, and Health* (ICF) to include environmental barriers and facilitators—systemic features—not only individual attributes. The ICF is now being adapted to educational contexts (see Florian et al. 2006).

At the system level, inclusive education itself risks simply becoming the new fashion without recognizing and achieving its fundamental paradigm shift that implies restructuring. In most visions of inclusive education, this requires not that students conform to the institutionalized structures of schooling, but that those structures be deeply reformed to acknowledge, respect, and value the inherent diversity of all student bodies. Some systems, in individualizing their support, simply do without the diagnostic, clinical categories that have so often been stigmatizing instead of emancipatory. Some countries, such as England and Norway, use only the general, umbrella category of "special educational needs." However, this does not solve the original problem of the medical model because it retains the causal equation of deficit within the child instead of focusing on disabling institutional practices and barriers (Barton and Armstrong 2001). Categorical shifts toward less stigmatizing labels evince a trend, but some criticize these changes as mere euphemism. Furthermore, over recent decades, members of the disability community, as other negatively-stigmatized minority groups, have in fact taken back certain pejorative terms—such as "cripple" turned into "crip"—from the oppressors, imbuing them with pride (Corbett 1995). *Parole* can be creatively used to subvert *langue*, but the latter remains powerful, especially when embedded in policies and regulations not amenable to rapid change.

Regardless of one's position on the decades-old controversy about labeling, the evolution of such categories must be analyzed as central to the institutionalized symbolic and social boundaries between general and special education that not only legitimate school systems' separation or segregation of students, but also produce the knowledge and norms that guide policymakers and professionals. Saussure's distinction held important methodological implications. The study of *langue* entails the formulation of models that represent the body of forms: what terms constitute the expanding world of "special educational needs"? Although this system determines the types and range of behaviors catalogued, the elementary structures of *langue* are largely invisible to individuals and groups and to traditional social scientific methods designed to explain them, as the necessity of having such terms is largely taken for granted on a daily basis. In contrast, *parole* is likened to statistical probabilities, for the types and range of behaviors reflect what is determined by the rules of combination. Which of the various categories of special educational needs are used, and how, in any given context? Critical studies of special education have rightly focused much attention on *langue*, the formal and thus visible, observable and measurable properties of the system. Classification systems are a most conspicuous example. However, how we talk about dis/ability and difference in everyday parlance has garnered increasing attention. Indeed, as Ian Hacking (1999: 59) points out, such classifications are interactive between "kind" and "person": when knowledge and beliefs change, this changes people via self-conscious knowledge and awareness, affecting their agency ("the looping effect of human kinds"). Thus, such analyses must be diachronic, analyzing changes in such categorical connotations, which reflect incremental shifts in social norms regarding dis/ability and behavior.

The distinction between "normative" and "nonnormative" categories bears a theoretical affinity to Saussure's distinction. The normative consensus about blindness, deafness, and physical impairments reflects a delimited range of expectations that are associated with the disability, largely because of their frequently biologically-based etiology. In contrast, for the nonnormative categories, the "mildly retarded," "socially maladjusted," and "learning disabled," "there are no adequate measuring instruments or agreed criteria in the social world to decide upon the particular categories, whether descriptive or statutory" (Tomlinson 1982: 65; see also Sternberg and Spear-Swerling

1999). The distinction between the two forms is a major fault line in special education systems. Divisions between countries can be found in classificatory systems that are dominated by nonnormative categories—which seem especially prevalent in Western countries owing to their long-established special education systems that generated these concepts through their professional praxis—or by normative categories. While the language of nonnormative categories parallels that of democracy / bureaucracy, the language of normative categories parallels neopatrimonialism.

From this point of view, the construction of disability and special education categories is intricately tied to the formation of the nation-state, exemplified throughout the preceding chapters. But the "nation" can also be thought in more social than political terms. As Lennard Davis (1995) has shown, the construction of the "Deaf" (capital D) as a category that coalesced a diversity of individuals was the construction of a societal category, akin to ethnicity, that entered the deep structure of national identity. Deafness entered the nation by way of Enlightenment thought and the stimulus it gave to residential institutions. Participation in life within state residential institutions—and the manual sign language that developed as the basis of a common culture—transformed deaf individuals into the Deaf *community* and raised the question of political inclusion, not of deaf individuals, but of the Deaf (Davis 1995: 83). The content of this question was not so much about some physical hearing impairment as it was about the social and political implications of the Deaf as a *linguistic* minority. The construction of the Deaf had more to do with the differences presented by sign as a transnational language than it had to do with physical limitations on hearing.

Davis's dissection of the interplay between "nationalism and Deafness" illustrates how certain behaviors or conditions come to signify a concept; in this example, how the *parole* of sign language signified the category of the Deaf. The process whereby certain behaviors become signifiers of categories begins at elementary levels of social organization. The divisions and boundaries of social life—those of class, gender, ethnicitiy, community, and so on—are the root sources of the rules that govern exclusion and accessibility, confinement and movement. In short, they are the rules of combination and transformation that link *parole* to *langue*.

This implies that the study of special education categories—their division into normative or nonnormative and their genealogical progression—is significantly incomplete without understanding the processes that select particular behaviors or conditions, from an endless range of possible behaviors and conditions, as signifiers within official classification systems maintained by international nongovernmental organizations and state bureaucracies. Inattention and inarticulateness have always been expected behaviors of schoolchildren, yet only recently have they been the critical signifiers of the categorical condition of "learning disability." To study how a learning disability "acquires a child" and not how a child acquires a learning disability reverses the causal logic and focus of study (McDermott 1988, 1993). It focuses on hierarchically linked social settings that have particular behaviors and perceptions associated with them. Such school settings structure how these behaviors and perceptions are interpreted, coming to signify learning difficulty or disability. The central question is how they become signifiers within official classification systems, managed by professions and codified in laws at multiple levels of governance.

The linking of certain behaviors to specific categories, of the *parole* of school behavior and praxis to the *langue* of special education categories defined by professional knowledge, is complicated by the core fact that the signifier and the signified "do not belong to the same language" (Barthes 2006: 42). Moreover, the task of linking the two joins a constancy of behaviors to a variable system that classifies these behaviors. The construction of new categories—such as "developmental delay," "traumatic brain injury," and "autism" in U.S. special education law since 1992—is effected in opposition to previous ones, which over time lose their legitimacy. Similar to Saussure's principle of negativity, "mental deficiency" was validated because it was *not* "backwardness"; "educable mentally retarded" was validated because it was *not* "mental deficiency"; and "learning disability" is currently validated because it is *not* "retardation." Yet although the system of classification is transformed, the behaviors that signify a category can remain essentially unchanged. New categories do not simply replace previous ones, they often redefine the rules of *access* and *passage* (see Richardson 1999) along the continuum from exclusion via segregation and separation to integration and inclusion. Indeed, in the United States today, a growing proportion of students in postsecondary education self-report having a learning disability. Higher education institutions have responded with enhanced efforts to accommodate students with disabilities by raising awareness, providing sign language interpreters or reducing architectural barriers (all specified by the International Convention, see

UN 2006). Once again, at a higher level, the classification threshold is lowered because the additional or specialized resources and accommodations are more highly valued than the stigma of belonging to the group of students with special educational needs is feared. The resource-labeling dilemma has, with enhanced access to postsecondary education, moved up a level as well. The status of higher education and the promised benefits of attainment encourage further classification when organizations provide measurable benefits to those belonging to the umbrella category of "special educational needs."

### The Associative Relations of Punitive and Paternalistic Benevolence

As we have shown, neither the establishment of special education organizations nor the drive to enact compulsory education, begun and led by European countries, was a homogenous, linear movement. On the contrary, the range of dates of enactment extended from the early nineteenth century to the mid-twentieth century. This variation paralleled the different historical sequences that structured benevolence along primarily punitive or paternalistic lines. The differences between these paths not only reflect the imprint of historical differences in how marginal groups and particular categories of people with disabilities were viewed and treated, but in effect channeled these differences in ways that would imprint the institutionalization of education systems and their organizational forms following enactment of compulsory schooling. This imprinting had—and has—significant implications for schooling—and not only for schooling of students with disabilities, difficulties, and disadvantages.

Institutional and policy emphases distinguished punitive and paternalistic benevolence and constituted very different paradigmatic structures, composed of very different associative relations. The two forms of benevolence penetrated deeply into perceptions and treatment of people with disabilities, connecting specific school interactions to the formal practices and procedures of special education. For example, the contemporary United States places tremendous emphasis on education at all levels but also expends vast resouces on punitive measures like prisons. Instead, Germany focuses efforts on paternalistic measures to "protect" students with disadvantages and disabilities, but this includes segregated special schooling that does little to qualify these individuals for vocational training; they remain marginalized in labor markets.

The decentralized systems that favored punitive benevolence grounded identification, assessment, and placement decisions within or close to the classroom level, thereby intertwining parental and school authority in a negotiated system of exchange. The classification threshold, measuring the relative ease with which children are classified as having special educational needs, was structurally low, reaching beyond such impairments as blindness and deafness to encompass a range of disadvantages and behavioral disruptions as sources of special educational needs. In contrast, paternalistic benevolence is structurally closer to centralized governance and seems to give priority to students with special educational needs who are less subject to parental or professional dispute. A seemingly paradoxical consequence is how punitive benevolence, compared with the paternalistic—and contrary to its connotation—actually can bolster learning opportunities for students with disabilities, based on traditions of individual rights and responsibility, even extending into the criminal justice system (see Chapter 7). In these countries, education for all goes hand in hand with meritocratic ideology, and even students with learning disabilities continue on in the contest, as schooling remains a reasonably viable, often preferable, option that competes with leaving school or an early, often state-subsidized, placement in vocational education. If the individual should fail or commit a crime, however, the punishment can be severe. Given the high correlation between low academic achievement, low attainment in education, and dropping out of school—and the resulting increased likelihood of labor market marginalization—juvenile justice systems exhibit disproportionately high rates of low attainers, many of whom had special educational needs. By contrast, paternalistically benevolent systems, by charitably providing services, protect students with disabilities and disadvantages from academic rigor and high expectations, albeit in highly segregated settings that often fail to prepare these youth for the world of work or participation in civil society (Pfahl in press). In such systems, education, especially at higher levels, remains reserved for the few, as class dis/advantages are reproduced. However, well-developed welfare states focus on outcome equality, via redistributive transfer payments, that reduce poverty; correspondingly less emphasis is placed on costly prisons and other punitive measures.

Again, independent of ideological debates and good or bad intentions, practices and outcomes of special education vary by their long-ago institutionalized ties to other fields, such as social welfare, health care, juvenile justice, and labor markets. These systemic interconnections also translate, as it were, the language of school behaviors as signifiers into the language of the signified categories of special education and into the language of social assistance, rehabilitation programs, criminal justice, and unemployment.

## GLOBAL DYNAMICS AND NATIONAL RESISTANCES

The distinction between punitive and paternalistic benevolence is an especially good fit for the experience of European nations, and matches the contextual climate through the late nineteenth century. When attention turns to non-European nations, the narrative changes as dramatically as do the institutionalization processes in schooling and social welfare. The European narrative centered around free and compulsory education with the working class as a central protagonist. The non-European narrative, beginning much later, has as much to do with national sovereignty as it does with global calls for certain types of education and human rights. The climate of recent decades—given advancing economic globalization and since the education and human rights revolutions—is different in content, but most of all it is different in *level*.

The level that defines the boundary of contemporary debates is now global, transcending national differences and colonial experiences, especially by way of transnational flows of information, capital, and labor. Rhetorically, international bodies that articulate human rights and schooling as prime generator of human capital—above what nations confer—are entities to which developing countries have attached themselves with considerable intensity. Yet while the power of such international (non)governmental organizations has grown tremendously, also in special education (see, for example, World Bank 2003; OECD 2007) the "world polity, increasingly influential in shaping national policies, has not yet broken free from global stratification" (Beckfield 2003: 420). Although the recommendations by international bodies suffer from a risk of nonreciprocity by individual nations, especially at the periphery, the rules behind the rhetoric have changed, highlighting a risk of exclusion if one doesn't participate (Molm 1994). Connections to the world polity have led to the near universal recognition of the necessity of education for all and of lifelong learning (Jakobi 2009) as well as the awareness of special education and, whether defined in culturally acceptable or adaptable terms or not, of inclusive education (see Muñoz 2007).

### An Alternative Trajectory to Benevolence, Education and Economic Development

Declarations of human rights, and the right to education in particular, reflect a shift in the locus and form of benevolence. Well illustrated by China, the emphasis is on "the caring society." Although this model deploys state authority as a benign agent of the new governmentality and a revised pastoral power (Foucault 2003), a counter-trend is shown in the one-child population policy that spawned new eugenic behavior—the killing of baby girls—leading to disproportionally more boys growing up. Different from welfare systems and their measures of compliance, often repressive and with little positive result, this new alliance in China joins the state and ascending middle classes whose citizenship is defined by "credentials, skills, and well-being    so critical to attracting foreign capital" (Ong 1999: 200–201). Fueled by the economic domain, foreign capital—and consumption—promise to allow developing and postcolonial societies to "skip the queue."

Within China, this accelerated economic growth is founded on a "bureaucratic benevolence"—an alternative trajectory to those of the punitive or paternalistic type that structured the West (see Chapter 1). As Aihwa Ong (1999: 202) notes: "While the welfare state developed as a way to deal with class conflict, the postdevelopmental strategy of pastoral care [*bureaucratic benevolence*] seeks to produce citizens attractive to capital." Yet government efforts in China to develop human capital production have depended not only on proliferating biopower that reflects global campaigns and development discourses, but also on state structures with their internal administrative logics as well as the officials and organizations that define disability, deviance, and difference, manage education and welfare provisions, and thus develop such biopolitical arenas (see Kohrman 2005).

The links between global culture, education systems, and financial capital in particular, seem to facilitate non-European countries to revise or at least condense not only Marshall's sequence of rights in the sphere of democracy, but Polanyi's double movement in the economic realm as well. Describing Asia's economic success stories, but with implications beyond, Ong pinpoints qualitative differences between the European and Asian experiences: "But while European states have confronted [contestations over civil, political, and economic rights] sequentially over decades, postcolonial Asian states have had to deal with them simultaneously, mostly in an era of globalization. Newly industrializing regimes . . . have evolved [what I call] a system of *graduated sovereignty*, whereby citizens in zones that are differently articulated to global production and financial circuits are subjected to different kinds of surveillance and in practice enjoy different sets of civil, political, and economic rights" (1999: 215–216, emphasis added). Indeed, as Andy Green (1997: chapter 2) has shown in his comparison of the relationship between economic and education development and state formation, the unprecedented economic development of the East Asian "little tigers" of Hong Kong, Singapore, South Korea, and Taiwan—and the closely related enormous expansion in education—resulted from the strategic actions of a "developmental state" investing heavily and intervening in education and economic capacity to legitimate state power, to assure national survival, and to construct national identity. Such examples suggest a necessary revision of the theorized movement between a laissez-faire market system and protections of collective welfare—via education. As these East Asian countries have matched or overtaken Europe in education participation rates and attainment levels within just a few decades, they showed their full understanding of human capital development as the engine of international economic competitiveness, utilizing and even surpassing the Western model for record growth.

The structuring of economies into "graduated zones," dictated by foreign capital, relocates market forces—outside of purely market forces. Among the forces that shape economic transactions, and thus the flow of capital, are family dynasties that forge interlocking networks on a regional and global level. In what may be more accurately termed "fraternal capitalism," the rules that govern family conduct initiate and enable economic transactions—and this may offer a strategy better suited to local demands, risks, and rewards. Removing both production and benevolence, if not schooling, from state institutions changes the terms of debates, for it also transforms conceptions of private and public. As the distinction between individualist and collectivist societies exemplified (see Table 4.1), this alters conceptions of dis/ability.

Families and states, through their schools and broader education and social policies, join forces to socialize and educate each new cohort. In those few attempts to compare student disability across a large number of countries, such as the UNESCO data analyzed here or in recent studies by the OECD (2007) entitled *Students with Disabilities, Learning Difficulties, and Disadvantages: Policies, Statistics and Indicators*, resource-based categories are used that reflect the provision of services, yet these counts reflect solely publically provided services, not the resources of families, which are inevitably greater in providing direct care and socialization, even as they differ considerably in the learning opportunities and economic activities they can offer. The perspectives of contemporary non-Western societies toward responsibilities for human and economic development underscore the importance of acknowledging the interconnectedness of spheres such as schools and families, rather than focusing solely on that which states officially provide their citizens and under what conditions. Yet both models show the importance of the nation-state, as it picks up influential ideas about how best to provide the education and economic channels in which family aspirations and activities can flourish—to the benefit of individuals and collectivities.

### *The Morphology of Inclusion: Alternative Conceptions*

As we have shown, variants of special education preceded compulsory schooling for all. Yet special education *within* regular schools remained organizationally nascent for decades following enactment and gradual universalization of compulsory education. Special education has diffused, along with the global call of "education for all," to the extent that it is largely taken for granted, especially in Western countries in which most schools provide additional resources to access the curriculum. Yet, ideologically and ethically, the institutions and organizations of special education have remained ambivalent. Originally, both the pedagogical theory and methods for the instruction of blind and deaf persons were elaborated within charitable residential institutions. Yet the schooling of children with disabilities and special educational needs within public schools did not readily inherit these tools. Among the factors were organizational differentiation, which grew largely based upon clinical, not educational, paradigms of dis/ability, and the failure of regular education to recognize the general applicability of these pedagogical advances. Nevertheless, in some highly successful education systems, additional and specialized supports for a large proportion of students are viewed as being integral to the overall educational performance and output, as in

Finland where a third of all students receive additional resources to access the curriculum.

Yet some technologies quickly spread beyond the bounds of special education. Alfred Binet originally constructed IQ tests to distribute pedagogical services among children to facilitate their development, not to sort individuals based on an amount of supposedly "natural" talent within an individual, as has become so commonplace today (Sarason and Doris 1979). The lack of common ground between special and general education undergirded not only techniques of instruction but also the logic of specialized and separate organizations. Within public education, subject to rules of compulsory attendance, instructors of students in special classes and schools sought their own rationales. Legitimation came from beyond the goal of protecting the integrity of the regular class, although that too has been a continuous feature of the discourses surrounding student disability and special education.

For years following the enactment of compulsory education on a global scale, special education was not a recognized participant in formulating curriculum. Despite ongoing professional specialization, its curriculum often remained merely a residual, shortened version of the courses of study that constituted general education.[1] Indeed, the enduring division between general and special education reinforces the normalcy of the former and the deviancy of the latter—instead of the collaborative problem solving and team-teaching at the heart of many models of inclusive education (see, for example, Gartner and Lipsky 1987; Skrtic 1991a, 1995; Biklen 1992; Booth and Ainscow 2002; Sapon-Shevin 2007).

The institutionalization processes of special education reach far beyond a consolidation of institutions and schools and the vesting of administrative authority in a single location. Moreover, the three major models of special education systems compared here—multitrack, dual track, and unitary/inclusive—almost without exception exhibit solely gradual, path-dependent institutional change reacting to incremental reforms. Indeed, almost everywhere, special education remains central in attempts to achieve inclusive education—sometimes as a facilitator, sometimes as a barrier, but always as a key point of reference. The opportunity for countries without a history of asylums, hospitals, and segregated or separated special schools and classrooms that goes back centuries is to learn from these experiences and proceed directly to inclusive education for all.

This poses the question, however, of what rights-based initiatives can accomplish if the prior development of the sequence of rights is either nonexistent or compressed. As we have discussed, T. H. Marshall's sequence was composed from English history and focused on the rights of males. Like the coupling of democracy and bureaucracy, the sequence may not transfer easily or at all to most non-Western nations. For these nations, the co-presence of categories of citizens who still do not enjoy such rights reflects, among many things, the persistent reality of "primordial publics." In many countries, peasants, "backward classes," indigenous populations (Sarker and Davey 2009: 3), and people with disabilities remain marginal to, if not insulated from, the political center, and efforts by central authorities to reach them can accentuate more than alleviate their insulation.[2] For non-Western regions, citizenship is often less a discourse about rights than a function of how individuals and groups live in communities and how they are connected to states and to the nation. Yet the principles of education for all, compulsory schooling, special education, and even inclusive education are being borrowed from the West, where they must be adapted to cultural contexts that have different ideals of education and dissimilar forms, or expectations, of schooling.

As we have seen since the Enlightenment, however, special education neither requires the enactment nor the actual attainment of universalized compulsory schooling to flourish, because impairment and disability are universal phenomena, even among children and youth. Nevertheless, in the West, its tremendous expansion has been associated with compulsory schooling. This growth reflects processes of differentiating school populations via relative norms of performance and behavior that have become increasingly relevant for local assessment and accountability and for international comparisons that more than ever empower international organizations to influence educational development throughout the world (see Baker and LeTendre 2005). Yet for non-European countries, the dramatic post–World War II expansion of special education may not come primarily as a response to purported organizational dilemmas of mass education, but, as we have suggested, are instead part and parcel of having a "modern" education system that reflects Western ideals—including defining "special educational needs" and serving children with them. As a consequence, depicting special education as illegitimate, as a lower-tiered and marginal organizational form, makes little sense. Moreover, the isomorphic pressure on all countries to attain education for all—in the West only realized through the intervention, innovation, and institutionalization of special education systems that overcame outright exclusion from public education—could prove more a local opportunity than a global dilemma. The schooling of children and youth with disabilities may provide the rationale and the direction for extensions of education access and equality across traditional boundaries of class, caste, gender, faith, ethnicity, and language.

The contributions of traditional groups and other societies to conceptions of dis/ability in general (see, for example, Ingstad and Whyte [1978] 1995; Jenkins 1998) and to the education of children with disabilities in particular could become instrumental. They demand attention to the implicit legitimacy of Western models in social and educational inclusion that rely heavily on welfare state bureaucracy and individualism. By contrast, in what Joseph Kisanji terms "customary education," members of extended kinship units are obligated to care for members with disabilities. The Turkana of Kenya believe children with disabilities are "the people of God," and thus often keep them close to kinship members even if a (special) school is nearby. Customary education is thus *indigenous* to many cultures, and therefore "education takes place everywhere and anytime" (Kisanji 1995a: 4; also Samuel 1983; Kisanji 1995b: 104). This "natural mode of inclusion, undifferentiated from time and place, emphasizes practical instruction and skill acquisition oriented toward community life. The introduction of the Western education model, with its adamant emphasis on individual autonomy and self-reliance, along with the ardent belief that schooling enhances economic development, conflicts with this indigenous customary education. The "crisis" in African education is not so much African as Western; "cultural alienation and destabilization of traditional values, life and cultural identity result from Western education" (Kisanji 1989: 4). Yet the "natural" inclusiveness of customary education can, of course, work against or completely hinder school participation. The primacy of obligations toward family members with disabilities can militate against special education if the school is seen as "outside." Despite school quality or national status, parents may confine their children with disabilities to places that are proximate and familiar. Thus, the potential of customary education is variable; it depends on *whether* and *how* it is linked to agents and institutions that are outside the primordial publics of developing nations.

In North America, Erica Neegan emphasizes, indigenous peoples of Canada "had a highly developed system of education" whereby "it was the duty and responsibility of the parents, Elders and members of the community as a whole to teach younger people and ensure they led a good life" (Neegan 2005: 4). Analogous to Kisanji's description of customary education in Africa, indigenous education in Canada was naturally inclusive; learning was experiential, closely linked to practical exigencies and their generational continuity. Neegan (2005) is equally emphatic about the damaging effects of residential schooling, alluding to the perpetuation of these effects if contemporary intentions to implement special or inclusive education are not mindful of this history. This discussion of indigenous education emphasizes once more the importance of questioning the different rationales and principles of special and inclusive education and which forms of community—within and outside schools—offer the support that children with disabilities need in order to participate. These contrasting social logics of course affect children's own aspirations, others' expectations for them, their developing capabilities, and their future life chances.

## THE FUTURES OF SPECIAL EDUCATION

The affirmation that no impairment or disability justifies restricting or denying access to education constitutes a decisive change, representing a new "policy paradigm" (Hall 1993). Yet the old paradigm in the West, derived from Enlightenment thought and influential in the institutionalization of special education systems operating today, persists. The maintenance of these paradigms side-by-side in expanding education systems has assisted the paradoxical situation revealed here, that of simultaneously rising rates of segregated schooling and inclusive education.

Three core elements of the new policy paradigm are: that children with disabilities have a right to an education that will fulfill their individual potential, extending to vocational training and higher education; that the education of all children regardless of recognized dis/ability is in the interest of and is an obligation of the state; and that general education—indeed, the general classroom in which all community children learn to interact with, challenge, and care for one another—be legitimatized as the optimal educational environment for most if not all students with disabilities (Powell 2011: chapter 1).

Thus, school systems are required to provide access and resources for the education of children with disabilities—and these children with disabilities are obliged to comply with the attendance requirements of compulsory education. Whether it is one or all of these stipulations, such international and national legislation does mark a significant change by declaring a perceived impairment or disability to be an illegitimate basis for exclusion from schooling. Invoking the "right to education" refers to state-supported general education, not to state-supported, segregated residential institutions.

International charters affirm this right and seek to broaden the democratic reach of education. Yet these intentions generate their own unintended consequences, not the least of which is a redrawing of the boundaries that define access to education and progression through schooling. Free and appropriate education can become graduated and hierarchical, especially dependent on the context in which opportunities to learn are to be provided. Furthermore, if linked to the classifications and categories of special education, these international recommendations can ignite resistance that relegitimatizes the legacy of segregated institutions or reinforces existing distinctions. If outright exclusion is no longer the key obstacle to educational rights in most developed countries, the segregation to inclusion continuum explored throughout this book becomes even more salient in a context that confers privilege on one (inclusion) over the other (segregation). As if in a mode of historical retaliation, the legacy of segregated institutions is invoked with the same rationales that embolden inclusive education—as a freely expressed, democratic choice that best fits the circumstances, which are known intimately better by those who experience them than by those who do not. Ironically, two major emancipatory communication technologies that today strengthen participation were developed within such then-progressive segregated settings. However, whereas Braille (and today's screen readers) can be used in any classroom and thus support inclusive education, manual sign language, by virtue of its interactive, interpretive form, has emboldened the Deaf as a linguistic minority interested in maintaining their own schools and colleges to carry forward their culture.

The susceptibility of special education to the law of unintended consequences is no longer confined to the boundaries of individual countries. On the contrary, the dramatic growth of the world polity intrudes into the legally protected division between state authority and civil society. A "cosmopolitan democracy" of regional and international governing agencies arises as a necessary adaptation to the new logic of a global order (Held 1996: part IV). As a consequence, the relation between state authority and civil society is necessarily rethought and restructured as they become more mutually integrated. In effect, the democratic intention is reversed, with the objective not so much to integrate the periphery to the center as to reorient the center to influence and incorporate groups long marginal or excluded. Thus, the (de)centralization dimension emphasized here has become more prominent in recent decades, partially because inclusive education has occupied a higher ground, but primarily because manipulations of national education systems can, in turn, affect the national locus of power. In societies dependent on education and science, investments in but also conflicts over learning opportunities are likely to continue to increase.

Whereas global initiatives forcefully declare universal human rights and the right to inclusive education for all, individual countries, especially developed ones, hesitate or remain beholden to highly institutionalized education systems that continue to segregate and separate students with officially recognized special educational needs. They may not ignore them; however, they are surely selective as they pick and choose elements of international ideas and charters to adapt to their own national context (Campbell 2004: 166). Whether through indifference or effective transfer via adequate translation, the outcomes are often similar: shielded by rhetorical conformity with global priorities and preferences, national differences remain, or even resurge depending on the political pressures and judiciary-based limits placed especially on expansive new rights provisions. For example, such policies as the Americans with Disabilities Act of 1990 broke new ground in establishing rights and providing tools to reduce discrimination, but also have sometimes led to backlash (Krieger 2003). Such diffusion processes have characterized the project of modernity since the eighteenth century: exported from western Europe, multiple modernities, instead of being replicated in fragments, now birth multiple identities and competing publics that link nations to an ever-more tightly interwoven international level of discourse, norms, and governance (Eisenstadt and Schluchter 2002: viii).

Surprisingly given the lack of recognition accorded it, special education has in some respects been at the center of the project of modernity. As the level above individual nations has enlarged, from the international writings of the eighteenth-century Enlightenment to the global knowledge networks of recent decades (Stone 2002), new bridging terms arise to mediate the "scale shift" in international contentions (della Porta and Tarrow 2005: 126) and collaborations. The disability movement within countries and its international networks championed national antidiscrimination laws, culminating in the first human rights treaty of the twenty-first century, the International Convention on the Rights of Persons with Disabilities (UN 2006; see Chapter 6). This treaty's Article 24 spells out a resolute vision of enhanced accessibility and inclusive education as fundamental to social, economic, and political participation and to reduce disablement and social inequality. But this call does not require the definition of particular categories to protect because everyone may become a member of the minority group of people with disabilities and inclusive education encompasses all types of human diversity.

As the pace and scale of social differentiation has expanded, groups once ignored as uneducable or excluded from schooling have themselves moved away from the margins and toward incorporation. The political incorporation of the European working class can be considered a historical mentor to the educational incorporation of children and youth with disabilities, difficulties, and disadvantages through special education. Similarly, the civil rights movement in the United States provided the necessary tools and nurtured the hopes of the disability rights movement (Barnartt and Scotch 2001), which has successfully fought for emancipation, recognition, and access—and not only in the United States (Charlton 1998). For both movements, organizational and substantive gains were marks of progress, necessary achievements in the larger project of modernity. Yet, like the only partial achievements of working class struggles, nationally specific special education systems have resisted fundamental reforms aimed at school integration and the restructuring of entire education systems to become more fully inclusive.

Resistance to inclusive education stems not only from a web of ideological positions, entrenched interests, and education and social policies, but also from the organizational location of special education: situated at the nexus of education and social policies (see Chapter 5), a row ahead of social assistance and labor market programs for disadvantaged youth and young adults with disabilities (see Chapter 6), and parallel to the juvenile justice system (see

Chapter 7). The opposition to inclusive education reflects entrenched instructional styles and expectations about who can and cannot be taught—and by whom. Yet prior to these assumptions are historical moments that set in place structural relations with exceedingly long-term ramifications. Among the decisive historical moments was the founding of asylums, residential institutions, and schools for children with disabilities as well as the enactment of compulsory education, which vastly expanded the heterogeneity of student bodies and thus paved the way for further differentiation. The takeoff of special education at the end of the nineteenth century was often portrayed in images of victimhood—children with disabilities and "maladjusted" youth were not genuinely invited to celebrate in the realization of free, compulsory education. After the Second World War, in a time of unparalleled affirmation of human rights, personhood was extended to all but the "uneducable." Today in developed countries, few children—if any—are considered "uneducable." Although via very different pathways, societies in the majority world long ago came to that conclusion, not knowing such categories as "learning disability," which results from schooling itself and continues to grow as a result of awareness-raising and advocacy—despite limited agreement as to etiology or effective treatment (see Jenkins 1998 on the construction of (in)competence).

Then as now, the main source of special education clients remains the "regular" classroom and "regular" educators, especially those who, even if well-meaning, suffer from a lack of resources and training and thus neglect to serve all students regardless of the students' individual characteristics. Conversely, general education is dependent on special education when it supplies additional and specialized pedagogies and services, offers an alternative educational environment when general education is challenged, and accepts those students removed from general education. Even the juvenile justice system now recognizes as legitimate the right to education, as evidenced in the United States (see Chapter 7). Special education (re)defines the boundaries of ab/normality, a process it began long before *all* children were expected to be part of formal schooling on their path toward adulthood and citizenship. Just as normality takes on contours via the boundaries of abnormality, so too does general education rely on special education to locate and affirm its boundaries.

As an ideal, inclusion may, in some parts of the world, now have nearly replaced the older visions of school integration and mainstreaming, at least discursively. As the ratification of the International Convention on the Rights of Persons with Disabilities progresses, in many countries the legal implications will force action, in the field of education and far beyond. At the very least, the Convention has given advocates and activists a tool by which to advance their cause. Yet in all but the most egalitarian and wealthy countries, the very real need to distinguish and count those students who are to legitimately receive additional resources to access the curriculum remains a requirement, continuing, to some extent, a dilemma that has been in existence since the passage of the Poor Laws in sixteenth-century England and Wales: who qualifies to receive charity or even state assistance to attain social norms in living standards or behavior and social participation? In receiving additional resources and support, how are people to be marked and treated? In contemporary (post)welfare states, the dilemma of classification, the construction of categories and indicators, and decisions about provision and receipt of support and services continues as the "distributive dilemma of disability" and the "resource-labeling dilemma" (see, for example, Stone 1984; Minow 1990; Füssel and Kretschmann 1993; Silvers, Wasserman, and Mahowald 1998). These have not been resolved by inclusion talk. On the contrary, inclusion talk is often intricately tied to exclusionary practices. Wariness of inflationary euphemism is warranted, as "inclusion" far too often seems to simply replace "integration" rhetorically, without any consequent restructuring of educational environments to accept, respect, and honor the diversity of learners in any community.

The persistence of segregation, indeed its rising simultaneously with inclusion demonstrated here (Chapter 6), indicates that although some international consensus on the importance of inclusive education has been reached at an abstract level, the deinstitutionalization of the dualism of special and general education is still just beginning in the countries analyzed most in-depth here, namely France, Germany, Great Britain, and the United States. Inclusive education reform implies the restructuring of nearly every aspect of schooling—too much for most involved interest groups to bear, especially where the will of national and local decision makers and community support lags behind the ideals and principles articulated at the global level.

By the middle of the twentieth century, the "sponsored admission" of "exceptional" students had become a mark of a progressive pedagogy and one that could travel across local and national boundaries, advancing the right to education in ways reminiscent of working-class struggles for the right to a primary education. For a number of decades, the struggle for inclusive schooling has profited from the power of myth resonating across nations, regardless of myriad substantive differences. The struggles to gain access to and accommodations within regular schools and classrooms were blunted, however, by the actual intent of compulsory education legislation. The growth of special classes, designed largely to defend the normal from the atypical, played the role of trickster—as special education grew *at the behest* of regular education, which could pass along to special education those students found most challenging to daily routines and with curricula imposed from above.

Without taking anything away from the struggles and achievements to advance first special and then inclusive education, two things stand out: the struggles have taken place largely in the West, led principally by European nations, and their social base has largely been middle class. Whereas the struggles of working-class organizations sought incorporation into societal domains from which they were excluded, the twentieth-century struggles by middle class organizations have sought inclusion into a domain—education for all— that was largely constructed by them. As major beneficiaries of compulsory education and on-going educational expansion, the European middle classes have led the reforms that have defined the structure and, in turn, the practices of special education. Alliances of lay and professional associations have been the architects of the classifications and organizational forms of their respective systems of special education. As a consequence, they have defined the landscapes of special education, including the segregated schools, the special resource rooms, and the inclusive classrooms. Yet when compared, the landscapes are significantly different and thus cannot be explained simply by invoking some common set of middle-class motives. On the contrary, as the comparison of the United States and Germany shows (Chapter 6), those interest groups that built special education systems did so according to the logic of the education system in which they grew up and knew best. For more than a century, based on class and ability groupings, Germany has constructed different school types (favoring segregation) and the United States has constructed different tracks within comprehensive schools (favoring separation), with major consequences for the educational environments and permeability between them that affects opportunities to learn, educational mobility, and life chances.

Case-based comparisons within Europe reveal more precisely the sources of difference between nations that otherwise seem largely similar. Even among the developed democracies, extraordinary contrasts in rates and patterns of classification as well as in form of schooling—segregation, separation, integration, inclusion—exist. These differences result from long-term institutionalization processes that produced categories of special educational needs varying in quantity and meanings, different classification thresholds, and dissimilar institutional and organizational potentials to achieve education for all and inclusive schooling.

When the range of countries is expanded beyond the European experience, alternative trajectories of benevolence and education are emerging that have not required the historical antecedents and sequences that so structured the European models. The role of the middle class in Asian countries and the role of traditional, customary education in African nations underscore the importance of resisting simple causal arguments crafted upon particular histories that are generalized beyond their boundaries.

The extension of education rights and provisions to children with disabilities in countries throughout the world has been shaped by a discourse of rights emanating from global organizations as well as from national and regional social movements and local advocacy coalitions. With the global revolution in education, debates over the inclusion of students with special educational needs have been internationalized; however, research on special education has remained focused primarily on individual diagnosis and instruction, largely ignoring what we can learn from other countries' very different approaches to the diversity of learners' needs. Comparative research on special education that explicitly compares and systematically links historical origins and contemporary patterns clarifies the social constructions of dis/ability. It reveals national and regional variation in special and inclusive education that emphasizes political choices made long ago—and the on-going reforms of education systems. And it sharpens judgments on culturally diverse practices that lead to the gap between global intentions and national and local persistence constraining attempts to provide schooling for all and inclusive education.

REFERENCE MATTER

# NOTES

## INTRODUCTION

1. For early revelations of overrepresentation, see Dunn (1968); Kirp (1973); Mercer (1973); Milofsky (1974); Tomlinson (1982). For more recent, mainly sociological interpretations of overrepresentation, see Carrier (1984, 1986a); Mehan, Hertweck, and Meihls (1986); Reschly (1988); Skrtic (1991, 2003); Artiles and Trent (1994); Harry and Anderson (1994); Gillborn (1995: 117–125); Agbenyega and Jiggets (1999); Richardson (1999); Losen and Orfield (2002). For the politics of integration/inclusion, see Oliver (1984, 1985, 1986); Swann (1985); Tomlinson (1985); Barton (1986, 1989); Borsay (1986); Fulcher (1989, 1991); Dyson (1990); Skrtic (1992); Skrtic, Sailor, and Gee (1996). As Booth showed for England, the rhetoric of integration was preceded by significant trends toward resegregation of disabled children in special schools (Booth 1981, 1983). Also, Drake (2001: 412) demonstrates how the primarily clinical understanding of disability that underlies the growth of modern welfare states "has been either the conceptual or, indeed, the actual segregation of disabled people from society at large." The evidence of overrepresentation in special education may thus be a microcosm of a broader paradox, for an increasing democratic participation and the legislation of a "rights discourse" exaggerates the internal organization of the very groups such efforts are designed to *include*, leading to new lines of segregation (see Mayhew 1968; see also Part 3 of this volume). Organizational interpretations of overrepresentation have played a crucial role in legitimizing the sociological study of special education. They demonstrated the explanatory power of *translating* the manifest intentions as well as unintended outcomes into more theoretically general processes.

2. In literature, the reading of a text is not a linear movement from beginning to end, but a dynamic process in which one encounters increased complexity that is reorganized

as one understands the interconnections of figures and events at a higher level (see Paulson 1988). In sociology, the concept of field has deepened the understanding of organizational structures, particularly the prevalence of isomorphic tendencies that are not explained by measures of internal size and composition (see Powell and DiMaggio 1991).

3. On the dynamics of collective action across a wide range of societies, see Olson (1965); Schelling (1978); Boudon (1981); Hedström and Swedberg (1998). While the former focus on the determinants and social mechanisms of collective action generally, Barnartt and Scotch (2001), focus specifically on the disability movement and protest activities.

4. See Baker (1999) on the ever-present developmentalism and love of the "progress" narrative in public schooling.

5. For documents and up-to-date information on the activities of the United Nations in the field of disability, see UN Rights and Dignity of Persons with Disabilities www.un.org/disabilities/default.asp?id=161 (last accessed 7 April 2010).

6. Stephan Fuchs is instructive: "The distinctions that do matter *matter in time and space*, there and then, here and now. Past and remote distinctions matter if they are adopted and go to work within a here and now" (2001: 19, emphasis added).

PART ONE
1. Following Paul DiMaggio (1988: 14), we can define "institutional entrepreneurs" as those who "create a whole new system of meaning that ties the functioning of disparate sets of institutions together."

CHAPTER ONE
1. For example, almshouses and poorhouses became workhouses, which often stood as models for the construction of reformatories and penitentiaries. Similarly, charitable hospitals could be highly punitive, for pauperism was largely associated with indebtedness and often with madness. Discourses about how to deal with pauperism and with perceived impairments or illnesses reiterated prevalent problems of delinquency and criminality (see Richardson 2006).

2. See Brunschwig (1974); Reill (1975); Beiser (1996).

3. Such real constraints, coupled with the scientific expertise that the British enjoyed from the seventeenth century, helped to immunize English philosophers from becoming mired in an intellectual alienation.

4. Jeremy Bentham began his treatise on the Panopticon with a summary of the intended benefits of such a penitentiary: "Morals reformed—health preserved—industry invigorated—instruction diffused—public burthens lightened—Economy seated, as it were, upon a rock—the gordian knot of the Poor-Laws are not cut, but untied—all by a simple idea in Architecture!" ([1787] 1995: 29). Although prisons were built on this model only after Bentham's lifetime (1748–1832), the surveillance system it espoused was made famous by Michel Foucault (1979) in *Discipline and Punish* as a metaphor for the modern "disciplinary" society, which intends to continuously observe and normalize individuals.

5. In 1784, Valentin Haüy founded the first school for blind people, in Paris, now named the French National Institute for Young Blind People (*Institut National des Jeunes Aveugles*), where Louis Braille (1809–52) was schooled and eventually became an instructor and where he devised his system of raised dots for reading texts by touch using the fingertips.

6. See, e.g., Heller (1979: 400). The worthiness of the blind was accentuated by the French revolution as equality and fraternity became national mandates (see Weiner 1974: 67).

7. Although the maze of schools was ripe for rationalization, quite the opposite occurred: the voluntary principle regained its prominence. Due in large part to the emergence of two competing, yet ideologically compatible voluntary organizations, the National Society and the British and Foreign School Societies (BFSS), education continued to be viewed as an extension of private philanthropy. Of the two, the BFSS had the greater impact, owing in large measure to the energies of Joseph Lancaster and his tireless promotion of the monitorial system for the efficient instruction of large numbers of students. Lancaster's method was seen by many as an organizational answer to the problem of inherited pauperism generally and to the labor problems facing manufacturing industries specifically. The problems of manufacturers were increasingly reiterated as educational and as reformable by means of a monitorial system. By 1815, the monitorial system had gained a wider sponsorship, one that forged links between the network of schools, official and otherwise, and the system of industrial factories. The movement toward more state controls was guided by the reiterated problem-solving (Haydu 1998) of the Factory Acts. The monitorial method was a bridge between the voluntary principle and state intervention as much as it was an organizational bridge between the factory and the school. The view of education as an extension of private philanthropy would be resistant to change, yet the course of the century was gradually moving toward more state control. The simultaneous occurrence of an untidy mass of educational endowments" with a movement toward more state control bears a striking resemblance to what Perry Anderson (1978) calls the "parcellization of sovereignty" characteristic of western European feudalism. There the "functions of the State were disintegrated in a vertical allocation downwards, at each level of which political and economic relations were, on the other hand, integrated" (1978: 148). The threat of disintegration contributed an ambiguity "at the vertex of the whole hierarchy of [feudal] dependencies" (Anderson 1978: 151), posing a contradiction in the whole system that led, over time, to the "absolute exigencies of a final centre of authority in which a practical recomposition could occur" (Anderson 1978: 152). The coexistence of a parcelization of sovereignty and an inherent tendency toward centralization is similarly characteristic of decentralized educational structures that exercise a punitive benevolence.

8. Jacob Viner (1968) observes a significant difference in the content of English and French charity sermons, an indicator of a cultural difference in the meaning of charity. Because English preachers were more constrained by the status of their audience, sermons needed to persuade members to give alms, "typically abounding in reservations." French preachers, in contrast, were far less constrained and thus could "address [his most aristocratic] audiences as sinners whose salvation was especially in jeopardy" if they did not fulfill requests for charity (Viner 1968: 33).

9. Edouard Seguin was a physician and educator of children with mental disabilities in France and, after his emigration, in the United States. Having worked under Jean Marc Gaspard Itard, a teacher of deaf-mute individuals (including the so-called Wild Boy of Aveyron), he established the first private school specifically for the education of children with mental disabilities in Paris around 1840. He published one of the earliest textbooks in this field: *Traitement Moral, Hygiène, et Education des Idiots* (The Moral Treatment, Hygiene, and Education of Idiots and Other Backward Children) in 1846 and *Idiocy and Its Treatment by the Physiological Method* in 1866.

10. Abbé Charles-Michel de l'Épée founded what is currently known as the National Institute for Deaf Youth in Paris (*Institut National de Jeunes Sourds de Paris*). He devised a system of sign language based on his observations of deaf people communicating and became an advocate of manualism in contrast to oralism.

11. There is an affinity between both institutional paths and Michel Foucault's discussion of the emergence of state governance as a problem in the eighteenth century. This problem was largely dichotomous, contrasting two forms: the "reason of state" and "pastoral power" (see Dean 2010: chapter 4). The former describes the late sixteenth and seventeenth century rationalization of state governance, as autonomous from a divine order. The latter describes the diffusion of an in-depth Christianization, principally the vehicles of the confession and its capacity for the social regulation of souls. The earlier establishment of prisons and reformatories tilts the cultural climate toward punitive benevolence, and the earlier establishment of charitable and educational institutions for blind and deaf people shapes the climate toward a paternal benevolence. Foucault's question was this: when did Europe enter the era of confinement, thereby ushering in disciplinary power? His answer was perceptive: "There is a *double movement,* then, of state centralization on the one hand and of dispersion and religious dissidence on the other: it is, I believe, at the intersection of these two tendencies that the problem comes to pose itself with this peculiar intensity, of how to be ruled, how strictly, by whom, to what end, by what methods, etc. There is a problematic of government in general" (Foucault 1991: 88).

The institutional sequences of paternal and punitive benevolence are indeed forms of power relations. As Foucault asserted, relations of power imply more than beneficent interaction or communication. They imply a "freedom" of those over whom power is exercised, not as some abstract state, but as a capacity or will to act in some way, particularly to resist (Ransom 1997: 124). Such a freedom was attributed to vagabonds and the poor and, with increasing intensity at the end of the eighteenth century, to disabled people. The construction of institutions reflected this exercise of power over marginal and disabled groups. Thus, a parallel may be discernible between the reason of state and punitive benevolence, facilitated within decentralized political systems, and pastoral power with paternalistic benevolence, facilitated by centralized systems (cf. Foucault 1997: 34, 2003: 177).

12. For a similar argument for the "historical contingency" of educationally deviant conduct, one that focuses on contemporary categories of learning disability, see Adams (2008).

13. The work of Jorge Arditi (1998) parallels that of Elias. In his study of the "genealogy" of manners from the fourteenth to the eighteenth centuries, Arditi relies on, but extends the work of Elias by exploiting its affinities with the work of Foucault, among others. His organizing term is the "infrastructure of social relations," defined as "the patterns of association and differentiation in a society and to the practices through which these patterns are produced and reproduced"—or, simply, how individuals and groups relate to other individuals and groups. The patterns that are exhibited by such relations have a "logic" to them, which Arditi terms their "pragmatics." Following Elias's lead, there is a common historical force that inaugurated a civilizing process, but for Arditi, this force is not merely the rising material improvement of the West; more specifically, it is the transformation of *honor*. Honor was the specific property of the upper strata, specifically the monarchy and the aristocracy. With the decline of absolutist power, it is the direction taken by honor that can explain national differences in the civilizing process.

The most prominent difference is that between England and France—a difference between two chains of interdependence, one in which power is multicentered and one in which power is centered. For England, the transformation of honor reflected the fate of the aristocracy in the eighteenth century. The power of the aristocracy, its cultural hegemony (as discussed earlier), did not stem from class unity, for it shared power with the monarchy and was pressured by the laboring poor. Rather, its power derived from its capacity to project the "pragmatics of relationality," that is, it derived from what Shaftesbury meant by civility, by the "natural affections" that can result only from proper socialization. The patterns of association between groups, those of similarity and difference, composed a multicentric plane. A decentralized, punitive benevolence, as it was called earlier, is in Arditi's terms a multicentric plane of power that is enforced by the pragmatics of relationality.

For France, the transformation of honor reflected the continued power of the monarchy. The patterns of association between groups are defined by the monarch, a centralized power that now replaces God. Patterns of similarity and difference approximate a series of concentric circles in which groups and individuals continue to be evaluated largely on their distance from the centralized power. Where the infrastructure of social relations mirrors the power of the monarchy, the pragmatics of "grace" constitute the logic that guides how individuals and groups relate. Under this logic, honor circulates like a form of currency, doing so "around the figure of the king."

Whereas Elias concentrates on the common force behind a civilizing process, Arditi concentrates on the variable ways in which this process has been materialized. The key to this, leading up to the eighteenth century and extending beyond, is the changing meanings of honor. These changing meanings reflect shifts in power, specifically in how dominant groups retain their domination. Like Elias, Arditi is quick to emphasize that retaining power is not the award of direct and intentional actions; rather, it results from two specific conditions: the extent to which the pragmatics of a dominant group "permeate a multitude of 'others'" and the extent to which a dominant group can "forge the institutions of society 'in their own image.'" Equal to an improvement in material conditions or to an advancing division of labor, the civilizing of "others" is a central indicator of a civilizing process. From this view, the education of pauper children in England and of blind and deaf people in France was just as significant and may indeed be seen as the causal force behind an improving material condition and an advancing division of labor (see Arditi 1998).

CHAPTER TWO

1. The development of *national* education systems was not simply a result of industrialization, even if economic competition gave emerging nation-states good reason to invest in free and compulsory schooling (see Richardson 2006). That primary emphasis must be placed on emergent processes, which lead to myriad unanticipated and unintended consequences, is a shared perspective among the major studies of such development (Vaughn and Archer 1971; Ramirez and Boli 1987). The former pair of authors emphasize that structural patterns elaborate to become something genetically rooted in their origins, with the goal of identifying the historical antecedents that led, almost inexorably, to a centralized education system and those that led to a decentralized education system. The latter pair outlines a general process of institutionalization from the Reformation forward, a process in which ideological myths converged in the late nineteenth

century around a trans-state exchange economy and structural patterns diffused outward into the world polity, linking national society and mass schooling.

2. Although a strategy that cross-classifies dimensions of power and infrastructure to produce types of nation-states can help to explain variation, it may unintentionally obscure fundamental similarities as well.

3. The dynamics captured by Corrigan and Sayer parallel the conception of the nation as an "imagined community" (Anderson 1983) but they parallel even more what Homi Bhabha (1994) calls the "ambivalence of the nation as a narrative strategy." Bhabha's conception of the nation is one that focuses on its "liminality," the margins and edges, gains and losses of cultural identification representation. Not only are the borders of the nation problematic, so too are the boundaries of cultural identity. Conceiving of the nation as a narration, the "people" are constructed "within a range of discourses as a double narrative movement." Claims to be representative (exemplified by "the colonized and women") provoke a "contested cultural territory" in which those who make such claims are both "objects of a nationalist pedagogy" and "subjects of a process of [renewed] signification." The production and reproduction of the nation as narration involves a tension between the pedagogical—a "continuist, accumulative temporality"—and the performative—the "repetitious, recursive strategy." Much like Corrigan and Sayers' great arch, constructed on categories of inclusion and exclusion, Bhabha locates the origins of this tension in the liminal spaces wherein live the social histories of marginal groups. Although Bhabha refers specifically to "the colonized and women," and Corrigan and Sayer refer to social classes, others whose histories of marginality have been situated between the pedagogical and the performative would be strong candidates for the structuring of national narratives: people with disadvantages and physical and mental disabilities as well as those perceived as delinquent and criminal (see Anderson 1983; Bhabha 1994: 292, 297).

4. For asylums, see Rothman (1971); Scull (1981, 1983); Foucault (1988). For poorhouses and workhouses, see Crowther (1981); Hurt (1988: 34–61); Wagner (2005). For prisons, houses of refuge, and industrial and reform schools, see Schlossman (1977); Ignatieff (1978); Foucault (1979); Brenzel (1983); Sutton (1983). For state hospitals for deaf and blind people, see Best (1914); Lane (1984).

5. An especially good example of an institutional study that corresponds to Marshall's thesis is Donzelot's (1979) rich theoretical inquiry into the origins of "the social"—embodied in the range of institutions he terms "the tutelary complex." Similar to Marshall's twin processes of fusion and separation, Donzelot's thesis begins with the transformation of the interior functions of the family, in what he terms the "propagation" of medical, educative, and relational norms surrounding children. The propagation of these norms was framed, historically, by a bourgeois pole that constructed an educative model around the child and a working-class pole, the basis of which was a set of institutional constraints. The twin of this interior transformation has been the change in the exterior status of family law, a change resulting in a "dual regime," a system of tutelage and a system of contract. The former reflects the bourgeois pole—how middle-class families are "brought into a relation of dependence vis-à-vis welfare and educative agents"; the latter fits the working-class pole, reflecting the transition from "a government of families to a government through the family." The transformation of the family, both its interior relations and exterior status, has resulted in an expansive "policing" over children, performed through the tutelary complex of state institutions. But it is the em-

pirical substance of this transformation that is most important, for the change is from "discreet protective measures" to "direct surveillance." Institutional structures are the concrete agents of this change and are the proper objects of study. Examples include: convents for the preservation and correction of young girls; foundling hospitals; poorhouses and general hospitals for vagrants, indigents, and the physically infirm; asylums for pauper children; protective societies for neglected children and the poor; and correctional establishments for delinquents. The transformation that Donzelot explores is, among other things, a change in the size and scope of institutional structures, from community-based mechanisms that were "discreet protective measures" to large, state-funded agencies that involve "direct surveillance." In terms relevant to education systems, this transition is from voluntary protective measures to compulsory institutions of surveillance.

6. See Keith Baker's (2003) hypothesis that the center point between the imagination of new institutions and old beliefs was the *invention* of society. As he concluded: "[Society] was rather the invention of a human middle-ground between certainty and doubt, religion and relativism, grace and despair, absolute power and anarchy. It was the institution of a bearable, imperfect—but possibly ameliaorable—human world" (Baker 2003: 104). Baker's insights here underscore a central and enduring tension that began with official and counter Enlightenment thought, namely the antinomy between individualism and its embodiment of rights and society as "a bearable, imperfect" construct. That society could be ameliorated was, however, a likely precondition for the subsequent invention of another middle ground: national systems of mass education.

## PART TWO
1. Jack Goldstone defines path dependency as "a property of a system such that the outcome over a period of time is *not determined* by any particular set of initial conditions" (1998: 834, emphasis in original).

## CHAPTER THREE
1. UNESCO (1988) published its *Review of the Present Situation of Special Education* in 1988, which summarized information received from fifty-seven countries. The information was confined to topics of special education policy, legislation, administration, and provisions (the information on provisions reports only those "forms" that are "currently available"). The *Review* does not present statistical data on special education enrollment/placement numbers.

2. Although often noted as a critical juncture in disability history, a catalog of 1981's direct impact and indirect influence awaits further scholarly attention. Many of the identified priorities—from basic physical accessibility to access to education to self-empowerment and self-supporting employment—continue to challenge societies worldwide, with ongoing policy reforms, disability movement advocacy, and protest activities interacting. On the disability movement in the United States and around the world, see Scotch ([1986] 2001); Driedger (1989); Percy (1989); Pfeiffer (1993); Shapiro (1994); Charlton (1998); Barnartt and Scotch (2001); Fleischer and Zames (2001); Groce (2002); Switzer (2003); Barnartt (2010).

3. In their especially insightful chapter on the association between educational psychology and special education in France, Bélanger and Garant (1999) critique the standard functionalist account. They note first that "teachers at the beginning of the twentieth

century did not ask for the creation of special educational settings . . . (and) . . . .when [Alfred] Binet asked teachers to say which of their pupils were presenting particular difficulties *most teachers did not seem able to identify them*" (138, emphasis added). After 1945, educational psychologists were met with resistance by teachers "who did not share" their perception that "problem pupils" were the source of instructional troubles (139). Such nuances suggest caution when interpreting the formalization of special education, particularly interpretations for the origins of categories. Formal categories may follow upon demographic, legislative or political events, but a more grounded interpretation must attend to those groups who succeed or fail in their implementation attempts. The power of lay and professional groups varies nationally and regionally, and thus the formal "origins" of special education vary accordingly.

4. The view follows a substantial body of cross-national research that demonstrates the significance of the "world culture" on the expansion of education enrollments and on national curriculum. This research seriously challenges "functional" interpretations, those akin to Putnam's *need* hypothesis for special education. For expansion of education enrollments, see Meyer et al. (1977); Meyer, Ramirez, and Soysal (1992); Schofer and Meyer (2005). For national curricula, see Benavot, Meyer, and Kamens (1992).

5. When all other organizations are tested, each is insignificant when International Association of Workers for Maladjusted Children (IAWMC) is included. Even for those with equally strong associations to levels of special education, particularly the World Council for the Welfare of the Blind and World Federation of the Deaf, when the IAWMC is included their contribution is erased. Moreover, when the total number of INGOs is included with the Institute for International Law (Civil) and the IAWMC, the three produce identical coefficients (standardized). The number of organizations seems to have negligible effect independent of the two specific organizations.

CHAPTER FOUR

1. The discussion of national differences in special education often revolves around four topical dimensions. One is quantitative: the number of students classified and placed in special and inclusive education, the number and type of categories implemented and applied, individual-level performance data on achievement and attainment, and rates of expansion and patterns of change over time in special education (see, e.g., Tomlinson 1985; Richardson 1992; Powell 2011). Another is the disability categories and patterns and consequences of classification and placement in single-, dual-, or multiple-tracked educational systems (see, e.g., Tomlinson 1982; Meijer, Pijl, and Hegarty 1994: 119; Powell 2006). A third is distinctly qualitative: differences in cultural conceptions of disability, ab/normality, and special educational needs and how such conceptions define educability, the content and extent of education, and the types of schools and institutions provided (see Biklen 1987; Shakespeare 1994; Oliver 1996; Powell 2010). All of these relate to the fourth: the complex interrelation of national laws and policies concerning the education of children with disabilities, difficulties, and disadvantages (see, e.g., Lewis and Vulliamy 1980; Oliver 1986; Fulcher 1991; Powell 2011).

2. The allure of taking the experience of western European nations as the model reference is a reminder of what Giambattista Vico called the "conceit of nations" in *The New Science of Giambattista Vico* (1991: Element II, 60–61).

3. Kathleen Thelen (2004: 292) states it well: "Contrary to strong punctuated equilibrium models that lead us to expect big changes in the context of big historic breaks, we

often find significant continuities through historically 'unsettled' times, and ongoing contestation and renegotiation in 'settled' periods that nonetheless over time add up to significant change."

4. The validity of this central premise of the Western narrative has been the target of direct and indirect critiques by post-colonial scholarship. As Partha Chatterjee (1993) notes, the dominance of Europe over subject peoples conferred an added legitimacy upon a theoretical framework wherein citizenship and the nation-state were central elements. And as Dipesh Chakrabarty concurred, this legitimacy was founded on an "asymmetric ignorance," one in which "Europe works as a silent referent in historical knowledge" (Chakrabarty 1992: 337). Similarly, Mahmood Mamdani denotes this asymmetry a "history by analogy," whereby postcolonial African states are caught in a "double distinction: between experiences considered universal and normal and those seen as residual or pathological" (Mamdani 1996: 9).

5. In studying the emergent world society, John Meyer and his colleagues (1977) found that massive worldwide educational expansion since the Second World War was related less to national economic, political, or social structural characteristics—given minor variation—than to the diffusion of powerful ideas about an educated citizenry that will bring about "human progress" and demand for economic development and competitiveness. More than ever, exclusion from schooling is illegitimate, as education is viewed around the world as a human right (Meyer 2001). However, even in the wealthiest Western countries, poor children and those with disabilities have only over recent decades fully realized this right (as we show in the following chapters).

6. A prominent assumption in statistical analyses is the presumption that countries, as the units of analysis, are independent; however, this assumption would be achievable only if units are randomly selected and have had no significant past interaction (Ebbinghaus 2005; see also Schweber 2006). Yet because almost all of the chosen countries in comparative special education research, for example those with membership in the Organization for Economic Cooperation and Development, are not independent of each other; the necessary conditions for such analyses are quickly violated. Indeed, today all macro comparisons must deal with the problems of contingency and network autocorrelation posed by global processes of nation-state formation and international cooperation.

7. Most significant in Weber's comparative analyses, and requiring explanation, was the aspect that action-orientations were "uprooted" from the "natural random flow" of daily exigencies. New actions arise that are distinguished from this natural random flow, either as rational (means-end deliberations), value-rational (ethical or aesthetic principles), affectual (emotional or "feeling states"), or traditional (habituation to routine responses). Each is, in its distinctive way, a deliberate orientation that uproots individuals from randomness, giving rise to new patterns that become "transformed into regularities."

8. The attribution of the model that joins democracy and bureaucracy as "distinctly Western" compared with its "diminished presence" in the East does overstate and overreach. Such a characterization could be a simplistic binary opposition if not tempered, explained, and reconceptualized. This is the specific intent here as the chapter proceeds. Initially, the distinction is drawn in terms that are intended to be consistent with Weber's own analytical objectives. Weber was keenly aware of the many ways the Occident and the Orient overlapped; but he was in search of the specific factors, or combination of factors, that best accounted for their different historical trajectories. As discussed above, and soon elaborated, Weber's real interest was on the mixture of types, not their presumed

homogenous reality. As the twentieth century unfolded, the mixture of democracy-bureaucracy and patrimonialism certainly was among the major determining forces that reshaped the West and the East.

9. In a lucid discussion of "complex phenomena," Frederick Hayek (1967) defined this self-reproducing property succinctly: "The 'emergence' of 'new' patterns as a result of the increase in the number of elements between which simple relations exist means that this larger structure as a whole will possess certain general or abstract features which will *recur independently* of the particular values of the individual data, so long as the general structure is preserved." The "certain general or abstract features" are, in essence, "the minimum number of distinct variables a formula or *model* must possess in order to reproduce the characteristic patterns of structures . . ." In short, phenomena, social as well as physical, may increase in complexity, yet there can remain a minimum number of features that will "recur independently" of that complexity. Our focus here is on the minimum number of features that recur, not the complexity. The recurrence of the whole exemplifies a "spontaneous social order" that recurs without individuals intending to (see Hayek 1967: 26, emphases added; also 1975).

10. The resilience of special education, the fact that it "replicates" itself through the process of "reconstructing" itself is a particularly evident feature of the more developed systems in advanced Western countries. Arguably the most salient example of this resilience is the persistence of racial overrepresentation in the face of court decisions mandating changes in diagnostic and classification practices (see *Diana v. State Board of Education*, 1970; *Larry P. v. Riles,* 1972; *Mills v. Board of Education* 1972). In spite of judicial mandates, attempts to reconstruct practices seemingly result in outcomes that replicate overrepresentation (Richardson 2000). A compelling explanation for this dynamic is sociological, emphasizing how practices are entrenched because they are routine and minimize uncertainty. Yet, the explanation may derive from the very nature of the "rules" that define what is routine and thus entrenched. Here, Giorgio Agamben (2005) offers an especially insightful view to the *paradoxical* relation between the "state of exception" and the juridical rules that constitute prevailing law. If challenges to racial overrepresentation are thought of as moments of "insurrection," their real significance (aside from their ethical meaning) lies not so much in their challenge to routine practices as in how they contest the legitimacy of the juridical rules that underlie such practices. It is easy, therefore, to see such challenges as intentionally disturbing, as transgressing established legal boundaries. Yet, as Agamben demonstrates, the state of exception, whether civil war, popular insurrection or legal challenge to improper classification, is not outside the rule, nor is it a transgression. On the contrary, the state of exception is the rule: "*Being-outside, and yet belonging*: this is the topological structure of the state of exception" (Agamben 2005: 35, emphasis original). The challenges to racial overrepresentation in special education reveal a state of exception, especially because they reveal the "threshold of indeterminancy" between exclusion and inclusion (Agamben 2005: 3).

To view attempts to reform special education, particularly ones that press for expanded inclusion as states of exception, helps to explain how responses to reforms and mandates often replicate pre-existing arrangements. For special education, the juridical structure is the body of law for a "free and compulsory education," a central element of which is the evolving specification of who is educable and admissible to (state financed) public schools. Challenges are not external to the juridical structure that defines educability and admissibility. Challenges are, on the contrary, logical expectations of the juridical structure itself. As Agamben (1998: 26) notes: "The law has a regulative character and is a 'rule' not because it commands and proscribes, but because it must first of all create the sphere of its own reference in real life and *make that reference regular* [emphasis original]. Since the rule both stabilizes and presupposes the conditions of this reference, the originary structure of the rule is always of this kind . . . in which *a fact is included in the juridical order through its exclusion* [emphasis added], and transgression seems to precede and determine the lawful case . . . . The juridical order does not originally present itself simply as sanctioning a transgressive fact but instead *constitutes itself through the repetition of the same act without any sanction* [emphasis added], that is, as an exceptional case". In sum, the "replication" of special education is indeed a repetition of practices, but it is not some pejorative comment on the psychology of teachers and school staff. It is, rather, the behavior of the juridical structure itself that *must* "make regular" the "sphere of its own reference", periodically and dramatically.

11. The genealogy may be extended further, linking both social maladjustment and learning disability to "backwardness"—the first behavioral category of special education (see, e.g., Franklin 1980; Carrier 1983, 1986b on learning disability).

12. Adherence to the rules that regulate the physical school, particularly those of space and time, may be an especially Western expectation. In developing nations with lower levels of school participation and limited educational resources, expectations and judgments about competence cannot so easily rely on such physical properties as measures. Evidence from post-communist Estonia, a nation that has entered into the climate that links schooling and market forces, suggests this (see Leino and Lahelma 2002: 80).

13. There are important differences between the United States and Britain, yet a significant commonality is their historically maintained decentralization of schooling. Nonetheless, as noted previously (Chapter 3), Great Britain has moved toward centralization, stimulated principally by the National Curriculum, and the United States is more centralized in special education than other types of education (see Chapter 5).

14. Alluding to the contradiction of "remedial education," but more pointedly as a hoax, J. E. Collins noted: "Our school system is at variance with evolutionary change . . . . What sort of institution is it that makes children 'ill' so that it can 'treat' them?" (1972: 9–10). As Jenny Corbett states: "I have deliberately abandoned the *linear model* for something far more haphazard and obtuse" (1997: 62, emphasis added).

15. Linda Molm accentuates the paradoxical outcomes that distinguish negotiated and reciprocal exchange systems: ". . . because disadvantaged actors must give more frequently to maintain their powerful partner's intermittent reciprocity, *they must forgo more of the potential rewards from alternative activities*" (Molm 2003: 14, emphasis added). "Children with disabilities and parental advocates" may be inserted for "disadvantaged actors" and "the commissions that initiate the evaluations and formulate statements that often lead to placement in restrictive environments or segregated institutions" may be inserted for "their powerful partners."

16. It is important to emphasize that the path is not so much determined by access to public or private goods as it is by the attitude ascriptive groups take toward these goods. The former presumes malign intentions to exclude marginalized groups who are, in turn, presumed to seek access. Under certain circumstances, marginal groups may seek access; under other circumstances, they may reject access.

17. Peasants and laborers—and people with disabilities—can be especially vulnerable to changes that weaken ties to land and local communities. As attention and resources

flow toward the political center, such groups can be marginalized in new ways, particularly by forces that emanate predominantly from an urban culture. It is here that clientelism can be crucial, filling in the open spaces created by the tensions wrought by modernization. Much like the forms of democracy, the forms of clientelism are highly variable, largely dependent on the degree of uprootedness and the realignments that tie subordinate groups to a new political center. There is substantial variation in those who become clients and those who become patrons. In addition, however, those who would be brokers is equally, if not more significant.

18. In his analysis of the elementary structures of kinship, Claude Lévi-Strauss distinguishes generalized (reciprocal) and restricted (negotiated) exchange in terms seemingly comparable to financial investments: "The belief is the basis of trust, and confidence opens up credit. In the final analysis, the whole system exists only because the group adopting it is prepared, in the broadest meaning of the term, to speculate . . . the speculation brings in a profit . . . whereas with restricted exchange, it can never function as a whole both in time and in space. By contrast, generalized exchange gains 'at every turn,' provided, of course, it takes the initial risk" (1969: 265). The apparent superiority of generalized exchange portrayed by Lévi-Strauss may not, however, be transferable to comparing educational structures. Indeed, it may be the reverse. Reciprocal systems fit centralized structures that may, in contrast to their decentralized counterparts, have a greater incentive—or need—to proclaim themselves as "a whole both in time and space." Such gains may, however, come at the cost of divisions between continued education opportunities and early vocational tracking. The latter is more unpredictable and noted for its messy accountings; the former is far more predictable and yields clearer records.

19. In contrast to the economy of affection, Jacques Godbout describes the "gift economy" of the modern (Western) state as a series of transactions "between strangers." It is instructive, and at minimum plausible, to conceive of special education in modern Western states as a form of the gift economy, but because it is bounded by the norms of democracy and the principles of bureaucracy, it is defined by the exchanges between strangers (see Godbout 2000: chapter 4).

20. The pervasive presence of corruption in many African societies demonstrates the proposition stated earlier that the course of institutional change is shaped by the *logics* of the preexisting institutional structures. In a lucid comparison to the European model, de Sardan (1999: 47) explains the persistence of African corruption: "Of course the norms of the public service or the legal definitions of corruption in Africa are the same as in Europe, being directly derived from the European model. But in Europe this model is in part the product of rather different sociocultural logics, inaugurated in the nineteenth century, on the basis of a distinction between pubic and private affairs, on Puritanism, on egalitarian and individualistic demands. In Europe, in other words, the norms of the public service and the legal definitions of corruption correspond or harmonize, even if only approximately, with the predominant sociocultural logics. In Africa, on the contrary, there is a glaring discrepancy. As a result, the functioning of the administrative apparatus, entirely copied from the European pattern, is a schizophrenic type. In law, official functioning and budget it is totally Western. In practice, it is otherwise, traversed by logics in drastic contradiction with the original model. Thus, what is considered to be corruption from the perspective of official norms is not, or very little viewed in the same light from the perspectives of practical norms and of practices."

CHAPTER FIVE

1. Here, we use the term "institutionalization" in the sense of the process of institutional stability and change, not in Goffman's (1961) definition of it as a patient's or inmate's response to bureaucratic structures and identity-altering processes of living in a "total institution," such as a mental hospital or prison.

CHAPTER SIX

1. See www.un.org/disabilities/.

2. The current recommendation of the Standing Conference of Culture Ministers of the *Länder* in the Federal Republic of Germany on special educational support in schools elaborates nine categories with specific guidelines on: hearing, seeing, instruction of students with illness, physical and motor development, speech, mental development, learning, emotional and social development, multiple categories or no classification, and upbringing and instruction of children and youth with autistic behavior (see KMK 2005, 2010).

3. Among the countries reported on here, special educational needs classification rates correlate only weakly with the total segregation rate (0.16) and modestly with the special educational needs group segregation rate (–0.30). Thus, higher integration or inclusion rates cannot be explained merely as a function of a larger population of students with special educational needs.

CHAPTER SEVEN

1. As Loïc Wacquant (2008) argues, the dramatic rise of the "penal state" is less a reaction to crime than it is a neoliberal form of governance of poverty that diverts attention from urban labor market marginality and the consequent social insecurity and melds restrictive "workfare" and expansive "prisonfare" policies.

2. Prevalence rates of disability by state for the civilian noninstitutionalized populations five years old and older, based on the 2006 American Community Survey, emphasize the regional disparities with a range from 12.3 percent in New Jersey and Utah via a mean for the United States of 15.1 percent to a high of 23.4 percent in West Virginia (Census Bureau 2008).

3. The source for the case challenges brought against correctional facilities is the National Center on Education, Disability, and Juvenile Justice. The cases for Table 7.1 are drawn from the document "Class Action Litigation Involving Special Education Claims for Youth in Juvenile and Adult Correctional Facilities," 2005 (available at www.edjj.org/Litigation/litchartOct05.pdf). Sources for the case law in special education are Thomas and Denzinger (1993) and Murdick, Gartin, and Crabtree (2002); see also Wright and Wright (1999); Boyle and Weishaar (2001).

4. For an overview of special education law and short summaries of major decisions from the U.S. Supreme Court, the Courts of Appeals, and the District Courts, see www.wrightslaw.com/caselaw.htm (last accessed 27 April 2010).

5. Studies of delinquency rates for European countries report inconsistencies in trends and in plausible explanations. There is agreement, however, that rates grew across several countries until the mid-1980s and then leveled off. Causes of the leveling off or declines are not easily identified, but changes in reporting practices and in convictions seem most plausible. Another explanation, rarely mentioned, is the absorption into

special education of youth who might otherwise likely be in a reformatory. For an analysis of the effects of the population of youth in reform schools on special education placement rates, see Richardson (1999: 92). For European trends, see Farrington (1992); Friday (1992); Estrada (1999); Stern (2001); Killia et al. (2004).

CHAPTER EIGHT

1. A key source of this dependency is the amendment in many compulsory education laws that *exempted* disabled children, thereby legally validating exclusion and segregation. For specific exemptions, see the *World Handbook of Educational Organization and Statistics* (UNESCO 1952: 30, 118, 151, 258, 356, 419; see also Dahl, Tangerud, and Vislie 1982: 16–17).

2. In his comprehensive study of compensatory discrimination and the backward classes in India, Marc Galanter noted: "Courts face the problem of keeping these categories *available* for carrying out policies of eliminating old inequalities without invigorating them as sources of symbolic sustenance for hierarchic patterns" (1972: 357, emphasis added).

# BIBLIOGRAPHY

Abang, T. B. "Disablement, Disability, and the Nigerian Society." *Disability, Handicap & Society* 3 (1988): 71–77.

Abbott, Andrew. *Chaos of Disciplines*. Chicago: University of Chicago Press, 2001.

Abrams, Irwin. "The Emergence of International Law Societies." *Review of Politics* 19 (1957): 361–380.

Abrams, Philip. "Towns and Economic Growth: Some Theories and Problems." In *Towns in Societies: Essays in Economic History and Historical Sociology*. Edited by Philip Abrams and E. A. Wrigley. Cambridge, UK: Cambridge University Press, 1997.

Adams, Paul. "Positioning Behavior, Attention Deficit/Hyperactive Disorder (ADHD) in the Post-Welfare Educational Era." *International Journal of Special Education* 12 (2008): 113–125.

Agamben, Giorgio. *Homo Sacer: Sovereign Power and Bare Life*. Stanford, CA: Stanford University Press, 1998.

———. *State of Exception*. Chicago: University of Chicago Press, 2005.

Agbenyega, Stephen, and Joseph Jiggets. "Minority Children and their Overrepresentation in Special Education." *Education* 119 (1999): 619–632.

Albrecht, Gary L., ed. *Encyclopedia of Disability*. Thousand Oaks, CA: Sage, 2005.

Albrecht, Gary L., Katharine D. Seelman, and Michael Bury, eds. *Handbook of Disability Studies*. Thousand Oaks, CA: Sage, 2001.

Alexander, Jeffrey C. *Theoretical Logic in Sociology: Vol. 3. The Classical Attempt at Theoretical Synthesis: Max Weber*. Berkeley: University of California Press, 1983.

Allan, Julie. *Rethinking Inclusive Education: The Philosophers of Difference in Practice*. A. A. Dordrecht, the Netherlands: Springer, 2008.

Allmendinger, Jutta, and Stephan Leibfried. "Education and the Welfare State: The Four Worlds of Competence Production." *Journal of European Social Policy* 13 (2003): 63–81.

Anderson, Benedict. *Imagined Communities: Reflections on the Origin and Spread of Nationalism.* London: Verso, 1983.

Anderson, Perry. *Passages from Antiquity to Feudalism.* London: Verso, 1978.

Andrews, Jack E., Douglas W. Carnine, Martha J. Coutinho, Eugene B. Edgar, Steven R. Forness, Lynn S. Fuchs, Dixie Jordan, James M. Kauffman, James M. Patton, James Paul, Jon Rosell, Robert Rueda, Ellen Schiller, Thomas M. Skrtic, and James Wong. "Perspective: Bridging the Special Education Divide." *Remedial and Special Education* 21.5 (2000): 258–260.

Archer, Margaret S. *The Social Origins of Educational Systems.* Beverly Hills, CA: Sage, 1979.

———. "Introduction: Theorizing About the Expansion of Educational Systems." In *The Sociology of Educational Expansion, Take-Off, Growth, and Inflation in Educational Systems.* Edited by Margaret S. Archer. Beverly Hills, CA: Sage, 1982.

———. *The Social Origins of Educational Systems* (University Edition). London: Sage, 1984.

———. "Cross-National Research and the Analysis of Educational Systems." *Cross-National Research in Sociology.* Edited by Melvin Kohn. London: Sage, 1989.

Arditi, Jorge. *The Genealogy of Manners: Transformations of Social Relations in France and England from the Fourteenth to the Eighteenth Century.* Chicago: University of Chicago Press, 1998.

Arendt, Hannah. *The Human Condition.* Chicago: University of Chicago Press, 1989.

Armstrong, Felicity. "Inclusion, Curriculum and the Struggle for Space in School." *International Journal of Inclusive Education* 3 (1999): 75–87.

———. "The Historical Development of Special Education: Humanitarian Rationality or 'Wild Profusion of Entangled Events'?" *History of Education* 31 (2002): 437–456.

———. *Spaced Out: Policy, Difference, and the Challenge of Inclusive Education.* Dordrecht, Netherlands: Kluwer, 2003.

Armstrong, Felicity, Derrick Armstrong, and Len Barton, eds. *Inclusive Education. Policy, Contexts and Comparative Perspectives.* London: David Fulton, 2000.

Artiles, Alfredo J., and Daniel P. Hallahan, eds. *Special Education in Latin America: Experiences and Issues.* Westport, CT: Praeger, 1997.

Artiles, Alfredo J., and Stanley C. Trent. "Overrepresentation of Minority Students in Special Education: A Continuing Debate." *Journal of Special Education* 27.4 (1994): 410–437.

Babler, Alan M. "Education of the Destitute: A Study of London Ragged Schools, 1844–1874." Ph.D. diss., Northern Illinois University, 1978.

Baker, Bernadette. "The Dangerous and the Good? Developmentalism, Progress, and Public Schooling." *American Educational Research Journal* 36.4 (1999): 797–834.

———. "The Hunt for Disability." *Teachers College Record* 104 (2002): 663–703.

Baker, David P., and Gerald K. LeTendre, eds. *National Differences, Global Similarities: World Culture and the Future of Schooling.* Stanford, CA: Stanford University Press, 2005.

Baker, David P., Gerald K. LeTendre, and Brian Goesling. "Rich Land, Poor Schools." In *National Differences, Global Similarities: World Culture and the Future of Schooling.* Edited by David P. Baker and Gerald K. LeTendre, 71–85. Stanford, CA: Stanford University Press, 2005.

Baker, Keith Michael. "Enlightenment and the Institution of Society: Notes for a Conceptual History." In *Civil Society: History and Possibilities.* Edited by Sudipta Kaviraj and Sunil Khilnani, 84–104. Cambridge, UK: Cambridge University Press, 2003.

Ball, Stephen J. *Politics and Policy Making in Education: Explorations in Policy Sociology.* London: Routledge, 1990.

———. "What is Policy? Texts, Trajectories and Toolboxes." *Discourse* 13 (1993): 10–17.

Barkey, Karen. *Bandits and Bureaucrats: The Ottoman Route to State Centralization.* Ithaca, NY: Cornell University Press, 1994.

Barnartt, Sharon N. "The Globalization of Disability Protests, 1970–2005: Pushing the Limits of Cross-Cultural Research?" *Comparative Sociology* 9.2 (2010): 222–240.

Barnartt, Sharon N., and Richard K. Scotch. *Disability Protests: Contentious Politics 1970–1999.* Washington, DC: Gallaudet University Press, 2001.

Barthes, Roland. *Elements of Semiology.* New York: Hill and Wang, 1977.

———. *The Fashion System.* New York: Hill and Wang, 1983.

———. *The Language of Fashion.* New York: Berg, 2006.

Barton, Len. "The Politics of Special Educational Needs." *Disability, Handicap & Society* 1 (1986): 273–290.

———, ed. *Integration: Myth or Reality?* London: Falmer, 1989.

———. "Sociology, Disability Studies, and Education." In *The Disability Reader.* Edited by Tom Shakespeare. London: Cassell, 1998.

Barton, Len, and Felicity Armstrong. "Disability, Education, and Inclusion: Cross-Cultural Issues and Dilemmas." In *Handbook of Disability Studies.* Edited by Gary L. Albrecht, Katherine D. Seelman, and Michael Bury, 693–710. Thousand Oaks, CA: Sage, 2001.

Beckfield, Jason. "Inequality in the World Polity: The Structure of International Organization." *American Sociological Review* 68.3 (2003): 401–424.

Beiser, Frederick C. *The Sovereignty of Reason: The Defense of Rationality in the Early English Enlightenment.* Princeton, NJ: Princeton University Press, 1996.

Bélanger, Nathalie. "Solicitude and Special Education Policies." *Cambridge Journal of Education* 31 (2001): 337–348.

Bélanger, Nathalie, and Nicolas Garant. "Educational Opportunities and Polysemic Notions of Equality in France." In *Disability, Human Rights and Education: Cross-Cultural Perspectives.* Edited by Felicity Armstrong and Len Barton. Philadelphia: Open University Press, 1999.

Bellah, Robert N., Richard Madsen, William M. Sullivan, Ann Swidler, and Steven M. Tipton. *Habits of the Heart.* Berkeley: University of California Press, 1985.

Below, Susanne von. *Bildungssysteme und soziale Ungleichheit.* Opladen, Germany: Leske & Budrich, 2002.

Benavot, Aaron, John W. Meyer, and David Kamens. *World Culture and the Curricular Content of Primary Education.* New York: Taylor & Francis, 1992.

Bender, John. *Imagining the Penitentiary: Fiction and the Architecture of Mind in Eighteenth-Century England.* Chicago: University of Chicago Press, 1987.

Bentham, Jeremy. *The Panopticon Writings.* London: Verso, [1787] 1995.

Berkeley, George. *A New Theory of Vision.* London: J.M. Dent & Sons, [1709] 1919.

Berlin, Isaiah. *Against the Current: Essays in the History of Ideas.* New York: Viking, 1968.

———. *The Roots of Romanticism.* Princeton, NJ: Princeton University Press, 1999.

Best, Harry. *The Deaf, Their Position in Society, and the Provision for Their Education in the United States.* New York: Thomas Crowell Co., 1914.

Bhabha, Homi K. "DissemiNation: Time, Narrative, and the Margins of the Modern Nation." In *Nation and Narration.* Edited by Homi K. Bhabha, 291–322. London: Routledge, 1994.

———. "What Is a Nation?" In *Nation and Narration*. Edited by Homi K. Bhabha. London: Routledge, 1994.

Biggart, Nicole W., and Mauro F. Guillén. "Developing Difference: Social Organization and the Rise of the Auto Industries of South Korea, Taiwan, Spain, and Argentina." *American Sociological Review* 64 (1999): 722–747.

Biklen, Douglas. "The Culture of Policy: Disability Images and Their Analogues in Public Policy." *Policy Studies Journal* 15 (1987): 515–535.

———. *Schooling Without Labels: Parents, Educators, and Inclusive Education.* Philadelphia: Temple University Press, 1992.

Bina, Michael. "Mainstreaming, Schools for the Blind, and Full Inclusion: What Shall the Future of Education for Blind Children Be?" In *The Illusion of Full Inclusion*. Edited by James M. Kauffman and Daniel P. Hallahan. Austin, TX: PRO-ED, 1995.

Birnbaum, Morton. "The Right to Treatment." *American Bar Association Journal* 46 (1960): 499–505.

Birnbaum, Morton, and Abraham Twerski. "Observations on the Right to Treatment." *Duquesne Law Review* 10 (1972): 554–578.

Black, Donald. *Sociological Justice.* New York: Oxford University Press, 1989.

Bloch, Marc. *The Historian's Craft.* New York: Vintage, 1964.

Boli, John. *New Citizens for a New Society: The Institutional Origins of Mass Schooling in Sweden.* Oxford: Pergamon Press, 1989.

Boli, John, and George Thomas. "World Culture in the World Polity: A Century of International Non-Governmental Organization." *American Sociological Review* 62 (1997): 171–190.

———, eds. *Constructing World Culture: International Nongovernmental Organizations Since 1875.* Stanford, CA: Stanford University Press, 1999.

Boli, John, and Michael A. Elliott. "Façade Diversity: The Individualization of Cultural Difference." *International Sociology* 23 (2008): 540–560.

Boli, John, Francisco Ramirez, and John W. Meyer. "Explaining the Origins and Expansion of Mass Education." *Comparative Education Review* 29 (1985): 145–170.

Booth, Tony. "Demystifying Integration." In *The Practice of Special Education*. Edited by Will Swann. Oxford: Blackwell, 1981.

———. "Policies Towards the Integration of Mentally Disabled Children in Education." *Oxford Review of Education* 9 (1983): 255–268.

Booth, Tony, and Mel Ainscow. *The Index for Inclusion.* Bristol, UK: Centre for Studies on Inclusive Education, 2002.

Borsay, Anne. "Personal Trouble or Public Issues? Towards a Model of Policy for People with Physical and Mental Disabilities." *Disability, Handicap & Society* 1 (1986): 179–195.

Boudon, Raymond. *The Logic of Social Action.* New York: Routledge & Kegan Paul, 1981.

Bourdieu, Pierre. *The Field of Cultural Production.* New York: Columbia University Press, 1993.

Bowker, Geoffrey C., and Susan Leigh Star. *Sorting Things Out: Classification and its Consequences.* Cambridge, MA: MIT Press, 1999.

Boyle, Joseph R., and Mary Weishaar. *Special Education Law with Cases.* Boston: Allyn and Bacon, 2001.

Braddock, David L., and Susan L. Parish. "An Institutional History of Disability." In *Handbook of Disability Studies*. Edited by Gary L. Albrecht, Katherine D. Seelman, and Michael Bury, 11–68. Thousand Oaks, CA: Sage, 2001.

Bradley, Karen, and John G. Richardson. "The Moral Career of Intelligence: Pedagogical Practices and Educational Psychology." In *Toolkits, Translation Devices, and Conceptual Accounts: Essays on Basil Bernstein's Sociology of Knowledge.* Edited by Parlo Singh, Alan R. Sadovnik, and Susan F. Semel, 197–216. New York: Lang, 2010.

Brantlinger, Ellen. "Using Ideology: Cases of Nonrecognition of the Politics of Research and Practice in Special Education." *Review of Educational Research* 67.4 (1997): 425–459.

———. "Winners and Losers: The Basis for School Competition and Hierarchies." In *Who Benefits from Special Education?* Edited by Ellen A. Brantlinger. Mahwah, NJ: Lawrence Erlbaum Associates, 2006.

Brenzel, Barbara M. *Daughters of the State: A Social Portrait of the First Reform School for Girls in North America, 1856–1905.* Cambridge, MA: MIT Press, 1983.

Brine, Jacky. "Education, Social Exclusion, and the Supranational State." *International Journal of Inclusive Education* 5.2/3 (2001): 119–131.

Broadbent, J. B. "Shaftesbury's Horses of Instruction." In *The English Mind, Studies in the English Moralists Presented to Basil Willey.* Edited by Hugh Sykes Davies and George Watson. Cambridge, UK: Cambridge University Press, 1964.

*Brown v. Board of Education,* 347 Supreme Court of the US 483 (1954).

Brubaker, Rogers. *Citizenship and Nationhood in France and Germany.* Cambridge, MA: Harvard University Press, 1992.

Brunschwig, Henri. *Enlightenment and Romanticism in Eighteenth-Century Prussia.* Chicago: University of Chicago Press, [1947] 1974.

Bühler-Niederberger, Doris. *Legasthenie: Geschichte und Folgen einer Pathologisierung.* Opladen, Germany: Leske & Budrich, 1991.

Burch, Susan. "Reading Between the Signs: Defending Deaf Culture in Early Twentieth-Century America." In *The New Disability History: American Perspectives.* Edited by Paul K. Longmore and Lauri Umansky, 214–235. New York: New York University Press, 2001.

Burleigh, Michael. *Death and Deliverance: "Euthanasia" in Germany c. 1900–1945.* Cambridge, UK: Cambridge University Press, 1994.

Burt, Robert A. "Judicial Action to Aid the Retarded." In *Issues in the Classification of Children, Vol. Two.* Edited by Nicholas Hobbs. San Francisco: Jossey-Bass, 1975.

Campbell, John L. "Ideas, Politics, and Public Policy." *Annual Review of Sociology* 28 (2002): 21–38.

———. *Institutional Change and Globalization.* Princeton, NJ: Princeton University Press, 2004.

Canguilhem, Georges. *The Normal and the Pathological.* New York: Zone Books, 1991.

Carey, Allison C. *On the Margins of Citizenship: Intellectual Disability and Civil Rights in Twentieth Century America.* Philadelphia: Temple University Press, 2009.

Carpenter, Mary. *Reformatory Schools for the Children of the Perishing and Dangerous Classes.* Montclair, NJ: Patterson Smith, 1970.

Carpenter, William Lant. *The Moral and Social Aspects of the Present Condition of Primary Education Discourse delivered in South Place Chapel, Finsburg, E.C.* London: E. W. Allen, 1888?.

Carrier, James G. "Masking the Social in Educational Knowledge: The Case of Learning Disability Theory." *American Journal of Sociology* 88 (1983): 948–974.

———. "Comparative Special Education: Ideology, Differentiation, and Allocation in England and the United States." In *Special Education and Social Interests.* Edited by Len Barton and Sally Tomlinson, 35–64. London: Croom Helm, 1984.

———. "Sociology and Special Education: Differentiation and Allocation in Mass Education." *American Journal of Education* 94.3 (1986a): 281–312.

———. *Learning Disability, Social Class and the Construction of Inequality in American Education.* New York: Greenwood Press, 1986b.

Carrington, Suzanne. "Inclusion Needs a Different School Culture." *International Journal of Inclusive Education* 3 (1999): 257–268.

Casey, Pamela, and Ingo Keilitz. "Estimating the Prevalence of Learning Disabled and Mentally Retarded Juvenile Offenders: A Meta-Analysis." In *Understanding Troubled and Troubling Youth.* Edited by Peter L. Leone. New York: Sage, 1990.

Chakrabarty, Dipesh. "Postcoloniality and the Artifice of History: Who Speaks for 'Indian' Pasts?" *Representations* 37 (1992): 1–26.

———. *Habitations of Modernity: Essays in the Wake of Subaltern Studies.* Chicago: University of Chicago Press, 2002.

Chance, William. *Children Under the Poor Law, Their Education, Traiining and After-Care.* London: Swan Sonnenschein and Co., 1897.

Charlton, James I. *Nothing About Us Without Us: Disability Oppression and Empowerment.* Berkeley: University of California Press, 1998.

Chatterjee, Partha. *The Nation and Its Fragments: Colonial and Postcolonial Histories.* Princeton, NJ: Princeton University Press, 1993.

Chayes, Abram. "The Role of the Judge in Public Law Litigation." *Harvard Law Review* 89 (1976): 1281–1316.

Cheselden, William. "An Account of Some Observations Made by a Young Gentleman, Who Was Born Blind, or Lost His Sight So Early, That He Had No Remembrance of Ever Having Seen and Was Couch'd Between 13 and 14 Years of Age." *Philosophical Transactions* 35 (1727–1728): 447–450.

Chisick, Harvey. *The Limits of Reform in the Enlightenment.* Princeton, NJ: Princeton University Press, 1981.

Clapham, Christopher. "Sovereignty and the Third World State." *Political Studies* XLVII (1999): 522–537.

Clark, Catherine, Alan Dyson, and Allan Millward. *Theorising Special Education.* London: Routledge, 1998.

Clark, Catherine, Alan Dyson, Allan Millward, and David Skidmore. *New Directions in Special Needs: Innovations in Mainstream Schools.* London: Cassell, 1997.

Cloerkes, Günther, ed. *Wie man behindert wird.* Heidelberg, Germany: Universitätsverlag Winter, 2003a.

———. "Zahlen zum Staunen. Die deutsche Schulstatistik." In *Wie man behindert wird.* Edited by G. Cloerkes. Heidelberg, Germany: Universitätsverlag Winter, 2003b. 11–23.

Cobban, Alfred. *Edmund Burke and the Revolt Against the Eighteenth Century.* London: George Allen & Unwin, 1962.

Cobbe, Frances Power. *Workhouse as an Hospital.* London: Emily Faithfull & Co., 1861.

Coleman, James S. *Equality and Achievement in Education.* Boulder, CO: Westview Press, 1990.

Collins, J. E. "The Remedial Education Hoax." *Remedial Education* 7.3 (1972): 9–10.

Collins, Randall. "Some Comparative Principles of Educational Stratification," *Harvard Educational Review* 47.1 (1977): 1–27.

Condillac, Étienne Bonnot de. *An Essay on the Origin of Human Knowledge.* New York: AMS Press, [1746] 1974.

———. *Treatise on the Sensations.* Manchester, UK: Clinamen Press, [1754] 2002.

Connor, David J. "Adding Urban Complexities into the Mix: Continued Resistance to the Inclusion of Students with Cognitive Impairments." Paper presented at the ninth Disability Studies in Education conference, Syracuse University, New York, 2009.

Cooke-Taylor, Richard W. *The Factory System and the Factory Acts.* London: Methuen, 1894.

Corbett, Jenny. *Bad Mouthing: The Language of Special Needs.* London: Falmer, 1995.

———. "Include/Exclude: Redefining the Boundaries." *International Journal of Inclusive Education* 1 (1997): 55–64.

Cornell, Stephen. *The Return of the Native.* New York: Oxford University Press, 1988.

Cornwell, John K. "CRIPA: The Failure of Federal Intervention for Mentally Retarded People." *Yale Law Journal* 97 (1988): 845–862.

Corrigan, Philip, and Derek Sayer. *The Great Arch: English State Formation as Cultural Revolution.* New York: Blackwell, 1985.

*Covarrubias v. San Diego Unified School District,* 70–394 (February 1971).

*Creek v. Stone,* 379 F.2d 106 DC Cir. (1967).

Crocker, L. G. "Rousseau and the Common People." In *Studies in the Eighteenth Century, III.* Edited by Robert G. Brissenden and J. C. Eade. Toronto: University of Toronto Press, 1976.

Crowther, Margaret Anne. *The Workhouse System, 1834–1929.* Athens: University of Georgia Press, 1981.

Crozier, Michel. *The Bureaucratic Phenomenon.* Chicago: University of Chicago Press, 1964.

Culler, Jonathan. *Ferdinand de Saussure.* New York: Penguin, 1976.

———. *Roland Barthes.* New York: Oxford University Press, 1983.

Cummings, William K. "The Institutions of Education: Compare, Compare, Compare!" *Comparative Education Review* 43.4 (1999): 413–437.

Dahl, Marit, Hans Tangerud, and Lise Vislie. *Integration of Handicapped Pupils in Compulsory Education in Norway.* Oslo, Norway: Universitetsforlaget, 1982.

Daly, Mary C. "Who Is Protected by the ADA? Evidence from the German Experience." *Annals of the American Academy of Political and Social Science* 549 (January 1997): 101–116.

Daniel, Philip T. K. "Educating Students with Disabilities in the Least Restrictive Environment." *Journal of Educational Administration* 35.2 (1997): 397–410.

Davis, Lennard J. *Enforcing Normalcy: Disability, Deafness, and the Body.* London: Verso, 1995.

Dean, Mitchell. *Governmentality, Power and Rule in Modern Society.* Los Angeles, CA: Sage, 2010.

Defoe, Daniel. *The Great Law of Subordination Consider'd; or, the Insolence and Unsufferable Behaviour of Servants in England duly enquir'd into.* London: S. Harding et al., 1724.

Degener, Theresia. "'Gesunder' juristischer Menschenverstand?" In *Normalität, Behinderung und Geschlecht.* Edited by Ulrike Schildmann, 43–61. Opladen, Germany: Leske & Budrich, 2001.

Delanty, Gerard. *Citizenship in a Global Age.* Buckingham, UK: Open University Press, 2000.

Delanty, Gerard, and Patrick O'Mahony. *Nationalism and Social Theory.* London: Sage, 2002.

della Porta, Donatella, and Sydney Tarrow, eds. *Transational Protest and Global Activism.* Lanham, MD: Rowan and Littlefield, 2005.

*Diana v. State Board of Education,* C-70 37 RFR ND Cal (1970).

Diderot, Denis. "Letter on the Blind for the Use of Those Who See." In *Thoughts on the Interpretation of Nature.* Edited by Denis Diderot. New York: Clinamen Press, [1749] 1999.

DiMaggio, Paul J. "Interest and Agency in Institutional Theory." In *Institutional Patterns and Organizations: Culture and Environment.* Edited by Lynne G. Zucker, 3–22. Cambridge, MA: Ballinger, 1988.

DiMaggio, Paul J., and Walter W. Powell. "The Iron Cage Revisited: Institutional Isomorphism and Collective Rationality in Organizational Fields." *American Sociological Review* 48 (1983): 147–160.

———. "Introduction." In *The New Institutionalism in Organizational Analysis.* Edited by Walter W. Powell and Paul J. DiMaggio, 1–38. Chicago: University of Chicago Press, 1991.

Diver, Colin S. "The Judge as Political Powerbroker: Superintending Structural Change in Public Institutions." *Virginia Law Review* 65 (1979): 43–106.

Dobbin, Frank. *Forging Industrial Policy.* New York: Cambridge University Press, 1994.

Donzelot, Jacques. *The Policing of Families.* New York: Pantheon, 1979.

Drake, Robert F. "Welfare States and Disabled People." In *Handbook of Disability Studies.* Edited by Gary L. Albrecht, Katherine D. Seelman, and Michael Bury. Thousand Oaks, CA: Sage, 2001.

Drewek, Peter. "Bildung und Erziehung im deutsch-amerikanischen Vergleich." In *Internationalisierung: Semantik und Bildungssystem in vergleichender Perspektive.* Edited by Marcelo Caruso and Heinz-Elmar Tenorth. Frankfurt am Main, Germany: Lang, 2002.

Driedger, Diane. *The Last Civil Rights Movement.* New York: St. Martin's Press, 1989.

Dunn, Lloyd M. "Special Education for the Mildly Retarded: Is Much of It Justified?" *Exceptional Children* 45 (1968): 5–22.

Dyson, Alan. "Special Educational Needs and the Concept of Change." *Oxford Review of Education* 16 (1990): 55–66.

Ebbinghaus, Bernhard. "When Less Is More: Selection Problems in Large-N and Small-N Cross-National Comparisons." *International Sociology* 20.2 (2005): 133–152.

Eisenstadt, Shmuel N. *Traditional Patrimonialism and Modern Neopatrimonialism.* London: Sage, 1973.

Eisenstadt, Shmuel N., and Luis Roniger. "Patron-Client Relations as a Model of Structuring Social Exchanges." *Comparative Studies in Society and History* 22 (1980): 42–77.

Eisenstadt, Shmuel N., and Wolfgang Schluchter. "Preface." In *Globality and Multiple Modernities.* Edited by Luis Roniger and Carlos H. Waisman. Brighton, UK: Sussex Academic Press, 2002.

Ekeh, Peter P. "Colonialism and the Two Publics in Africa: A Theoretical Statement." *Comparative Studies in Society and History* 17 (1975): 91–112.

Elias, Norbert. *The Civilizing Process: Sociogenetic and Psychogenetic Investigations*. Malden, MA: Blackwell, 2000.

Ellger-Rüttgardt, Sieglind. "Das Sonderschulwesen." In *Handbuch der Deutschen Bildungsgeschichte. Vol. VI.II: Deutsche Demokratische Republik und neue Bundesländer*. Edited by Chrisoph Führ and Carl-Ludwig Furck, 233–254. Munich: C. H. Beck, 1997a.

———. "Entwicklung des Sonderschulwesens." In *Handbuch der Deutschen Bildungsgeschichte. Vol. VI.I: Bundesrepublik Deutschland*. Edited by Chrisoph Führ and Carl-Ludwig Furck, 356–377. Munich: C. H. Beck, 1997b.

Entwisle, Doris R., Karl L. Alexander & Linda Steffel Olson. *Children, Schools, and Inequality*. Boulder, CO: Westview, 1997.

Ertman, Thomas. *Birth of the Leviathan, Building States and Regimes in Early Modern Europe*. New York: Cambridge University Press, 1997.

Estrada, Felipe. 1999. "Juvenile Crime Trends in Post-War Europe." *European Journal on Criminal Policy and Research* 7: 23–42.

European Agency for Development in Special Needs Education. *Integration in Europe: Provision for Pupils with Special Educational Needs: Trends in 14 European Countries*. Middelfart, Denmark: EADSNE, 1998.

———. *Transition from School to Employment: Main Problems, Issues and Options Faced by Students with Special Educational Needs in 16 European Countries. Summary report*. Middelfart, Denmark: EADSNE, 2002.

———. *Special Education Across Europe in 2003: Trends in Provision in 18 European Countries*. Middelfart, Denmark: EADSNE, 2003.

———. *Special Needs Education: Country Data 2006*. Middelfart, Denmark: EADSNE, 2006.

European Union. *Resolution on the Situation of Persons with Disabilities in the European Union* (6941/08). Brussels, 2008.

Eurydice. *Key Data on Education in Europe*. Brussels: European Commission, 2005 and prior years.

Evans, Peter, with Suzanne Bronheim, John Bynner, Stephan Klasen, Phyllis Magrab, and Stewart Ranson. "Social Exclusion and Students with Special Educational Needs." Paper for the Organisation for Economic Cooperation and Development's Centre for Educational Research and Development. Paris: OECD/CERI, 2002.

Farber, Bernard. *Mental Retardation: Its Social Context and Social Consequences*. Boston: Houghton Mifflin, 1968.

Farr, James R. *Artisans in Europe, 1300–1914*. Cambridge, UK: Cambridge University Press, 2000.

Farrington, David P. "Trends in English Juvenile Delinquency and Their Explanation." *International Journal of Comparative and Applied Criminal Justice* 16 (1992): 151–163.

Fischl, Richard Michael. "Some Realism About Critical Legal Studies." *University of Miami Law Review* 41 (1987): 505–532.

Fleischer, Doris Zames, and Frieda Zames. *The Disability Rights Movement: From Charity to Confrontation*. Philadelphia: Temple University Press, 2001.

Florian, Lani, Judith Hollenweger, Rune J. Simeonsson, Klaus Wedell, Sheila Riddell, Lorella Terzi, and Anthony Holland. "Cross-Cultural Perspectives on the Classification of Children with Disabilities: Part I." *Journal of Special Education* 40.1 (2006): 36–45.

Florian, Lani, and Margaret J. McLaughlin. *Disability Classification in Education: Issues and Perspectives.* Thousand Oaks, CA: Corwin Press, 2008.

Florian, Lani, and Julia Rafal. "Transitions of People with Disabilities Beyond Secondary Education in the United States." Background paper. Paris: OECD, 2008.

Forrest, Alan. *The French Revolution and the Poor.* New York: St. Martin's, 1981.

Foucault, Michel. *Discipline and Punish.* New York: Vintage, 1979.

———. *Madness and Civilization: A History of Insanity in the Age of Reason.* New York: Vintage, 1988.

———. "Governmentality." In *The Foucault Effect: Studies in Governmentality.* Edited by Graham Burchell, Colin Gordon, and Peter Miller. Chicago: University of Chicago Press, 1991.

———. *Ethics, Subjectivity and Truth.* Edited by Paul Rabinow. New York: The New Press, 1997.

———. *Abnormal. Lectures at the Collége de France.* New York: Picador, 2003.

Francis, Martin. "Disruptive Units—Labelling a New Generation." *Where* 158 (1980): 12–14.

Franklin, Barry M. "From Backwardness to LD: Behaviorism, Systems Theory, and the Learning Disabilities Field Historically Reconsidered." *Journal of Education* 162 (1980): 5–22.

Friday, Paul C. "Delinquency in Sweden: Current Trends and Theoretical Implications." *International Journal of Comparative and Applied Criminal Justice* 16 (1992): 231–246.

Friedland, Roger, and Robert R. Alford. "Bringing Society Back In." In *The New Institutionalism in Organizational Analysis.* Edited by Walter W. Powell and Paul J. DiMaggio, 232–263. Chicago: University of Chicago Press, 1991.

Fuchs, Dieter. "Die demokratische Gemeinschaft in den USA und in Deutschland." In *Die Vermessung kultureller Unterschiede: USA und Deutschland im Vergleich.* Edited by Jürgen Gerhards, 33–72. Wiesbaden, Germany: Westdeutscher Verlag, 2000.

Fuchs, Stephan. *Against Essentialism: A Theory of Culture and Society.* Cambridge, MA: Harvard University Press, 2001.

Fulcher, Gillian. "Integrate and Mainstream? Comparative Issues in the Politics of These Policies." In *Integration: Myth or Reality?* Edited by Len Barton. London: Falmer, 1989.

———, ed. *Disabling Policies? A Comparative Approach to Education Policy and Disability.* London: Falmer, 1991.

Füssel, Hans-Peter, and Rudolf Kretschmann. *Gemeinsamer Unterricht für behinderte und nichtbehinderte Kinder.* Witterschlick/Bonn, Germany: Verlag Marg. Wehle, 1993.

Gabel, Susan, Svjetlana Curcic, Justin J. W. Powell, Khaled Kader, and Lynn Albee. "Migration and Ethnic Group Disproportionality in Special Education: An Exploratory Study." *Disability & Society* 24.5 (2009): 625–639.

Galanter, Marc. "The Abolition of Disabilities—Untouchability and the Law." In *The Untouchables in Contemporary India.* Edited by J. Michael Mahar. Tucson: University of Arizona Press, 1972.

Gardner, Phil. *The Lost Schools of Victorian England: The People's Education.* London: Croom Helm, 1984.

Garland-Thomson, Rosemarie. *Staring: How We Look*. New York: Oxford University Press, 2009.

Garnier, Maurice A. "Education as Loosely Coupled Systems in West Germany and the US." In *Comparative Public Policy and Citizen Participation*. Edited by C. R. Foster, 87–98. New York: Pergamon Press, 1980.

Gartner, Alan, and Dorothy Kerzner Lipsky. "Beyond Special Education: Toward a Quality System for All Students." *Harvard Educational Review* 57 (1987): 367–395.

Gillborn, David. *'Race,' Ethnicity: Teaching and Learning in Multi-ethnic Schools*. London, Boston: Unwin Hyman, 1990.

Godbout, Jacques T. *The World of the Gift*. Montreal: McGill-Queen's Uuniversity Press, 2000.

Goffman, Erving. *Asylums: Essays on the Social Situation of Mental Patients and Other Inmates*. New York: Doubleday, 1961.

Goldstein, Jan. *Console and Classify: The French Psychiatric Profession in the Nineteenth Century*. Cambridge, UK: Cambridge University Press, 1987.

Goldstone, Jack A. "Initial Conditions, General Laws, Path Dependency, and Explanation in Historical Sociology." *American Journal of Sociology* 104 (1998): 829–845.

Gomolla, Mechthild, and Frank-Olaf Radtke. *Institutionelle Diskriminierung: Die Herstellung ethnischer Differenz in der Schule*. Opladen, Germany: Leske & Budrich, 2002.

Gordon, Beth Omansky, and Karen E. Rosenblum. "Bringing Disability into the Sociological Frame: A Comparison of Disability, Race, Sex, and Sexual Orientation Status." *Disability & Society* 16.1 (2001): 5–19.

Graham, Linda J., and Roger Slee. "An Illusory Interiority: Interrogating the Discourse/s of Inclusion." *Educational Philosophy and Theory* 40 (2008): 277–293.

Granovetter, Mark. "The Strength of Weak Ties." *American Journal of Sociology* 78 (1973): 1360–1380.

Graser, Alexander. "Integration aus rechtlicher Perspektive." In *Die integrative Beschulung behinderter Kinder*. Edited by Ulrich Becker and Alexander Graser, 63–92. Baden-Baden, Germany: Nomos, 2004.

Green, Andy. *Education, Globalization, and the Nation State*. Basingstoke, UK: Palgrave, 1997.

Greif, Avner. "Cultural Beliefs and the Organization of Society: A Historical and Theoretical Reflection on Collectivist and Individualist Societies." *Journal of Political Economy* 102.5 (1994): 912–950.

Groce, Nora Ellen. *Everyone Here Spoke Sign Language: Hereditary Deafness on Martha's Vineyard*. Cambridge, MA: Harvard University Press, 1985.

———. *From Charity to Disability Rights: Global Initiatives of Rehabilitation International, 1922–2002*. New York: Rehabilitation International, 2002.

*Guadalupe Organization Inc. v. Tempe Elementary School District*, Civil Action No. 71-435, Phoenix District, AZ (24 January 1972).

Guillén, Mauro F. *Models of Management*. Chicago: University of Chicago Press, 1994.

———. *The Limits of Convergence: Globalization and Organizational Change in Argentina, South Korea, and Spain*. Princeton, NJ: Princeton University Press, 2001.

Guthrie, Thomas. *Seed-Time and Harvest of Ragged Schools; Or Three Pleas for Ragged Schools*. Montclair, NJ: Patterson Smith, [1860] 1973.

Hacking, Ian. *The Social Construction of What?* Cambridge, MA: Harvard University Press, 1999.

―――. *Historical Ontology*. Cambridge, MA: Harvard University Press, 2002.

Hahn, Harlan. "Towards a Politics of Disability: Definitions, Disciplines, and Policies." *Social Science Journal* 22.4 (1985): 87–105.

Hall, Peter A. "Policy Paradigms, Social Learning, and the State: The Case of Economic Policymaking in Britain." *Comparative Politics* 25 (1993): 275–296.

Hall, Peter A., and David Soskice. "An Introduction to Varieties of Capitalism." In *Varieties of Capitalism: The Institutional Foundations of Comparative Advantage*. Edited by Peter A. Hall and David Soskice, 1–68. Oxford: Oxford University Press, 2001.

Hamilton, Stephen F., and Klaus Hurrelmann. "The School-to-Career Transition in Germany and the United States." *Teachers College Record* 96 (1994): 329–344.

Harrington, Joel F. "Escape from the Great Confinement: The Genealogy of a German Workhouse." *The Journal of Modern History* 71 (1999): 308–345.

Harry, Beth, and Mary G. Anderson. "The Disproportionate Placement of African American Males in Special Education Programs: A Critique of the Process." *Journal of Negro Education* 63 (1994): 602–619.

Haüy, Valentin. *An Essay on the Education of the Blind*. London: Sampson, Low, Marston, and Co., 1894.

Haydu, Jeffrey. "Making Use of the Past: Time Periods as Cases to Compare and as Sequences of Problem Solving." *American Journal of Sociology* 104 (1998): 339–371.

Hayek, Friedrich A. *Studies in Philosophy, Politics, and Economics*. Chicago: University of Chicago Press, 1967.

Hayles, N. Katherine. *The Cosmic Web: Scientific Field Models and Literary Strategies in the Twentieth Century*. Ithaca, NY: Cornell University Press, 1984.

―――. *Chaos Bound: Orderly Disorder in Contemporary Literature and Science*. Ithaca, NY: Cornell University Press, 1990.

Hazard, Paul. *European Thought in the Eighteenth Century*. Cleveland and New York: World Publishing Company, 1963.

Hedström, Peter, and Richard Swedberg. *Social Mechanisms: An Analytic Approach to Social Theory*. Cambridge, UK: Cambridge University Press, 1998.

Hegarty, Seamus, Keith Pocklington, and Dorothy Lucas. *Educating Pupils with Special Needs in the Ordinary School*. Windsor, UK: NFER-NELSON, 1981.

Heidenheimer, Arnold. "Education and Social Security Entitlements in Europe and America." In *The Development of Welfare States in Europe and America*. Peter Flora and Arnold Heidenheimer, 269–304. New Brunswick, NJ: Transaction, 1984.

Held, David. *Democracy and the Global Order, from the Modern State to Cosmopolitan Governance*. Stanford, CA: Stanford University Press, 1995.

Helvétius, Claude Adrien. *De L'Esprit, or Essays on the Mind*. Boston: Adamant Media Corporation, [1758] 2005.

Her Majesty's Inspectorate (HMI). *Behaviour Units: A Survey of Special Units for Pupils with Behavioural Problems*. London: Department of Education and Science, 1978.

Hernes, Gudmund. "Structural Change in Social Processes." *American Journal of Sociology* 82 (1976): 513–547.

Herzog, Tamar, and Luis Roniger. "Conclusions: Collective Identities and Public Spheres in Latin America." In *The Collective and the Public in Latin America: Cultural Identities and Political Order*. Edited by Luis Roniger and Tamar Herzog. Brighton, UK: Sussex Academic Press, 2000.

Heyer, Peter. "Integration und Selektion als gegenläufig wirksame Kräfte deutscher Schulentwicklung." In *Kinder und Schule auf dem Weg: Bildungsreformpolitik für das 21. Jahrhundert.* Edited by Helga Z. Thomas and Norbert H. Weber, 97–105. Weinheim, Germany: Beltz, 2000.

Heyl, Barbara Sherman. "Parents, Politics, and the Public Purse: Activists in the Special Education Arena in Germany." *Disability & Society* 13.5 (1998): 683–707.

Heywood, Colin. *Childhood in Nineteenth Century France: Work, Health, and Education Among the "Classes Populaires."* Cambridge, UK: Cambridge University Press, 1988.

Hobbes, Thomas. *Leviathan.* New York: Cambridge University Press, [1651] 1991.

Hobbs, Nicholas. *Issues in the Classification of Children: A Sourcebook on Categories, Labels, and Their Consequences.* 2 vols. San Francisco, CA: Jossey-Bass, 1975.

Hofsäss, Thomas R. *Die Überweisung von Schülern auf die Hilfsschule und die Schule für Lernbehinderte.* Berlin: Marhold, 1993.

Hofstede, Geert. *Culture's Consequences: Comparing Values, Behaviors, Institutions, and Organizations Across Nations.* Thousand Oaks, CA: Sage, 2001.

Holbach, Paul Henry Thiery d'. *The System of Nature.* 2 vols. Teddington, Middlesex, UK: Echo Library, [1770] 2007.

Holman, Barry, and Jason Ziedenberg. *The Dangers of Detention: The Impact of Incarcerating Youth in Detention and Other Secure Facilities.* Washington, DC: Justice Policy Institute, 2006.

*Honig v. Doe,* 484 US 305, 108 S. Ct. 592 (1988).

Horowitz, Donald L. "Decreeing Organizational Change: Judicial Supervision of Public Institutions." *Duke Law Journal* 6 (1983): 1265–1307.

Howe, Richard H. "Max Weber's Elective Affinities: Sociology Within the Bounds of Pure Reason." *American Journal of Sociology* 84.2 (1978): 366–385.

Hufton, Owen H. "Begging, Vagrancy, Vagabondage, and the Law: An Aspect of the Problem of Poverty in 18th-Century France." *European Studies Review* 2.2 (1972): 97–123.

———. *The Poor of Eighteenth-Century France, 1750–1789.* Oxford: Clarendon Press, 1974.

Humphries, Stephen. *Hooligans or Rebels? An Oral History of Working-Class Childhood and Youth, 1889–1939.* Oxford: Basil Blackwell, 1981.

Humphries, Stephen, and Pamela Gordon. *Out of Sight: Experiences of Disability, 1900–1950.* London: Northcote House Publisher, 1992.

Hurt, John S. *Outside the Mainstream: A History of Special Education.* London: B. T. Batsford, 1988.

Hyden, Goran. *No Shortcuts to Progress: African Development Management in Perspective.* Berkeley: University of California Press, 1983.

Ignatieff, Michael. *A Just Measure of Pain: The Penitentiary in the Industrial Revolution, 1750–1850.* New York: Pantheon Books, 1978.

Imrie, Rob. "Disabling Environments and the Geography of Access." *Disability & Society* 15 (2000): 5–24.

Ingstad, Barbara, and Susan R. Whyte, eds. *Disability and Culture.* Berkeley: University of California Press, [1978] 1995.

*In re Harris,* 2 2412, Cook County Circuit Court, Illinois Court, Juvenile Division, *Criminal Law Reporter* (1967).

Jackson, Robert H. "Quasi-States, Dual Regimes, and Neoclassical Theory: International Jurisprudence and the Third World." *International Organization* 41 (1987): 519–549.

————. *Quasi-States: Sovereignty, International Relations, and the Third World*. Cambridge, UK: Cambridge University Press, 1990.

Jakobi, Anja P. *International Organizations and Lifelong Learning: From Global Agendas to Policy Diffusion*. Basingstoke, UK: Palgrave Macmillan, 2009.

Janoski, Thomas. *Citizenship and Civil Society*. New York: Cambridge University Press, 1998.

Jenkins, Richard, ed. *Questions of Competence: Culture, Classification, and Intellectual Disability*. New York: Cambridge University Press, 1998.

Jepperson, Ronald. "Institutions, Institutional Effects, and Institutionalism." In *The New Institutionalism in Organizational Analysis*. Edited by Walter W. Powell and Paul J. DiMaggio, 143–163. Chicago: University of Chicago Press, 1991.

*Johnson v. Upchurch*, No. 86-195 D. AZ (filed August 1986).

Jones, Colin. *Charity and "Bienfaisance": The Treatment of the Poor in the Montpellier Region, 1740–1815*. Cambridge, UK: Cambridge University Press, 1982.

————. *The Charitable Imperative: Hospitals and Nursing in Ancien Regime and Revolutionary France*. London: Routledge, 1989.

Jones, Colin, and Roy Porter. *Reassessing Foucault, Power, Medicine, and the Body*. London: Routledge, 1994.

Jones, M. G. *The Charity School Movement: A Study of Eighteenth Century Puritanism in Action*. London: Frank Cass and Co. [1938] 1964.

"Juvenile Court Orders Treatment for Deaf-Mute." *Criminal Law Reporter* 2 (1968): 2401.

Kalberg, Stephen. *Max Weber's Comparative-Historical Sociology*. Chicago: University of Chicago Press, 1994.

Kauffman, James M., and Daniel P. Hallahan. *The Illusion of Full Inclusion*. Austin, TX: PRO-ED, 1995.

Kavale, Kenneth A., and Steven R. Forness. "History, Rhetoric, and Reality: Analysis of the Inclusion Debate." *Remedial and Special Education* 21 (2002): 279–296.

Kay, James Phillips. *The Training of Pauper Children*. Manchester, UK: E. J. Morten, [1838] 1970.

————. *Memorandum on Popular Education*. London: Ridgway, 1868.

Keane, John. *Democracy and Civil Society*. London: Verso, 1988.

Kerschensteiner, Georg. *The Schools and the Nation*. London: Macmillan and Co., 1914.

Kettering, Sharon. *Patrons, Brokers, and Clients in Seventeenth-Century France*. New York: Oxford University Press, 1986.

————. "The Historical Development of Political Clientelism." *Journal of Interdisciplinary History* 18 (1988): 419–447.

Killias, Martin, Sonia Lucia, Philippe Lamon, and Mathieu Simonin. "Juvenile Delinquency in Switzerland over 50 Years: Assessing Trends Beyond Statistics." *European Journal on Criminal Policy and Research* 10 (2004): 111–122.

Kirby, Peter. *Child Labour in Britain, 1750–1870*. New York: Palgrave Macmillan, 2003.

Kirp, David L. "Schools as Sorters: The Constitutional and Policy Implications of Student Classification." *University of Pennsylvania Law Review* 121 (1973): 705–797.

Kisanji, Joseph. "The Relevance of Indigenous Customary Education Principles in the Formulation of Special Needs Education Policy." Paper presented at the Fourth International Special Education Congress, Birmingham, 10–13 April 1995 (1995a).

————. "Interface Between Culture and Disability in the Tanzanian Context: Part I." *International Journal of Disability, Development and Education* 42 (1995b): 93–108.

————. "The March Towards Inclusive Education in Non-Western Countries: Retracing the Steps." *International Journal of Inclusive Education* 2 (1998): 55–72.

————. "Historical and Theoretical Basis of Inclusive Education." Keynote Address for the Workshop on "Inclusive Education in Nambia: The Challenge for Teacher Education." Manchester, UK: Centre for Educational Needs, School of Education, 1999.

Klein, Lawrence E. *Shaftesbury and the Culture of Politeness*. Cambridge, UK: Cambridge University Press, 1994.

Klemm, Klaus, and Ulf Preuss-Lausitz. *Gutachten zum Stand und zu den Perspektiven der sonderpädagogischen Förderung in den Schulen der Stadtgemeinde Bremen*. Essen and Berlin: Authors, 2008.

KMK. *Empfehlungen zur sonderpädagogischen Förderung in Schulen in der Bundesrepublik Deutschland*. Bonn, Germany: Sekretariat der Kultusministerkonferenz, 1994.

————. *Datengewinnungsstrategie für die Bildungsstatistik, Dokumentation des Beratungszwischenstandworkshops am 13.02.07 in Berlin*. Bonn, Germany: Sekretariat der Kultusministerkonferenz, 2007.

————. *Sonderpädagogische Förderung in Schulen 1999 bis 2008. Statistische Veröffentlichungen der Kultusministerkonferenz. Dokumentation Nr. 189—März 2010*. Bonn, Germany: Sekretariat der Kultusministerkonferenz, 2010 and prior years.

Knight, Isabel F. *The Geometric Spirit: The Abbé de Condillac and the French Enlightenment*. New Haven, CT: Yale University Press, 1968.

Koepp, Cynthia Joan. "The Order of Work: Ideas, Attitudes, and Representations in Eighteenth-Century France." Ph.D. diss., Cornell University, 1992.

Kohrman, Matthew. *Bodies of Difference: Experiences of Disability and Institutional Advocacy in the Making of Modern China*. Berkeley: University of California Press, 2005.

Komardjaja, Inge. "The Malfunction of Barrier-Free Spaces in Indonesia." *Disability Studies Quarterly* 21.4 (2004): 97–104.

Konsortium Bildungsbericht. *Bildung in Deutschland. Ein indikatorengestützter Bericht mit einer Analyse zu Bildung und Migration*. Frankfurt am Main, Germany: Deutsches Institut für Internationale Pädagogische Forschung, 2006.

Kontopoulos, Kyriakos M. *The Logics of Social Structure*. Cambridge, UK: Cambridge University Press, 1993.

Kors, Alan Charles, and Paul J. Korshin, eds. *Anticipations of the Enlightenment in England, France, and Germany*. Philadelphia: University of Pennsylvania Press, 1987.

Kottmann, Brigitte. *Selektion in die Sonderschule: Das Verfahren zur Feststellung von sonderpädagogischem Förderbedarf als Gegenstand empirischer Forschung*. Bad Heilbrunn, Germany: Klinkhardt, 2006.

Krappmann, Lothar, Achim Leschinsky, and Justin Powell. "Kinder, die besonderer pädagogischer Förderung bedürfen." In *Das Bildungswesen in der Bundesrepublik Deutschland*. Edited by Kai S. Cortina, Jürgen Baumert, Achim Leschinsky, Karl Ulrich Mayer, and Luitgard Trommer, 755–786. Reinbek, Germany: Rowohlt, 2003.

Krieger, Linda Hamilton, ed. *Backlash Against the ADA: Reinterpreting Disability Rights*. Ann Arbor: University of Michigan Press, 2003.

Kydd, Samuel H. G. *The History of the Factory Movement*. New York: Augustus M. Kelley, [1857] 1966.

Lane, Harlan. *When the Mind Hears: A History of the Deaf*. New York: Random House, 1983.

―――. "The Education of Deaf Children: Drowning in the Mainstream." In *The Illusion of Full Inclusion*. Edited by James M. Kauffman and Daniel P. Hallahan. Austin, TX: PRO-ED, 1995.

*Larry P. vs. Riles,* 343 F. Supp. 1306 (1972).

Lavia, Jennifer. "Repositioning Pedagogies and Postcolonialism: Theories, Contradictions, and Possibilities." *International Journal of Inclusive Education* 11 (2007): 283–300.

Lazerson, Marvin. "The Origins of Special Education." In *Special Education Policies: Their History, Implementation, and Finance*. Edited by Jay G. Chambers and William T. Hartman. Philadelphia: Temple University Press, 1983.

League of Nations. *Institutions for Erring and Delinquent Minors*. 1934.

Lechner, Frank J. and John Boli. *World Culture: Origins and Consequences*. Oxford, UK: Blackwell, 2005.

Leino, Mare, and Elina Lahelma. "Constructing and Educating 'Problem Children': The Case of Post-Communist Estonia." *International Journal of Inclusive Education* 6 (2002): 79–90.

Lemann, Nicholas. *The Big Test: The Secret History of the American Meritocracy*. New York: Farrar, Straus & Giroux, 1999.

Lemarchand, Rene. "Political Clientelism and Ethnicity in Tropical Africa: Competing Solidarities in Nation-Building." *American Political Science Review* 46 (1972): 68–90.

Lenhardt, Gero. *Hochschulen in Deutschland und in den USA*. Wiesbaden, Germany: VS Verlag für Sozialwissenschaften, 2005.

Leone, Peter E., and S. M. Meisel. "Improving Education Services for Students in Detention and Confinement Facilities." *Children's Legal Rights Journal* 17 (1997): 2–12.

Leone, Peter E., Ted Price, and Richard K. Vitolo. "Appropriate Education for All Incarcerated Youth: Meeting the Spirit of EAHCA in Youth Detention Facilities." *Remedial and Special Education* 7 (1987): 9–14.

Leschinsky, Achim, and Karl Ulrich Mayer. "Comprehensive Schools and Inequality of Opportunity in the FRG." In *The Comprehensive School Experiment Revisited*. Edited by Achim Leschinsky and Karl Ulrich Mayer. New York: Lang, 1999.

Leuze, Kathrin. Bildungswege besser verstehen: das Nationale Bildungspanel. *WZBrief Bildung* 2008/04. Berlin: Wissenschaftszentrum Berlin für Sozialforschung, 2008.

Lévi-Strauss, Claude. "The Structural Study of Myth." *The Journal of American Folklore* 68 (1955): 428–444.

―――. *The Elementary Structures of Kinship*. Boston: Beacon Press, 1969.

Lewis, Ian, and Graham Vulliamy. "Warnock or Warlock? The Sorcery of Definitions: The Limitations of the Report on Special Education." *Educational Review* 32 (1980): 3–10.

Lippman, Leopold, and I. Ignacy Goldberg. *Right to Education: Anatomy of the Pennsylvania Case and Its Implications for Exceptional Children*. New York: Teachers College Press, 1973.

Lipset, Seymour Martin. *The First New Nation: The United States in Historical and Comparative Perspective*. New York: W.W. Norton & Co., [1963] 1979.

Lloyd-Smith, Mel. *Disrupted Schooling*. London: John Murray, 1984.

Locke, John. *An Essay Concerning Human Understanding*. Hertfordshire, UK: Wordsworth Editions Limited, [1689] 1998.

———. *Two Treatises of Government*. Cambridge, UK: Cambridge University Press, [1690] 1988.

———. *Some Thoughts Concerning Education* [1693] and *Of the Conduct of the Understanding* [1689]. Indianapolis: Hackett Publishing Company, 1996.

Lomnitz, Claudio. "Passion and Banality in Mexican History: The Presidential Persona." In *Deep Mexico, Silent Mexico: Anthropology of Nationalism*. Edited by Claudio Lomnitz. Minneapolis: University of Minnesota Press, 2001.

Losen, Daniel J., and Gary Orfield, eds. *Racial Inequality in Special Education*. Cambridge, MA: Harvard Education Press, 2002.

Loveless, Tom. *The Tracking Wars: State Reform Meets School Policy*. Washington, DC: Brookings Institution Press, 1999.

Lucas, Samuel R. *Tracking Inequality: Stratification and Mobility in American High Schools*. New York: Teachers College Press, 1999.

Mackay, Thomas. *A History of the English Poor Law, Volume III, from 1834 to the Present Time*. London: P. S. King & Company, 1899.

Maddison, Arthur J. S. *The Law Relating to Child-Saving and Reformatory Efforts*. London: Reformatory and Refuge Union, 1896.

Mahoney, James. "Strategies of Causal Assessment in Comparative Historical Analysis." In *Comparative Historical Analysis in the Social Sciences*. Edited by James Mahoney and Dietrich Rueschemeyer. New York: Cambridge University Press, 2003.

Maistre, Joseph de. *Considerations on France*. Montreal: McGill-Queen's University Press, [1797] 1974.

Malacrida, Claudia. *Cold Comfort: Mothers, Professionals, and Attention Deficit (Hyperactivity) Disorder*. Toronto: University of Toronto Press, 2003.

Malloy, James M., ed. *Authoritarianism and Corporatism in Latin America*. Pittsburgh: University of Pittsburgh Press, 1977.

Mamdani, Mahmood. *Citizen and Subject: Contemporary Africa and the Legacy of Late Colonialism*. Princeton, NJ: Princeton University Press, 1996.

Mandeville, Bernard. "An Essay on Charity and Charity-Schools." In *The Fable of the Bees*. Edited by Bernard Mandeville. Indianapolis: Liberty Classics, [1714] 1988.

Mann, Michael. *The Sources of Social Power, Vol. II*. Cambridge, UK: Cambridge University Press, 1993.

Mannheim, Karl. "Conservative Thought." In *Essays on Sociology and Social Psychology*. Edited by Karl Mannheim. London: Routledge & Kegan Paul, 1966.

Marder, Camille, and Ronald D'Amico. *How Well Are Youth with Disabilities Really Doing?* Menlo Park, CA: SRI International, 1992.

Marfo, Kofi, Sylvia Walker, and Bernard Charles, eds. *Childhood Disability in Developing Countries: Issues in Habilitation and Special Education*. New York: Praeger, 1985.

Marin, Louis. "Toward a Semiotic of Utopia: Political and Fictional Discourse in Thomas More's Utopia." In *Structure, Consciousness, and History*. Edited by Richard H. Brown and Stanford M. Lyman. Cambridge, UK: Cambridge University Press, 1978.

Marshall, T. H. *Class, Citizenship, and Social Development*. Chicago: University of Chicago Press, [1950] 1964.

Maschke, Michael. *Behindertenpolitik in der Europäischen Union*. Wiesbaden, Germany: VS Verlag für Sozialwissenschaften, 2008.

Mauss, Marcel. *The Gift*. Glencoe, IL: Free Press, 1954.

Mayer, Karl Ulrich. "Life Courses and Life Chances in a Comparative Perspective." In *Analyzing Inequality: Life Chances and Social Mobility in Comparative Perspective*. Edited by Stefan Svallfors, 17–55. Stanford, CA: Stanford University Press, 2005.

Mayer, Karl Ulrich, and Walter Müller. "The State and the Structure of the Life Course." In *Human Development and the Life Course: Multidisciplinary Perspectives*. Edited by Aage B. Sørensen, Franz E. Weinert, and Lonnie R. Sherrod, 217–245. Hillsdale, NJ: Lawrence Erlbaum Associates, 1986.

———. "Lebensverläufe im Wohlfahrtsstaat." In *Soziale Ungleichheit. Klassische Texte zur Sozialstrukturanalyse*. Edited by Heike Solga, Justin Powell, and Peter A. Berger, 427–446. Frankfurt am Main, Germany: Campus Verlag, [1986] 2009.

Mayhew, Leon. "Ascription in Modern Society." *Sociological Inquiry* 38 (1968): 105–20.

———. *The New Public, Professional Communication and the Means of Social Influence*. Cambridge, UK: Cambridge University Press, 1997.

Mazurek, Kas, and Margret Winzer, eds. *Comparative Studies in Special Education*. Washington, DC: Gallaudet University Press, 1994.

McDermott, R. P. "Inarticulateness." In *Linguistics in Context*. Edited by Deborah Tannen. Norwood, NJ: Ablex, 1988.

———. "The Acquisition of a Child by a Learning Disability." In *Understanding Practice*. Edited by N. Seth Chaiklin and Jean Lave. New York: Cambridge University Press, 1993.

McLaughlin, Margaret J., and Martin Rouse, eds. *Special Education and School Reform in the United States and Britain*. London: Routledge, 2000.

Mehan, Hugh, Alma Hertweck, and J. Lee Meihls. *Handicapping the Handicapped: Decision Making in Students' Educational Careers*. Stanford, CA: Stanford University Press, 1986.

Meijer, Cor J. W., Sip Jan Pijl, and Seamus Hegarty. *New Perspectives in Special Education: A Six-Country Study of Integration*. London: Routledge, 1994.

Melnick, R. Shep. "Separation of Powers and the Strategy of Rights: The Expansion of Special Education." In *The New Politics of Public Policy*. Edited by Marc K. Landy and Martin A. Levin, 23–46. Baltimore, MD: Johns Hopkins University Press, 1995.

Melosi, Dario, and Massimo Pavarini. *The Prison and the Factory: Origins of the Penitentiary System*. Totowa, NJ: Barnes & Noble Books, 1981.

Mercer, Jane R. "Institutionalized Anglocentricism: Labeling Mental Retardates in Public Schools." In *Race, Change and Urban Policy*. Edited by P. Orleans and W. Russell. New York: Sage, 1971.

———. *Labeling the Mentally Retarded*. Berkeley: University of California Press, 1973.

Meyer, Heinz-Dieter. "Saying What We Mean and Meaning What We Say: Unpacking the Contingencies of Decentralization." *American Journal of Education* 115, 3 (2009): 457–474.

Meyer, John W. "Innovation and Knowledge Use in American Education." In *Organizational Environments: Ritual and Rationality*. Edited by John W. Meyer and W. Richard Scott, 233–260. Newbury Park, CA: Sage, 1992.

———. "Reflections: The Worldwide Commitment to Educational Equality." *Sociology of Education* 74, Extra Issue (2001): 154–158.

———. *Weltkultur: Wie die westlichen Prinzipien die Welt durchdringen*. Frankfurt am Main, Germany: Suhrkamp Verlag, 2005.

————. "World Society, Institutional Theories, and the Actor." *Annual Review of Sociology* 36 (2010): 1–20.

Meyer, John, W., John Boli, George Thomas, and Francisco Ramirez. "World Society and the Nation-State." *American Journal of Sociology* 103 (1997): 144–181.

Meyer, John W., and Michael Hannan, eds. *National Development and the World System.* Chicago: University of Chicago Press, 1979.

Meyer, John W., Francisco O. Ramirez, Richard Rubinson, and John Boli-Bennett. "The World Educational Revolution, 1950–1970." *Sociology of Education* 50.4 (1977): 242–258.

Meyer, John W., Francisco O. Ramirez, and Yasemin N. Soysal. "World Expansion of Mass Education, 1870–1980." *Sociology of Education* 65.2 (1992): 128–149.

Meyer, John W., and Brian Rowan. "Institutionalized Organizations: Formal Structure as Myth and Ceremony." *American Journal of Sociology* 83 (1977): 340–63.

————. "The Structure of Educational Institutions." In *Organizational Environments.* Edited by John W. Meyer and W. Richard Scott, 71–97. Newbury Park, CA: Sage, [1977] 1992.

Midelfort, H. C. Erik. *A History of Madness in Sixteenth-Century Germany.* Stanford, CA: Stanford University Press, 1999.

Miles, M. "Special Education in Pakistan: Developmental Issues." *International Journal of Special Education* 3 (1988): 39–50.

*Mills v. Board of Education*, 348 F. Supp. 866 DDC (1972).

Milofsky, Carl. "Why Special Education Isn't Special." *Harvard Educational Review* 44 (1974): 437–458.

Ministry of Education. *Report of the Committee on Maladjusted Children.* London: Her Majesty's Stationery Office, 1955/56.

Minow, Martha. *Making All the Difference: Inclusion, Exclusion, and American Law.* Ithaca, NY: Cornell University Press, 1990.

Mitchell, David, ed. *Contextualizing Inclusive Education: Evaluating Old and New International Perspectives.* London: Routledge, 2005.

Molm, Linda D. "Dependence and Risk: Transforming the Structure of Social Exchange." *Social Psychology Quarterly* 57 (1994): 163–176.

————. "Theoretical Comparisons of Forms of Exchange." *Sociological Theory* 21 (2003): 1–17.

Molm, Linda, David R. Schaefer, and Jessica L. Collett. "Fragile and Resilient Trust: Risk and Uncertainty in Negotiated and Reciprocal Exchange." *Sociological Theory* 27 (2009): 1–32.

Mongon, Denis. "Behaviour Units, 'Maladjustment' and Student Control." In *Discipline and Schools: A Curriculum Perspective.* Edited by Roger Slee. Melbourne: Macmillan, 1988.

*Morales v. Texas*, U.S. District Court, E. D. Texas, Sherman Division (August 1974).

Mortier, Roland. "The '*Philosophes*' and Public Education." *Yale French Studies— Literature and Society: The Eighteenth Century* 40 (1968): 62–76.

Muller, Johan. "The Well-Tempered Learner: Self-Regulation, Pedagogical Models, and Teacher Education Policy." *Comparative Education* 34 (1998): 177–193.

Münch, Richard. "Politische Kultur, Demokratie und politische Regulierung: Deutschland und USA im Vergleich." In *Die Vermessung kultureller Unterschiede: USA und Deutschland im Vergleich.* Edited by Jürgen Gerhards, 189–207. Wiesbaden, Germany: Westdeutscher Verlag, 2000.

————. *Nation and Citizenship in the Global Age.* Basingstoke, UK: Palgrave Macmillan, 2001.

Muñoz, Vernor. *The Right to Education of Persons with Disabilities: Report of the Special Rapporteur on the Right to Education.* UN General Assembly A/HRC/4/29, 19 February 2007.

Murdick, Nikki L., Barbara C. Gartin, and Terry Crabtree. *Special Education Law.* Upper Saddle River, NJ: Merrill Prentice Hall, 2002.

Murdock, Charles W. "Civil Rights of the Mentally Retarded: Some Critical Issues." *The Notre Dame Lawyer* 48 (1972): 133–188.

Myrdal, Gunnar. *An American Dilemma: The Negro Problem and Modern Democracy.* New York: Carnegie Corporation, 1944.

*Nason v. Superintendent of Bridgewater State Hospital,* 353 Mass. 604, 233 N.D. 2d 908 1968.

National Center for Education Statistics. *120 Years of American Education: A Statistical Portrait.* Washington, DC: NCES, 1993.

————. *Education Indicators: An International Perspective.* Washington, DC: NCES, 1996a.

————. *120 Years of Historical Statistics.* Washington, DC: NCES, 1996b.

————. *Common Core of Data.* Washington, DC: NCES, 2001.

————. *Digest of Education Statistics.* Washington, DC: NCES, 2005.

Neal, David, and David L. Kirp. "The Allure of Legalization Reconsidered: The Case of Special Education." In *School Days, Rule Days.* Edited by David L. Kirp and Donald N. Jensen, 343–365. Philadelphia: Falmer, 1996.

Neegan, Erica. "Excuse Me: Who Are the First Peoples of Canada? A Historical Analysis of Aboriginal Education in Canada Then and Now." *International Journal of Inclusive Education* 9 (2005): 3–15.

Nelson, C. Michael, Robert B. Rutherford Jr., and Bruce I. Wolford. *Special Education in the Criminal Justice System.* Columbus, OH: Merrill, 1987.

Ness, Arlin E., and Martin L. Mitchell. "AIEJI: Creating a Profession to Work with Troubled Children and Youth." *Child & Youth Care Quarterly* 19.3 (1990): 199–207.

Nilholm, Claes. "Special Education, Inclusion, and Democracy." *European Journal of Special Needs Education* 21 (2006): 431–445.

Nussbaum, Martha Craven. *Frontiers of Justice: Disability, Nationality, Species Membership.* Cambridge, MA: Harvard University Press, 2006.

Obiakor, Festus E., Dorothy Aramburo, Gregory Maltby, and Earl Davis. "Comparison of Special Education in Nigeria and the United States of America." *International Journal of Special Education* 6 (1991): 341–352.

O'Hanlon, Christine. "The European Dimension in Integration and Special Needs Education." *Research Papers in Education* 8 (1993): 19–32.

Oliver, Michael. "The Politics of Disability." *Critical Social Policy* 11 (1984): 21–32.

————. "The Integration-Segregation Debate: Some Sociological Considerations." *British Journal of Sociology of Education* 6 (1985): 75–92.

————. "Social Policy and Disability: Some Theoretical Issues." *Disability, Handicap and Society* 1 (1986): 5–17.

————. *Understanding Disability: From Theory to Practice.* London: Macmillan, 1996.

Olson, Mancur. *The Logic of Collective Action: Public Goods and the Theory of Groups.* Cambridge, MA: Harvard University Press, 1965.

Olzak, Susan. *The Global Dynamics of Racial and Ethnic Mobilization*. Stanford, CA: Stanford University Press, 2006.

Ong, Aihwa. *Flexible Citizenship*. Durham, NC: Duke University Press, 1999.

Oorschot, W. van. "European Comparative Data on the Situation of Disabled Persons: An Annotated Review." Academic Network of European Disability Experts (ANED), 2008.

Organisation for Economic Co-operation and Development. *Reviews of National Policies for Education: France*. OECD Working Papers, Vol. II, No. 39. Paris: OECD, 1994.

————. *Inclusive Education at Work*. Paris: OECD, 1999.

————. *Special Needs Education: Statistics and Indicators*. Paris: OECD, 2000.

————. *Education at a Glance: OECD Indicators*. Paris: OECD, 2002 and prior years.

————. *Transforming Disability into Ability*. Paris: OECD, 2003a.

————. *Disability in Higher Education*. Paris: OECD, 2003b.

————. *Reviews of National Policies for Education: Bulgaria*. Paris: OECD, 2004.

————. *Students with Disabilities, Learning Difficulties, and Disadvantages: Statistics and Indicators*. Paris: OECD, 2005.

————. *Students with Disabilities, Learning Difficulties, and Disadvantages: Policies, Statistics, and Indicators*. Paris: OECD, 2007.

Owen, David. *English Philanthropy, 1660–1960*. Cambridge, MA: Belknap Press, 1964.

Parent, Dale G., Valerie Leiter, Stephen Kennedy, Lisa Livens, Daniel Wentworth, and Sarah Wilcox. *Conditions of Confinement: Detention and Corrections Facilities*. Washington, DC: U.S. Department of Justice, Office of Juvenile Justice and Delinquency and Prevention, 1994.

Parrish, Thomas B. *Special Education in an Era of School Reform: Special Education Finance*. Palo Alto, CA: American Institutes for Research, 2001.

Paulson, William R. *Enlightenment, Romanticism, and the Blind in France*. Princeton, NJ: Princeton University Press, 1987.

————. *The Noise of Culture: Literary Texts in a World of Information*. Ithaca, NY: Cornell University Press, 1988.

Payne, Harry C. "Elite Versus Popular Mentality in the Eighteenth Century." *Historical Reflections* II (1975): 183–208.

————. *The Philosophes and the People*. Yale Historical Publications, Miscellany 109. New Haven, CT: Yale University Press, 1976.

*Pennsylvania Association for Retarded Children* [PARC] *v. Commonwealth of Pennsylvania*, 343 F. Supp. 279 Ed.D.PA (1972).

Percy, Stephen L. *Disability, Civil Rights, and Public Policy*. Tuscaloosa: University of Alabama Press, 1989.

Peters, Susan J., ed. *Education and Disability in Cross-Cultural Perspective*. New York: Garland, 1993.

————. *Inclusive Education: Achieving Education for All by Including Those with Disabilities and Special Educational Needs*. Washington, DC: World Bank, 2003.

Pfahl, Lisa. *Techniken der Behinderung. Der deutsche Lernbehinderungsdiskurs, die Sonderschule und ihre Auswirkungen auf Bildungsbiografien*. Bielefeld, Germany: Transcript Verlag, in press.

Pfeiffer, David. "Overview of the Disability Movement: History, Legislative Record, and Political Implications." *Policy Studies Journal* 21.4 (1993): 724–734.

Pitcher, George. *Berkeley*. London: Routledge & Kegan Paul, 1977.

Plaisance, Éric. "The Integration of 'Disabled' Children in Ordinary Schools in France: A New Challenge." In *Policy, Experience and Change: Cross-Cultural Reflections on Inclusive Education*. Edited by Len Barton and Felicity Armstrong. Dordrecht, Netherlands: Springer, 2007.

Poggi, Gianfranco. *The Development of the Modern State*. Stanford, CA: Stanford University Press, 1978.

Polanyi, Karl. *The Great Transformation*. Boston: Beacon Press, 1957.

Poore, Carol. *Disability in Twentieth-Century German Culture*. Ann Arbor: University of Michigan Press, 2007.

Popkewitz, Thomas S. *Cosmopolitanism and the Age of School Reform*. New York: Taylor & Francis, 2008.

Potts, Patricia. *Unit 9 Origins*. Milton Keynes, UK: Open University, 1982.

Powell, Justin J. W. "Constructing Disability and Social Inequality Early in the Life Course: The Case of Special Education in Germany and the United States." *Disability Studies Quarterly* 23.2 (2003a): 57–75.

———. "Hochbegabt, behindert oder normal? Klassifikationssysteme des sonderpädagogischen Förderbedarfs in Deutschland und den Vereinigten Staaten." In *Wie man behindert wird*. Edited by Günther Cloerkes, 103–140. Heidelberg, Germany: Universitätsverlag Winter, 2003b.

———. "Special Education and the Risk of Becoming Less Educated." *European Societies* 8.4 (2006): 577–599.

———. "To Segregate or to Separate? The Institutionalization of Special Education in the United States and Germany." *Comparative Education Review* 53.2 (2009): 161–187.

———. "Change in Disability Classification: Redrawing Categorical Boundaries in Special Education in the United States and Germany, 1920–2005." *Comparative Sociology* 9.2 (2010): 241–267.

———. *Barriers to Inclusion: Special Education in the United States and Germany*. Boulder, CO: Paradigm Publishers, 2011.

Powell, Justin J. W., Kai Felkendorff, and Judith Hollenweger. "Disability in the German, Swiss, and Austrian Higher Education Systems." In *Disability and the Politics of Education: An International Reader*. Edited by Susan Gabel and Scot Danforth, 517–540. New York: Lang, 2008.

Powell, Justin J. W. and Heike Solga. "Internationalization of Vocational and Higher Education Systems—A Comparative-Institutional Approach." *WZB Discussion Papers* SP I 2008–501. Berlin: Wissenschaftszentrum Berlin für Sozialforschung, 2008.

———. "Analyzing the Nexus of Higher Education and Vocational Training in Europe: A Comparative-Institutional Framework." *Studies in Higher Education* 35.6 (2010): 705–721.

Powell, Walter W., and Paul J. DiMaggio, eds. *The New Institutionalism in Organizational Analysis*. Chicago: University of Chicago Press, 1991.

Preuss-Lausitz, Ulf. "Gemeinsamer Unterricht Behinderter und Nichtbehinderter." *Zeitschrift für Erziehungswissenschaft* 4.2 (2001): 209–224.

———. "Untersuchungen zur Finanzierung sonderpädagogischer Förderung in integrativen and separaten Schulen." In *Integrationspädagogik*. Edited by Hans Eberwein and Sabine Knauer, 514–524. Weinheim, Germany: Beltz, 2002.

Priestley, Mark, ed. *Disability and the Life Course: Global Perspectives*. Cambridge, UK: Cambridge University Press, 2001.

————. *Disability: A Life Course Approach*. Cambridge, UK: Polity, 2003.

Pritchard, D. G. *Education and the Handicapped, 1760–1960*. London: Routledge & Kegan Paul, 1963.

Prokou, Eleni. "International Influences on Educational Policy—with Special Reference to the Technological Sector of Higher Education—in Greece as a European Semi-Periphery." *Compare* 33 (2003): 301–313.

Propp, Vladimir. *Morphology of the Folktale*. Austin: University of Texas Press, [1928] 1968.

Putnam, Rosemary Werner. "Special Education—Some Cross-National Comparisons." *Comparative Education* 15 (1979): 83–98.

Pye, Lucian W. "Civility, Social Capital, and Civil Society: Three Powerful Concepts for Explaining Asia." *Journal of Interdisciplinary History* 29 (1999): 763–782.

Quinn, Gerard, and Theresia Degener. *Human Rights and Disability*. New York: United Nations, 2002.

Ragin, Charles C. *The Comparative Method*. Berkeley: University of California Press, 1987.

————. "Turning the Tables: How Case-Oriented Research Challenges Variable-Oriented Research." *Comparative Social Research* 16 (1997): 27–42.

Ramirez, Francisco O., and John Boli. "The Political Construction of Mass Schooling: European Origins and Worldwide Institutionalization." *Sociology of Education* 60.1 (1987): 2–17.

Ramirez, Francisco O., and John Boli Bennett. "Global Patterns of Educational Institutionalization." In *Comparative Education*. Edited by Philip Altbach, Robert Arnove, and Gail Kelly. New York: Macmillan, 1982.

Ramirez, Francisco O., and Richard Rubinson. "Creating Members: The Political Incorporation and Expansion of Public Education." In *National Development and the World System*. Edited by John W. Meyer and Michael Hannan. Chicago: University of Chicago Press, 1979.

Ransom, John S. *Foucault's Discipline: The Politics of Subjectivity*. Durham, NC: Duke University Press, 1997.

Redekop, Benjamin W. *Enlightenment and Community: Lessing, Abbt, Herder, and the Quest for a German Public*. Montreal: McGill-Queen's University Press, 2000.

Reill, Peter Hanns. *The German Enlightenment and the Rise of Historicism*. Berkeley: University of California Press, 1975.

Renn, Donna E. "The Right to Treatment and the Juvenile." *Crime and Delinquency* 19 (1973): 477–484.

Reschly, Daniel J. "Minority MMR Overrepresentation and Special Education Reform." *Exceptional Children* 54 (1988): 316–323.

Resnick, Judith. "Managerial Judges." *Harvard Law Review* 96 (1982): 374–448.

Reynolds, Cecil R., and Elaine Fletcher-Janzen, eds. *Encyclopedia of Special Education*. New York: Wiley, 2007.

Richardson, John G. "The Expansion of Special Education." In *The Political Construction of Education*. Edited by Bruce Fuller and Richard Rubinson. New York: Praeger, 1992.

————. "Common, Delinquent, and Special: On the Formalization of Common Schooling in the American States." *American Educational Research Journal* 31 (1994): 695–723.

————. *Common, Delinquent, and Special: The Institutional Shape of Special Education*. New York: Falmer, 1999.

————. "The Variable Construction of Educational Risk." In *The Handbook of the Sociology of Education*. Edited by Maureen Hallinan, 307–323. New York: Kluwer, 2000.

————. "Institutional Sequences, Pedagogical Reach, and Comparative Educational Systems." In *The Impact of Comparative Education Research on Institutional Theory*. Edited by David P. Baker and Alexander W. Wiseman. Amsterdam: Elsevier, 2006.

————. "Institutional Sequences and Curriculum History: Classical Versus Scientific Knowledge and the Formation of a New Nation." In *New Curriculum History*. Edited by Bernadette Baker. Rotterdam, Netherlands: Sense Publishers, 2009.

Ringer, Fritz. *Max Weber's Methodology: The Unification of the Cultural and Social Sciences*. Cambridge, MA: Harvard University Press, 1997.

Robson, Adam Henry. *The Education of Children Engaged in Industry in England, 1833–1876*. London: Kegan Paul, Trench, Trubner & Co., 1931.

Roller, Edeltraud. "Marktwirtschaftliche und wohlfahrtsstaatliche Gerechtigkeitsprinzipien in Deutschland und den USA." In *Die Vermessung kultureller Unterschiede: USA und Deutschland im Vergleich*. Edited by Jürgen Gerhards, 89–110. Wiesbaden, Germany: Westdeutscher, 2000.

Roniger, Luis. "Democratic Transitions and Consolidation in Contemporary Southern Europe and Latin America." *International Journal of Comparative Sociology* 30 (1989): 216–230.

————. *Hierarchy and Trust in Modern Mexico and Brazil*. New York: Praeger, 1990.

————. "The Comparative Study of Clientelism and the Changing Nature of Civil Society in the Contemporary World." In *Democracy, Clientelism, and Civil Society*. Edited by Luis Roniger and Ayse Günes-Ayata. Boulder, CO: Lynne Rienner, 1994.

Roniger, Luis, and Carlos H. Waisman, eds. *Globality and Multiple Modernities: Comparative North American and Latin American Perspectives*. Brighton, UK: Sussex Academic Press, 2002.

Rossi, Ino. *Structural Sociology*. New York: Columbia University Press, 1982.

Roth, Guenther. "Sociological Typology and Historical Explanation." In *Scholarship and Partisanship: Essays on Max Weber*. Edited by Reinhard Bendix and Guenther Roth. Berkeley: University of California Press, 1971.

Rothman, David J. *The Discovery of the Asylum*. Boston: Little Brown, 1971.

*Rouse v. Cameron,* 373 F.2d 451 DC Cir (1966).

Rousseau, Jean-Jacques. *Emile, or Treatise on Education*. Translated by William H. Payne. Amherst, NH: Prometheus Books, 2003.

Rubinson, Richard. "Class Formation, Politics, and Institutions: Schooling in the United States." *American Journal of Sociology* 92 (1986): 519–548.

Rubinstein, David. *School Attendance in London, 1870–1904: A Social History*. New York: Augustus M. Kelley, 1969.

Rusche, Georg, and Otto Kirchheimer. *Punishment and Social Structure*. Piscataway, NJ: Transaction, 2003.

Russett, Bruce M. *World Handbook of Political and Social Indicators*. New Haven, CT: Yale University Press, 1964.

Rutherford, Robert B., Jr., C. Michael Nelson, and Bruce I. Wolford. "Special Education in the Most Restrictive Environment: Correctional/Special Education." *The Journal of Special Education*, 19 (1985): 59–71.

Sainsbury, Sally. *Deaf Worlds: A Study of Integration, Segregation and Disability*. London: Hutchinson, 1986.

Samuel, Ojwang' N. "EARS: Working in Kenya's Turkana District." In *Special Education: New Dimensions in Developing Nations*. Wellington, New Zealand: Rehabilitation International, 1983.

Sapon-Shevin, Mara. *Widening the Circle: The Power of Inclusive Classrooms*. Boston: Beacon Press, 2007.

Sarason, Seymour B., and John Doris. *Educational Handicap, Public Policy, and Social History: A Broadened Perspective on Mental Retardation*. New York: Free Press, 1979.

Sardan, J.P. Olivier de. "A Moral Economy of Corruption in Africa?" *The Journal of Modern African Studies* 37 (1999): 25–52.

Sarker, Ila, and Gareth Davey. "Exclusion of Indigenous Children from Primary Education in Rajshahi Division of Northwestern Bangladesh." *International Journal of Inclusive Education* 13 (2009): 1–11.

Saussure, Ferdinand de. *Course in General Linguistics*. New York: McGraw-Hill, [1916] 1966.

Savelsberg, Joachim J. "Knowledge, Domination, and Criminal Punishment." *American Journal of Sociology* 99.4 (1994): 911–943.

Sayed, Yusef, Crain Soudien, and Nazir Carrim. "Discourses of Exclusion and Inclusion in the South: Limits and Possibilities." *Journal of Educational Change* 4 (2003): 231–248.

Schafer, Sylvia. *Children in Moral Danger and the Problem of Government in Third Republic France*. Princeton, NJ: Princeton University Press, 1997.

Schelling, Thomas. *Micromotives and Macrobehavior*. New York: W.W. Norton, 1978.

Schlossman, Steven. *Love and the American Delinquent*. Chicago: University of Chicago Press, 1977.

Schofer, Evan, and John W. Meyer. "The Worldwide Expansion of Higher Education in the 20th Century." *American Sociological Review* 70 (2005): 898–920.

Schriner, Kay, and Richard Scotch. "Disability and Institutional Change: A Human Variation Perspective on Overcoming Oppression." *Journal of Disability Policy Studies* 12 (2001): 100–106.

Schweber, Libby. *Disciplining Statistics: Demography and Vital Statistics in France and England, 1830–1885*. Durham, NC: Duke University Press, 2006.

Scotch, Richard K. *From Good Will to Civil Rights: Transforming Federal Disability Policy*. Philadelphia: Temple University Press, [1986] 2001.

Scott, Elizabeth S., and Laurence Steinberg. *Rethinking Juvenile Justice*. Cambridge, MA: Harvard University Press, 2008.

Scott, W. Richard. *Institutions and Organizations*. Thousand Oaks, CA: Sage, 2003.

Scull, Andrew, ed. *Madhouses, Mad-Doctors, and Madmen*. Philadelphia: University of Pennsylvania Press, 1981.

———. "Humanitarianism or Control? Some Observations on the Historiography of Anglo-American Psychiatry." In *Social Control and the State*. Edited by Stanley Cohen and Andrew Scull. New York: St. Martin's Press, 1983.

*Seattle School District v. State*, 90 Wn. 2d at 513, n. 13 (1978).

Seguin, Edouard. *Idiocy and Its Treatment by the Physiological Method*. New York: William Wood & Co., 1866.

Sellin, Thorsten. *Pioneering in Penology: The Amsterdam Houses of Correction in the Sixteenth and Seventeenth Centuries*. Philadelphia: University of Pennsylvania Press, 1944.

Serres, Michel. *The Parasite*. Baltimore, MD: Johns Hopkins University Press, 1982.

———. *Hermes: Literature, Science, Philosophy*. Baltimore, MD: Johns Hopkins University Press, 1983.

Sewell, William H., Jr. *Work and Revolution in France: The Language of Labor from the Old Regime to 1848*. Cambridge, UK: Cambridge University Press, 1980.

———. "Three Temporalities: Toward an Eventful Sociology." In *The Historic Turn in the Human Sciences*. Edited by Terrence J. McDonald. Ann Arbor: University of Michigan Press, 1996.

Shaftesbury, Anthony, Earl of. *Characteristics of Men, Manners, Opinions, Times*. Indianapolis: Bobbs-Merrill Co., [1711] 1964.

Shakespeare, Tom. "Cultural Representation of Disabled People: Dustbins for Disavowal?" *Disability & Society* 9 (1994): 283–299.

Shapiro, Joseph P. *No Pity: People with Disabilities Forging a New Civil Rights Movement*. New York: Times Books, 1994.

Shils, Edward. *The Virtue of Civility: Selected Essays on Liberalism, Tradition, and Civil Society*. Edited by Steven Grosby. Indianapolis: Liberty Fund, 1997.

Silver, Harold. *Education as History*. London: Methuen, 1983.

Silvers, Anita, David Wasserman, and Mary B. Mahowald. *Disability, Difference, Discrimination: Perspectives on Justice in Bioethics and Public Policy*. Lanham, MD: Rowman & Littlefield, 1998.

Skocpol, Theda. *States and Social Revolutions*. New York: Cambridge University Press, 1979.

———. *Social Policy in the United States: Future Possibilities in Historical Perspective*. Princeton, NJ: Princeton University Press, 1995.

Skrentny, John D. *The Minority Rights Revolution*. Cambridge, MA: Harvard University Press, 2002.

Skrtic, Thomas M. *Behind Special Education: A Critical Analysis of Professional Culture and School Organization*. Denver, CO: Love, 1991a.

———. "The Special Education Paradox: Equity as the Way to Excellence." *Harvard Educational Review* 61.2 (1991b): 148–206.

———, ed. *Disability and Democracy: Reconstructing (Special) Education for Postmodernity*. New York: Teachers College Press, 1995.

———. "An Organizational Analysis of the Overrepresentation of Poor and Minority Students in Special Education." *Multiple Voices* 6 (2003): 41–57.

Skrtic, Thomas M., Wayne Sailor, and Kathleen Gee. "Voice, Collaboration, and Inclusion: Democratic Themes in Educational and Social Reform Initiatives." *Remedial and Special Education* 17 (1996): 142–157.

Slater, R. O. "On Centralization, Decentralization, and School Restructuring: A Sociological Perspective." In *Restructuring Schools: An International Perspective on the Movement to Transform the Control and Performance of Schools*. Edited by Hedley Beare and W. Lowe Boyd. London: Falmer, 1993.

Slee, Roger. *Changing Theories and Practices of Discipline*. London: Falmer, 1995.

———. "Social Justice and the Changing Directions in Educational Research: The Case of Inclusive Education." *International Journal of Inclusive Education* 5.2/3 (2001): 167–177.

Slee, Roger, and Julie Allan. "Excluding the Included: A Reconsideration of Inclusive Education." *International Studies in Sociology of Education* 11.2 (2001): 173–191.

Smith, Barbara J., Bruce A. Ramirez, and Robert B. Rutherford. "Special Education in Youth Correctional Facilities." *Journal of Correctional Education* 34 (1983): 108–112.

Smith, Daniel Jordan. "Kinship and Corruption in Contemporary Nigeria." *Ethnos* 66 (2001): 344–364.

Snyder, Howard N., and Melissa Sickmund. *Juvenile Offenders and Victims: 1999 National Report*. Washington, DC: Office of Juvenile Justice and Delinquency Prevention, 1999.

Snyder, Susan L., and David T. Mitchell. *Cultural Locations of Disability*. Ann Arbor: University of Michigan Press, 2006.

Solga, Heike. "Stigmatization by Negative Selection: Explaining Less-Educated People's Decreasing Employment Opportunities." *European Sociological Review* 18.2 (2002): 159–178.

———. *Ohne Abschluss in die Bildungsgesellschaft: Die Erwerbschancen gering qualifizierter Personen aus soziologischer und ökonomischer Perspektive*. Opladen, Germany: Barbara Budrich, 2005.

———. "Lack of Training—The Employment Opportunities of Low-Skilled Persons from a Sociological and Micro-Economic Perspective." In *Skill Formation—Interdisciplinary and Cross-National Perspectives*. Edited by Karl Ulrich Mayer and Heike Solga, 173–204. New York: Cambridge University Press, 2008.

Soltan, Karol, Eric M. Uslaner, and Virginia Haufler, eds. *Institutions and Social Order*. Ann Arbor: University of Michigan Press, 1998.

Soysal, Yasemin Nuhoglu. *Limits of Citizenship: Migrants and Postnational Membership in Europe*. Chicago: University of Chicago Press, 1994.

*Spangler v. Pasadena City Board of Education*, 311 F. Supp. 501 D.C. CA (1970).

Statistisches Bundesamt. *Bildung und Kultur, Allgemeinbildende Schulen. Fachserie 11, Reihe 1*. Wiesbaden, Germany: Statistisches Bundesamt, 2006.

Steiner-Khamsi, Gita, ed. *The Global Politics of Educational Borrowing and Lending*. New York: Teachers College Press, 2004.

Stephen, Leslie. *History of English Thought in the Eighteenth Century*. 2 vols. New York: G.P. Putnam's Sons, and London: Smith, Elder & Co., 1902.

Stern, Vivien. "An Alternative Vision: Criminal Justice Developments in Non-Western Countries." *Social Justice* 28 (2001): 88–104.

Sternberg, Robert J., and Louise Spear-Swerling, eds. *Perspectives on Learning Disabilities: Biological, Cognitive, Contextual*. Boulder, CO: Westview, 1999.

Stiker, Henri-Jacques. *A History of Disability*. Ann Arbor: University of Michigan Press, 1999.

Stinchcombe, Arthur. "The Deep Structure of Moral Categories, Eighteenth-Century French Stratification, and the Revolution." In *Structural Sociology*. Edited by Ino Rossi, 66–95. New York: Columbia University Press, 1982.

———. "Social Structure and Organizations." *Advances in Strategic Management* 17 (2000): 229–259.

Stone, Deborah. *The Disabled State*. Philadelphia: Temple University Press, 1984.

Stone, Diane. "Non-Governmental Policy Transfer: The Strategies of Independent Policy Institutes." *Governance* 13 (2000): 45–70.

———. "Introduction: Global Knowledge and Advocacy Networks." *Global Networks* 2.1 (2002): 1–12.

Streeck, Wolfgang, and Kathleen Thelen, eds. *Beyond Continuity: Institutional Change in Advanced Political Economies*. Oxford: Oxford University Press, 2005.

Stronach, Ian. "The Rituals of Recovery, UK Education and Economic 'Revival' in the 70s and 80s." *Anthropology Today* 6 (1990): 4–8.

*Sunsirae Tunstall et al. v. Teresa Bergeson*, Memorandum in Support of Plaintiffs' Motion for Summary Judgment (1998).

Sutherland, Gillian. "The Origins of Special Education." In *The Practice of Special Education*. Edited by Will Swann. London: Basil Blackwell, 1981.

———. "Endpiece: Integrating Historical and Contemporary Studies on Special Education Policy." *Oxford Review of Education* 9 (1983): 277–279.

Sutton, John R. "Social Structure, Institutions, and the Legal Status of Children in the United States." *American Journal of Sociology* 24 (1983): 915–947.

Swann, Will. "Is the Integration of Children with Special Needs Happening? An Analysis of Recent Statistics of Pupils in Special Schools." *Oxford Review of Education* 11 (1985): 3–18.

Switzer, Jacqueline Vaughn. *Disabled Rights: American Disability Policy and the Fight for Equality*. Washington, DC: Georgetown University Press, 2003.

Taylor, Charles. "Modes of Civil Society." *Civil Society and the State* 3 (1990): 95–118.

Taylor, Charles L., and Michael C. Hudson. *World Handbook of Political and Social Indicators*. 2nd ed. New Haven, CT: Yale University Press, 1972.

Thelen, Kathleen. *How Institutions Evolve: The Political Economy of Skills in Germany, Britain, the United States, and Japan*. New York: Cambridge University Press, 2004.

Thomas, Stephen B., and Carol A. Denzinger. *Special Education Law: Case Summaries and Federal Regulations*. Topeka, KS: National Organization on Legal Problems of Education, 1993.

Thompson, E. P. "Patrician Society, Plebeian Culture." *Journal of Social History* 8 (1974): 382–405.

———. "Eighteenth-Century English Society: Class Struggle Without Class?" *Social History* 3 (1978): 133–165.

Thomson, J. J. "Molyneux's Problem." *Journal of Philosophy* 71 (1974): 637–650.

Thousand, Jacqueline S., and Richard A. Villa, eds. *Creating an Inclusive School*. Baltimore, MD: Paul H. Brookes, 2005.

Tilly, Charles. *Coercion, Capital, and European States, AD 990–1990*. Cambridge, MA: B. Blackwell, 1990.

———. *Durable Inequality*. Berkeley: University of California Press, 1998.

Tocqueville, Alexis de. *Democracy in America*. New York: Knopf, 1945.

———. *The Old Regime and the French Revolution*. New York: Doubleday Anchor Books, 1955.

Tomlinson, Sally. *Educational Subnormality*. London: Routledge & Kegan Paul, 1981.

———. *A Sociology of Special Education*. London: Routledge, 1982.

———. "The Expansion of Special Education." *Oxford Review of Education* 11 (1985): 157–165.

———. *Education in a Post-Welfare Society*. Milton Keynes, UK: Open University Press, 2001.

———. *Education in a Post-Welfare Society*. 2nd rev. ed. Maidenhead, UK: Open University Press, 2005.

———. *Race and Education: Policy and Politics in Britain*. Maidenhead, UK: Open University Press, 2008.

Trent, James W., Jr. *Inventing the Feeble Mind: A History of Mental Retardation in the United States.* Berkeley: University of California Press, 1994.

Tröhler, Daniel. "The Educationalization of the Modern World: Progress, Passion, and the Protestant Promise of Education." In *Educational Research: The Educationalisation of Social Problems.* Edited by Paul Smeyers and Marc Depaepe, 31–46. Dordrecht, Netherlands: Springer, 2008.

———. "Globalizing Globalization: The Neo-Institutional Concept of a World Culture." In *Globalization and the Study of Education.* Edited by Thomas S. Popkewitz and Fazal Rizvi. Malden, MA: Wiley-Blackwell, 2010.

Trow, Martin. "The Second Transformation of American Secondary Education." In *The School in Society: Studies in the Sociology of Education.* Edited by Sam D. Sieber and David E. Wolder. New York: Free Press, 1963.

Turnbull, H. Rutherford, III, and Ann P. Turnbull. *Free Appropriate Public Education: The Law and Children with Disabilities.* Denver, CO: Love, 2000.

Turner, Ralph. "Sponsored and Contest Mobility and the School System." *American Sociological Review* 25.6 (1960): 855–867.

Tushnet, Mark. "Critical Legal Studies and Constitutional Law: An Essay in Deconstruction." *Stanford Law Review* 36 (1984): 623–47.

Tuveson, Ernest. "The Importance of Shaftesbury." *ELH,* 20 (1953): 267–299.

Tyack, David. *The One Best System.* Cambridge, MA: Harvard University Press, 1974.

Tyack, David, and Larry Cuban. *Tinkering Toward Utopia: A Century of Public School Reform.* Cambridge, MA: Harvard University Press, 1995.

Tyack, David, Thomas James, and Aaron Benavot. *Law and the Shaping of Public Education, 1785–1954.* Madison: University of Wisconsin Press, 1987.

Unger, Roberto M. *The Critical Legal Studies Movement.* Cambridge, MA: Harvard University Press, 1986.

Union of International Associations. *Yearbook of International Organizations.* 10th ed., 1964–65. Brussels: UIA, 1965.

United Nations. *International Convention on the Rights of Persons with Disabilities.* New York: UN, 2006.

United Nations Educational, Scientific, and Cultural Organization. *World Handbook of Educational Organization and Statistics,* 1st ed., 1951. Paris: UNESCO, 1952.

———. *World Survey of Education Handbook, 1960–1971.* Geneva: UNESCO, 1960–71.

———. *Statistical Yearbooks, 1960–1995.* Louvain, Belgium: UNESCO, 1960–95.

———. *A Study of the Legislation Concerning the Special Education and Young People.* Paris: UNESCO, 1969.

———. *A Study of the Present Situation of Special Education,* ED/MD/16, 15 March 1971. Paris: UNESCO, 1971a.

———. *World Survey of Education V: Educational Policy, Legislation, and Administration.* Paris: UNESCO, 1971b.

———. *The Present Situation and Trends of Research in the Field of Special Education: Four Studies.* Paris: UNESCO, 1973.

———. "Special Education: Teachers and Pupils." In *Statistical Yearbook.* Paris: UNESCO, 1974a.

———. *Case Studies in Special Education: Cuba, Japan, Kenya, Sweden.* Paris: UNESCO, 1974b.

————. *Review of the Present Situation of Special Education*. Paris: UNESCO, 1988.

————. *The Salamanca Statement and Framework for Action on Special Needs Education*. Paris: UNESCO, 1994.

————. *Review of the Present Situation of Special Education* (review conducted by Seamus Hegarty). Paris: UNESCO, 1995.

————. *Legislation Pertaining to Special Needs Education*. Paris: UNESCO, 1996.

————. *Global Education Digest 2007: Comparing Education Statistics Across the World*. Montreal: UNESCO Institute for Statistics, 2007.

U.S. Census Bureau. *Disability Status and the Characteristics of People in Group Quarters: A Brief Analysis of Disability Prevalence Among the Civilian Noninstitutionalized and Total Populations in the American Community Survey 2006* (written by Matthew Brault). Washington, DC: U.S. Census Bureau, 2006.

U.S. Department of Education. *Annual Report to Congress on the Implementation of the Individuals with Disabilities Education Act*. Washington, DC: U.S. DOE, 2007 and prior years.

Üstün, T. Bedirhan, Somnath Chatterji, Jerome E. Bickenbach, Robert T. Trotter II, Robin Room, Jürgen Rehm, and Shekhar Saxena. "Disability and Cultural Variation: The ICIDH-2 Cross-Cultural Applicability Research Study." In *Disability and Culture: Universalism and Diversity*. Edited by T. Bedirhan Üstün, et al., 3–19. Göttingen, Germany: Hogrefe & Huber, 2001.

Vaughn, Michalina, and Margaret S. Archer. *Social Conflict and Educational Change in England and France, 1789–1848*. Cambridge, UK: Cambridge University Press, 1971.

Vico, Giambattista. *The New Science of Giambattista Vico*. Ithaca, NY: Cornell University Press, 1991.

Viner, Jacob. "Man's Economic Status." In *Man Versus Society in Eighteenth-Century Britain: Six Points of View*. Edited by James L. Clifford. Cambridge, UK: Cambridge University Press, 1968.

Vislie, Lise. "From Integration to Inclusion: Focusing Global Trends and Changes in the Western European Societies." *European Journal of Special Needs Education* 18 (2003): 17–35.

Vlachou-Balafouti, Anastasia. "Equality and Full Participation for All? School Practices and Special Education/Integration in Greece." In *Disability, Human Rights and Education: Cross-Cultural Perspectives*. Edited by Felicity Armstrong and Len Barton. Buckingham, UK: Open University Press, 1999.

Voltaire, François-Marie. *The Elements of Sir Isaac Newton's Philosophy*. London: Frank Cass & Co. [1738] 1967.

Wacquant, Loïc. "Ordering Insecurity: Social Polarization and the Punitive Upsurge." *Radical Philosophy Review* 11.1 (2008): 9–27.

Wagner, David. *The Poorhouse: America's Forgotten Institution*. New York: Rowman & Littlefield, 1967.

Wagner, Mary M., Jose Blackorby, Renée Cameto, and Lynn Newman. *The Transition Experiences of Young People with Disabilities*. Menlo Park, CA: SRI International, 2003.

Wagner, Mary, Lynn Newman, Renée Cameto, and Phyllis Levine. *Changes over Time in the Early Postschool Outcomes of Youth with Disabilities: A Report of Findings from the National Longitudinal Transition Study (NLTS) and the National Longitudinal Transition Study-2 (NLTS2)*. Menlo Park, CA: SRI International, 2005.

Wagner, Mary M., Lynn Newman, Renée Cameto, Phyllis Levine, and Nicolle Garza. *An Overview of Findings from Wave 2 of the National Longitudinal Transition Study-2 (NLTS2)*. Menlo Park, CA: SRI International, 2006 (www.nlts2.org/reports/2006_08/nlts2_report_2006_08_complete.pdf).

Walters, Pamela Barnhouse. "The Limits of Growth: School Expansion and School Reform in Historical Perspective." In *The Handbook of the Sociology of Education*. Edited by Maureen T. Hallinan, 241–261. New York: Kluwer Academic/Plenum, 2000.

Wang, Margaret C., and Maynard C. Reynolds. "'Progressive Inclusion': Meeting New Challenges in Special Education." *Theory into Practice* 35.1 (1996): 20–25.

Ware, Linda, ed. *Ideology and the Politics of (In)Exclusion*. New York: Lang, 2004.

Warren, Jenifer. *One in 100: Behind Bars in America 2008*. Washington, DC: Pew Charitable Trusts, 2008.

Warren, Leland. "Turning Reality Round Together: Guides to Conversation in Eighteenth-Century England." *Eighteenth Century Life* VIII (1982): 65–87.

Weatherly, Richard, and Michael Lipsky. "Street-Level Bureaucrats and Institutional Innovation: Implementing Special Education Reform." *Harvard Educational Review* 47.2 (1977): 171–197.

Webb, Sidney, and Beatrice Webb. *The Development of English Local Government, 1689–1835*. Oxford: Oxford University Press, 1963.

Weber, Max. *The Protestant Ethic and the Spirit of Capitalism*. New York: Scribner, [1904] 1958 (http://xroads.virginia.edu/~HYPER/WEBER/cover.html) (last accessed 27 March 2010).

———. *Economy and Society*. 2 vols. Berkeley: University of California Press, [1922] 1978.

Weick, Karl E. "Educational Organizations as Loosely Coupled Systems." *Administrative Science Quarterly* 21.1 (1976): 1–19.

Weiner, Dora B. "The Blind Man and the French Revolution." *Bulletin of the History of Medicine* xlviii (1974): 60–89.

Wellisz, Stanislaw, and Ronald Findlay. "Central Planning and the 'Second Economy' in Soviet-Type Systems." *The Economic Journal* 96 (1986): 646–658.

Wells, Thomas, Gary D. Sandefur, and Dennis P. Hogan. "What Happens After the High School Years Among Young Persons with Disabilities?" *Social Forces* 82.2 (2003): 803–832.

Weygand, Zina. *The Blind in French Society from the Middle Ages to the Century of Louis Braille*. Stanford, CA: Stanford University Press, 2009.

*Willie M. v. Hunt*, C. A. No. CC/79-0249 W.D.N.C. (1979).

Wocken, Hans. "Leistung, Intelligenz und Soziallage von Schülern mit Lernbehinderungen." *Zeitschrift für Heilpädagogik* 12 (2000): 492–503.

Wolfensberger, Wolf. "The Origins and Nature of Our Institutional Models." In President's Committee on Mental Retardation, *Changing Patterns in Residential Services for the Mentally Retarded*. Washington, DC: U.S. Government Printing Office, 1976.

Woloch, Isser. "From Charity to Welfare in Revolutionary Paris." *The Journal of Modern History* 58 (1986): 779–812.

Wood, Frank H. "Special Education Law and Correctional Education." In *Special Education in the Criminal Justice System*. Edited by C. Michael Nelson, Robert B. Rutherford, and Bruce I. Wolford. Columbus, OH: Merrill Publishing, 1987.

World Health Organization. *International Classification of Functioning, Disability, and Health*. Geneva: WHO, 2001.

Wright, Peter W. D., and Pamela Darr Wright. *Wright's Law: Special Education Law.* Hartfield, VA: Harbor House Law Press, 1999.

Wrigley, Owen. *The Politics of Deafness.* Washington, DC: Gallaudet University Press, 1996.

Wuthnow, Robert. "State Structures and Ideological Outcomes." *American Sociological Review* 50 (1985): 799–821.

*Wyatt v. Stickney,* 325 F. Supp. 781 M.D. Ala. (1971).

Yang, Mayfair Mei-hui. *Gifts, Favors, and Banquets: The Art of Social Relationships in China.* Ithaca, NY: Cornell University Press, 1994.

*Youngberg v. Romeo,* 457 US 307 (1982).

Zola, Irving Kenneth. *Missing Pieces: A Chronicle of Living with a Disability.* Philadelphia: Temple University Press, 1982.

———. "Self, Identity, and the Naming Question: Reflections on the Language of Disability." *Social Science and Medicine* 36.2 (1993): 167–173.

# INDEX